MILTON STUDIES

XL ❧ Edited by

Albert C. Labriola

UNIVERSITY OF PITTSBURGH PRESS

MILTON STUDIES

is published annually by the University of Pittsburgh Press as a forum for Milton scholarship and criticism. Articles submitted for publication may be biographical; they may interpret some aspect of Milton's writings; or they may define literary, intellectual, or historical contexts—by studying the work of his contemporaries, the traditions which affected his thought and art, contemporary political and religious movements, his influence on other writers, or the history of critical response to his work.

Manuscripts should be upwards of 3,000 words in length and should conform to *The Chicago Manual of Style*. Manuscripts and editorial correspondence should be addressed to Albert C. Labriola, Department of English, Duquesne Unviersity, Pittsburgh, Pa., 15282–1703. Manuscripts should be accompanied by a self-addressed envelope and sufficient unattached postage.

Milton Studies does not review books.

Within the United States, *Milton Studies* may be ordered from the University of Pittsburgh Press, c/o CUP Services, Box 6525, Ithaca, N.Y., 14851, 607–277–2211.

Published by the University of Pittsburgh Press, Pittsburgh, Pa. 15260

Copyright © 2002 by the University of Pittsburgh Press

Manufactured in the United States of America

Printed on acid-free paper

10 9 8 7 6 5 4 3 2 1

ISBN 0-8229-4167-8

ISSN 0076-8820

CONTENTS

MILTON STUDIES

XL

"THE MELTING VOICE THROUGH MAZES RUNNING": THE DISSOLUTION OF BORDERS IN *L'ALLEGRO* AND *IL PENSEROSO*

Eric C. Brown

CRITICS OF MILTON'S *L'Allegro* and *Il Penseroso* have long explored the sophisticated interrelationship of these companion poems. None has succeeded more admirably than have Casey Bowen and Peter Finch, who write that "these poems, forever performing the strange oscillations of dreaming and undreaming, of twisting and untwisting, at once defer satisfaction and grant it; for what each companion dreams, what each desires, will always be the other. And it is precisely this desire for the other that makes it impossible for us ever to read either poem absolutely in isolation or to read them simultaneously."[1] Their cautiously deconstructive reading of the poems' "solitary companionship" continues the tradition of viewing these works as interpenetrating, a tradition begun with Samuel Johnson's famous remark, "No mirth can, indeed, be found in his melancholy; but I am afraid that I always meet some melancholy in his mirth."[2] Peter C. Herman finds that the poems "problematize the defense of poetry by undoing any firm distinctions between right and wrong forms of imagination. Both speakers exorcise what each considers the wrong form of imagination, and yet each is implicated in precisely what he denounces."[3] The poems divulge their concern with the borders between themselves in their paradoxical imagery of limitless horizons, unbounded enclosures, and other sites of liminality.

The repeated dissolution of these borders creates a sense of instability between the poems, contributing to the constant flux in which one poem melts into the other. This pattern provides an aesthetic model akin to the chiaroscuro play of light and shadow prevalent in the visual arts of Milton's day, a parallel reinforced by the attention Milton pays to visual art in the poems.[4] Additionally, an equally significant model may be the informing myth of both poems, that of Orpheus and Eurydice.[5] Critics have given much attention to his near obsession with this myth, but Milton mined Ovid for these poems even more deeply than has been previously argued. In particular, Orpheus and Eurydice signify the poems' power to draw one to the brink but never conclusively over it; each poem strains, like Orpheus, toward a

1

closure it never quite realizes. The rhetoric of the poems—swaying from harsh dismissals to enchanting enticements—thus matches the play of borders *inside* the poems with those *between* the poems.

I

Milton had explored these aesthetics elsewhere. E. M. W. Tillyard first noted the links between *L'Allegro* and *Il Penseroso* and *Prolusion 1,* primarily in their similar treatment of light and dark.[6] *Prolusion 1* debates "Whether day or night is the most excellent," with Milton taking the side of day, and Tillyard concludes that *Il Penseroso* balances the discussion by championing the previously debased night. Rather than dichotomizing night and day, however, *L'Allegro* and *Il Penseroso* continue an idea at which Milton arrives only near the conclusion of that oration where he writes, "For when night falls . . . no difference can then be seen between a Helen and a Canidia, a precious jewel and a common stone. . . . Then too the loveliest spots strike horror to the heart."[7] The two points display a paradox also evident in *L'Allegro* and *Il Penseroso:* on the one hand, night dissolves difference, so that physical descriptors no longer apply; on the other hand, night imposes a difference, so that the same locale can seem alternately lovely and horrific. What Milton begins to investigate here is the interrelated effect of each on the other. *Prolusion 1* suggests the line of inquiry Milton would continue in the paired poems: How do things of light appear in the dark? And how things of dark in light?

Milton at times treats such queries fatuously in *Prolusion 1,* but they need not be so treated, for broader aesthetic and metaphysical ideas spring from them. These germinations will grow into a similar expression in *Areopagitica,* for instance. Milton there asserts that "Good and evill we know in the field of this World grow up together almost inseparably; and the knowledge of good is so involv'd and interwoven with the knowledge of evill, and in so many cunning resemblances hardly to be discern'd, that those confused seeds which were impos'd on Psyche as an incessant labour to cull out, and sort asunder, were not more intermixt."[8] Good and evil share with darkness and light the same paradox of borders, wherein difference is established only to be dissolved, and one knows of good through evil and evil through good until they intermingle almost inseparably.[9]

Such principles in the abstract had already shaped the visual art world of the Renaissance. Primarily relevant to this discussion is the development throughout Europe of chiaroscuro, or the utilization of stark contrasts in light and shadow to create illusions of depth and holism.[10] Chiaroscuro eventually became the hallmark of Caravaggio, Rembrandt, La Tour, and hosts of others, but it probably was begun by Leonardo da Vinci. Leonardo saw chiaroscuro as part of the "first intention of the painter," namely "to produce a flat surface that shows itself as an object in relief and standing out from this surface," by which the art of painting "exceeds all the others."[11] To make figures stand out from their background, one must "contrive to accommodate the bodies . . . such that the part of these bodies which is dark terminates against a bright background and that the illuminated part of the body terminates against a dark background."[12] Milton, too, takes as his launching point these ideas: the effect of stark contrasts when overlapped with each other, the nature of separation between light and dark. But for Leonardo as for Milton, chiaroscuro in its mastered form works by means of separation to approach seamless integrity. Kim Veltman writes that by the time of the *Mona Lisa* (1503–1505), the "basic principle of a light filled face surrounded by a dark frame remains the same." However, the effect has developed such that "Mona Lisa's face is filled with shadows. . . . Moreover, they obscure the transition from light to dark. . . . When we look at Mona Lisa from the side as Leonardo recommends, and specifically from the right, we realize that it is precisely this absence of a clear line separating light from dark which is the essential ingredient in her appearing lifelike."[13]

This idea was current in Milton's day as well. One seventeenth-century treatise suggests that "the art of colouring . . . lies in a certain contention . . . between the light and the shades, which by means of colours, are brought to unite with other."[14] Indeed, the highest perfection of light and shadow was believed to be an image in which "the bodies enlightened may appear by the opposition of your shadows . . . and also, that there be an imperceptible passage from your shadows to your lights."[15] This "absence of a clear line," this "imperceptible passage from your shadows to your lights," lies at the heart of Milton's companion pieces. And just as Leonardo creates the absence of contrast from ostensibly its opposite—that is, from stark contrast—so too Milton dissolves borders in and between his poems, even as the poems disclose in their imagery a hyperawareness of such borders, of light on dark and dark on light.

Roland Frye alludes to the latter effect when he writes of *Il Penseroso*'s "storied Windows richly dight, / Casting a dim religious light" (159–60).[16] He points out "the special properties of stained glass windows," which "can be properly revealed only by the 'dim' light which they themselves transmit; any other light, far from revealing their beauty, will in fact deface it."[17] The effect of light here recalls the paradoxes of *Prolusion 1*, as less light brings not shadows but a more intense illumination. The dim light might be said to fall somewhere between light and dark, a realm in which the poems cohabit. Frye's observation might also be made of a passage in *L'Allegro* mirroring *Il*

Penseroso's stained glass: when the mirthful man makes his sunrise pere-
grination, he observes not "storied windows richly dight," but "clouds in
thousand Liveries dight" (62). The rays of sunrise, a kind of in-between light
dividing night and day, create a kaleidoscope of clouds quite unlike the
washed-out whites of a midday nimbus.

Many of the preoccupations of artists working in other visual forms
during the seventeenth century, preoccupations often cited by critics as in-
fluencing Milton's verbal art, involve both the dissolution and observance of
borders.[18] Frye notes that Milton's use in *L'Allegro* of "lantskip" (70) reflects knowledge of the term's "artistic significance" even though as a distinct genre landscape art in England was only a little older than the poet
himself.[19] According to Frye, "Milton refers to 'landscape' more often than to
any other form of the arts," the term first entering English to "describe the
well-known products of Dutch art."[20] One important aspect of such landscape art was its paradoxical treatment of enclosure. G. Stanley Koehler
proposes Eden in *Paradise Lost* as an ideal landscape garden, in which "Milton resolved the issue of boundaries" by composing "a region so broad that
any notion of enclosure is forgotten," effects that, he argues, Milton forecasts
in *L'Allegro* and *Il Penseroso*.[21] "Visual images of *L'Allegro* are properly
accompanied by details implying uninterrupted space," and the "closed
spaces of *Il Penseroso* . . . imply also an auditory image not impeded by the
barriers that block vision."[22] Milton's dexterous combination of apparent
boundaries with "uninterrupted space," and "closed spaces" with unconfin-
able sound, amplifies the similar results of intertwining light and dark. For
Koehler, this produces an Eden that serves as "the ideal mean between those
extremes of negation and fulfillment, destruction and perfection for which
hell and heaven are emblems."[23] The knowledge of good and evil, heaven and
hell, finds early metaphoric expression in *L'Allegro* and *Il Penseroso;* the
movement in extremes constructs in them an amalgamated world hovering
always at the horizon.

From the beginning of *L'Allegro,* much of the action takes place at the
juncture of two worlds. The speaker dismisses "loathed Melancholy / Of
Cerberus and blackest midnight born" to an "uncouth cell" in a "dark *Cimmerian* desert," and so juxtaposes a bleak, Stygian enclave with the trip-
pingly fantastic realm of Mirth (1–10). The convergence of worlds is even
more remarkable in the genealogy of Melancholy. She is born of Midnight—
horizonal figure embodying the midpoint of night and dividing one day from
another—and Cerberus, the watchdog of the underworld. One role of the
mythical three-headed sentinel is to ensure the separation of one world from
another—in effect, to prevent one from seeping into the other, an action I will
show to be ironically extensive in Milton's poems. Such parentage super-

ficially maintains the borders that these poems collectively undermine, as figured by Melancholy's banishment to a "dark Cimmerian desert," a featureless terrain that purposefully erases all such borders and distinctions.

Critics seem to have overlooked the connection of these opening lines to the myth of Orpheus (discussed in greater detail below) with which *L'Allegro* concludes: as a figure who in his underworld descent also serves to dissolve the borders between the living and dead, Orpheus dismisses Cerberus as well. (Although in one contemporary translation of the *Metamorphoses* the poet claims, "I come not hither to discover Hell, / Nor bind that scouling Curre, who barking shakes / About his triple browes *Medusa's* snakes" [10.23].)[24] The banishment of Melancholy leads to the invocation of Mirth, who has, as her counterpart, a horizonal lineage. Indeed, Mirth is by one account the daughter of Aurora, goddess of the dawn. She presides over that time between night and day even as she emanates from the junction of earth and sky. A descendant of such a goddess might well, then, embody a great many seemingly contradictory qualities; but like her mother, Mirth exhibits no pure dichotomy between any extremes. Rather, she is always at the border, suspended at a threshold between opposing qualities. Thus if Mirth at times represents liberty, as Melancholy might tend toward restraint, it is a liberty that needs much qualification. For Liberty herself, personified in *L'Allegro,* is ironically grasped by the hand of Mirth, when one might expect the contrary from an unfettered spirit.

The path of the mirthful man notably leads over spatial thresholds as well. The regularity of such images helps establish that the poems, even as they question the violability of their own separation, depend on the idea of borders in general. Dawn returns in line 44, when the scene shifts from the processions of Mirth's confederates to the meanderings of the mirthful man. A window is fittingly the site for an exchange between the lark, harbinger of sunrise, and the mirthful man; it both allows for interaction and forms a barrier. The window scene, an infamous syntactical crux, is hardly less challenging when one considers it as a convergence not simply for bird and man but for inside and outside as well.[25] Gazing through windows seems to be a favorite pastime of several figures. Enclosed in "Towers and Battlements," the "beauty" who serves as "The Cynosure of neighboring eyes" (77, 79–80) appears at first to be the object of some wandering voyeur, and in *Il Penseroso,* a "Lamp at midnight hour" might "Be seen in some high lonely Tow'r" (85–86). The sequence culminates in the "storied Windows richly dight" of the latter poem, through which passes "a dim religious light" (159–60). The first reference in *L'Allegro* anticipates all these images and also leads into the mirthful man's walk, where he is positioned as if gazing still through a window. He proceeds, "Some time walking not unseen / By Hedgerow Elms, on Hillocks green, / Right against the Eastern gate, / Where the great Sun begins his state" (57–60). Pressed up against the pane of a horizon, "right against the Eastern gate," he wanders with a sense of anonymity even as he encounters ploughmen, milkmaids, mowers, and shepherds. A constant sensation here is of a window that somehow keeps Mirth apart even as it nevertheless allows worlds to fuse. Such a path, along the horizon, is perfect for one accompanied by the child of Aurora.

The mood of the poems, as Cleanth Brooks noticed years ago, is set in part by the light imagery (of which the dawn is certainly a part). Brooks corrected earlier critics, notably Tillyard, who had seen the operation of light and dark as ruling exclusively over *L'Allegro* and *Il Penseroso*, respectively. Brooks notes both the "tendency for the opposed items to cross over from their usual antitheses in a fashion which associates the same object with both mirth and melancholy" and the "predominantly cool half-lights."[26] But in calling the light imagery of the two poems "the most important device used to bring the patterns of opposites together," he betrays the predominance of these "half-lights" that sift through in shades of grey.[27] These poems create a world of crepuscular shadows to which a description as either light or dark does not particularly apply. The mixture of light with dark in these poems, then, presents something quite unlike Brooks's unification: indeed their most important effects derive from their *not* being brought together. In *L'Allegro* the pattern is marked by the chessboard-style cavorting of "many a youth, and many a maid / Dancing in the Checker'd shade" (95–96). Even on this "Sunshine holiday" (98), the light dances on a kind of parquet. The filtering of light and dark bears a kind of variegated beauty, a Hopkinsesque "Glory be to God for dappled things," which echoes Milton's own "dappled dawn" and "Meadows trim with Daisies pied" (44, 75). When the "great Sun begins his state," he does so in a sky that bears "laboring clouds" (74). *Il Penseroso* answers these conditions in the shrouded lines, "And when the Sun begins to fling / His flaring beams, me Goddess bring / To arched walks of twilight groves, / And shadows brown that *Sylvan* loves" (131–34). The imagery suggests a conflation of borders; night and day are less important than the imaginary line that arbitrarily separates, or absorbs, them. Sunny skies are clouded, dark nights lunar lit.

John Keats undoubtedly noticed these movements when he composed "A Song of Opposites," modeled on Milton's companion pieces. After an epigraph by Milton, Keats begins, "Welcome joy, and welcome sorrow, / Lethe's weed, and Hermes' feather, / Come to-day, and come to-morrow, / I do love you both together!" Keats's love for "sad faces in fair weather" and "Muses bright, and muses pale" suggests that the heritage of Milton's companion poems is not limited to the various melancholic odes written in the than the inside? And as to the stars—their "containment" in the sky, fixed in constellations—they are themselves knocked out of orbit by Milton's subsequent conceits, as he unspheres them and places them with the "Ladies, whose bright eyes / Rain influence" (121–22), a property normally assigned to the stars themselves. (C. S. Lewis called the line a "fully conscious metaphor from astrology.")[33] In further weaving the stellar with the ocular, the *influence* serves importantly not as a part of either but rather as permeating the air between and around. As does the music that later awakes Penseroso from his slumbers, "Above, about, or underneath" (152), the stars' influence seems to melt into every available "fleshly nook."

The surreality in these poems (stars becoming eyes, towers' outsides becoming insides) can be effectively traced through the overt dream sequences, in which the borders between waking and dreaming are confounded. Over a "Spicy Nut-brown Ale" (100), storytellers begin to tell of pinching fairies and drudging goblins. Within the stories themselves, an entire night passes, anticipating the "actual" night that will pass once the storytellers creep to bed. The "stories told of many a feat" (101) contain the tale of a Robin Goodfellow–type creature who can thresh, in one night, corn "That ten day-laborers could not end" (109). The goblin then sleeps a night in the chimney, "Basks at the fire," and leaves "Ere the first Cock his Matin rings" (112, 114). The stories within stories anticipate the endlessly digressive Alice in Wonderland, who relates on several occasions her own story, and thus the telling of her own story, ad infinitum. That Milton should anticipate the dreams of the storytellers with the imaginary, virtual night-passing suggests that one might view the dreams as recalling earlier imagery in a surreal, looking-glass manner. And indeed, just such a recollection takes place.

In *L'Allegro*, a drowsiness begins to settle around line 117, when the storytellers have gone to bed and are "By whispering Winds soon lull'd asleep" (116). The ensuing images are dreamlike, if not dreams outright: "Tow'red Cities please us then / And the busy hum of men, / Where throngs of Knights and Barons bold, / In weeds of Peace high triumphs hold" (117–20). Thomas Greene rightly remarks that the youthful poet's dream, of lines 129–30, "forces us to consider the possibility that the revelry and the triumphs and ladies and barons bold, even the urban hum of men, have all been fictions of a 'dream.' "[34] The first image of "towered cities" recasts what the measuring eye witnessed earlier in the poem, "Towers and Battlements . . . / Bosom'd high in tufted Trees" (77–78). The "throngs of knights and barons bold," along with the "store of Ladies" who "judge the prize / Of Wit, or Arms" (121, 122–23), perhaps metamorphose the youths and maids dancing in the shade. As dreams themselves dissolve borders between realities, so too the dreams of the companion poems dissolve the realities purported by them. It is startling that the

wake of *Il Penseroso*.[28] Indeed, the "moods" have much in common, too, w.
the occasionally Miltonic *Moby-Dick,* as when Ishmael observes one levi
than raising its tail above the water: "So in dreams have I seen majestic Sata
thrusting forth his tormented colossal claw from the flame Baltic of Hell. But
in gazing at such scenes, it is all in all what mood you are in; if in the Dantean,
the devils will occur to you; if in that of Isaiah, the archangels."[29] Accordingly,
these two poems, so concerned with effecting a mood of *some* sort, not only
play off one another as foils but also express two moods motivated by the
same scene. Although some have supposed Milton's two pieces to be indeed
"songs of opposites," both Keats's and Milton's poems manifest the inter-
penetration and juxtaposition of tendencies as well.

The dawns and dusks, clouded suns and moonlit evenings, all impart a
kind of perpetual twilight, but other sequences contribute vividly to this
paradigm as well. The stars and towers have been much explicated. Finch
and Bowen offer that there is "no reason to doubt that the tower Allegro
discovers 'high in tufted trees' is the selfsame tower from which Penseroso
ponders the dawn of day. . . . One poem, as it were, 'sees' the other, if only as a
distant, dreamlike vision."[30] Without repeating previous treatments, it suf-
fices to say that Milton fully exploits the borders between waking and dreaming, and that he constantly challenges their rigidity. There is a great deal of
surreality in *L'Allegro*'s "Cynosure of neighboring eyes" (80) transforming,
through some sidereal word-play, into the "Bear" of *Il Penseroso.* Ursa Minor
(the "cynosure") grows into Ursa Major (though it does not, as has been
suggested, "literally surround Ursa Minor in the northern sky").[31] Milton's
pattern seems to support Louis Martz's observation that a sibling rivalry exists
between the two poems: *Il Penseroso,* the older brother, watches the great
bear, while *L'Allegro,* the younger brother, watches the lesser bear. To dif-
ferentiate these parallel figures and the stars that steer them, however, is to
neglect the comparable properties that tie them together. Hermes thought
the Great Bear to represent perfection, since it never set during the night;
meanwhile, Ursa Minor, the constellation containing the North Star, Polaris,
might stand watching even more than Ursa Major in its role as never-setting,
boreal guide. The alternative to stargazing, for Penseroso, is an activity that
still resembles what this gazing accomplishes—the dissolving of apparent
difference. Penseroso seeks to "unsphere / the spirit of *Plato* to unfold / What
Worlds, or what vast Regions hold / The immortal mind that hath forsook /
Her mansion in this fleshly nook" (88–92). The question of enclosure—what
parameters can measure the immortal mind, forever voyaging?—is repeatedly demanded by these two poems.[32] Taken together, the towers in each
poem offer a kind of fragmented, cubistic perspective: indeed, what artistic
representation can hold even an image of a tower? Is the outside more crucial

vision in *L'Allegro* of "pomp, and feast, and revelry, / With mask, and antique Pageantry" (127–28), which constitutes "Such sights as youthful Poets dream / On Summer eves by haunted stream" (129–30), evokes the very scene that appears in *Il Penseroso*. The pensive man hides "from Day's garish eye, / While the Bee with Honied thigh, / That at her flow'ry work doth sing, / And the Waters murmuring / . . . Entice the dewy-feather'd Sleep" (141–44, 145). The pensive man's "strange mysterious dream" then "Wave[s] at his Wings in Airy stream, / Of lively portraiture display'd, / Softly on my eyelids laid" (146–50). The interaction of the two poems is clearly evident: Melancholy intrudes upon the sights the youthful poet dreams just as "singing" and "murmuring" intrude upon the pensive dreamer. That the latter actions are intrusions by Mirth is envisioned in the opening lines of *Il Penseroso*, when the "vain deluding joys" and "fancies fond" are banished, as they are "likest hovering dreams / The fickle Pensioners of *Morpheus'* train" (1–10). Whereas the pensive man should have no capacity or desire for dreams, "lively portraiture" is yet displayed upon his eyelids.

II

Epitomizing the idea of dissolution and of a suspension of borders, the myth of Orpheus and Eurydice is explicit in both texts (as Michael Fixler notes, "the only cluster exactly common to the two") and occupies the focal point of the poems' relationship to each other.[35] Most critics have given sole attention to the figure of Orpheus—as poetry incarnate or as the holder of esoteric wisdom. In doing so, they have missed the love story that resonates so powerfully in *L'Allegro* and *Il Penseroso*.[36] Finch and Bowen point to the importance of marriage imagery, and they "indeed regard Hymen, though officially present only in *L'Allegro*, as the presiding deity of the companion poems; everywhere in them marriages (official or otherwise, sanctioned or almost scandalous) are proposed, described, and enacted."[37] The "presiding deity" appears some twenty lines before the reference to Orpheus: "There let *Hymen* oft appear / In Saffron robe, with Taper clear, / And pomp, and feast, and revelry, / With mask, and antique Pageantry" (124–27). These lines in fact prepare for the later reference, as they invert the beginning of the Orpheus myth in the *Metamorphoses:*

> Hence, to the *Cicones*, through boundlesse skies,
> In saffron mantle, *Hymenaeus* flies:
> By *Orpheus* call'd. But neither usuall words
> Nor chearefull lookes, nor happy signes affords.
> The torch his hand sustain'd, still sputtering, rais'd
> A sullen smoke: nor yet, though shaken, blaz'd.[38]   (10.1–6)

In Milton's inversion, the speaker asks that Hymen appear—in familiar saffron robes—"with taper clear." The sputtering smoke Hymen's torch produced before the wedding of Orpheus and Eurydice spelled their doom; for hardly had Hymen appeared, clouding up the air, then Eurydice is bitten on the ankle by a serpent.[39] The mirthful man wants none of this. So in his lyrical conclusion, he asks for a song to bring a different ending to Orpheus's sad tale:

> That *Orpheus'* self may heave his head
> From golden slumber on a bed
> Of heapt *Elysian* flow'rs, and hear
> Such strains as would have won the ear
> Of *Pluto,* to have quite set fee
> His half-regain'd *Eurydice.*   (145–50)

The inversion seems perfect, and *L'Allegro* concludes, "These delights if thou canst give, / Mirth, with thee I mean to live" (151–52). But the intervening portions of the Orpheus and Eurydice myth, so nicely elided by the mirthful man, disclose a frustrated search for such resolution. Rather, at the heart of the tale is the idea that the dissolution of boundaries can effect only so much, the very idea confronted by these two poems. Ultimately, the failure of Orpheus is one of contingency: Eurydice is only "half-regained" because her freedom depends on his not looking back at her as they leave the underworld. An echo of that conditional stipulation resounds in the concluding lines of *L'Allegro*, offering a very different treatment of the myth than first appears. Stanley Fish makes an interestingly orphic observation of *L'Allegro*, arguing that the poem demands no sequential interpretation of the reader. That is, the poem moves in discrete packets of scenic non sequiturs; it verily requires one not to look back upon it.[40] Thus, like Pluto to the bard, the poem asks us not to review its paths; to do so would be to lose all promised joy. And yet, as with Orpheus, we must look back when we arrive at *Il Penseroso*, whose banishment of "vain deluding joys" (1) seems a recognition of Eurydice's disappearance. She is half regained but twice missed. And *Il Penseroso* often seems the tale of one who has lost at love and yet finds some melancholy pleasure in this loss.

    The power of "divinest Melancholy" in *Il Penseroso* is triumphant enough to "bid the soul of *Orpheus* sing / Such notes as, warbled to the string, / Drew iron tears down *Pluto's* cheek, / And made Hell grant what Love did seek" (12, 105–8). Yet here too the poem asserts resolution even as it questions the very foundations of completion. *L'Allegro* already has shown that ultimately hell did *not* grant what love did seek. The subsequent allusion to Chaucer's "Squire's Tale" is also relevant for it having been "left half-told"

(109). The tale was continued by Spenser in Book Four of *The Faerie Queene* and thus indirectly links the fantastic scenes conjured up by Spenser's epic to the fairies and goblins of *L'Allegro.* More importantly, the concept meshes with the overriding theme of dissolution, for the entire premise of an "unfinished" story is extremely problematic.[41] In general, one can question whether calling something "half-told," like Coleridge's *Kubla Khan,* is simply oxymoronic. What constitutes the borders within which a story or poem must be contained? Moreover, the intertextual loopings created by including an "unfinished" story in *Il Penseroso* contribute to a sense of indeterminacy in the poem itself.[42] This allusion to a story "half-told" at once recalls Eurydice's epithet in *L'Allegro,* "half-regained." The melancholic pleasure in reading a tale without ending mimics the melancholic wanderings of Orpheus after his frustrated harrowing of the underworld, a solitary ambulation evoked quietly in *Il Penseroso.*

When in the *Metamorphoses* Eurydice (fittingly) dissolves into thin air, Orpheus is stunned, "With equall terror unto his, who spi'd / Three-headed Cerberus: whome feare alone, / Oppressing nature, turn'd into a stone" (10.67–69).[43] Such petrification is perfectly within the sphere of Melancholy: the speaker in *Il Penseroso* implores the goddess, "Forget thyself to Marble" (42), an imperative reminiscent of the lines in *On Shakespeare:* "Then thou our fancy of itself bereaving, / Dost make us Marble with too much conceiving" (13–14).[44] After the loss of Eurydice Orpheus is unable to recross into the underworld. The borders between realities—waking and dreaming, life and death—are suddenly solidified, as well. Though Milton ignores Orpheus's ensuing change in affection, preferring young boys to women (unless one takes the "Attic boy" pursued by Aurora in line 124 as a sort of conversion), he does seem still to be thinking of the myth in his description of the "arched walks of twilight groves, / And shadows brown that *Sylvan* loves" (133–34).[45] Orpheus abandons civilization for a hill, where he gathers about him, by playing his music, a catalogue of greenery to provide shade. Milton mentions only two trees in his grove of the two-dozen or so enumerated in Ovid, but they are notably the first and last: "pine" and "monumental oak" (135). This setting provides the context not only for the pensive man's "mysterious dreams" but also for the "sweet music . . . / Above, about, or underneath" (151–52), appropriate harmonies for an Orphic grove. In the *Metamorphoses,* from this hill Orpheus is finally espied by the troupe of Maenads who tear apart the singer. Aligned with Bacchus (as is, ironically, Mirth in Milton's first genealogy, "Whom lovely *Venus* at a birth / . . . / To Ivy-crowned *Bacchus* bore" [14–16]), the women are punished in turn by the god for murdering his favorite disciple. The women, of course, also restore him to Eurydice, upon whom he is now free to gaze without restraint; he might well say with *Il Penseroso,* "Dissolve me into ecstasies, / And bring all Heav'n before mine eyes" (165–66). Additionally, the death of Orpheus, treated in Book Eleven of the *Metamorphoses,* brings us full circle as the "vain deluding joys" of Mirth in *Il Penseroso* recall the images of Cerberus and Melancholy in the opening lines of *L'Allegro.*

Following the death of the famed musician, Ovid relates the story of Ceyx and Alcyone. The tale is noteworthy for its depiction of the realm of Morpheus—who even more than Hymen might be called the presiding deity of Milton's two poems. It resembles the dwelling place of Melancholy and further conflates her and Mirth together as consorting with "the fickle Pensioners of *Morpheus'* train" (10). Ovid describes the dwelling place of the dream god as follows:

> Neere the *Cimmerians* lurks a Cave, in steepe
> And hollow hills; the Mansion of dull *Sleepe:*
> Not seene by *Phoebus* when he mounts the skies,
> At height, nor stooping: gloomie mists arise
> From humid earth, which still a twi-light make.
> No crested fowles shrill crowings here awake
> The chearfull Morne: no barking Sentinell
> Here guards; nor geese, who wakefull dogs excell.
> Beasts tame, nor salvage; no wind-shaken boughs,
> Nor strife of jarring tongues, with noyses rouse
> Secured Ease.[46]   (11.593–603)

The Cimmerian cave, which brings to mind Milton's "*Stygian* Cave forlorn" and "dark *Cimmerian* desert" (3, 10), and its position hidden from "Day's garish eye" (141), is a fitting place for Melancholy. But this description is most remarkable for what it lacks: no "Cock with lively din" to "Scatter the rear of darkness thin" (49–50), no "Hounds and horn" to "Cheerly rouse the slumb'ring morn / . . . Through the high wood echoing shrill" (53–55), and certainly no "Shepherd" to "tell his tale / Under the Hawthorn in the dale" (67–68). Instead, Ovid's account dismisses "crested fowles shrill crowings," "barking Sentinell" and "wakefull dogs," and "strife of jarring tongues." The place exudes Melancholy (in part, both despite and because of the absence of the barking Cerberus-sentinel). Yet Milton expressly melds Mirth and Morpheus.

Considering the importance of the Orpheus myth, it is somewhat surprising that the Morpheus myth, in the same book of Ovid, has gone generally unnoticed; but Morpheus, as god of dreams, is a fitting deity to associate with the idea of dissolution. In the *Metamorphoses,* he brings resolution to Ceyx and Alcyone. In *L'Allegro* and *Il Penseroso,* he at once ties the two poems together and imbues them with a sense of ephemerality. For although concord is an insistent aim, union is fleeting. In overemphasizing the importance of marriage (and Hymen), for instance, Finch and Bowen suggest "Aurora's sensual companionship with Cephalus, 'the Attic boy' (112)."[47] Yet the Orpheus and Eurydice myth overlays this, too: Aurora is not sensual but "civil-suited . . . / Not trickt and frounc't as she was wont" (122–23). She is not "With the Attic boy" but distanced from him and "kercheift in a comely Cloud" (124–25). And if this "comely cloud" is informed by the "laboring clouds" of *L'Allegro*, which rest on "barren" mountains, the fruitfulness of this couple is further destabilized by an implicit sterility. In these poems relationships are dreamed far more often than consummated; the dreams of fruition comply with the call to Mirth and Melancholy. The imagination can suggest cohabitation with one goddess or another, but the calls end with contingency right at the moment the poems conclude. The speakers both, in a sense, awake from their reveries at such moments. To look back, as in the Orpheus and Eurydice myth, or to pursue with too much ardor, as one chasing a dream that recedes more quickly the harder one tries to capture it, forces disappearance and dissolution. In the case of *L'Allegro* and *Il Penseroso*, the text itself is no less subject to such effects than the figures in the text.

Ultimately, these poems do not only demonstrate aesthetic concerns; in challenging the nature of borders, enclosures, and space, Milton also vividly begins treatments that would continue into *Paradise Lost*. As in *Areopagitica*, Milton in his epic recasts themes of dissolution and interrelation into broadly conceived metaphors for good and evil. In beginning a work that must depict the illimitable qualities of eternity in spatial terms, Milton could find the writing of *L'Allegro* and *Il Penseroso* to have been ample preparation. Continually positioned at the horizons of seemingly separate worlds (or separate poems), the poems challenge the very notion of separation, not unlike the insurrections of Satan in both heaven and Eden. One is reminded of Satan's plan to "make a Heav'n of Hell, a Hell of Heav'n" and "Earth with hell / To mingle and involve."[48] And the importance of Milton's own dissolution of borders in Eden is demonstrated by his succession of epic similes in Book Four (178–93). The paradoxes of chiaroscurists, generating visual dimensions by the careful, distinct placement of light and shadow that nevertheless dissolve their own borders, are after all akin to the seeds Psyche sorted in absence of distinguishing light—the seeds, for Milton, of more than artistry. *L'Allegro* and *Il Penseroso* are indeed mazes through which a melting voice runs; even as each ends in an ecstatic address that seems to beg for union with eternal forces, the path to such atonement is a labyrinthine one, full of negotiations and interminglings. That these convolutions and distinctions—

light and dark, waking and dreaming, good and evil—can be dissolved Milton successfully depicts; it remains for his later works, perhaps, to demonstrate how they might be resolved.

University of Louisiana at Lafayette

NOTES

1. Casey Finch and Peter Bowen, "The Solitary Companionship of *L'Allegro* and *Il Penseroso*," in *Milton Studies* 26, ed. James D. Simmonds (Pittsburgh, 1991), 20. For the contrary view, see Herbert J. Phelan, "What Is the Persona Doing in *L'Allegro* and *Il Penseroso?*" in *Milton Studies* 22, ed. James D. Simmonds (Pittsburgh, 1987), 3–20.

2. Samuel Johnson, *Lives of the English Poets*, 3 vols., ed. George Birkbeck Hill (Oxford, 1905), vol. 1, 167. Or as Thomas M. Greene distinguishes, "allegedly melancholic experiences turn up as mirthful in 'L'Allegro.'" See his "The Meeting Soul in Milton's Companion Poems," *English Literary Renaissance* 14 (1984): 161. The pensive and the mirthful man have been variously referred to as older and younger brothers, as Milton's options for his future writing paths, or as the contemporaneous manifestations of one being, perhaps Milton, at various stages of life. See Stella P. Revard, "'L'Allegro' and 'Il Penseroso': Classical Tradition and Renaissance Mythography," *PMLA* 101 (1986): 338–50, who sees a complementary sorority in the presiding feminine deities. Gary Stringer, "The Unity of 'L'Allegro' and 'Il Penseroso,'" *Texas Studies in Literature and Language* 12 (1970): 221, argues that "'L'Allegro' portrays a young man who loves Mirth and that 'Il Penseroso' concerns an older man who has come to prefer Melancholy." Stanley Fish, "What It's Like to Read *L'Allegro* and *Il Penseroso*," in *Milton Studies* 7, ed. Albert C. Labriola and Michael Lieb (Pittsburgh, 1975), 95, concludes that "*L'Allegro* and *Il Penseroso* are the reader; that is, they stand for modes of being which the reader realizes in his response to the poems bearing their names." In the manner of Fish, Dana Brand, "Self-Construction and Self-Dissolution in 'L'Allegro' and 'Il Penseroso,'" *Milton Quarterly* 15 (1981): 116–19, reads the two poems as near antitheses: one speaker seeks to lose himself in discontinuity, whereas the other seeks to edify a consistent self.

3. Herman, "Milton and the Muse-Haters: *Ad Patrem*, *L'Allegro/Il Penseroso*, and the Ambivalences of Poetry," *Criticism* 37 (1995): 37–56. See also George L. Geckle, "Miltonic Idealism: *L'Allegro* and *Il Penseroso*," *Texas Studies in Literature and Language* 9 (1967–1968): 455–73, who writes, "The companion poems do not, however, express simple contrasts. . . . The complexities of the poems result from the fact that each one contains within itself the framework of the other, but the other seen from a different perspective" (457); and Gerard H. Cox, "Unbinding 'The Hidden Soul of Harmony': *L'Allegro*, *Il Penseroso*, and the Hermetic Tradition," in *Milton Studies* 18, ed. James D. Simmonds (Pittsburgh, 1983), 45–62. Kathleen M. Swaim succinctly adds that these poems "impel a continually deferred resolution in which presence emphasizes absence and difference emphasizes likeness. . . . The resulting oscillation . . . is aptly imaged by a Möbius strip" (79–80); see "Myself a True Poem: Early Milton and the (Re)Formation of the Subject," in *Milton Studies* 38, ed. Albert C. Labriola and Michael Lieb (Pittsburgh, 2000), 66–95.

4. For instance, Roy Flannagan notes, in the recent *Riverside Milton* (Boston, 1998), 76n. 63, that *Il Penseroso*'s "lively portraiture display'd" (150) is "one of Milton's rare references to visual art, in this case lifelike portraiture, the image of a dream as depicted by a painter."

5. Finch and Bowen, "The Solitary Companionship," write similarly without addressing the myth: the poems "[deploy] a vocabulary of companionship even as they remain ultimately apart, not only from each other, but from everything else around them" (5). Michael Fixler, "The Orphic Technique of 'L'Allegro' and 'Il Penseroso,'" *English Literary Renaissance* 1 (1970): 165–77, alludes to an importance of this myth when he writes of *L'Allegro*, "By virtue of the sleeping Orpheus and his half-regained Eurydice the poem is left suspended, awaiting completion" (174). On the role of Orpheus in these poems and Milton's work in general, see also Douglas Bush, *Mythology and the Renaissance: Tradition in English Poetry* (New York, 1963); Patricia Vicari, "The Triumph of Art, the Triumph of Death: Orpheus in Spenser and Milton," in *Orpheus: The Metamorphosis of a Myth*, ed. John Warden (Toronto, 1982), 207–30; Richard J. DuRocher, who writes that the "paired allusions in these poems are further proof that Milton habitually saw ethical and aesthetic issues from two sides before moving toward a resolution," in *Milton and Ovid* (Ithaca and London, 1985), 66; John Mulryan, *"Through a Glass Darkly": Milton's Reinvention of the Mythological Tradition* (Pittsburgh, 1996); and Melissa F. Zeiger, *Beyond Consolation: Death, Sexuality, and the Changing Shapes of Elegy* (Ithaca and London, 1997). Revard, "Classical Tradition," 349–50n. 26, concludes instead that a Hercules tale is the operative myth. The hero's choice at a crossroads between two women, "one carefree and light, the other somber and serious, . . . was as well-known in the Renaissance as it was in antiquity." Nevertheless, in *Milton and the Tangles of Neaera's Hair: The Making of the 1645 Poems* (Columbia and London, 1997), 116–17, Revard sees the appearance of Orpheus as further indicating Milton's desire to work out a "theory of poetry," in which "the archetypal poet and father of song is supreme master of the kinds of poetry both goddesses, Mirth and Melancholy, inspire."

6. E. M. W. Tillyard, *The Miltonic Setting* (London, 1938), 1–27; for some other modifications, see Kathleen M. Swain, "Cycle and Circle: Time and Structure in *L'Allegro* and *Il Penseroso*," *Texas Studies in Literature and Language* 18 (1976): 422–32.

7. Milton, *Prolusions*, in *Complete Prose Works of John Milton*, ed. Douglas Bush et al., 7 vols. (New Haven, 1959), vol. 1, 230.

8. Milton, *Areopagitica*, in *Complete Prose Works*, vol. 4, 514.

9. William Kerrigan, *The Sacred Complex: On the Psychogenesis of Paradise Lost* (Cambridge, Mass., 1983), 144, suggests something similar for Milton's theodicy, as "even the light of Genesis required as a receptacle" the existence of chaos. In *Matter of Glory: A New Preface to Paradise Lost* (Pittsburgh, 1987), 62, John Rumrich further asserts that "the material state of chaos thus represent[s] the dark, silent, female dimension of God—the infinite power to bring forth," helpfully articulating Milton's resistance in his theology to clear cut divisions and preference instead for interplay, even between such seemingly oppositional forces as God and Chaos.

10. On the influence of the visual arts upon Milton, in addition to the works cited below, see especially Edward William Tayler, *Nature and Art in Renaissance Literature* (New York and London, 1964); Marcia Pointon, *Milton and English Art* (Toronto, 1970); Beverly Sherry, "Approaches to Milton via the Visual Arts," *AUMLA* 57 (May 1982): 31–39; *Milton in Italy: Contexts, Images, Contradictions*, ed. Mario A. Di Cesare (Binghamton, 1991); Diane Kelsey McColley, *A Gust for Paradise: Milton's Eden and the Visual Arts* (Urbana and Chicago, 1993).

11. Quoted in Kim H. Veltman, *Studies on Leonardo da Vinci I: Linear Perspective and the Visual Dimensions of Science and Art* (München, 1986), 336.

12. Veltman, *Studies on Leonardo*, 329.

13. Ibid., 348.

14. William Aglionby, *Painting illustrated in three diallogues* (London, 1685), 18–19.

15. Ibid., 112.

16. Unless otherwise noted, quotations from Milton's poetry are from *Complete Poems and Major Prose*, ed. Merritt Y. Hughes (New York, 1957), hereafter cited parenthetically in the text.

17. Roland Mushat Frye, *Milton's Imagery and the Visual Arts: Iconographic Tradition in the Epic Poems* (Princeton, 1978), 37.

18. Roy Daniells provides an enthusiastically representative example: "Mannerism canvasses the elements of a fixed traditional pattern, unexpectedly combines them to achieve effects of dissonance, dislocation, and surprise, and illuminates the reader's mind, enabling him to reconsider the whole traditional pattern of their relationship." See *Milton, Mannerism, and Baroque* (Toronto, 1963), 11.

19. Frye, *Milton's Imagery*, 227.

20. Ibid., 34.

21. G. Stanley Koehler, "Milton and the Art of Landscape," in *Milton Studies* 8, ed. James D. Simmonds (Pittsburgh, 1975), 3–40.

22. Ibid., 13.

23. Ibid., 3.

24. Translation of George Sandys, *Ovid's Metamorphosis: Englished, Mythologized, and Represented in Figures*, ed. Karl K. Hulley and Stanley T. Vandersall (London, 1632; rpt. Lincoln, 1970), 10.21–23. Subsequent references to this edition will be made parenthetically in the text, by book and line number. The Latin reads "non hue, ut opaca viderem / Tartara, descendi, nec uti villosa colubris / terna Medusaei vincirem guttura monstri," from Ovid's *Metamorphoses*, trans. Frank Justus Miller, 2 vols. (1916; rpt. Cambridge, Mass., 1976), vol. 2, 64.

25. On the much-chronicled difficulties of this window scene, see especially Fish, "What It's Like to Read," 77–100.

26. Cleanth Brooks, "The Light Symbolism in 'L'Allegro–Il Penseroso,'" in *The Well Wrought Urn* (1947; rpt. London: Dobson, 1968), 53, 55.

27. Ibid., 55.

28. Keats, "A Song of Opposites," in the Oxford *John Keats* (New York, 1990), lines 1–4, 5, 20. On the influence of Milton on Keats and in general, see, among others, A. R. Malagi, "Versions of Melancholy: Keats's 'Ode on Melancholy' and Milton's 'Il Penseroso,'" *Journal of Karnatak University* 18 (1974): 69–88; Meg Harris Williams, *Inspiration in Milton and Keats* (London, 1982); John T. Shawcross, *John Milton and Influence: Presence in Literature, History, and Culture* (Pittsburgh, 1991).

29. Herman Melville, *Moby-Dick*, ed. Charles C. Walcutt (New York, 1967), 350. Henry F. Pommer proposes that "Melville knew 'L'Allegro' and 'Il Penseroso' well, and used them in his own writing," in *Milton and Melville* (New York, 1970), 106. See also Leslie E. Sheldon, "Another Layer of Miltonic Allusion in *Moby-Dick*," *Melville Society Extracts* 35 (1978): 15–16; "Surmising the Infidel: Interpreting Melville's Annotations on Milton's Poetry," *Milton Quarterly* 26 (December 1992): 103–13; Daniel Goske, "Melville's Milton," *Princeton University Library Chronicle* 54 (winter–spring 1993): 296–302.

30. Finch and Bowen, "Solitary Companionship," 15.

31. Ibid., 23n. 25.

32. See also Greene, "The Meeting Soul," who notes that in reading the poems, one is "obliged to shift levels of reality," and that "the companion poems . . . play elusively with inside and outside" (165).

33. Lewis, *The Discarded Image* (Cambridge, Eng., 1967), 110.

34. Greene, "The Meeting Soul," 164.

35. Fixler, "The Orphic Technique," 174.

36. A recent example is Rachel Falconer, *Orpheus Dis(re)membered: Milton and the Myth of the Poet-Hero* (Sheffield, U.K., 1996), 22–23, who despite acknowledging that the "two major classical sources, *Georgics* 4 and *Metamorphoses* 10, both place the romance element at the center of their narratives," spends most of her discussion on the "civilizing influence of Or-

pheus's song." Her subsequent treatment of the "double nature of Orphic song," Epicurean in *L'Allegro* and Stoic in *Il Penseroso,* is conventional in criticism of the myth in these poems. See also Kenneth R. R. Gros Louis, "The Triumph and Death of Orpheus in the English Renaissance," *SEL* 9 (1969): 63–80, who sees Orpheus in both *L'Allegro* and *Il Penseroso* as ultimately triumphant; and Marilyn L. Williamson, "The Myth of Orpheus in 'L'Allegro' and 'Il Penseroso,'" *Modern Language Quarterly* 32 (1971): 377–86, who points out the dual traditions "of Orphic song for both the social order and religious worship" (378). Revard, *Milton and the Tangles of Neaera's Hair,* relegates "Orpheus's power to conquer hell with the impulse of his love for his wife" to a footnote (117n. 54).

37. Finch and Bowen, "The Solitary Companionship," 8.

38. "Inde per inmensum crocco velatus amictu / aethera digreditur Ciconumque Hymenaeus ad oras / tendit et Orphea nequiquam voce vocatur. / adfuit illequidem, sed nec sollemnia verba / nec laetos vultus nec felix attulit omen. / fax quoque, quam tenuit, lacrimoso stridula fumo / usque fuit nullosque invenit motibus ignes" (*Met.* 2.64).

39. In *A Variorum Commentary on the Poems of John Milton, II, The Minor English Poems,* ed. A. S. P. Woodhouse and Douglas Bush (New York, 1972), pt. I, 307, the editors note that Milton "perhaps remembers that the torch's smoking was a fatal omen at the marriage of Orpheus and Eurydice"; Williamson, "The Orphic Myth," 382–83, also observes this possibility, concluding that in *L'Allegro,* "the sexual drive begins in careless encounter and ends as part of the social order."

40. Fish's essay "What It's Like to Read" sets forth a kind of quantum theory for *L'Allegro* and *Il Penseroso.* The first poem, writes Fish, moves with "abruptness," the second "fluidity" (90). If Brooks emphasizes the symbolic importance of light, Fish justifiably asks that it adhere to wave-particle theory.

41. Fixler, "Orphic Technique," appropriately sees "the half-told tale as a kind of model of how these poems work together and upon us, for the function of the irregularly disposed related sets of images within both 'L'Allegro' and 'Il Penseroso' is to set up certain tensions, suggesting pervasive but elusive latencies of exact correspondences the mind is attracted to complete" (174). On Orpheus as embodiment of horizonal boundaries, see also Robert McGahey, *The Orphic Moment: Shaman to Poet-Thinker in Plato, Nietzsche, and Mallarmé* (Albany, 1994); he borrows an epigraph from the last writer: "Orpheus is the sunset and the sunrise: those moments when the sun just touches the principle of darkness."

42. Jonathan Goldberg finds this also conspicuous in Spenser's continuation of Chaucer's *Squire's Tale.* See his *Endlesse Worke: Spenser and the Structures of Discourse* (Baltimore, 1981), 34–46.

43. "Quam tria qui timidus, medio portante catenas, / colla canis vidit, quem non pavor ante reliquit, / quam natura prior saxo per corpus oborto" (*Met.* 2.68).

44. Cleanth Brooks and John Edward Hardy, in their edition of *Poems: The 1645 Edition* (New York, 1951), gloss these lines as "turned to stone . . . not by losing all power of thought, but by being overwhelmed with thought; not by becoming dead, but by being awaked to more intense life" (126). In many ways, such is the case for Orpheus, who though not dead himself nevertheless experiences a kind of death-in-life that intensifies his experience.

45. Some critics see the role of Orpheus here as diminished. Geckle, "Miltonic Idealism," says that "the speaker of *Il Penseroso* passes over the Orpheus myth as merely one of many subjects, whereas it occupied an important place at the end of *L'Allegro*" (472). Somewhat contrastingly, Don Cameron Allen, *The Harmonious Vision: Studies in Milton's Poetry* (Baltimore, 1970), describes the passive role of Orpheus in *L'Allegro,* and his active singing in *Il Penseroso* (19).

46. "Est prope Cimmerios longo spelunca recessu, / mons cavus, ignavi domus et penetralia

SPENSER, MILTON, AND THE RENAISSANCE CAMPE: MONSTERS AND MYTHS IN *THE FAERIE QUEENE* AND *PARADISE LOST*

George F. Butler

I N *PARADISE LOST*, when Satan confronts Sin and Death at the gates of hell, Sin is described as a grotesque monster:

> The one seem'd Woman to the waist, and fair,
> But ended foul in many a scaly fold
> Voluminous and vast, a Serpent arm'd
> With mortal sting: about her middle round
> A cry of Hell Hounds never ceasing bark'd
> With wide *Cerberean* mouths full loud, and rung
> A hideous Peal: yet, when they list, would creep,
> If aught disturb'd thir noise, into her womb,
> And kennel there, yet there still bark'd and howl'd
> Within unseen. Far less abhorr'd than these
> Vex'd *Scylla* bathing in the Sea that parts
> *Calabria* from the hoarse *Trinacrian* shore.[1]   (*PL* 2.650–61)

Death is depicted less vividly, but the monster is nonetheless terrifying:

> The other shape,
> If shape it might be call'd that shape had none
> Distinguishable in member, joint, or limb,
> Or substance might be call'd that shadow seem'd,
> For each seem'd either; black it stood as Night,
> Fierce as ten Furies, terrible as Hell,
> And shook a dreadful Dart; what seem'd his head
> The likeness of a Kingly Crown had on.   (*PL* 2.666–73)

Milton's two goblins have attracted considerable scholarly and critical attention. Sin in particular has drawn the comments of Miltonists, who have pointed to several sources for Milton's description, including Phineas Fletcher's Hamartia, or "Sinne," from *The Purple Island* (1633); Chiurca, from Guillaume de Salluste, Sieur du Bartas's *Les Semaines,* which was translated into English by Joshua Sylvester as *Bartas: His Devine Weekes and Workes* (1605); and various emblems of Opinion and Error that were current

19

in Milton's time.² As Milton's editors have noted, the most obvious classical source for Sin is Ovid's account of Scylla:

> Scylla venit mediaque tenus descenderat alvo,
> cum sua foedari latrantibus inguina monstris
> adspicit ac primo credens non corporis illas
> esse sui partes, refugitque abigitque timetque
> ora proterva canum, sed quos fugit, attrahit una
> et corpus quaerens femorum crurumque pedumque
> Cerbereos rictus pro partibus invenit illis:
> statque canum rabie subiectaque terga ferarum
> inguinibus truncis uteroque exstante coercet.

[Then Scylla comes and wades waist-deep into the water; when all at once she sees her loins disfigured with barking monster-shapes. And at the first, not believing that these are parts of her own body, she flees in fear and tries to drive away the boisterous, barking things. But what she flees she takes along with her; and, feeling for her thighs, her legs, her feet, she finds in place of these only gaping dogs'-heads, such as a Cerberus might have. She stands on ravening dogs, and her docked loins and her belly are enclosed in a circle of beastly forms.] (*Met.* 14.59–67)³

In addition to the general similarity between the two accounts, Milton directly refers to Scylla (*PL* 2.660), and the phrase "*Cerberean* mouths" (*PL* 2.655), translates Ovid's "Cerbereos rictus" (*Met.* 14.65). Critics have also noted the strong influence of Spenser and have argued that Milton's Sin is largely based on Spenser's Error, "A monster vile, whom God and man does hate" (*FQ* 1.1.13, 7).⁴ A generally disregarded model for Sin and Death is Campe, a little-known monster from classical mythology.⁵ The figure of Campe influenced Milton's account directly through classical and Renaissance texts and may also have influenced Milton indirectly, through Spenser's portrait of Error.

Though relatively obscure, Campe is mentioned by several classical authors. The story of Campe is told in the *Bibliotheca,* or *Library* of classical mythology, popularly ascribed to Apollodorus and probably written in the first or second century A.D. According to that work, Zeus had to slay Campe in order to free the hundred-handed Giants from Tartarus, whose help he needed to defeat Cronos and the Titans:

μαχομένων δὲ αὐτῶν ἐνιαυτοὺς δέκα ἡ Γῆ τῷ Διὶ ἔχρησε τὴν νίκην, τοὺς καταταρ-
ταρωθέντας ἂν ἔχῃ συμμάχους· ὁ δὲ τὴν φρουροῦσαν αὐτῶν τὰ δεσμὰ Κάμπην
ἀποκτείνας ἔλυσε. καὶ Κύκλωπες τότε Διὶ μὲν διδόασι βροντὴν καὶ ἀστραπὴν καὶ
κεραυνόν, Πλούτωνι δὲ κυνέην, Ποσειδῶνι δὲ τρίαιναν· οἱ δὲ τούτοις ὁπλισθέντες
κρατοῦσι Τιτάνων, καὶ καθείρξαντες αὐτοὺς ἐν τῷ Ταρτάρῳ τοὺς ἑκατόγχειρας
κατέστησαν φύλακας.

[They fought for ten years, and Earth prophesied victory to Zeus if he should have as allies those who had been hurled down to Tartarus. So he slew their gaoleress Campe, and loosed their bonds. And the Cyclopes then gave Zeus thunder and lightning and a thunderbolt, and on Pluto they bestowed a helmet and on Poseidon a trident. Armed with these weapons the gods overcame the Titans, shut them up in Tartarus, and appointed the Hundred-handers their guards.] (*Lib* 1.2.1)[6]

In the *Theogony*, which was probably composed in the eighth century B.C., Hesiod names the beings imprisoned by Campe, though he does not mention their keeper. During the battle between the gods and Titans, "Οἳ δ' ἄρ' ἐνὶ πρώτοισι μάχην δριμεῖαν ἔγειραν / Κόττος τε Βριάρεώς τε Γύης τ' ἄατος πολέμοιο" [amongst the foremost Cottus and Briareos and Gyes insatiate for war raised fierce fighting] (*Theog.* 713–14).[7] They are the Hundred-handers:

τῶν ἑκατὸν μὲν χεῖρες ἀπ' ὤμων ἀίσσοντο
ἄπλαστοι, κεφαλαὶ δὲ ἑκάστῳ πεντήκοντα
ἐξ ὤμων ἐπέφυκον ἐπὶ στιβαροῖσι μέλεσσιν·
ἰσχὺς δ' ἄπλητος κρατερὴ μεγάλῳ ἐπὶ εἴδει.

[From their shoulders sprang an hundred arms, not to be approached, and each had fifty heads upon his shoulders on their strong limbs, and irresistible was the stubborn strength that was in their great forms.] (*Theog.* 150–53)

Cronos, in Hesiod's account, chained the three monstrous brothers beneath the earth, and Zeus and the other Olympians, at Earth's advice, brought them up to help overthrow Cronos and the Titans (*Theog.* 617–53). Diodorus Siculus, in his *Bibliotheca Historica*, or *Library of History* (ca. 30 B.C.), a lengthy history of the world from the origin of humanity to 59 B.C., mentions that Dionysos fought and defeated Campe at Zabirna, a city in Libya:

πρὸς δὲ ταύτῃ γηγενὲς ὑπάρχον θηρίον καὶ πολλοὺς ἀναλίσκον τῶν ἐγχωρίων, τὴν ὀνομαζομένην Κάμπην, ἀνελεῖν καὶ μεγάλης τυχεῖν δόξης ἐπ' ἀνδρείᾳ παρὰ τοῖς ἐγχωρίοις.

[Near this city an earth-born monster called Campê, which was destroying many of the natives, was slain by him, whereby he won great fame among the natives for valour.] (Diod. Sic. 3.72.3)[8]

Perhaps the most vivid description of Campe is found in the *Dionysiaca*, a massive epic written by the Byzantine poet Nonnos of Panopolis in Egypt, who flourished around A.D. 470. In his epic, Nonnos details the exploits of Dionysos and tells of the conquest of India. Staphylos, king of Assyria, inspires Dionysos to fight the Indians by telling the god of Zeus's conquest of Campe, whom Nonnos also refers to as Enyo (*Dion.* 18.226, 238–39) and "Κρονίην . . . ἐχιδνήεσσαν Ἐνυώ" [the snaky Enyo of Cronos] (*Dion.* 18.264).[9]

συμφερτῇ δὲ φάλαγγι πολυσκυλάκων κεφαλάων
Σκύλλης ἰσοτέλεστον ἔην μίμημα προσώπου·
καὶ χροϊ μεσσατίῳ διφυὴς ἀνεφαίνετο νύμφη
ἰοβόλοις κομόωσα δρακοντείοισι κορύμβοις.

[her countenance was the very image of Scylla with a marshalled regiment of throng-
ing dogs' heads. Doubleshaped, she appeared a woman to the middle of her body,
with clusters of poison-spitting serpents for hair.] (*Dion.* 18.246–49)

Thus Campe is part woman and also has canine and serpentine characteristics. And she has a scorpion:

ἐξ ὑπάτου δὲ τένοντος ἀμαιμακέτων διὰ νώτων
σκορπίος αὐτοέλικτος ἐπήορος αὐχένος οὐρῇ
εἷρπε χαλαζήεντι τεθηγμένος ὀξέι κέντρῳ.

[From her neck over her terrible shoulders, with tail raised high over her throat, a
scorpion with an icy sting sharp-whetted crawled and coiled upon itself.] (*Dion.*
18.254–56)

These classical texts were available to varying degrees throughout the
Renaissance. Apollodorus' *Bibliotheca,* Hesiod's *Theogony,* and Diodorus
Siculus' *Bibliotheca Historica* were published in numerous editions during the sixteenth and seventeenth centuries. The works of Apollodorus
and Hesiod, in particular, formed the foundation of the Renaissance mytho-
graphic tradition. Though relatively obscure, the *Dionysiaca* nonetheless
appeared in several Renaissance editions. The French scholar Jean Dorat
(1508–88) had read and commented on the *Dionysiaca* prior to its initial
publication by Christopher Plantin at Antwerp in 1569. Later editions included Διονυσιαχά. *Dionysiaca; nunc denuo in lucem edita, et Latine reddita
per Eilhardvm Lvbinvm* (Hanover, 1605), which made the work available in
Latin and provided a commentary by Gerhard Falkenburg from the 1569
edition; and a French translation by C. Boitet de Frauville, *Les Dionysiaques
ou les metamorphoses, les voyages, les amours, les adventures et les con-
questes de Bacchus aux Indes. Nouvellement traduittes du Grec de Nonnus*
(Paris, 1625). But the most significant edition was the *NONNOY ΠΑΝΟ-
ΠΟΛΙΤΟΥ ΔΙΟΝΥΣΙΑΚΑ. Nonni Panopolitæ Dionysiaca. Petri Cvnæi Animadversionvm liber. Danielis Heinsii Dissertatio de Nonni Dionysiacis &
ejusde Paraphrasi. Iosephi Scaligeri Coniectanea. Cum vulgata versione, &
Gerarti Falkenburgi lectionibus* (Hanover, 1610). That edition included the
Greek and Latin text of the poem on facing pages, along with Falkenburg's
commentary; a 174-page literary critique by Peter van der Kun, known as
Cunaeus; a 27-page discussion by Daniel Heinsius; and 13 pages of comments and conjectures by Joseph Scaliger. The extent of the volume's critical

apparatus and the involvement of Heinsius and Scaliger, two of the most important classical scholars of the Renaissance, testify to the value of that work and the place of Nonnos in the Renaissance canon of classical authors.[10]

In light of his voracious reading and high regard for the classics, Milton was doubtlessly familiar with most of these texts.[11] In his *Prolusion 1*, on "Whether Day or Night is the More Excellent," which he delivered while a student at Cambridge, he shows particular knowledge of the *Theogony* and cites Hesiod as an authority (YP 1:223).[12] And in *Of Education* (1644), he includes the Greek poet in his ideal curriculum (YP 2:394). Aside from these explicit references to Hesiod, the *Theogony* is generally believed to inform much of *Paradise Lost*, especially Milton's account of the war in heaven and Satan's fall into hell.[13] The same can be said about Apollodorus' *Bibliotheca*. Though Milton says little, if anything, about Apollodorus, his familiarity with the Greek mythographer's works is generally accepted.[14] And although Diodorus Siculus is relatively obscure to modern readers, Milton quotes the ancient historian several times in *A Defence of the People of England* (1651 and 1658), thus displaying his knowledge of that author (YP 4:433–36). More difficult to ascertain is Milton's reading of the *Dionysiaca*. He does not refer to the poem in his writings, nor does he cite Nonnos in his *Commonplace Book* (YP 1:344–513). But Milton does not habitually identify the sources of his mythological material, so this does not imply that he did not know the Greek poet. Both Ruth Mohl and James Holly Hanford have studied the *Commonplace Book* in detail. As Mohl observes, "the number of entries made from an author may not be an indication of Milton's later dependence on him." Hanford makes an even more forceful statement: "There are only three quotations from the classics and none at all from Scripture. Nor did he ordinarily, as we shall see, use [the *Commonplace Book*] for materials gathered in the immediate process of research, but rather as a permanent aid to his thought and memory." The citations in the *Commonplace Book* thus do not adequately reflect Milton's thorough knowledge of the Bible and broad command of classical literature.

The *Dionysiaca* was read and commented on throughout the Renaissance. Angelo Ambrogini (1454–94), more commonly known as Politian, had read the *Dionysiaca* in October 1485 and had studied the Laurentian codex of the manuscript, which had been written around A.D. 1280. In his *Mythologiae*, a popular Renaissance mythological handbook that appeared in numerous editions throughout Europe between 1551 and 1669, Natale Conti quotes Nonnos' explanation of Dionysos' name, indicating that Jove walked with a limp, or "nysus," when he carried Dionysos in his thigh. Lodovico Castelvetro refers to the *Dionysiaca* in his *Poetica d' Aristotele Vulgarizzata et Sposta* (1570), where he cites the work as an example of an epic that recounts multiple adventures in the life of a hero. And Edward, Lord Herbert of Cherbury repeats Nonnos' account of Dionysos talking to a dog in his *De Religione Gentilium* (1645), a comprehensive overview of pagan religions.[15] Moreover, Nonnos had special standing in the Renaissance because he was considered a Christian. Though his epic was not widely known, he was acclaimed as the author of a hexameter paraphrase of the Gospel of John. Nonnos is mentioned in the *Dictionarium Historicum, Geographicum, Poeticum* of Charles Stephanus, one of the standard Renaissance classical dictionaries. First published in 1553 and originally an expansion of the widely popular *Elucidarius* of Herman Torrentinus (ca. 1450–1520), Stephanus' *Dictionarium* appeared in at least nine editions through 1600, and eleven more were issued during the seventeenth century. In the 1609 edition Stephanus calls the Greek author "poeta egregius, qui carmine hexametro Ioannis Euangelium scripsit" [an illustrious poet, who wrote the Gospel of John in a hexameter poem]. The paraphrase attributed to Nonnos was part of the Renaissance grammar school curriculum. In his *Certain Epistles of Tully* (1611), for instance, William Hayne listed chapter five of the work as a text that should be read by students.[16]

Scholars have said little about Milton's familiarity with the *Dionysiaca*, but nonetheless some have commented on his likely use of that epic. In his early-twentieth-century survey of Milton's use of classical mythology, Charles Grosvenor Osgood suggests that *Dionysiaca* 44.107–18 influenced Milton's allusion to Cadmus and Hermione in *Paradise Lost* 9.506; that the invocations in *Paradise Lost* might be indebted to Nonnos' invocation of the muse in *Dionysiaca* 1.1; and that Milton's reference to Typhon dwelling in the den by Tarsus (*PL* 1.199–200) may have come from Nonnos' account of Typhon's actions at Tarsus and Corycium (*Dion.* 1.258). J. Douglas Bruce notes that Milton's account of Creation may have come from *Dionysiaca* 4.427–40, and Douglas Bush repeats Bruce's claim. Thomas O. Mabbott has likewise suggested that Nonnos may have shaped Milton's representation of the animals playing around Adam and Eve (*PL* 4.340–47). John Kevin Newman has detected similarities between Milton's war in heaven and the battles in the *Dionysiaca*, and between the serpent's temptation of Eve (*PL* 9.496–503) and the seduction of Proserpina by Zeus, who appears to her in the form of a snake (*Dion.* 6.155–62). Stella Revard notes the availability of the poem in several Renaissance editions; the dependence of many Renaissance accounts of the war in heaven, such as Erasmo di Valvasone's *Angeleida* (1590), Giovandomenico Peri's *La Guerra Angelica* (ca. 1612), and Odorico Valmarana's *Daemonomachiae* (1623) on details from the *Dionysiaca;* and Milton's likely use of the poem in Raphael's tale of celestial warfare. And George F. Butler has cited the *Dionysiaca* as a background for the "vast *typhœan* rage" of the demons in Milton's hell (*PL* 2.539–46).[17]

The texts of antiquity were popular during the Renaissance, but the classical myths also reached Renaissance authors through mythological reference works. In his *Mythologiae* Conti, probably drawing on Apollodorus, says that in the tenth year of the war between the Olympians and the Titans, "Tellus (or the earth) predicted to Jove that he would be victorious if he would receive in his ranks the comrades that had been thrown into Tartarus. Accordingly, Jove then liberated them, killing their guard Campe and, joining with them, he allegedly gained victory." Stephanus does not provide an entry for Campe in the 1609 edition of his *Dictionarium Historicum, Geographicum, Poeticum.* Nor is Campe listed in the tables of contents of the 1606 edition of Giuseppe Betussi's Italian translation of Giovanni Boccaccio's *Della Geneologia de gli Dei* or the 1571 edition of Vincenzo Cartari's *Le Imagini De i Dei de gli Antichi*, which were, with Conti's book, probably the three most significant Renaissance mythographies. But Nonnos referred to Campe several times as "Enyo," and Stephanus explains that Enyo is "soror Martis, quam Latini Bellonam vocant" [sister of Mars, whom the Latins call Bellona]. In the account of Campe in Book Eighteen of the Hanover, 1610, edition of the *Dionysiaca*, the Latin translation consistently mentions Bellona where Enyo appears in the Greek text. Homer speaks of "πτολίπορθας Ἐνυώ" [Enyo, sacker of cities] (*Iliad* 5.333) and later tells how she brings with her "Κυδοιμὸν ἀναιδέα δηϊοτῆτος" [ruthless Din of War] (*Iliad* 5.593). Boccaccio notes that Bellona is the sister of Mars, the god of war; and in a chapter on Minerva, Cartari offers a discussion of Bellona the war goddess, in which he stresses her ferocity. In his discussion, Cartari quotes from the epic *Punica* of Silius Italicus (ca. A.D. 96), who describes Bellona steering Mars' chariot of war: "frenisque operata regendis / quadriiugos atro stimulat Bellona flagello" [Bellona, busy with the reins, urged on the four coursers with her fatal scourge] (4.438–39). And later, in describing a battle, Silius refers to Bellona as Enyo (10.202). Statius, in his *Thebaid* (A.D. 92), mentions "Martia . . . Enyo" [Martian Enyo] (5.155), and Bellona's torches (11.413) and battle spear (2.718–19); and he describes Enyo provoking war: "Dumque ea per Thebas, aliis serpentibus ardens / et face mutata bellum integrabat Enyo" [While these things were happening in Thebes, Enyo, afire with torch fresh-charged and other serpents, was restoring the fight] (*Theb.* 8.655–56). Virgil, too, mentions Bellona in the *Aeneid* (7.319), and he says that the goddess follows Discord "cum sanguineo . . . flagello" [with bloody scourge] (8.703); and in his *Pharsalia* (A.D. 65), an unfinished epic about the Roman civil war between Caesar and Pompey, Lucan likewise writes of "Sanguineum . . . quatiens Bellona flagellum" [Bellona brandishing her bloody scourge] (*Phars.* 7.568). When Ovid relates the myth of Perseus returning to Ethiopia and the fighting that ensues at the palace of Cepheus, he says that "pollutosque simul multo Bellona penates / sanguine perfundit renovataque proelia miscet" [Bellona drenches and pollutes with blood the sacred home, and ever renews the strife] (*Met.* 5.155–56).[18]

In these classical texts the figures of Bellona, Enyo, and Campe were sometimes the same figure, or they shared certain roles and features. Although this association may seem recondite, there is good reason to believe that Milton was aware of it. Milton mentions both Enyo and Bellona in his writings. In *Elegy 4*, which he wrote when he was only eighteen, Milton associates Enyo with the horror of war: "Te circum late campos populatur Enyo, / Et sata carne virum iam cruor arva rigat" [All around you Enyo is laying waste the fields and blood is watering the ground which has been sown with human flesh] (75–76). In *Paradise Lost*, shortly after Sin opens the gates of hell Milton attributes a similar role to Bellona, as Satan stands on the brink of Chaos, listening to noises no less "loud and ruinous" (*PL* 2.921) than "when *Bellona* storms, / With all her battering Engines bent to rase / Some Capital City" (*PL* 2.922–24). This passage evidently alludes to Homer's Enyo bringing with her the Din of War. In both passages, Enyo and Bellona have identical roles as a war goddess.

In an anonymous life of Milton written sometime between 1676 and 1691, the biographer comments that "hee began that laborious work of amassing out of all the Classic Authors, both in Prose and Verse, a *Latin Thesaurus* to the emendation of that done by Stephanus; Also the composing *Paradise Lost*," and "had begun a *Greek Thesaurus*."[19] DeWitt T. Starnes and Ernest William Talbert have noted that "with respect to proper names, the poet most frequently consulted the *Thesaurus* of Robert Stephanus and the *Dictionarium Historicum, Geographicum, Poeticum* of Charles Stephanus."[20] In addition, Milton was familiar with the *Thesaurus Graecae Linguae* of Henry Stephanus (1572), for he had consulted that work in annotating his copy of Aratus.[21] In preparing his own reference works, both for Greek and Latin, Milton would have become familiar with Charles Stephanus' *Dictionarium Historicum, Geographicum, Poeticum*, which identifies Enyo with Bellona; with reference handbooks of Boccaccio, Conti, and Cartari, which summarize the myths and which, in the case of Conti, discuss Campe; and with the classical texts cited by these mythographers, including the detailed account of Campe's appearance in the *Dionysiaca* of Nonnos.

Spenser's Error, as with Milton's Sin, is an allegorical composite of many figures, including Scylla and Echidna. Among these figures is Nonnos' Campe. According to John M. Steadman, "Error's speckled tail recalls that of

Hesiod's Echidna, while her scorpion-like sting is also characteristic of Nonnus' Campe." Steadman also notes that the Echidna-like features of Error, along with her other attributes, link her to popular superstitions about vipers; and he suggests that Spenser's monster might thus be related to Nonnos' Campe, who is a "viperish Enyo" with "viperish feet." As with the monster from the *Dionysiaca*, Spenser's Error is part woman, with serpentine and canine attributes. Steadman shows Error has a place in a long line of serpent-women, including Nonnos' Campe, and that Milton's Sin continues that tradition.[22] Spenser would have been able to learn about Campe through many of the same classical texts, mythographies, and dictionaries available to Milton.[23] Although the *Dionysiaca* was published relatively late, Steadman's implication that Spenser may have read Nonnos is plausible. Nonetheless, Steadman himself has cautioned that "the extent of Spenser's reading has often been greatly exaggerated," and that "Spenser was hardly a polymath." In his biography of the poet, Alexander C. Judson notes the difficulty of establishing Spenser's knowledge of Greek. "The question as to whether Spenser had a real command of Greek has been debated," says Judson; "he seems, at any rate, to have had the opportunity to ground himself early in that language." Judson then notes that Lodowick Bryskett, whom Spenser had known in Ireland, had called Spenser "perfect in the Greek tongue" and that Spenser had encouraged Bryskett in his study of that language.[24]

In *The Faerie Queene* Spenser presents the Wandering Wood as a type of hell. When the Redcrosse Knight enters the wood, the dwarf tells him that "this is no place for liuing men" (*FQ* 1.1.13, 9), which suggests that the wood is a more appropriate abode for the lifeless. And Spenser says that it is a "darksome hole" (*FQ* 1.1.14, 3), which recalls the pit of Tartaros. Because Error traps and entangles those who stumble into her den, she is a type of infernal gatekeeper. That is a role which she shares with Campe, who guards Tartaros. Steadman has noted that Error's sting recalls the sting of Campe's scorpion, and Error's tail is similarly poised. Spenser says that she

> rushed forth, hurling her hideous taile
> About her cursed head, whose folds displaid
> Were stretcht now forth at length without entraile. (*FQ* 1.1.16, 2–4)

The image is strikingly similar to Nonnos' account of Campe's scorpion, holding its tail over Campe's neck and shoulders, the tail wrapped in coils (*Dion.* 18.254–56), although Error's tail is unfolded.

Spenser uses the myth of Campe to underscore the larger significance of Error in his poem. He links Error with the Fall, since the Fall was caused by the initial error of Adam and Eve. Error, too, is dragon-like, and the dragon is associated with Satan in Christian tradition. So too, Satan's rebellious error led to his fall from heaven. The Redcrosse Knight's encounter with Error anticipates his apocalyptic battle with the Great Dragon near the end of Book One. The Dragon draws near, "Halfe flying, and halfe footing in his hast" (*FQ* 1.11.8, 2); "His flaggy wings" were like "two sayles" (*FQ* 1.11.10, 1–2); and his body "all with brasen scales was armd" (*FQ* 1.11.9, 1). He has a "huge long tayle wound vp in hundred foldes" (*FQ* 1.11.11, 1). The tail ends in "two stings," "Both deadly sharpe" (*FQ* 1.11.11, 8–9); and Spenser later refers to the Dragon's "mortall sting" (*FQ* 1.11.38, 5). In these admittedly generic details, the Dragon recalls the dusky wings, seamonster's scales, and coiled stinger of Nonnos' Campe.

The Dragon, too, is associated with error and rebellion. The battle between Redcrosse and the Dragon takes place in the fallen Eden. There is *"The tree of life, the crime of our first fathers fall"* (*FQ* 1.11.46, 9); and in that fertile soil "all good things did grow" (*FQ* 1.11.47, 2), until "that dread Dragon all did ouerthrow" (*FQ* 1.11.47, 5). In keeping with biblical myth, the tree of knowledge of good and evil, "That tree through one mans fault hath doen vs all to dy" (*FQ* 1.11.47, 9). When the Dragon appears, he reminds one of the classical monsters or Titans who sided with Campe and threatened Jove: "The cloudes before him fled for terrour great, / And all the heauens stood still amazed with his threat" (*FQ* 1.11.10, 8–9).

Through such references Spenser weaves a web of associations among the rebellion of Satan, the error and fall of Adam, and the classical Titanomachy. References to rebellion likewise appear in Spenser's account of Redcrosse's battle with Error. Just before Una and the knight become lost in the Wandering Wood, the weather changes:

> Thus as they past,
> The day with cloudes was suddeine ouercast,
> And angry *Ioue* an hideous storme of raine
> Did poure into his Lemans lap so fast.   (*FQ* 1.1.6, 4–7)

This storm prompts them to seek shelter in the wood. But the trees are full of "sommers pride" (*FQ* 1.1.7, 4), and the sheltering branches "Did spred so broad, that heauens light did hide" (*FQ* 1.1.7, 5). The den of Error opposes the classical Jove and the Christian God. The opposition is repeated when Error vomits "bookes and papers" (*FQ* 1.1.20, 6), which probably included heretical theological works.

Classical texts describe Campe in terms similar to the Giants, who later rebelled against Jove. Ovid, for example, tells the myth as follows:

> Neve foret terris securior arduus aether,
> adfectasse ferunt regnum caeleste gigantas

altaque congestos struxisse ad sidera montis.
tum pater omnipotens misso perfregit Olympum
fulmine et excussit subiecto Pelion Ossae.

[And, that high heaven might be no safer than the earth, they say that the Giants essayed the very throne of heaven, piling huge mountains, one on another, clear up to the stars. Then the Almighty Father hurled his thunderbolts, shattered Olympus, and dashed Pelion down from underlying Ossa.] (*Met.* 1.151–55)

Jove later considers the rebelliousness of the humans who were born from the blood of the fallen Giants:

Non ego pro mundi regno magis anxius illa
tempestate fui, qua centum quisque parabat
inicere anguipedum captivo bracchia caelo.

[I was not more troubled than now for the sovereignty of the world when each one of the serpent-footed giants was in act to lay his hundred hands upon the captive sky.] (*Met.* 1.182–84)

Ovid describes the Giants as being serpent-footed, an image which became a commonplace of Renaissance iconography.[25] As are the Giants, Campe is γηγενὲς, or earth-born, as Diodorus Siculus noted (Diod. Sic. 3.72.3). And according to Nonnos, Campe has "ἐχιδναίων . . . ταρσῶν" ("viperish feet," *Dion.* 18.240), a feature that links her with Ovid's serpent-footed Giants.[26]

As Ovid and other classical writers influenced Spenser, Spenser's allegorization of Error in *The Faerie Queene* shaped Milton's description of Sin and Death in *Paradise Lost.* Error is "Halfe like a serpent horribly displaide, / But th'other halfe did womans shape retaine" (*FQ* 1.1.14, 7–8). Thus the creature is part woman and part serpent, as is Milton's Sin. Error is surrounded by her monstrous children:

Of her there bred
A thousand yong ones, which she dayly fed,
Sucking vpon her poisonous dugs, eachone
Of sundry shapes, yet all ill fauored.   (*FQ* 1.1.15, 4–7)

These beasts are like the dogs that surround both Scylla and Sin. When they are disturbed, they crawl into Error's mouth: "Soone as that vncouth light vpon them shone, / Into her mouth they crept, and suddain all were gone" (*FQ* 1.1.15, 8–9). In imitation of Spenser, Milton has Sin's canine offspring retreat into her womb (*PL* 2.656–59). And in an appropriation of Spenser's language, Milton says that Sin is "a Serpent arm'd / With mortal sting" (*PL* 2.652–53), while Error's tail is "Pointed with mortall sting" in Spenser's poem

(*FQ* 1.1.15, 4). Spenser's Great Dragon may also have informed Milton's allegory of Sin and Death. The Dragon's "mortall sting" brings to mind the "mortal Dart" of Milton's Death (*PL* 2.729) and the "mortal sting" of Sin (*PL* 2.653). Everything the Dragon touches with its claws is doomed to die, and so the Dragon is a form of death:

> But stings and sharpest steele did far exceed
> The sharpnesse of his cruell rending clawes;
> Dead was it sure, as sure as death in deed,
> What euer thing does touch his rauenous pawes,
> Or what within his reach he euer drawes.   (*FQ* 1.11.12, 1–5)

The Dragon is explicitly linked with hell. His "deepe deuouring iawes / Wide gaped, like the griesly mouth of hell" (*FQ* 1.11.12, 7–8), a description that recalls the ravenous appetite of Death at hell gate in *Paradise Lost* (2.805–7). Spenser's Dragon is an "infernall Monster" (*FQ* 1.11.31, 5) and a "hell-bred beast" (*FQ* 1.11.40, 3), and it belches fire and smoke "from hellish entrailes" (*FQ* 1.11.45, 5).

To the extent that Spenser's Error is derived from Campe, the classical monster indirectly shaped Milton's description of Sin and Death. But Milton's indebtedness to the myth of Campe is even more explicit and direct. While Spenser only suggests that the Wandering Wood is a type of hell and Error is its guardian, Milton says that Sin is "the Portress of Hell Gate" (*PL* 2.746). And like Campe, she is very much the "Νύμφη Ταρταρίη," the "nymph of Tartaros" (*Dion.* 18.261). Sin tells Satan that God has

> thrust me down
> Into this gloom of *Tartarus* profound,
> To sit in hateful Office here confin'd.   (*PL* 2.857–59)

Campe travels through the cosmos, causing chaos:

> τοίη ποικιλόμορφας ἕλιξ κουφίζετο Κάμπη,
> καὶ χθόνα δινεύουσα καὶ ἠέρα καὶ βυθὸν ἅλμης
> ἵπτατο κυανέων πτερύγων ἑτερόζυγι παλμῷ,
> λαίλαπας αἰθύσσουσα καὶ ὁπλίζουσα θυέλλας,
> Νύμφη Ταρταρίη μελανόπτερος.

[Such was manifoldshaped Campe as she rose writhing, and flew roaming about earth and air and briny deep, and flapping a couple of dusky wings, rousing tempests and arming gales, that blackwinged nymph of Tartaros.] (*Dion.* 18.257–61)

So too, Sin and Death, though initially confined to hell, eventually cross the primordial abyss to earth, where they bring misery to humanity. Milton even says that Sin and Death can fly, for Satan tells his daughter that

> Thou and Death
> Shall dwell at ease, and up and down unseen
> Wing silently the buxom Air.   (*PL* 2.840–42)

After the Fall, Milton explicitly says that Sin grew wings:

> Methinks I feel new strength within me rise,
> Wings growing, and Dominion giv'n me large
> Beyond this Deep.   (*PL* 10.243–45)

Similar to the figure of Campe as it flew through the primitive world, Sin and Death

> Both from out Hell Gates into the waste
> Wide Anarchy of *Chaos* damp and dark
> Flew diverse, and with Power (thir Power was great)
> Hovering upon the Waters.   (*PL* 10.282–85)

Sin and Death resemble Campe in other details. Nonnos specifically refers to a "σκορπίος" or "scorpion" in his account (*Dion.* 18.255). When Milton describes Death's lethal powers, he follows Nonnos by mentioning scorpions. Death warns Satan:

> Back to thy punishment,
> False fugitive, and to thy speed add wings,
> Lest with a whip of Scorpions I pursue
> Thy ling'ring, or with one stroke of this Dart
> Strange horror seize thee, and pangs unfelt before. (*PL* 2.699–703)

The whip which Milton mentions additionally recalls the bloody scourge of Bellona, Campe's Latin counterpart. Sin has "many a scaly fold" (*PL* 2.651), and Campe is covered by "πτύχα . . . κητείαις," ("sea-monsters' scales," *Dion.* 18.250–51).

In Nonnos' account, Zeus vanquished Campe when he fought his battle against Cronos and the Titans so that he could free Briareos (*Dion.* 18.217–38), although Nonnos does not explain the full role of Campe in that war. In *Paradise Lost* Milton compares Satan to Briareos and alludes to the battles of the classical gods. Satan is

> in bulk as huge
> As whom the Fables name of monstrous size,
> *Titanian*, or *Earth-born*, that warr'd on *Jove*,
> *Briareos* or *Typhon*, whom the Den
> By ancient *Tarsus* held.   (*PL* 1.196–200)

Both Sin and Campe are the keepers of "Briareos." In confronting Sin and Death to free himself—and eventually the other demons—from hell, Satan recalls Zeus slaying Campe to liberate Briareos and the Hundred-handers. And while God is analogous to Zeus, and Satan to the Titans, Milton explicitly condemns the actions of Zeus as a rebellion, as he includes among the demons "Th' *Ionian* Gods, of *Javan's* Issue held / Gods" (*PL* 1.508–9). He then mentions

> *Titan* Heav'n's first born
> With his enormous brood, and birthright seiz'd
> By younger *Saturn*, he from mightier *Jove*
> His own and *Rhea's* Son like measure found;
> So *Jove* usurping reign'd.   (*PL* 1.510–14)

Because Milton casts Jove—or Zeus—as a rebel, Satan is also analogous to Zeus when he encounters Sin and Death. As Milton indicates, Sin grew out of Satan's head in a way that parallels Athena's springing from the head of Zeus (*PL* 2.752–58).

Milton's implicit comparison of Sin to Athena may at first seem odd, since Athena is usually not depicted as a misshapen monster. But Athena (or Pallas or Minerva) was sometimes identified with Bellona by the Renaissance mythographers. Spenser, in fact, makes this association and explains it. In "October" of *The Shepheardes Calender*, he mentions "queint *Bellona*" (114). In a gloss on the line, Spenser's E. K. explains:

Queint) strange Bellona; the goddesse of battaile, that is Pallas, which may therefore wel be called queint for that (as Lucian saith) when Iupiter hir father was in traueile of her, he caused his sonne Vulcane with his axe to hew his head. Out of which leaped forth lustely a valiant damsell armed at all poyntes, whom Vulcane seeing so faire and comely, lightly leaping to her, preferred her some cortesie, which the Lady disdeigning, shaked her speare at him, and threatned his saucinesse. Therefore such straungenesse is well applyed to her. (*Works* 7:102–3)

And in *The Faerie Queene* he similarly considers Athena and Bellona as interchangeable. In the 1596 edition of the poem, Britomart is "Like as *Minerua*, being late returnd / From slaughter of the Giaunts conquered" (*FQ* 3.9.22,1–2). But the 1590 edition read "Bellona" instead of "Minerva."[27] Milton, then, could find in Spenser a precedent for associating Athena with Bellona, who in turn was identified with Sin and Campe.

In *The Faerie Queene* and *Paradise Lost*, the legacy of the ancient poets is continued, as Spenser and Milton translate Campe into Error and then into Sin and Death. For Spenser, the figure of Campe was a source of monstrous detail for Error and the Dragon. Because of Campe's opposition to Zeus in his battle against the Titans, and the monster's fight against Dionysos, Campe was also an appropriate classical antecedent for the foes of the Redcrosse Knight. Milton, in turn, uses the myth of Campe to underscore Satan's role as a prisoner of hell and as a rebel. By suggesting a parallel between Satan and Zeus in their confrontations with infernal gatekeepers, Milton additionally reminds the reader that classical myth is but an imperfect rendering of biblical truth, and that Zeus is far from identical to the Christian God.

Fairfield, Connecticut

NOTES

1. Milton's poetry is cited parenthetically from *Complete Poems and Major Prose*, ed. Merritt Y. Hughes (Indianapolis, 1957).

2. These likely sources are mentioned in *Paradise Lost*, ed. Alastair Fowler, 2d ed. (New York, 1998), glosses on 2.650–66 and 2.653–59. For an extensive discussion of the literary and mythological background of Milton's Sin, see John M. Patrick, *Milton's Conception of Sin as Developed in Paradise Lost* (Logan, Utah, 1960). For a brief review of Milton's sources, with special attention to *The Faerie Queene*, see John N. King, "Milton's Cave of Error: A Rewriting of Spenserian Satire," in *Worldmaking Spenser: Explorations in the Early Modern Age*, ed. Patrick Cheney and Lauren Silberman (Lexington, Ky., 2000), 148–55. King says that "Milton styles Sin retrospectively as the ultimate ancestress of Spenserian Error" (148), and he explores Milton's episode as a comment on religious controversy. King considers the matter further in "Milton's Sin and Death: A Rewriting of Spenser's Den of Error," in *Form and Reform in Renaissance England: Essays in Honor of Barbara Kiefer Lewalski*, ed. Amy Boesky and Mary Thomas Crane (Newark, Del., 2000), 306–20, and in *Milton and Religious Controversy: Satire and Polemic in Paradise Lost* (New York, 2000), 73–78.

Fletcher describes Hamartia as follows: "A woman seem'd she in her upper part" (12.17.5), "The rest (though hid) in serpents form arayd, / With iron scales, like to a plaited mail" (12.28.1–2). She has a "knotty tail" (12.28.3), which ends "with a double sting" (12.28.5). Her hair hangs loosely in "viperous locks" (12.30.1), and in a gloss on her name in 12.28.2, Fletcher indicates that she is "Sinne." Fletcher's poetry is cited from Giles and Phineas Fletcher, *Poetical Works*, ed. Frederick S. Boas, 2 vols. (1908–1909; rpt. Cambridge, 1970).

Du Bartas, in his account of the sixth day of the first week of Creation, writes: "Heare the Beast, bred in the bloodie Coast / Of *Canibals*, which thousand times (almost) / Re-whelpes her whelpes, and in her tender wombe, / She doth as oft her liuing brood re-toomb." Du Bartas is cited from *Bartas: His Devine Weekes and Works*, trans. Joshua Sylvester (1605; rpt. Delmar, N.Y., 1977), 201–202. Du Bartas identifies this creature as Chiurca in a marginal gloss. In his note on *Paradise Lost* 2.653–59, Fowler calls this creature "Du Bartas's untameable chiurca, or opposum," and he directs the reader to John Illo, "Animal Sources for Milton's Sin and Death," *Notes and Queries* 205 (1960): 425–26. George Coffin Taylor, *Milton's Use of Du Bartas* (1934; rpt. New York, 1967), says: "Upon *Paradise Lost* ii, even less of the influence of Du Bartas is to be detected than upon the first book" (67).

3. Ovid is cited parenthetically by book and line number from *Metamorphoses*, 2 vols., trans. by Frank Justus Miller, 3d ed. (Cambridge, Mass., 1977).

4. Spenser is cited parenthetically from *The Works of Edmund Spenser: A Variorum Edition*, ed. Edwin Greenlaw et al., 11 vols. (Baltimore, 1932–57). Critics who have noted similarities between Spenser's Error and Milton's Sin include Richard J. DuRocher, *Milton and Ovid* (Ithaca, N.Y., 1985), 138–39; Anne Ferry, *Milton's Epic Voice: The Narrator in Paradise*

Lost (1963; rpt. Chicago, 1983), 123–25; Maureen Quilligan, *Milton's Spenser: The Politics of Reading* (Ithaca, N.Y., 1983), 79–98. *The Faerie Queene* is also an obvious source for Phineas Fletcher's Hamartia in *The Purple Island.*

5. Campe is not mentioned in the notes on Milton's allegory of Sin and Death in the editions by Hughes and Fowler or in a succession of other editions, including *The Complete Poetical Works of John Milton,* ed. Harris Francis Fletcher (Cambridge, Mass., 1941); *The Complete Poetical Works of John Milton,* ed. Douglas Bush (Boston, 1965); *Paradise Lost and Paradise Regained,* ed. Christopher Ricks (New York, 1968); *The Complete Poetry of John Milton,* ed. John T. Shawcross, rev. ed. (New York, 1971); *John Milton,* ed. Stephen Orgel and Jonathan Goldberg (New York, 1991); *Paradise Lost,* ed. Roy Flannagan (New York, 1993); *Paradise Lost: An Authoritative Text, Backgrounds and Sources, Criticism,* ed. Scott Elledge, 2d ed. (New York, 1993); *The Riverside Milton,* ed. Flannagan (Boston, 1998); and *John Milton: The Complete Poems,* ed. John Leonard (New York, 1998).

6. Apollodorus is cited parenthetically by book, chapter, and section number from *The Library,* trans. by James George Frazer, 2 vols. (Cambridge, Mass., 1921).

7. Hesiod is cited parenthetically by line number from *Hesiod, the Homeric Hymns, and Homerica,* trans. by Hugh G. Evelyn-White (Cambridge, Mass., 1914).

8. Diodorus Siculus is cited parenthetically by book, chapter, and section number from *The Library of History,* trans. by C. H. Oldfather et al., 12 vols. (Cambridge, Mass., 1933–67).

9. Nonnos is cited parenthetically by book and line number from *Dionysiaca,* trans. by W. H. D. Rouse, 3 vols. (Cambridge, Mass., 1940).

10. The first edition of Apollodorus' *Bibliotheca,* a Greek text accompanied by a Latin translation and some notes, was published in Rome by Benedictus Aegius in 1555. The second, which contained the Greek text and the Latin translation of Aegius, was edited by Hieronymus Commelinus and published at his press in Heidelberg in 1599. The third was published in 1661, by Tanaquil Faber. That edition was followed by Thomas Gale's *Historiae Poeticae Scriptores Antiqui* (Paris, 1675), a compendium of the *Bibliotheca* and several other mythological texts. Ironically, the first edition of the *Theogony* was published in Latin hexameters by Boninus Mombritius at Ferrara in 1474, while the Greek text was initially published by Aldus Manutius at his press in Venice in 1495. The Aldine text and a manuscript formed the basis for Eufrosyno Bonini's Florence, 1516 edition. That edition along with the Aldine were used by Ioannes Frobenius in editing his Basel, 1521 text. Later editions were printed in Venice (1537, 1543), Florence (1540), Basel (1542, 1544), Paris (1544, 1566), Cambridge (1635), Leiden (1603, 1612, 1622), and Amsterdam (1650, 1657, 1667). Gian Francesco Poggio Bracciolini's Latin translation of Diodorus Siculus' *Bibliotheca Historica,* Books One–Five, was first published at Bologna in 1472 and was reprinted many times in Lyons, Paris, and Venice. The first Greek edition, by Vincentius Opsopoeus, was published at Basel in 1539 and included Books Sixteen–Twenty. Henry Stephanus published a Greek edition at Geneva in 1559, which contained Books One–Five, Eleven–Twenty, and fragments of Books Twenty-One–Forty. John Skelton translated Poggio's Latin text into English, though his translation remained unpublished during his lifetime; and Henry Cogan issued an English translation in 1653. See J. G. Frazer, introduction, in Apollodorus, *The Library,* xxxvii; Don Cameron Allen, *Mysteriously Meant: The Rediscovery of Pagan Symbolism and Allegorical Interpretation in the Renaissance* (Baltimore, 1970), 59, 201–203; Hesiod, *Theogony,* ed. M. L. West (Oxford, 1966), 61–63, 101; Rudolf Pfeiffer, *History of Classical Scholarship: From 1300 to 1850* (Oxford, 1976), 34, 104, 119, 129; J. E. Sandys, *A History of Classical Scholarship,* 3 vols., (1908–21; rpt. Mansfield Centre, Conn., and Beverly Hills [1997]), 2:38, 66, 98, 104–105, 175, 271–72, 313; C. H. Oldfather, introduction, in Diodorus Siculus, *The Library of History,* xxiii; Claire Carroll, "Humanism and English Literature in the Fifteenth and Sixteenth Centuries," in *The Cambridge Companion to Renaissance*

Humanism, ed. Jill Kraye (New York, 1996), 247; N. G. Wilson, *From Byzantium to Italy: Greek Studies in the Italian Renaissance* (London, 1992), 107, 180; L. D. Reynolds and N. G. Wilson, *Scribes and Scholars: A Guide to the Transmission of Greek and Latin Literature,* 3d ed. (Oxford, 1991), 178–79.

11. For a thorough overview of Milton's use of classical mythology and its Renaissance interpretations, see John Mulryan, *"Through a Glass Darkly": Milton's Reinvention of the Mythological Tradition* (Pittsburgh, 1996).

12. References to Milton's prose are to *The Complete Prose Works of John Milton,* 8 vols., ed. Don M. Wolfe et al. (New Haven, 1953–82), hereafter designated YP and cited parenthetically by volume and page number in the text.

13. See, for example, William M. Porter, *Reading the Classics and Paradise Lost* (Lincoln, Neb., 1993), 54: "The overwhelming preponderance of Milton's allusions to the *Theogony,* then, is striking. . . . Milton's war in heaven, of course, had numerous specific precedents besides Hesiod's titanomachy. . . . But no other single work is alluded to in *Paradise Lost* 6 so extensively or to such purpose as the *Theogony."*

14. Harris Francis Fletcher, *The Intellectual Development of John Milton,* 2 vols. (Urbana, Ill., 1956–61), vol. 1, 256, notes that Apollodorus was an important author in the Renaissance grammar school curriculum. Charles Grosvenor Osgood, *The Classical Mythology of Milton's English Poems* (New York, 1900), xlii, counts Apollodorus among Milton's many classical sources. The passage is repeated by Bush, *Mythology and the Renaissance Tradition in English Poetry* (1932; rpt. New York, 1957), 249, who stresses the difficulty of identifying a single source for any one of Milton's classical allusions.

15. Mohl, *John Milton and His Commonplace Book* (New York, 1969), 35; Hanford, "The Chronology of Milton's Private Studies," in *John Milton, Poet and Humanist: Essays by James Holly Hanford* (Cleveland, 1966), 81; Wilson, *From Byzantium to Italy,* 107, 180; *Natale Conti's Mythologies: A Select Translation,* ed. Anthony DiMatteo (New York, 1994), bk. 5, ch. 13, 272–73; *Castelvetro on the Art of Poetry: An Abridged Translation of Lodovico Castelvetro's Poetica d' Aristotele Vulgarizzata et Sposta,* ed. Andrew Bongiorno (Binghamton, N.Y., 1984), 88; Edward, Lord Herbert of Cherbury, *Pagan Religion: A Translation of De Religione Gentilium,* ed. John Anthony Butler (Binghamton, N.Y., 1996), 247. Butler's edition of *De Religione Gentilium* cites Book Fifteen of Nonnos' poem as the source for the quotation from the *Dionysiaca,* but the passage appears as *Dion.* 16.199–203 in the Loeb edition and is in Book Sixteen, 450–51, of the Hanover, 1610, edition.

16. DeWitt T. Starnes and Ernest William Talbert, *Classical Myth and Legend in Renaissance Dictionaries: A Study of Renaissance Dictionaries in Their Relation to the Classical Learning of Contemporary English Writers* (Chapel Hill, N.C., 1955), 8–9; Stephanus, *Dictionarium Historicum, Geographicum, Poeticum* ([Geneva,] 1609), 319v; T. W. Baldwin, *William Shakspere's Small Latine and Lesse Greeke,* 2 vols. (Urbana, Ill., 1944), vol. 1, 400. Nonnos' authorship of the paraphrase of the Gospel of John is presently disputed. While most scholars hold that stylistic similarities between the epic and the paraphrase are sufficient to demonstrate the common authorship of both works, though the paraphrase may have been written earlier, Dennis Ronald MacDonald, *Christianizing Homer: The Odyssey, Plato, and The Acts of Andrew* (New York, 1994), 25, says that the paraphrase was written by "An anonymous Christian poet who imitated the verse of Nonnos of Panopolis."

17. Osgood, *The Classical Mythology of Milton's English Poems,* 18, 57, 84; Bruce, "A Note on *Paradise Lost,* vii, 463–74," *Englische Studien* 41 (1909): 166–70; Bush, *Mythology and the Renaissance Tradition in English Poetry,* 278 n.79; Mabbott, "Milton and Nonnos," *Notes and Queries* 197 (1952): 117–18; Newman, *The Classical Epic Tradition* (Madison, Wisc., 1986), 383, 388–90; Revard, *The War in Heaven: Paradise Lost and the Tradition of Satan's Rebellion*

(Ithaca, N.Y., 1980), 149–50 n.45, 192–94; Butler, "Nonnos and Milton's 'vast *Typhœan rage*': The *Dionysiaca* and *Paradise Lost*," *Milton Quarterly* 33 (1999): 71–76.

18. Conti, *Mythologies*, bk. 2, ch. 1, 37. Homer is cited parenthetically by book and line number from *The Iliad*, trans. by A. T. Murray, 2 vols. (Cambridge, Mass., 1924–25); Boccaccio, *Della Geneologia de gli Dei*, trans. Betussi (Venice, 1606), bk. 9, 146; Cartari, *Le Imagini De i Dei de gli Antichi* (Venice, 1571), 363–64; Stephanus, *Dictionarium Historicum, Geographicum, Poeticum*, 198r; *NONNOΥΠΑΝΟΠΟΛΙΤΟΥ ΔΙΟΝΥΣΙΑΚΑ. Nonni Panopolitæ Dionysiaca. Petri Cvnæi Animadversionvm liber. Danielis Heinsii Dissertatio de Nonni Dionysiacis & ejusde Paraphrasi. Iosephi Scaligeri Coniectanea. Cum vulgata versione, & Gerarti Falkenburgi lectionibus* (Hanover, 1610), 500–503; Silius Italicus is cited parenthetically by book and line number from *Punica*, trans. by J. D. Duff, 2 vols. (Cambridge, Mass., 1934); Statius is cited parenthetically by book and line number from *Status*, trans. by J. H. Mozley, 2 vols. (Cambridge, Mass., 1928); Virgil is cited parenthetically by book and line number from *Virgil*, trans. by H. Rushton Fairclough, 2 vols., rev. ed. (Cambridge, Mass., 1934–35); Lucan is cited parenthetically by book and line number from *Lucan: The Civil War*, trans. by J. D. Duff (Cambridge, Mass., 1928).

19. Helen Darbishire attributes the life to John Phillips, but this attribution has been debated. See William Riley Parker, *Milton: A Biography*, 2d ed., ed. Gordon Campbell, 2 vols. (Oxford, 1996), vol. 1, xiii–xiv. Parker attributes it to Cyriack Skinner. The life is quoted from "The Life of Mr. John Milton," in *The Early Lives of Milton*, ed. Helen Darbishire (London, 1932), 29. Several of the other "early lives" of Milton edited by Darbishire mention his Latin dictionary. John Aubrey, in his "Minutes of the Life of Mr John Milton" (ca. 1681–1682), says, "I heard that after he was blind, that he was writing in the hands of Moyses Pitt a Latin Dictionary" (Darbishire, *Early Lives*, 4); Anthony à Wood, in "*Fasti Oxonienses* or *Annals* of the University of Oxford" (1691), notes: "he began that laborious work of amassing out of all the classick Authors both in prose and verse a Latin *Thesaurus*, to the emendation of that done by *Stephanus*" (Darbishire, *Early Lives*, 45–46); Edward Phillips writes in his "The Life of Mr. John Milton" (1694) that the poet began "a New *Thesaurus Linguæ Latinæ*, according to the manner of *Stephanus*; a work he had been long since Collecting from his own Reading, and still went on with it at times, even very near to his dying day" (Darbishire, *Early Lives*, 72); John Toland, in *The Life of John Milton* (1698), says that he worked on "his new *Thesaurus Linguæ Latinæ*" (Darbishire, *Early Lives*, 166), "design'd as a Supplement to *Stephanus*" (Darbishire, *Early Lives*, 192); and Jonathan Richardson, in his *Explanatory Notes and Remarks on Milton's Paradise Lost* (1734), remarks that Milton "set himself to Collect out of all the Classicks in Verse and Prose, a Latin *Thesaurus*, in Emendation of That done by *Stephanus*" (Darbishire, *Early Lives*, 268). Though the Latin dictionary was never completed, Darbishire (*Early Lives*, 339–40) explains that the manuscript apparently was the basis for the *Linguae Romanae Dictionarium Luculentum Novum. A New Dictionary in Five Alphabets* (1693). Katherine D. Carter, "Dictionaries and Encyclopedias," in *A Milton Encyclopedia*, ed. William B. Hunter Jr. et al., 9 vols. (Lewisburg, Penn., 1978–83), vol. 2, 153, notes that several later authors also claimed to have used Milton's Latin dictionary.

20. Starnes and Talbert, *Classical Myth and Legend in Renaissance Dictionaries*, 226. See ch. 8, "Milton and the Dictionaries," for a survey of the topic.

21. Maurice Kelley and Samuel D. Atkins, "Milton's Annotations of Aratus," *PMLA* 70 (1955): 1100; Starnes and Talbert, *Classical Myth and Legend in Renaissance Dictionaries*, 227.

22. "Error," in *The Spenser Encyclopedia*, ed. A. C. Hamilton et al. (Toronto, 1990), 253; *Nature into Myth: Medieval and Renaissance Moral Symbols* (Pittsburgh, 1979), 168–69, 175–79. See also Steadman's essays: "Spenser's *Errour* and the Renaissance Allegorical Tradition,"

Neuphilologische Mitteilugen 62 (1961): 22–38; "Tradition and Innovation in Milton's 'Sin': The Problem of Literary Indebtedness," *Philological Quarterly* 39 (1960): 93–103.

23. For a review of Spenser's classical learning, see Starnes and Talbert, *Classical Myth and Legend in Renaissance Dictionaries,* ch. 4; Alice Elizabeth Randall, *The Sources of Spenser's Classical Mythology* (New York, 1896); Bush, *Mythology and the Renaissance Tradition in English Poetry,* ch. 5; Mulryan, "Mythographers," in *The Spenser Encyclopedia,* ed. Hamilton, 493–94; Steadman, "Reading, Spenser's," in *The Spenser Encyclopedia,* ed. Hamilton, 587; Stephen A. Barney, "Reference Works, Spenser's," in *The Spenser Encyclopedia,* ed. Hamilton, 590–93. Not to be overlooked is James Nohrnberg, *The Analogy of The Faerie Queene* (Princeton, N.J., 1976), which makes passing discussions of Spenser's mythological background throughout.

24. Steadman, "Reading, Spenser's," 587; Judson, *The Life of Edmund Spenser,* in *The Works of Edmund Spenser: A Variorum Edition,* ed. Greenlaw, vol. 11, 14; Bryskett, *A Discourse of Ciuill Life: Containing the Ethike part of Morall Philosophie. Fit for the instructing of a Gentleman in the course of a vertuous life* (London, 1606), 25, quoted in Judson, *The Life of Edmund Spenser,* 106.

25. Andrea Alciato, *Emblemata,* trans. and annotated by Betty I. Knott (1550; rpt. Brookfield, Vt., 1996), 11, shows a snake-footed man and says: "sic gigantes terra mater protulit" [in such a form did Mother Earth once bring forth the Giants].

26. Steadman, *Nature into Myth,* 179, says that "Nonnos apparently took Hesiod's Typhoeus as the model for Campe." Hesiod describes the monster, who fought against Zeus, as having a hundred serpent-heads (*Theog.* 824–25). In the first two books of the *Dionysiaca,* Nonnos relates the battle between Typhoeus and Zeus, thus demonstrating his familiarity with the monster. For Milton's use of the myth of Typhoeus and the conflation of Typhoeus and Typhaon into Typhon in classical and Renaissance texts, see George F. Butler, "Milton's Typhon: Typhaon and Typhoeus in the Nativity Ode and *Paradise Lost,*" *Seventeenth-Century News* 55, (1997): 1–5. For Milton's use of Typhon as a classical model for the rebellious Satan, see Albert C. Labriola, "The Titans and the Giants: *Paradise Lost* and the Tradition of the Renaissance Ovid," *Milton Quarterly* 12 (1978): 9–16.

27. See the note in the variorum edition of Spenser's works (vol. 3, 279; note to *FQ* 3.9.22). The note additionally remarks that Spenser's Bellona in *FQ* 7.6.3 "is represented as quite different from that of Pallas, who does not delight in war for its own sake; while Bellona, like the Greek Enyo, revels in the spirit of battle, and arouses enthusiasm in armies."

MILTON'S WEDDED LOVE:
NOT ABOUT SEX (AS WE KNOW IT)

Thomas H. Luxon

THIS ESSAY WILL TRY to correct a widely accepted misconception about what John Milton meant by "wedded Love" in the hymn-like verses from Book Four of *Paradise Lost:*

> Haile wedded Love, mysterious Law, true source
> Of human ofspring, sole proprietie,
> In Paradise of all things common else.[1]

Some of the best recent commentaries on this topic allow too easy an equation of "wedded Love" with what we today call sexuality. James Grantham Turner, one of the most learned and otherwise careful authorities on this topic, substitutes "sexuality" for "wedded Love" in a paraphrase of a key part of the passage from Book Four of *Paradise Lost* with which this essay opens: "In both *Paradise Lost* and the divorce tracts *sexuality* is the 'sole proprietie / In Paradise of all things common else'—the term connotes privacy, closeness, and exclusive mystery as well as ownership—but in the prose this served only to explain what an 'intimate evil' it becomes when the marriage turns sour. Now [in *Paradise Lost*] this intimacy is a source of delight rather than horror" (italics mine).[2]

Modern readers associate the word *sexuality* with sexual dimorphism, reproduction, genital sensual pleasures, and all the attributes and activities that arouse and satisfy the physical desires associated with sexual intercourse of any kind. But Milton's voluminous writings on marriage and divorce repeatedly insist, with what sometimes seems hysterical frequency, that marriage is essentially and principally a conjunction of minds, hearts, and souls and is only secondarily, as "an effect and fruit" of such conjunction, concerned with the reproduction and delight of bodies.[3] Even those authors whose opinions on marriage Milton most admired—Martin Bucer, Desiderius Erasmus, and Nicolaus Hemming—stopped short of Milton's radical view that the proper purpose of marriage was single, not threefold. God made marriage to remedy the first man's loneliness (Gen. 2:18), a mental and spiritual loneliness that yearned for the rational rather than sensual delights of a fit partner in conversation. Physical procreation was a secondary (though quite necessary) purpose, and sensual delight an incidental effect. "God in the first ordaining of marriage, taught us to what end he did it, in words expresly implying the apt and cheerfull conversation of man with woman, to comfort and refresh him against the evill of solitary life, not mentioning the purpose of generation till afterwards, as being but a secondary end in dignity, though not in necessitie" (*The Doctrine and Discipline of Divorce;* YP 2:235).[4]

Most Protestant writers before Milton—established churchmen and Puritans alike—held that marriage had three ends, differing only about which was most important: procreation, the avoidance of vice or sin, and mutual society.[5] Milton's radical contributions to Protestant marriage theory (which earned him estrangement and abuse from his co-religionists) were to degrade the end of physical procreation, as a matter largely beneath the dignity of manliness, and to redefine matters of physical pleasure or desire as not properly ends but coincident effects of spiritual and mental conjugation. Milton knew that this required some hermeneutic agility, since according to Genesis Adam's first exclamation at seeing the partner God created for him was: "This is now bone of my bones, and flesh of my flesh. . . . Therefore shall a man . . . cleave unto his wife: and they shall be one flesh" (2: 23–24). Adam's initial reaction to his wife and his marriage thus seems to focus on the physical. Milton's strategy was first to claim that God's purpose, stated in verse eighteen (to make "an help meet"), must take precedence over anything Adam says, and second to redefine the meaning of the expression *one flesh:*

For *one flesh* is not the formal essence of wedloc, but one end, or one effect of *a meet help;* The end oft-times beeing the effect and fruit of the form, as Logic teaches: Els many aged and holy matrimonies, and more eminently that of *Joseph* and *Mary,* would bee no true mariage. And that *maxim* generally receiv'd, would be fals, that *consent alone, though copulation never follow, makes the mariage.* Therefore to consent lawfully into one flesh, is not the formal cause of Matrimony, but only one of the effects. (*Tetrachordon;* YP 2:610–11)

When the hymn to marriage in Book Four of *Paradise Lost* invites readers to celebrate "wedded Love" as the "sole proprietie, / In Paradise of all things common else," it defines such a relationship as quintessentially human; marriage was instituted for Adam's manly, not his animal, nature. Wedded love was to be a kind of love altogether different from that practiced and enjoyed by all others in Paradise. Animals, the poem teaches, know nothing of wedded love. Adam notices that the beasts pair off for some sort of solace and conversation (8.392–94), but nowhere is it suggested that they marry each other. Milton's Adam seeks a mate who can offer "rational delight" (8.391–92), a sort of pleasure beasts probably know little or nothing about and certainly cannot supply to Adam. The poem clearly distinguishes between sexuality and wedded love: sexuality belongs to both men and beasts, even plants and planets; wedded love is "the sole proprietie" of what Milton called mankind.

John Halkett's path-breaking *Milton and the Idea of Matrimony* appears to make the same mistake as Turner's *One Flesh* when it refers to Book Four's praise of wedded love (*PL* 4.750–70) as "a hymn in praise of matrimonial sexuality" (Halkett, 27–28). Halkett, Turner, and most other modern Miltonists assume that in the time between writing the divorce tracts (1643–1645) and composing Book Four of *Paradise Lost,* Milton softened in his attitudes toward sexuality. The generally accepted story is that the Milton of the divorce tracts is still bitter over a marriage apparently gone sour and so cannot bring himself to speak of sexuality "without tension, violence, and open disgust" (Turner, *One Flesh,* 232). The Milton of *Paradise Lost,* however, is older and mellower. Mary Paul returned to him in 1645 (and in 1646 brought her entire royalist family to live with them) and Milton would marry again (to Katherine Woodcock in 1656, and to Elizabeth Minshull—aged 24—in 1663). The later Milton is prepared not only to speak of sensual matters with a civil tongue but even to praise and celebrate sexuality as an essential element, even a defining aspect, of wedded love. This Milton, in Stephen M. Fallon's words, wants very much "to debrutalize and redeem sexuality," to proclaim "the refining of the 'quintessence of an excrement' into a 'fountain' of peace and love."[6] I do not think that this account, accepted for so long, will stand closer scrutiny.

Milton often speaks frankly and openly, without disgust, about copulation and sensuality in the divorce tracts, especially in *Tetrachordon.* When he does exhibit disgust, especially in *Colasterion,* it is usually directed toward those who cannot bring themselves to understand the expression "one flesh" from Genesis 2:24, or to understand that what Milton in *The Doctrine and Discipline* called "conversation" signified anything other than sexuality. Conversely, in *Paradise Lost* Milton reserves words of praise and celebration, not for sexuality (matrimonial or other), but for "wedded Love"—that form of human eros that tends away from the body and toward heavenly love. According to Milton's tracts and poems, wedded love does not debrutalize or redeem sexuality. Both beasts and humans enjoy sensual pleasures and both generate offspring. According to the archangel Raphael, there is nothing impure about either activity until the first disobedience permanently taints both. When he describes the angel erotics toward which wedded love will lead Eden's blest pair, Raphael indicates that sensuality is not impure and so needs no redemption:

mane respects of civilitie" (*Doctrine and Discipline;* YP 2:238). Men have
other, more effective means for controlling their physical appetites, says
Milton. Exercise and a "frugal diet without mariage would easily chast'n" the
most insistent sexual desire (YP 2:269).[7] Marriage was instituted to address
altogether higher, more manly, desires. Throughout the divorce tracts Milton's insists that bad marriages and the laws that refuse to dissolve them
depress "the high and Heaven-born spirit of Man, farre beneath the condition wherein either God created him or sin hath sunke him" (YP 2:223).

I recommend a closer look at the praise of wedded love in Book Four of
Paradise Lost. What warrant does this passage provide for equating wedded
love as understood by Milton with sexuality? The passage opens with a string
of appositions, as if the narrator knows that the term has often been misunderstood and is likely to be misunderstood again; he is anxious to be very
clear about what counts as "wedded Love." Can any of these appositives—
"mysterious Law, true source / Of human ofspring, sole proprietie, / in Paradise of all things common else"—legitimately be glossed as a euphemism for
sexuality? In what follows I will argue that in each instance the best answer is
no. I find myself in basic agreement with Irene Samuel's contention, made
long ago in *Plato and Milton,* that Milton declares Adam and Eve's married
love to be "unlibidinous," utterly devoid of passion, and devoted to a mode of
procreation largely unconcerned with matters of the body.[8] Milton's poem insists that in Paradise there was nothing impure about sexual reproduction. As
did Augustine, Milton imagines prelapsarian copulation as entirely free of
"any lust," an absolutely rational act of the will in obedience to God, not to
passion or physical desire.[9] That is why the poem celebrates a bed "undefil'd
and chaste" (*PL* 4.761). The words allude to the advice given in Hebrews
13:14 to early Christians eager for the apocalypse: don't abandon your marriages and families, says the anonymous elder, "whore mongers and adulter-
ers God will judge." Adam and Eve's first copulation is undefiled and chaste,
not because it excludes other partners, but because it is free of the desires and
passions that transform partners into others, into objects of one's physical
desire. Were it not, their copulation would be adulterous, as the poem suggests it is shortly after the Fall (9.1034–45). Book Four reserves its praise for
"wedded Love" rather than copulation, however pure and chaste. And wedded love has nothing whatever to do with the "amorous play" of Book Nine.

There is more at stake in these matters than my efforts to correct three
talented scholars from whom I have learned so much, and to whom all
Miltonists are indebted. If what follows is convincing, we may have to abandon the widely held notion that Milton gradually abandoned his youthful
and almost cultish devotion to purity (as articulated in *Comus, Epitaphium
Damonis,* and the *Apology against a Pamphlet* [1642]) and came to embrace

a more broad-minded appreciation for the God-given pleasures of the human body. And since Milton often serves as a representative for English Puritanism, we may wish either to reconsider assigning him that role or reconsider the merits of a once popular but lately frowned upon sense of the word *puritanical.*

My analysis also supports the contention that Milton was more of a Platonist than a Neoplatonist.[10] Milton read Plato's *Symposium* with the same energy and independence that he brought to his interpretations of Scripture. He does not conflate all of the symposiasts' erotic theories and hymns of praise into one teaching called Platonic. He explicitly rejects Aristophanes' fables and Pausanius' detailed prescriptions about when it is proper and dignified to gratify a lover, and he embraces Socrates' (or Diotima's) teaching about the procreancy of the soul. Unlike the Neoplatonists, and much more like Plato's Diotima, Milton tends to regard the differences between spirit and flesh as differences of degree on a continuum, rather than as differences of kind or binary opposites. This is an aspect of what Miltonists refer to as his monism, although Milton's sense of a matter-spirit continuum does assign a greater moral value to the spiritual than to the physical end of that continuum; thus the opposite ends of the matter-spirit continuum remain effectively a moral binary. Even opposite vectors along that continuum count as moral opposites: "more refin'd, more spiritous, and pure / As neerer to him plac't or neerer tending" (*PL* 5.475–76).[11]

Finally, my analysis suggests that Milton's monism need not always have the effect most often ascribed to it—that of redeeming the body from the detestation it suffers at the hands of Neoplatonic dualism. Raphael teaches Adam that the *telos* of all bodies well exercised by obedience is to "turn all to Spirit, / . . . and wingd ascend / Ethereal" as angels (5.497–99). Persistence in the body, according to this teaching, must be evidence of stubborn disobedience. A body that does not improve by "tract of time" into "all Spirit" is a body of sin. On this score, Milton's monistic continuum supports an ethics no less dualistic than Paul's *kata sarx* and *kata pneuma* in Romans 7 and 8. We shall even find that Milton often resorts to the quasi-allegorical practice of regarding spiritual things as *true,* or more truly real, or more fully realized, versions of bodily things.

MYSTERIOUS LAW

Milton spent much time and effort between 1643 and 1645 trying to redefine marriage for a reluctant, even reactionary, English Parliament. For his pains he earned the ridicule of his friends and Presbyterian allies, and his efforts, however impressive to us, appear to have had no effect on marriage law in

England during his lifetime.[12] Milton's epic narrator, therefore, is careful about the way he deploys the term "wedded Love." That is why he tells readers right away that the practices of "connubial Love" (*PL* 4.743) are "Mysterious" and repeats the word *mysterious* again in his hymn to wedded love (750). The word *mysterious* designates something that is not what it appears to be, not what the many, especially the rabble or uninitiated, suppose it to be. In *Colasterion* Milton derides his anonymous Answerer, calling him a boar and a bayard, because when Milton speaks of a "fit conversing Soul" the Answerer still hears nothing but sex (*Colasterion;* YP 2:747). Milton probably expected him to hear nothing more elevated in Book Four's hymn to wedded love.

The word *mysterious* also appears in Book Three, where it describes the stairs to heaven, similar to those Jacob dreamed of, in a place called Luz (Gen. 28:12). "Each Stair mysteriously was meant," says the narrator, to make it clear that these are not literally stairs but a representation of the stages along a soul's journey toward or away from heaven and spiritual being (*PL* 3.516). In Book Ten we read that God punishes the serpent "in mysterious terms" (10.173). This means, as we know, that the curse is not literally about heads, heels, and bruises. The poem ridicules Satan's willful carnal-mindedness when he later boasts "A World who would not purchase with a bruise" (10.498–500) and carefully explains the mysterious sense to the fit audience in lines 183–90. These examples suggest that "mysterious" in this poem means something that is not literal, not what it superficially appears to be, and not what unfit readers are likely to think it means.

The word *mysterious* in this passage from Book Four also alludes to the Pauline midrash on Genesis and marriage in Ephesians 5. There Paul explains that when Adam proclaims Eve "bone of my bones and flesh of my flesh" (Gen. 2:23), we should understand such language as signifying a "great mystery."[13] However much the Genesis Adam appears to speak about flesh and bones, marriage as instituted by God in Paradise is not about fleshly matters at all but a *mega mysterion* signifying Christ's love for his church. The love Christ has for his church may be erotic, but it is not sexual. When Paul invokes such love as a model for husbands, his intention is to promote something other than sexual love between husbands and wives, perhaps even something meant to *replace* sexual love in what he believed were the last days of life in this world (1 Thess. 4, esp. 3–8 and 16–18). Milton's Adam adopts this midrash in Book Eight when, on first seeing Eve up close, he exclaims:

> I now see
> Bone of my Bone, Flesh of my Flesh, my Self
> Before me; Woman is her Name, of Man

Extracted; for this cause he shall forgoe
Father and Mother, and to his Wife adhere;
And they shall be one Flesh, one Heart, one Soule.   (*PL* 8.494–99)

This passage is more than 80 percent quotation from Genesis, but the language Milton's narrator adds, as a hermeneutic gloss on the passage, is important, for it is the language of classical friendship—"my Self . . . one Heart, one Soule."[14] The Genesis Adam appears to speak of flesh and bone, but Milton's Adam gives such language the Pauline interpretation Milton believed it always already had. By "flesh" and "bone," heart, soul, and self mysteriously are meant. Marriage is a law pronounced and a rite enacted not literally but in figures.

Thus with his first appositional definition of "wedded Love" Milton takes pains to remind readers that the phrase "one flesh" of Genesis 2:24 should not be taken literally to mean that marriage itself has anything to do with flesh. "One flesh" should be read mysteriously, allegorically, to signify those distinctly non-sensual aspects of marriage, aspects that might be understood as similar to Christ's attentions to his church. Milton's invocation of "mysterious Law" here is all of a piece with his argument in *Tetrachordon* that we should no more take the words "one flesh" as a literal description of marriage than we should hear "Take eat, this is my body. . . . This is my blood" (Mark 14:22–24) as a literal description of the Lord's Supper:

Why did *Moses* then set down thir uniting into one flesh? And I again ask, why the Gospel so oft repeats the eating of our Saviours flesh, the drinking of his blood? *That wee are one body with him, the members of his body, flesh of his flesh, and bone of his bone. Ephes.* 5. Yet lest wee should be Capernaitans, as wee are told there, that the flesh profiteth nothing, so wee are told heer, if wee be not deaf as adders, that this union of the flesh proceeds from the union of a fit help and solace. Wee know that there was never a more spiritual mystery then this Gospel taught us under the terms of body and flesh; yet nothing less intended then that wee should stick there. What a stupidnes then is it, that in Mariage, which is the neerest resemblance of our union with Christ, wee should deject our selvs to such a sluggish and underfoot Philosophy, as to esteem the validity of Mariage meerly by the flesh; though never so brokn and disjoynted from love and peace, which only can give a human qualification to that act of the flesh, and distinguish it from the bestial. (*Tetrachordon;* YP 2:606)

The "act of the flesh" that most of us value so dearly Milton considered simply bestial; marriage, a partnership of "fit help and solace," qualifies that bestial act as fit for humans. Men and women may copulate, and they may experience sensual pleasures, but that has nothing to do with marriage as God instituted it. Indeed, marriage is the mysterious conjunction of minds, hearts, and souls that keeps such brutish activities and pleasures in their properly subordinated places.

Before moving on to the next appositive phrase defining wedded love, I want to draw attention to another use of the word *mysterious* in Book Four: the narrator refers to Adam and Eve's genitals as "mysterious parts" (4.312). This may be nothing more than a rhetorically graceful way to say, "the parts we normally conceal were not then concealed." But if the rest of what I have said about the word *mysterious* is right, we are entitled to hear Milton's narrator here insisting that what *we* call sexual organs are not really about sex at all but are, as are the "Rites" of "connubial Love," mysterious. They are organs of generation in only the most shallowly literal sense; Milton would not have us remain satisfied with the literal sense, for they signify, mysteriously, another mode of procreation that is not of the body but of the soul, and thus peculiarly human. *Paradise Lost* teaches that the advent of shame followed closely on the heels of disobedience (9.1058–63). The body's shame focuses on the genitals, and most apparently the penis because it now obeys "upstart passions" more readily than reason, and so man is reduced from manly freedom to brutal servitude (12.88–90).

True Source of Human Offspring

When Milton called wedded love the "true source" of human offspring, he implied that readers are apt to be mistaken in their notions of procreation. Eve had difficulty in learning to distinguish between what is "fair" and what "truly fair" (*PL* 4.477–91). Adam has to resort to physical pedagogy to get her to yield, and thus to see that things "truly fair" are invisible—the inward traits of "manly grace / And wisdom."[15] Much the same is implied by calling wedded love the "true source / Of human ofspring." *True* here means something that is not what you expect, not what you see, invisible and mysterious as opposed to visible and obvious.

If wedded love is, as the next appositional phrase insists, unique to humans, something proper only to Adam and Eve and not "common" to the rest of creation, then it cannot refer to the physical acts of sexual intercourse. Certainly the animals in Eden enjoy coital relations with each other. Sensual pleasures are among the "all things common else," whereas wedded love is peculiar to the human pair. The wedded love this poem celebrates is something distinctly unsensual, something utterly devoid of "touch" and "passion." The archangel Raphael, sent by God the Father to teach Adam all he that needs to know to remain obedient, specifically identifies "the sense of touch whereby mankind / Is propagated" as common to beasts and therefore not proper to the "true Love" Adam was meant to feel for Eve:

> But if the sense of touch whereby mankind
> Is propagated seem such dear delight
> Beyond all other, think the same voutsaf't
> To Cattel and each Beast; which would not be
> To them made common and divulg'd, if aught
> Therein enjoy'd were worthy to subdue
> The Soule of Man, or passion in him move.   (8.579–85)

Milton expected his fit audience to hear in this passage an echo of his claim in *Doctrine and Discipline* that "God does not principally take care for such cattell"; God did not provide an institution like marriage for the remedy of "carnal lust" (which Adam does not experience before the Fall) or "sensitive desire" (the dangers of which Raphael carefully warns him about). Adam confesses to Raphael that he sometimes fears he might be inordinately moved by "touch" and "passion" when he beholds and touches Eve's outward fairness:

> transported I behold,
> Transported touch; here passion first I felt,
> Commotion strange, in all enjoyments else
> Superiour and unmov'd, here onely weake
> Against the charm of Beauties powerful glance.   (8.529–33)

According to this poem, wedded love was meant to be the remedy against that charm, the very charm that subdues Adam, when he falls, and renders him unmanly, "fondly overcome by Femal charm" (9.999). Marriage keeps sensuality in proper subordination and thus keeps passion at bay. What does the poem mean by saying that wedded love is the "true source of human ofspring," then? Are we mistaken in thinking that heterosexual coitus is what makes offspring?

Yes and no. Sensual arousal, touching and rubbing, and orgasm and ejaculation are indeed necessary to propagate the flesh, but that is not, the poem implies, what makes offspring *human*. Only wedded love can make offspring that are truly human. Animals and people both make young through the fleshly act of coitus, but Adam and Eve will make human offspring by a kind of love that is distinct from and higher than coitus, a love of which coitus is the mere earthly sign—wedded love.[16] Not only is this kind of love distinct from sensual erotics; when properly practiced, it will discipline and eventually displace sensuality. After the string of appositions, the hymn continues in apostrophic address to wedded love itself:

> By thee adulterous lust was driv'n from men
> Among the bestial herds to raunge, by thee
> Founded in Reason, Loyal, Just, and Pure,

Relations dear, and all the Charities
Of Father, Son, and Brother first were known.   (4.753–57)

Wedded love drives lust out of men, replacing it with something more god-like. "Adulterous" here does not specify a certain kind of lust; it designates lust as adulterous by definition.[17] Lust is unconcerned with the humanity of its object; indeed it objectifies human subjects as mere flesh or remedies of fleshly desire. This is why most animals are not monogamous; they reproduce by lust and so range from partner to partner unconcerned with anything that makes one sexual partner unique. Humans, the poem insists, because they are flesh, can also love in this way, but truly human love and truly human reproduction is something else. When people reproduce, their bestial nature may be what brings forth young, but only human nature can reproduce human relations that are "Founded in Reason," relations that are "Loyal, Just, and Pure." Animal reproduction knows nothing of fatherhood, brother-hood, filial devotion. Animals reproduce flesh; humans reproduce human relations.[18] Heterosexual coitus can do the former, but only wedded love can do the latter. Thus the poem distinguishes wedded love from anything we might recognize as sexuality.

SOCRATES, PLATO, AND HEAVENLY LOVE

Being so quick to find in Milton's epic a celebration of the sort of sensual erotics we frankly and unashamedly enjoy, we have mostly missed the poem's celebrations of non-sensual, and often non-hetero, erotics. Milton says in the 1642 *Apology against a Pamphlet* that his primary teachers in the lore of love were "the divine volumes of *Plato,* and his equall *Xenophon*" (YP 1:891). From them, he says, he learned of both "chastity and love" together, by which he means something other than physical, or what Neoplatonists called "earthly," love. Plato and Xenophon teach a doctrine of manly love, or "that which is truly so, whose charming cup is only vertue which she bears in her hand to those who are worthy. The rest are cheated with a thick intoxicating potion which a certaine Sorceresse the abuser of loves name carries about; and how the first and chiefest office of love, begins and ends in the soule, producing those happy twins of her divine generation knowledge and vertue" (*Apology;* YP 1:891–92). In other words, he learned from Xenophon and Plato to distinguish between vulgar love and what Xenophon refers to as heavenly love. The Socrates of Xenophon's *Symposium* largely echoes the Pausanius of Plato's in this matter. He is not convinced, as is Plato's Pausa-nius, that there are actually two Aphrodites, each with her own son, but he does affirm that there are two different temples, altars, and distinct rituals for the followers of earthly, carnal, vulgar love, on the one hand, and the noble, spiritual "love of friendship and noble conduct," on the other.[19] Xenophon's Socrates teaches not only that "spiritual love is far superior to carnal" but also that spiritual love is altogether distinct from carnal love. It is "less liable to satiety" (Xenophon 8.16), noble rather than servile (8.23–27), and grows stronger with age rather than weaker because, unlike carnal love, it "progresses towards wisdom" (8.15).

Milton's Adam feels this sort of insatiable, wisdom-directed love in conversation with his heavenly guest, Raphael. He says to his angel guest:

> while I sit with thee, I seem in Heav'n,
> And sweeter thy discourse is to my eare
> Then Fruits of Palm-tree pleasantest to thirst
> And hunger both, from labour, at the houre
> Of sweet repast; they satiate, and soon fill,
> Though pleasant, but thy words with Grace Divine
> Imbu'd, bring to thir sweetness no satietie.   (8.210–16)

Hence Adam's transparent devices aimed at detaining his heavenly guest (206–8); hence also what Linda Gregerson correctly identifies as the hyperbolic compliments typical of fond love poets: suggesting that the sun itself may be charmed to a halt by Raphael's voice and "Sleep list'ning to thee will watch" (7.99–100, 106).[20] In Raphael's company, Adam finds, as it were, that his "conversation is in heaven," as Paul says of his heaven-bound followers in Philippians 3:20–21.

The insatiable desire Adam feels for unending conversation with Raphael may be Milton's finest image of heavenly love; it reminds one of the love he expressed for his own friend Charles Diodati even, or perhaps especially, after his death.[21] In *Epitaphium Damonis* Milton eulogized his friend under the pastoral name of Damon:

Damon dwells in the purity of heaven, for he himself is pure. He has thrust back the rainbow with his foot, and among the souls of heroes and the everlasting gods he quaffs the heavenly waters, and drinks of joys with his sacred lips. But now that the rights of heaven are yours, stand by my side and gently befriend me, whatever be now your name, whether you would still be our Damon, or whether you prefer to be called Diodati, by which divine name all the dwellers in heaven will know you, but in the forests you will still be called Damon. Because a rosy blush, and a youth without stain were dear to you, because you never tasted the pleasure of marriage, lo! for you are reserved a virgin's honours. Your noble head bound with a glittering wreath, in your hands the glad branches of the leafy palm, you shall for ever act and act again the immortal nuptials, where song and the lyre, mingled with the blessed dances, wax rapturous, and the joyous revels rage under the thyrsus of Zion.[22]

Milton imagines his friend as enjoying the ultimate erotic experience reserved for the pure in body when they finally reach heaven—the "immortal
nuptials" and the Dionysiac "rage" only possible when the flesh has been
turned "all to Spirit" (*PL* 5.497). Milton remembers his friend in heaven
when he imagines the archangel Raphael in *Paradise Lost.* He imagines
Charles playing Raphael to his Adam. When Raphael admires Adam's graceful lips (8.218) and smiles "Celestial rosie red" (8.619) as he describes "Union
of Pure with Pure / Desiring," we witness Milton's idealized version of the
love he shared with Charles—centered on highly erotic conversation, intensely and exclusively masculine, intellectual, and strictly non-sexual.[23]
Gregerson is surely right to remark that Milton runs the risk of making
Raphael seem more appropriate a lover, more fit a conversation partner, than
Eve (*The Reformation of the Subject,* 171). And that entails the even more
startling risk of suggesting that the paederasty of the soul Socrates recommended in Plato's *Symposium* might be more fitting than marriage as a
means of leading Adam toward heaven.

But Milton staunchly rejected the notion that Adam might have been
better off with a male partner, even though he was clearly attracted to the
idea. In *Tetrachordon* he explains that "alone" in Genesis 2:18 means specifically without a woman: "And heer *alone* is meant alone without woman;
otherwise *Adam* had the company of God himself, and Angels to convers
with; all creatures to delight him seriously, or to make him sport. God could
have created him out of the same mould a thousand friends and brother
Adams to have been his consorts; yet for all this till *Eve* was giv'n him, God
reckn'd him to be alone" (YP 2:595). Milton strained to redefine marriage as
the friendship Socrates recommended—an erotics beyond the sexual. As a
result, his notion of marriage sometimes looks a lot like a heteroerotic paederasty, with Adam as the paederast and Eve the philerast destined never to
outgrow the role of student and beloved. However disappointing his own
marriages may have been, Milton tried hard to imagine Adam and Eve before
the Fall as enjoying a heavenly erotics, free of earthly passion, perfectly free
of lust.

The conventional wisdom is that Milton abandoned his fantasy of chaste
love, and that he gave up his youthful and cultish devotion to the heavenly
Aphrodite or the "Celestial Cupid" of the Attendant Spirit's closing song in
Comus (1002–11).[24] Stephen Fallon argues that in *Paradise Lost* Milton
manages to shrug off the "dualist drag" of the divorce tracts and, in imagining
Adam and Eve's love life, comes close to a monist blending of body with spirit
that appears as "frank eroticism" (Fallon, "The Metaphysics of Milton's Divorce Tracts," 81). I agree that *Paradise Lost* frankly celebrates eros. I have
already cited the erotics of Adam's conversation with Raphael, and I could

dwell for some time on the erotics of Adam's conversation with God, but the eros there celebrated and hailed as wedded love is not sensuality. In Milton's Paradise, as I have already argued, sensuality needed no redemption, but it also was never meant to be mistaken for wedded love.

Many will object that Milton must somehow have mended the breach between body and spirit that yawns so largely in Neoplatonist erotics, if only to make sense out of God's injunction to "Be fruitful, and multiply, and replenish the earth" (Gen. 1:28). Does not God command the practice of earthly love? Must there not be, then, some pure form of procreation, both in body and in soul? In pursuit of this question we should turn to Milton's other teacher, Plato's Socrates.

From Plato's *Symposium* Milton learned the love lore of Diotima, or, according to Milton, the erotic doctrine Socrates "fain'd to have learnt from the Prophetesse *Diotima*" (*Doctrine and Discipline* 1.4, YP 2:252). This doctrine, somewhat at odds with those of the other symposiasts, teaches that love is centrally a matter of procreation: "it is giving birth in beauty both in body and in soul" (*Symposium* 206b). The sharp distinction Neoplatonists routinely drew between earthly carnal love and heavenly spiritual love follows Pausanius' doctrine of carefully regulated paederasty, articulated in *Symposium* 180d–185c.[25] Christian and Jewish Neoplatonists quietly adapted the symposiasts' explicit homoerotic assumptions and examples to the implicitly heteroerotic nature of the first pair of humans according to Genesis. Most Neoplatonists also merged the various doctrines articulated in the *Symposium* into one, despite the contradictions and inconsistencies between Pausanius, Aristophanes, Phaedrus, Eryximachus, and Diotima. Milton, I believe, read Plato somewhat more critically than they. He dismisses Aristophanes' myth of originary hermaphrodites, one of the Neoplatonists' favorite parts of the *Symposium*, as "*Plato's* wit" and opposes it to Socrates' doctrine of love. He rejects the Neoplatonic conflation of Genesis 1:27 and Aristophanes' primeval androgyne, a reading the Jewish Neoplationist Leone Ebreo embraced. Milton regarded such conflation as typical of the way "the Jewes fable, and please themselvs with the accidentall concurrence of *Plato's* wit" (*Tetrachordon;* YP 2:589).[26] Milton singles out Socrates' teaching, which he "fain'd to have learnt from the Prophetesse *Diotima*," as Plato's true teaching on love. This doctrine, and not Pausanius' meticulous rules of paederasty or Aristophanes' anthropological just-so stories, is the teaching that "divinely sorts" with what Moses teaches in Genesis (*Doctrine and Discipline;* YP 2:252).

Socrates teaches that love is principally about giving birth. Some people, so the doctrine goes, understand procreation as what Milton in the *Doctrine and Discipline* derides as "the purpose of generation" or "the work of male and female," but for a more dignified sort of people, those Milton calls "all generous persons," procreation is altogether a matter of the soul rather than the body (YP 2:235, 240, 246). Here is this understanding of procreation, as Socrates says he learned it from Diotima:

> Now those who are pregnant in body are more oriented toward women and are lovers in that way, providing immortality, remembrance, and happiness for themselves for all time, *as they believe*, by producing children. Those who are pregnant in soul how-ever—for there are people who are even more pregnant in their souls than in their bodies, . . . these people are pregnant with and give birth to what is appropriate for the soul. . . . Good sense [*phronësis*] and the rest of virtue, of which all poets are procre-ators, as well as artisans who are said to be inventors. But much the most important and most beautiful aspect of good sense . . . is that which deals with the regulation of cities and households, the name of which is judiciousness [*söphronsunë*] and justice. (*Symposium* 208e–209b, emphasis mine)

Poets, lawgivers, artists, great men of virtue—these procreate in the soul and give birth to children more truly immortal than fleshly children. "Everyone," says Diotima "would prefer to bring forth this sort of children rather than human offspring" (209d). That is why people envy Homer, Lycurgus, and Solon. Milton certainly imagined he was one of that sort, and he could not have imagined that Adam was anything less. Indeed, Eve often calls Adam her "Author" (*PL* 4.635; 5.397), in a sense virtually synonymous with parent (4.660). Some people must procreate in the body, and no doubt Adam and Eve will do so at some point, but Milton would hardly waste his efforts at celebrating the first nuptials in Paradise on "such cattell" as bodily procre-ation. Indeed, Milton quietly leaves intact the almost universal assumption that Adam and Eve do not procreate *in the body* until after the Fall.[27] The procreation Milton celebrates as wedded love in Paradise is the procreancy of the soul, the first purposes of the Author and Disposer of humankind. Only a reader such as the anonymous Answerer to the *Doctrine and Discipline of Divorce* would hear any note of sensuality in Milton's celebration of wedded love.[28]

   With this in mind, let's take a fresh look at what critics have long under-stood as Milton's radical description of prelapsarian sex.[29] The poem tells us that the "Blest pair" (4.774) finish their evening devotion to God and go to bed.

> This said unanimous, and other Rites
> Observing none, but adoration pure
> Which God likes best, into thir inmost bowre
> Handed they went; and eas'd the putting off
> These troublesom disguises which wee wear,

> Strait side by side were laid, nor turnd I weene
> *Adam* from his fair Spouse, nor *Eve* the Rites
> Mysterious of connubial Love refus'd. (*PL* 4.736–43)

Consistent with what we already have inferred from the poem's celebration of wedded love, which follows this narration, this passage says nothing about desires of the flesh.[30] Adam and Eve may indeed be "one flesh" in some mysterious sense, but their nuptial relations are not about bodily desire. We're told that Adam *did not turn away* from Eve, and that Eve *did not refuse* "the Rites / Mysterious of connubial Love." Everywhere is talk of spontaneous obedience and ritual; nowhere is there talk of desire, unless it is the desire to adore and obey God, who "bids increase" (748). The repeated word "Rites" (736 and 742) should, in any fit reader's mind, evoke images of spontaneous expressions of gratitude to and adoration of God both times it is used. Desire here, in both instances, is vertical toward God, never horizontal between Adam and Eve. They perform the spontaneous ritual of evening prayer unanimously, and they also perform the mysterious rites of connubial love unanimously; that is to say, their desire is unanimously directed toward God.[31] So far from any sort of earthly desire are the two, they seem put to bed by another hand: "Strait side by side were laid." The poet uses the word *mysterious* here, as before, to guard against the possibility of misinterpretation. To see this as a description of sensual copulation is to read in the way that the Answerer reads, and so to earn the poet's condemnation: "But what should a man say more to a snout in this pickle? What language can be low and degenerat anough?" (*Colasterion; YP* 2:747). *Mysterious,* as I have argued, means something that is not what it appears to be at first glance, or not literally what you see, or not what the unlettered rabble mistake it for. Milton argued that Jesus' words about "body" and "blood" in Mark 14:22–24 are meant mysteriously; so also Adam's declaration of marriage as becoming "one flesh." Jacob thought at first that he saw a ladder, but the ladder "mysteriously" meant something else. The mysterious rites of connubial love are meant to be understood this way. This may look like sex at first. Men like the Answerer will always see this as sex, but the fit few see something else: utterly lust-free connubial rites undertaken without any passion or compulsion but in deliberate rational obedience to God, by two perfectly free wills. No one and nothing is swept up or away; here reason does not sleep, or even nod.

Pure procreation is procreation without the least hint of fleshly desire, performed out of a desire to adore and gratify God, not each other or one's self, and to produce more human beings who will stand in proper "filial" relation to the God in whose image they were procreated (4.294). Although Adam and Eve apparently do not conceive children on their wedding night, they do

conceive, mentally and spiritually, the "Relations dear, and all the Charities /
Of Father, Son, and Brother" that are "Founded in Reason, Loyal, Just, and
Pure" (4.755–57). Those who complain that such activity is insufficiently
pure for Paradise are called "Hypocrites" (4.744) not because they have an
unjustly low opinion of sex—Milton also has a low opinion of sex—but because in such complaints they betray their carnal minds; as with the Answerer,
they cannot read "wedded Love" without thinking it means sex. Thus the
famous sex scene in Book Four turns out not to be about sex as we know it.

Adam, who confesses to Raphael that sometimes he feels passion and
has much ado to keep it subjected to his reason, knows that the "genial Bed"
is a place for procreation of quite a different sort than that "common to
all kindes" and thus requires a "mysterious reverence" (8.596–99). Indeed,
when Raphael upbraids him for tending to overvalue passionate feelings and
the object toward which they yearn, Adam corrects himself, "half abash't," by
thinking about marriage and the special mysteries of the nuptial bed. These
thoughts help him to drive off lust and carnal desire. Milton imagines Adam
and Eve as practicing the *true* procreation of human offspring; this does not
exclude, but need not include, what we think of as sexual activity. And in
either case, what we think of as heterosexual coitus is more an accidental
aspect of their "true" intercourse—imagining into being the "Relations dear"
that will be formed amongst their children. This truer form of intercourse
always succeeds in conceiving.

Before I conclude, at least one objection raised by Turner still needs
answering. Turner makes much of the poem's description of Adam as "only
'half abasht'" at Raphael's condemnation of passion and his warnings about
overvaluing "the sense of touch whereby mankind / Is propagated" (*One
Flesh*, 277–78). Adam, he says, is only half abashed because Raphael, though
normally an "impeccably orthodox speaker," is on this score only half correct. The angel does not really understand, Turner suggests, human lovemaking. Turner argues that Adam successfully "challenges the archangel's
estimation of sexual desire, and so redeems some of the rhapsodic 'Passion'
that had inspired his high valuation of Eve and thus caused the [Raphael's]
frowning interruption" (*One Flesh*, 278). Turner plays masterfully on his
reader's biases here, portraying Raphael as insensitively doctrinaire, a masculinist martinet of orthodoxy. Condemning passion, Raphael appears to
condemn Adam's passion-inspired vision of Eve as an equal, even sometimes
superior, being:

> yet when I approach
> Her loveliness, so absolute she seems
> And in her self compleat, so well to know

> Her own, that what she wills to do or say,
> Seems wisest, vertuousest, discreetest, best;
> All higher knowledge in her presence falls
> Degraded, Wisdom in discourse with her
> Looses discount'nanc't, and like folly shewes;
> Authority and Reason on her waite,
> As one intended first, not after made
> Occasionally; and to consummate all,
> Greatness of mind and nobleness thir seat
> Build in her loveliest, and create an awe
> About her, as a guard Angelic plac't.   (*PL* 8.546–59)

Raphael frowns at this speech because he is indeed a masculinist martinet of orthodoxy, but the poem as a whole endorses his position on this score. The sensations Adam here confesses to his heavenly teacher are not in themselves sinful sensations, any more than are the fantastic images of Eve's dream (5.35–93). But they are, just as is her dream, mistaken sensations and notions that, if approved by Adam's reason, could lead to more than mistakenness. Everything we have heard so far about this heaven-blest pair, even from Eve's own mouth, indicates that Eve is neither "absolute" nor "in her self compleat," let alone "wisest, vertuousest, best." The very ugliness of the word *vertuousest* suggests that what we are hearing from Adam strikes wide of the mark. When he is not on the verge of passionate sensual commotion, Adam knows that Eve was formed *for* him and *from* him and that without him she is pointless (4.440–42). She sometimes may seem absolute and self-complete, especially to Adam, because unlike Adam she was not created lonely. She was created as the remedy for human loneliness. Upon her first experience of an apparent other—the "watry" shape in the lake—her response was not, as Turner supposes, desire for the other or for the self but the excitement of being desired (*One Flesh*, 267). She says she thought that the shape was "Bending to look on me" (4.461); her primary desire is to be desired. That is the end for which she was created. That is why in the divorce tracts Milton refers to the husband as "the wanting soul" and mutual pleasure in marriage as "the mutual enjoyment of that which the wanting soul needfully seeks" (*Doctrine and Discipline* 1.4; YP 2:252). He desires; she desires to be desired. Because of this asymmetric mutuality, Eve might well be mistaken as complete in herself, for unlike Adam she is not constitutively lonely. But this is a mistake born of passion, not the well-managed rational "self esteem" Raphael recommends (8.572).

As Adam experiences the oncoming rush of passion prompted by his inordinate attention to Eve's loveliness, he risks forgetting that only the inward qualities—"manly grace / And wisdom"—are "truly fair." As "Best Image" of himself and his "dearer half" (5.95), Eve displays as "an outside" (8.568) the inward virtues that count as truly human and truly fair, because truly in the image of the invisible God. But Adam, says the poet and Raphael, must take care not to let "an outside" dazzle him into forgetting that he, not she, properly possesses such beauties. Eve possesses them only insofar as she is part of Adam, his "Best Image." Apart from him, such loveliness deceives. This passage is Milton's frontal attack on those protofeminist pamphlets that asserted Eve's and women's superiority; such notions, alleges Milton, are the mistakes passion makes when it overcomes reason.[32]

Adam's account of his first experience of sensual erotics complements that of Eve's dream in Book Five; the two are companion pieces. Just as Adam reassured Eve that evil images and notions, unapproved by reason and not activated by consent, "leave / No spot or blame behind" (5.118–19), so Adam, prompted by Raphael's frown and disapproval, reassures himself that he has not been foiled by his experiences of passion and carnal delight because they have not won his approval or his following. Adam is only "half abash't," because he has not sinned; he has merely left Raphael with a mistaken, or incomplete, impression of his nuptial experience. Actually, Raphael interrupted Adam before he could finish his story, before he could reassure Raphael that he left "passion," "the sense of touch," and "carnal pleasure" unapproved and followed instead the delights he experiences in Eve's graceful acts of wedded conversation—what Milton in *Tetrachordon* called "a thousand raptures . . . farre on the hither side of carnall enjoyment" (YP 2:597)[33] Adam, that is to say, already knew what Raphael was going to say, and he agrees completely with Raphael's point.

> Neither her out-side formd so fair, nor aught
> In procreation common to all kindes
> (Though higher of the genial Bed by far,
> And with mysterious reverence I deem)
> So much delights me as those graceful acts,
> Those thousand decencies that daily flow
> From all her words and actions mixt with Love
> And sweet compliance, which declare unfeign'd
> Union of Mind, or in us both one Soule;
> Harmonie to behold in wedded pair
> More grateful then harmonious sound to the eare.
> Yet these subject not; I to thee disclose
> What inward thence I feel, not therefore foild,
> Who meet with various objects, from the sense
> Variously representing; yet still free
> Approve the best, and follow what I approve.

To Love thou blam'st me not, for love thou saist
Leads up to Heav'n, is both the way and guide.   (*PL* 8.596–613)

Turner may not be wrong in endorsing a proper appreciation of sensuality in marriage. I for one agree that frank sensuality and physical erotics deserve more praise than Christianity traditionally has allowed. But Turner is wrong in claiming to side with Adam against Raphael, for Adam fully agrees with Raphael on this score as on all others. After all, God sent Raphael to help Adam get and keep all the most important matters clear; Milton does not mean us to regard him as misleading Adam on any matter, least of all this one. Milton, Raphael, and Adam all share the same, rather sophisticated, misogynist convictions.

SAGE AND SERIOUS DOCTRINE

Milton's doctrine of wedded love, I have argued, is not principally about sex. It does not embrace a "frank eroticism," if by erotic we mean anything lusty or passionate; it does not try to redeem sensuality or celebrate it as "wedded Love." Sensuality, the poem teaches, is always something low and brutal, though in Paradise it once was pure. Milton never retreated from the doctrine of "rational burning" he developed in the *Doctrine and Discipline* (YP 2:251). We might even say that the mysterious rites of wedded love are not as different from the Lady of *Comus*'s "sage / and Serious doctrine of Virginity" as many have supposed (786–87). Milton's sense of manly dignity, especially Father Adam's, requires that marriage and *true* procreation, as with *true* beauty, be a matter of the soul rather than the body. Milton's monism, after all, does not erase dualism; it simply translates a binary opposition into a hierarchical scale—an important adjustment, certainly, but not a thorough departure from body-spirit dualism. "All Spirit" is still the desired country; all body is still the great fear.

Dartmouth College

NOTES

Since its first version, this essay has been improved by discussions with Stephen Fallon, Sharon Achinstein, Shari Zimmerman, Nigel Smith, and Rachel Trubowitz at the Sixth International Milton Symposium in York in July 1999. Rachel Trubowitz also kindly and carefully read yet another draft and made comments that changed the essay dramatically. An anonymous reader for *ELH* made key suggestions, and William Hunter's assessment for *Milton Studies* suggested important improvements. For all of these and for the constructive ways Miltonists in general mix friendship and rigor, I am deeply grateful. The errors signify my inattention or stubbornness.

1. *PL* 4.750–52. Except in the one instance noted, all quotations from Milton's poetry are from *The Milton Reading Room*, ed. Thomas H. Luxon (www.dartmouth.edu/~milton), and will be hereafter cited parenthetically in the text by book and line number, or, when appropriate, simply by line number.

2. James Grantham Turner, *One Flesh: Paradisal Marriage and Sexual Relations in the Age of Milton* (Oxford, 1987), 233.

3. *Tetrachordon*, in *The Complete Prose Works of John Milton*, 8 vols., ed. Don M. Wolfe et al. (New Haven, 1953–82), vol. 2, 610. Further quotations from Milton's prose will be from this volume and cited hereafter parenthetically in the text as YP, with volume and page number. Biblical quotations will be from the Authorized or King James Version throughout.

4. See Richard Strier's interesting discussion of the unresolved tension in Milton's poetry between positive and negative conceptions of necessity in "Milton's Fetters, Or, Why Eden is Better than Heaven," in *Milton Studies* 38, ed. Albert C. Labriola and Michael Lieb (Pittsburgh, 2000), 182–84. As Strier notes on pages 173–74, the God described in *Christian Doctrine* carries out the first act of begetting " 'not from any natural necessity but of his own free will'—a method, Milton assures us, 'more excellent and more in keeping with paternal dignity' (*CD*, YP 6:209)." For Adam, unlike God, procreation may be necessary (indeed, it is commanded by God), but the manly dignity of begetting has to do with an act of free will, not necessity.

5. See Halkett's survey, in *Milton and the Idea of Matrimony: A Study of the Divorce Tracts and Paradise Lost* (New Haven, 1970), of Protestant authors on marriage (5–30).

6. Stephen M. Fallon, "The Metaphysics of Milton's Divorce Tracts," in *Politics, Poetics, and Hermeneutics in Milton's Prose*, ed. David Loewenstein and James Grantham Turner (Cambridge, 1990), 80–81. As are Turner and Halkett, Fallon is a careful and extremely helpful scholar and one of Milton's most attentive readers.

7. See also *Doctrine and Discipline* 1.4: "strict life and labour, with the abatement of a full diet may keep that low and obedient anough" (YP 2:251).

8. Irene Samuel, *Plato and Milton* (Ithaca, 1947), 162. Samuel quotes from and refers to *PL* 5.499.

9. See Augustine's *Concerning the City of God against the Pagans*, trans. Henry Bettenson (London, 1984), book 14, chap. 23–24. Unlike Milton, Augustine believed that Adam fell by disobedience before there was time to copulate rationally. Milton performs the additional move of detaching the rational procreation between souls that results in human society from the purpose of generation. Milton devotes only a rather short (for him) paragraph to explication in *Tetrachordon* of the Genesis injunction to "be fruitful and multiply" (1:28). Even here he cites Plato to help define what he calls an "honest and pious" desire for children, that is not for children as mere offspring but as "continuall servants of God" (YP 2:593).

10. Irene Samuel, in *Plato and Milton*, measures quite carefully and sensibly Milton's relation to his Neoplatonist predecessors (27–43).

11. Stephen Fallon makes a similar point in "The Metaphysics of Milton's Divorce Tracts," 81.

12. On the reception of the divorce tracts see Ernest Sirluck's introduction to *Doctrine and Discipline* (YP 2:137–141). Also consider the vituperative bile of *Colasterion* as Milton's response to their reception (YP 2:719–58).

13. See the entry for *mysterion* in William F. Arndt and F. Wilbur Gingrich, *A Greek-English Lexicon of the New Testament*, 4th ed. (Chicago, 1952), 532. On Milton's reading of Ephesians 5 in *Tetrachordon*, see Rachel Trubowitz, " 'The Single State of Man': Androgyny in *Macbeth* and *Paradise Lost*," *Papers on Language and Literature* 26 (1990): 329. See also the classic treatment of mysterious meaning in Renaissance culture, Don Cameron Allen, *Mysteriously Meant: The Rediscovery of Pagan Symbolism and Allegorical Interpretation in the Re-*

naissance (Baltimore, 1970). For wonderful discussions of Pauline teaching as Platonic versions of traditional midrash, see Daniel Boyarin, *A Radical Jew: Paul and the Politics of Identity* (Berkeley, 1994), 57–85.

14. For a fine collection of classical literature on friendship, emphasizing the "other self" tradition, see *Other Selves: Philosophers on Friendship*, ed. Michael Pakaluk (Indianapolis, 1991).

15. I rely on observations and analyses here, and later, from John Guillory's brilliant reading of this distinction, and of the distinction between Adam and Eve in general, in "Milton, Narcissism, Gender: On the Genealogy of Male Self-Esteem," in *Critical Essays on John Milton*, ed. Christopher Kendrick (New York, 1995), 194–223, esp. 209–15.

16. That not all babies born are necessarily truly human is implied by Michael's teaching in *PL* 12.97–110. Presumably Ham's children were born with the face of God turned from them, justly doomed or cursed to be servants of servants with no legitimate claim to humanity. Milton was, contrary to what many modern Miltonists believe, quite comfortable with the notion of race-based slavery. See Steven Jablonski's convincing arguments in "Ham's Vicious Race: Slavery and John Milton," *Studies in English Literature, 1500–1900* 37 (1997): 173–90.

17. In Plato's *Symposium* (191e) Aristophanes expresses the conviction that adulterous lust was most typical of heterosexuals, those who originally were hermaphrodites; presumably homosexuals, or those from originally male and female wholes, made more faithful partners, and in general were less moved by lust. See *The Symposium and the Phaedrus: Plato's Erotic Dialogues*, trans. William S. Cobb (Albany, 1993). Cited hereafter parenthetically in the text as *Symposium*.

18. According to most classical teaching the paradigmatic human relationship was manly friendship. Milton follows Genesis, which teaches that the first and therefore paradigmatically human relationship is heterosexual marriage. In many ways, however, Milton's redefinition of marriage seems a lot like classical paederasty and classical friendship. In both *Paradise Lost* and the divorce tracts this had the unexpected effect of suggesting that women are human enough— "Manlike" enough—to serve as friends and protégés to men (*PL* 8.471). Perhaps this is why some readers find the poem mildly protofeminist.

19. Xenophon, *Symposium* 8.11–12, in *Symposium and Apology*, trans. O. J. Todd, vol. 4 of *Xenophon in Seven Volumes* (Cambridge, Mass., 1979). Cited hereafter as Xenophon.

20. On the homoerotic tone of Adam's conversation with Raphael, see Linda Gregerson, *The Reformation of the Subject: Spenser, Milton, and the English Protestant Epic* (Cambridge, Mass., 1995), 171.

21. The two most interesting and useful essays on the Milton's friendship with Diodati are John Rumrich, "The Erotic Milton," *Texas Studies in Literature and Language* 41 (1999): 128–41, and John Shawcross, "Milton and Diodati: An Essay in Psychodynamic Meaning," in *Milton Studies* 7, ed. Albert C. Labriola and Michael Lieb (Pittsburgh, 1975), 127–63. Still indispensable after many years is Donald Clayton Dorian, *The English Diodatis* (New Brunswick, 1950).

22. *Epitaphium Damonis* 203–19. The translation is from *The Oxford Authors: John Milton*, ed. Stephen Orgel and Jonathan Goldberg (Oxford, 1991), 161.

23. I cannot agree with the speculations of Shawcross and William Kerrigan about a sexual relationship between the two young friends. Their relationship was certainly erotic; even a brief glance at the surviving correspondence betrays that, but their bond also involved a deep appreciation of and perhaps commitment to sexual purity. For Kerrigan, see *The Sacred Complex: On the Psychogenesis of Paradise Lost* (Cambridge, Mass., 1983), 49.

24. Amor or Cupid appears again in *PL* 4.763–64; his "constant Lamp" distinguishes him as the fully spiritualized lover of the human soul rather than the younger son of Venus who hides in the dark.

25. The Neoplatonist uses to which Plato's *Symposium* was put are fascinating. For exam-

ple, in Aristophanes' rather funny just-so story about where desire comes from, Neoplatonists imagined they had found a solution to the problem of the apparently divergent accounts of human creation in Genesis. Genesis 1:27 articulated the creation of a spiritual or ideal Adam, both male and female. Genesis 2:7–23 told how the corporeal Adam was formed from the dust of the ground, and the female made from a piece of his body. Milton rejected such interpretations as Jewish fables, by which I take him to mean traditional midrash, and insisted that Paul's teaching in 1 Corinthians settled the matter: "But *St. Paul* ends the controversie by explaining that the woman is not primarily and immediatly the image of God, but in reference to the man. *The head of the woman, saith he, 1 Cor. 11. is the man: he the image and glory of God, she the glory of the man:* he not for her, but she for him" (*Tetrachordon;* YP 2:589). See also Turner, *One Flesh,* 65–68; Philo, *On the Creation,* in vol. 1 of the Loeb Classical Library *Philo,* trans. F. H. Colson and G. H. Whitaker (London, 1929), 55–61; Leone Ebreo, *The Philosophy of Love,* trans. F. Friedeberg-Seeley and Jean H. Barnes (London, 1937), 367–73.

26. See also Turner, *One Flesh,* 70–71.

27. In *Paradise Lost* 9.270, the narrator refers to Eve's "Virgin Majestie" at a point chronologically after to the "Rites / Mysterious of connubial Love" celebrated in 4.742–43. After the Fall Eve implies that Adam has not yet begotten, nor she conceived, fleshly children (10.986–89), even though they have certainly experienced the "wedded Love" that is the "true source of human ofspring" (4.750–51).

28. See Milton's frequent berating in *Colasterion* of the Answerer for always having sex on his mind when Milton speaks of a "fit conversing soule" (YP 2:741–43).

29. Turner even refers to this episode as "the normal process of sexuality" (*One Flesh,* 258).

30. Halkett, without any explanation or paraphrase, quotes lines 738–43 as evidence of the "fully sexual" nature of Adam and Eve's relationship (*Milton and the Idea of Matrimony,* 102).

31. Turner notes that Luther imagined prelapsarian lovemaking as a form of worship, and that Milton here realizes Luther's "wistful conjecture" (*One Flesh,* 236). In this I think Turner was exactly right, but this observation does not lead Turner to conclude that Adam and Eve's coupling here is something other than "making love" as we use the term today.

32. For examples, see *Jane Anger, Her Protection for Women* (London, 1589); *Ester Hath Hang'd Haman* (London, 1617); and Mary Tattle-well, *The Woman's Sharpe Revenge* (London, 1640). These texts are conveniently reprinted in *Half Humankind: Contexts and Texts of the Controversy about Women in England, 1540–1640,* ed. Katherine Usher Henderson and Barbara F. McManus (Urbana, 1985).

33. Turner's frequent assumption that Milton understood the rhetoric of the Song of Solomon as sensually erotic cannot stand in the face of this passage, in which Milton explains that the "jolliest expressions" of the Song of Songs are not about sex: "Wherof lest we should be too timorous, in the aw that our flat sages would form us and dresse us, wisest *Salomon* among his gravest Proverbs countenances a kinde of ravishment and erring fondnes in the entertainment of wedded leisures; and in the Song of Songs, which is generally beleev'd, even in the jolliest expressions to figure the Spousals of the Church with Christ, sings of a thousand raptures between those two lovely ones farre on the hither side of carnall injoyment" (*Tetrachordon;* YP 2:597).

THE PORTRAYAL OF EVE IN *PARADISE LOST:*
GENIUS AT WORK

Ken Hiltner

The hardness and smell of the oakwood began to speak clearly of the slow and lasting way in which the tree grew. The oak itself proclaimed that all that lasts, and bears fruit is founded on such growth alone: that growth means to lie open to the span of the heavens and, at the same time, to have roots in the dark earth: that everything real and true only prospers if mankind fulfills at the same time the two conditions of being ready for the demands of the highest heaven and of being safe in the shelter of the fruitful earth.

Martin Heidegger

IN THIS ESSAY I intend to argue that Milton deconstructed medieval theology's dualistic representations of Christianity. To suggest that Milton "deconstructed" anything (let alone Christianity) may seem little more than a thinly veiled attempt to attach this essay to an influential movement; nonetheless, I hope to bring attention to recent scholarship that has traced deconstruction from Derrida (through Heidegger) to a surprising Reformation antecedent in Luther, and also to approach Milton's "monism" in a new way.[1] I will argue that his monism may be the result of Milton's de-structuring of medieval theology's dualistic Christianity, Christianity understood as being con-structed within what I will call the "Christian-pagan" dyad.

Derrida's method of deconstruction was not only derived from Heidegger's *destruction (Destruktion)*; as the translator of *Of Grammatology* tells us, deconstruction in Derrida's sense was originally so similar to destruction that "in the first published version of *De la grammatologie,* Derrida uses the word 'destruction' in place of 'deconstruction.'"[2] Though deconstruction in Derrida's sense would come to be associated with the belief that signifiers are so freely (perhaps mischievously) at play within texts that all authority is undermined, destruction's counter aim, as Heidegger defines it in *Being and Time,* is an effort to "stake out the positive possibilities of . . . tradition" and *not* (as in deconstruction) to succumb to "a vicious relativizing of . . . standpoints"[3]—a remarkable prefiguring of Derrida in 1927.

When confronted with dualistic thinking in the form of binary structures in opposition, such as the subjectivity-objectivity dyad, Heidegger sought to de-structure the structure to arrive at the origin of the structure itself; in the case of the subjectivity-objectivity dyad this origin was Heidegger's much celebrated *Dasein*. The "origin" not only because both halves of the dyad are derived from this source, but, as Heidegger's analysis was historical, after the "hardened tradition" was "loosened up, and the concealments which it [the tradition] has brought about" were "dissolved,"[4] it would be found that the dyadic structure was historically preceded by the "origin" (Heidegger generally held that the subjectivity-objectivity binary structure had yet to emerge in pre-Socratic thought). Whereas destruction has a negative aspect in that it destabilizes the binary structure, as does deconstruction, its aim is nonetheless positive, because it attempts to recover something precious (concealed by the dyadic structure) that the tradition no longer sees.

The relevance of this to Milton studies becomes clear when we look for an historical precedent to Heidegger's destruction. Because Heidegger destroyed many of his early notes, his precedent had been something of a mystery. Though some scholars suggested Nietzsche as a source, recent scholarship by Edward John Van Buren and others into Heidegger's previously unavailable early lecture notes discovered a surprising Reformation origin for destruction.[5] As John D. Caputo succinctly puts it, the young Heidegger, "who identified himself . . . as a Christian theologian," had as "model in this project" of destruction none other than Martin Luther, who "even used the word 'destruction' [*Destruktion*] to describe his project of recovering an authentic scriptural Christianity beneath the conceptual scaffolding of medieval theology."[6] As with Heidegger centuries later, Luther found himself mired in a tradition of duality, particularly with respect to the spirit-flesh dyadic structure propounded by the Church. As Luther puts it with characteristic directness, "Metaphysical theologians deal with a silly and crazy fiction when . . . they invent the notion that the spirit, i.e., reason, is something absolute or separate by itself and in its own kind an integral whole and that, similarly, opposite to it also sensuality, or the flesh, constitutes equally an integral whole."[7] For Luther the spirit-flesh structure, as a mutually exclusive dichotomy, was con-structed by medieval theologians and was without scriptural support.

Luther himself adopted the name and idea of destruction from an interpretive reading of 1 Corinthians, in which God declares, " 'I will *destroy* the wisdom of the wise' " (1:19; italics mine). As Van Buren puts it, "fatefully for the young Heidegger, Luther's Theses 19 and 20 [of the *Heidelberg Disputation*] translate the term 'destroy' in I Corinthians into the Latin *destruere* [cognate for the German *Destruktion*], to pull down, to dismantle, to destroy, to deconstruct." This suggested to Luther that the spirit's desire to pull free of the body, especially for the purpose of abstract theoretical thought, amounts to a very dangerous sort of pride that, as Van Buren states it, "will-fully and hyperbolically oversteps its limits, elevates itself into the Beyond (*super*) of its speculative visions, and thereby seeks to satisfy its desire for do-minion (*dominium*), power (*potestas*), empire (*imperium*)."[8] Luther's sug-gestion—that the spirit-flesh dichotomy as a means of understanding human nature tempts the spirit to overstep its limits and to elevate itself (desiring dominion and power)—can help us, I will argue, understand the Fall in *Paradise Lost*. Although it is beyond the scope of this essay to link destruction in Luther's sense with Milton, I will suggest that the mature Milton's monism follows from his similar de-struction of dualistic (as being of the earth or *not* of the earth) Christianity into a Christianity rooted in the earth.

Before moving to Milton, however, I shall explore the Christian-pagan dyad through a type of etymological destruction of the word *pagan* to arrive at its historical origin. The historian Oswald Spengler, though more inter-ested in our Decline than our Fall, has an interesting viewpoint on our original relationship to the earth. A deep transformation occurred, he argues, when humans first entered into a relationship with the earth, not as hunters or gatherers, but as *planters:*

To plant implies, not to take something, but to produce something. *But with this, man himself becomes plant*—namely, as peasant. He roots in the earth that he tends, the soul of man discovers a soul in the countryside, and a new earth-boundness of being, a new feeling, pronounces itself. Hostile Nature becomes the friend; earth becomes *Mother* Earth. Between sowing and begetting, harvest and death, the child and grain, a profound affinity is set up. A new devoutness addresses itself in chthonian cults to the fruitful earth that grows up along with man. (Italics Spengler's.)[9]

What I find most fascinating about this account is the association of plants with peasants. Though Spengler does not expound further, an etymological consideration of our English word *peasant* will help us understand this asso-ciation. *Peasant* derives from the Latin *pangere* (and, as we shall see, so does *pagan*), which means literally to place something into the earth, to fix it there, establish it, join and unite it (with the earth), or simply, "to plant in the earth."[10] As it carries the meaning of "something joined together," *pangere* has a common root with *pax*, from which our words *pact* and *peace* derive, since people at "peace" with each other are, by way of a "pact," joined together. *Peasant* then means (as Spengler noted) not only to be a planter but at the same time to be rooted in the earth, literally by a pact between the peasant and the earth in which each is at peace. A pact, as Spengler puts it, is "not to take something, but to produce something" (*Decline of the West*, 89).

The modern sense of *pagan* (the idea and the meaning attached to *pangere*) was brought about by an early interpretation of Christianity that sought to *construct* itself in opposition to what Spengler called "chthonian cults" and also created the Christian-pagan dyadic structure—and a thoroughly dualistic manner of thinking.[11] Following from this interpretation, the pagans became those who, as rooted in and connected to the earth, were thoroughly earth-bound, whereas Christians, who had the capacity to transcend the earthly shell, suffered no such bondage.[12] The earth and spirit (as well as body and mind) were thus separated, and Christians ran the risk of undoing that blessed union between human beings and the earth that typifies peasants. If Milton is to overcome this dualism, he must undertake the destruction of the Christian-pagan dyad by reclaiming the original sense of *pangere* (as peasant, rootedness in the earth) from pagan.[13] The difficulty of this enterprise can be seen in the ease in which Spengler moves from his perception of earth as friend, then as mother, then as the object of devotion at the center of "chthonian cults" (*Decline of the West,* 90). If Milton fails to reclaim our original peasantry, then this remarkable connection between human beings could be lost to Christianity. To show just how devastating this lapse into dualism could be for us and the earth, I will first discuss Friedrich Nietzsche, before moving on to Milton.

In what some would see as an anticipation of deconstruction, Nietzsche set about from his first work, *The Birth of Tragedy,* to invert the privileged position that the Christian (interpreted as spirit) had over the pagan (the earthly). The ecological significance of Nietzsche's interpretation of Christianity lies in his belief that the Christian wished to have the spirit pull free of the earthly and be with God in a super-sensible realm. But since the spirit is still connected to the earth by way of the body, the Christian spirit lashes back at the body (and the Earth) out of anger at having its dream of ascension thwarted. As I noted earlier, this line of thinking was intimated by Luther, but Nietzsche saw this anger in Christianity as a more general need for power and dominion not only over the body but over all that was earthly, indeed, the earth itself. As environmental writer Bruce W. Foltz puts it, "And as Nietzsche saw so lucidly . . . this metaphysical hostility to the earth . . . is the very essence of revenge."[14] What is forgotten here, however, is what Nietzsche only came to see in the last few months of his sanity: this potential for ecological disaster *only necessarily occurs* when the super-sensible realm is inaccessible for the embodied human being.[15] To understand why Milton is not vulnerable to such a critique, it will be first helpful to consider the *genius loci* figures in Milton's poetry.

In an influential essay, Lynn White Jr. emphasizes the environmental significance of the *genius loci*: "In Antiquity every tree, every spring, every stream, every hill had its own *genius loci*, its guardian spirit. . . . Christianity of course also had angels and demons. . . . But these were all as mobile as the Saints themselves. The spirits *in* natural objects, which formerly had protected nature from man, evaporated."[16] Christianity, which White argues opposed belief in the *genius loci*, "made it possible to exploit nature in a mood of indifference to the feelings of natural objects" as "the old inhibitions to the exploitation of nature crumbled." White's understanding of "guardian spirits" is that their sole function (as guardians) is to protect nature from human beings. However, in Milton's poetry, the classical idea of the *genius loci* is substantially revised, as a human *spirit* joins with a specific *place* to become a "spirit of place" that guards both the place *and* human beings.

Each of five major works of Milton's 1645 *Poems* contains a *genius loci* (in most actually named *genius*) who figures prominently. In *Lycidas*, for example, the figure is critical in ameliorating the tragedy of the story. Lycidas (Edward King), a human being in peril, drowns but is saved by the beneficent nature of the place, which transforms the human being into the spirit of the place: "Hence forth thou [King] art the Genius of the shore" (183). The story of Lycidas is not a transformation myth in the sense of the Daphne story, since the shore did exist before King and continues on with Lycidas made "Genius of the shore" (183). At a moment of complete powerlessness, King's spirit unites with the shore to become imbued with the immense saving power of the place, which enables him to save "all that wander in that perilous flood" (185).

In the oft-quoted reference to the "parting Genius" (186) in the Nativity ode, a *genius loci,* along with a host of pagan gods, is forced out of each "haunted spring, and dale" (184) to make room for Christ. In *Il Penseroso* there is only a brief mention of a *genius loci*—a "sweet musick" (151) that was either sent by a spirit, "Or th' unseen Genius of the Wood" (154). Yet in *Arcades* a *genius loci* again has a central role. Why? To begin, the twenty-one-year-old Milton is not necessarily exiling his *genius loci* in the Nativity ode. As Stella Revard remarks of Apollo (another outcast in the Nativity ode), though it would seem that the pagan god must "either be a symbol for Christ or a rival," Milton's novel approach to this either-or dilemma was to "embrace it as he endows his Christ in the Nativity ode with Apollonian splendor and to reject it as he dismisses Apollo himself."[17] That a *genius loci* later appears in *Arcades* indicates just such a refusal to accept the *either* pagan *or* Christian dyadic structure. As Cedric Brown notes, in the genius of the northern wood's speech, "fifteen lines go to the description of plant doctoring. Ten lines play out 'the caelestiall sirens harmonie.' And each balances the other in a 'puritan' rhythm."[18] In *Arcades* we have the vocation of the *genius loci* clearly defined as caring for the nature of the place (through plant doctoring), over which the Genius presides, yet seemingly in contrast to this rootedness in place there is a near equal concern for "the celestial Sirens harmony" (63). We are witness in *Arcades* to an early reemergence of the pagan *genius loci* within the Christian tradition—a spirit rooted in place, yet with an ear for a spirit realm.

This Miltonic idea of *genius loci* as both rooted in the earth and spiritually aware is probably nowhere clearer in the earlier works than in *Comus*. As Richard Neuse noted of *Comus's genius loci*, "Sabrina becomes a symbolic expression of man's lower nature seen in a truly new light, transformed, namely as no longer in conflict with spirit and reason, but as harmoniously responsive to them."[19] Neuse continues by suggesting that this thought would find fruition in *Paradise Lost*: "It would seem that Milton envisioned the essential harmony and continuity between the sensual and spiritual faculties long before he wrote the Tree of Life passage in Book Five of *Paradise Lost*." (At this point Neuse quotes lines 479–87 of Book Five, in which Creation is figured as a plant rooted in the earth that ultimately flowers as spirit while still connected to the earth.) Although we might substitute Milton's own coinage of "sensuous" for Neuse's sexually evocative "sensual," in his phrase "sensual and spiritual faculties," and see Sabrina more literally as an expression of the "Nature of the place" and not "man's lower nature," Neuse does make a provocative case for a spirituality rooted in the earth as being further developed in *Comus* in the form of a *genius loci*, Sabrina.

Adapting the Sabrina myth for this purpose did present something of a problem for Milton: as it appears in Spenser, Drayton, and Geoffrey of Monmouth, and even in his own *The History of Britain*, the river Severn is not the mechanism by which Sabrina is saved but, quite the contrary, the instrument of her destruction, as she is murdered by being thrown into its swift current.[20] Undaunted, Milton simply rewrites the tale to ascribe a saving power to a now beneficent river—a saving power that Sabrina will come to share in as she will be able to free the Lady of *Comus*. As in *Lycidas* Edward King is made the rescuing "Genius of the shore" (183) by the power of the place, in *Comus* Sabrina is transformed into the saving "Goddess of the River" (842).

Having gone to such pains to adapt the *genius loci* of antiquity to Christian thinking, Milton, rather surprisingly, abandoned the idea of a *genius loci* for the most part in the great works of his maturity: there is no mention of a *genius loci* in *Paradise Lost, Paradise Regained,* or *Samson Agonistes*. Or did he? A careful look at *Arcades* and *Paradise Lost* together will reveal the remarkable final form that the "spirit of place" will take in Milton's mature thought. Consider the description of the Genius of the Wood's vocation of caring for the earth in *Arcades:*

For know by lot from Jove I am the powr
Of this fair Wood, and live in Oak'n bowr,
To nurse the Saplings tall, and curl the grove
With Ringlets quaint, and wanton windings wove.
And all my Plants I save from nightly ill,
Of noisom winds, and blasting vapours chill.
And from the Boughs brush off the evil dew,
And heal the harms of thwarting thunder blew,
Or what the cross dire-looking Planet smites,
Or hurtfull Worm with canker'd venom bites.
When Eev'ning gray doth rise, I fetch my round
Over the mount, and all this hallow'd ground,
And early ere the odorous breath of morn
Awakes the slumbring leaves, or tasseld horn
Shakes the high thicket, haste I all about,
Number my ranks, and visit every sprout
With puissant words, and murmurs made to bless. (44–60)

The similarities between this Genius and Sabrina are obvious. Both actively visit the place they inhabit: "oft at Eeve" (843) Sabrina "Visits the herds along the twilight meadows" (844), and the Genius in *Arcades* informs us that "When Eev'ning gray doth rise, I fetch my round / Over the mount, and all this hallow'd ground" (54–55). Sabrina "with pretious voild liquors heals" (847) the effect of "all urchin blasts, and ill luck signes" (845), and in *Arcades* the Genius explains not only that he undertakes to "heal the harms of thwarting thunder blew" (51) but also that "all my plants I save from nightly ill, / Of noisom winds, and blasting vapours chill" (48–49). What may be less obvious, however, is just how closely the Genius of the Wood in *Arcades* resembles Eve in *Paradise Lost*.

Diane McColley first noticed the likeness between the genius in *Arcades* and Eve. In order to give evidence of Milton's "lifelong insistence on the responsible use of creative energy" toward the earth, McColley draws our attention to Milton's early spirit of place: "In *Arcades*, the Genius of the northern Wood says that it is his job to 'nurse the saplings,' save plants 'from nightly ill,' 'heal the harms' of thunder, unpropitious planets, and 'hurtfull Worm,' and, like Eve, hasten forth early to 'Number my ranks, and visit every sprout / With puissant words, and murmurs made to bless.' "[21] If we consider, on a line-by-line basis, just how much this Genius is "like Eve," it becomes clear that he is an early formulation of Eve (and to a lesser extent, Adam).

Both the Genius in *Arcades* and humanity in *Paradise Lost* have been given, by divine decree, "dominion"[22] over the place where they dwell: the Genius knows that because of "Jove I am the powr / Of this fair Wood" (44–

45), and one of Adam's earliest memories is of God informing him that "This Paradise I give thee, count it thine / To Till and Keep" (8.319–20). The idea that human beings have dominion over the entire earth is sure to make environmentalists cringe, but as this early formulation in Arcades shows, the *domain* of the Genius (as a *genius loci*) is limited to a specific place (the "fair Wood"), as are Adam and Eve in *Paradise Lost*. Adam realizes that while "other Creatures all day long / Rove idle unimploid . . . And of thir doings God takes no account" (4.616–22), human beings must remain rooted to do their work of tilling and keeping their place: "Man hath his daily work of body or mind / Appointed, which declares his Dignitie" (4.618–19) by caring for the small part of the earth where they are rooted—their "pleasant labour" (4.625).

Both Adam and Eve realize that if human beings are to have dominion over the entire earth (to be guardians of the entire earth), many more will be necessary to "Till and Keep" all the specific places: Adam remarks to Eve that the work will "require / more hands than ours" (4.628–29), and Eve realizes that "till more hands / Aid us, the work under our labor grows" (9.207–8). There is a hint that the need for more human guardians of place has already been provided for: when Adam is first brought into the Garden, he notices that it is "Planted, with Walks, and Bowers" (8.305), suggesting that there were many places (with bowers in place) in need of spirits to tend them. The idea that a "Spirit of a Place" would dwell in a bower was introduced in *Arcades:* the Genius lives in an "Oak'n bowr" (45), and Adam and Eve similarly live in a "blissful Bower" of "Laurel and Mirtle" (4.690–94).

Continuing with *Arcades,* the tilling the Genius practices is described in the next line: "To nurse the Saplings tall" (46). This "nursing" of plants will mature into the dual image of fertility (as in a child's nursery) and fecundity (as in a plant nursery) coming together in the single personage of the nurturing Eve, whose plants "at her coming sprung" in "Her Nurserie" (8.46).[23] As the words *nurse, nursery,* and *nurture* have a common root in the Latin *nutrire* ("to nourish"), keeping and tilling their place are first and foremost to the Genius and Eve a nurturing of the plants in the place they inhabit.

Milton further elaborates on this vocation of tilling and keeping a place on earth. In *Arcades* the Genius must "curl the grove / With Ringlets quaint, and wanton windings wove" (46–47). In *Paradise Lost* this activity is portrayed in two ways: first as the practical work of nurturing, as Eve (with Adam) must work to ensure that no "Fruit-trees overwoodie reachd too farr" (5.213) and must lead "the Vine / to wed her Elm" (5.215–16). The immense fecundity of the Earth itself will prove a liability without the judicious gardening of a spirit of the place. Secondly, with the phrase "Ringlets quaint" (47), *Arcades* introduces the aesthetic aspect of gardening that Eve would beautifully practice in the bower: "Here in close recess / With Flowers, Garlands, and sweet-smelling Herbs / Espoused Eve deckt first her nuptial bed" (4.708–10), and that she would remember after the Fall, "Thee lastly nuptial Bowre, by mee adornd / With what to sight or smell was sweet" (11.280–81). In both of these works a "guardian of the place" is needed to ensure both the bounty and beauty of their place.

The next lines of *Arcades* concern a postlapsarian world in which ills and evils come at night. Though the Genius must save his plants "from nightly ill, / Of noisom winds, and blasting vapours chill" (48–49) and more ominously "from the Boughs brush off the evil dew" (50), in the prelapsarian world, the "nightly ill" that Milton retains is far more benign, as Eve fears that "one night or two with wanton growth derides / Tending to wilde" (9.211–12). Incidentally, not only is there an early formulation of Eve in *Arcades;* in the postlapsarian night there also lurks a prototype of the threat to her, the "hurtfull Worm with canker'd venom bites" (53). After the references to the night, the Genius tell us he is so concerned with his vocation that with "the odorous breath of morn . . . haste I all about" (56–58). This deep sense of vocation (and with it deep joy) emerges again in *Paradise Lost* (as morning "haste") when "On to thir morning work they [Eve and Adam] haste" (5.211)[24]

The Genius in *Arcades* next further expounds on how he tends his place. Part of his task is to "Number my ranks" (59) of plants in order to keep track of them through a sort of classification system. In the parallel passage in *Paradise Lost*, Eve, when faced with exile from the Garden, asks her plants, "Who now shall reare ye to the Sun or ranke / Your Tribes" (11.278–79). So tilling and keeping mean not only nurturing but also keeping track of the plants in the domain of the "guardian." As Milton quickly reminds us, nurturing is of the utmost importance, as the Genius makes sure to "visit every sprout / With puissant words, and murmurs made to bless" (59–60). The idea of "visiting" plants returns in *Paradise Lost* as Eve goes "forth among her Fruits and Flours, / To visit how they prosper'd, bud and bloom" (8.44–45) and after the Fall remembers the flowers and her "early visitation" (11.275). (Note also that to Eve they are *"her* Fruits and Flours" [8.44; italics mine] that she visits, in the same way that the Genius proclaims that "all *my* plants I save from nightly ill" [48; italics mine]: both the Genius and Eve understand their responsibility, in that these plants are within their domain—these plants are "theirs" to till and keep.) Whereas in *Arcades* the Genius only "blesses" the plants "With puissant words, and murmurs," the metaphor is varied and strengthened in *Paradise Lost*: it is not "words" or "murmurs" of Eve's voice but her touch that affects the plants, and whereas there may be doubt that the Genius's blessing was felt by his plants, there is no question that Eve's flowers felt the work of her hands as "they at her coming sprung / And toucht by her fair tendance gladier grew" (8.46–47).[25]

Continuing with our comparison, in *Arcades* the Genius has a split nature, being not only rooted in the earth, as we have been suggesting, but also having an ear for a transcendental spirit realm:

> But els in deep of night when drowsines
> Hath lockt up mortal sense, then listen I
> To the celestial Sirens harmony.   (61–63)

This idea reappears in *Paradise Lost,* although there the celestial music is a hymn to God. As it is spoken by Adam to Eve:

> how often from the steep
> Of echoing Hill or Thicket have we heard
> Celestial voices to the midnight air,
> Sole, or responsive to each others note
> Singing thir great Creator.   (4.680–84)

Arcades's Genius and Eve (as well as Adam) are not merely rooted in the Earth but also have celestial awareness, as Creation in general is figured as a plant rooted in the earth that is also rising to Heaven.

If human beings are spirits rooted in place, the new *genius loci* for a Christian world, then what do we make of medieval theology's conviction that Christians, as spirit, should attempt to pull free of the earthly aspect of Creation? Should Christians uproot themselves from the earth and renounce their peasantry? Milton's description of the Fall may offer a startling answer to these questions.

The image of human beings kept *low* on Earth while Heaven stands *above* the Garden is persistent in *Paradise Lost.* When Satan first hears of the command regarding the Tree of Knowledge, he assumes that God intends "To keep them [human beings] low whom knowledge might exalt / Equal with Gods" (4.525–26). In many respects his temptation of Eve is an effort to convince her of this conviction: "Why then was this forbid? . . . / Why but to keep ye low and ignorant" (9.703–4). The idea that Eve can rise above the earth is first offered by Satan in the dream he induces, as he tempts Eve to "Taste this, and be henceforth among the Gods / Thy self a Goddess, not to Earth confind" (5.77–78). But as *genius loci,* Eve is thoroughly connected to her place on the Earth—not in the pejorative sense of Satan's "confind," but in the sense that she is nurtured by and nurturer of what she and Adam recognize in their nightly prayer as their "delicious place" (4.729).

Nonetheless, Satan induces Eve to dream that she can pull free of her place on the Earth:

> Forthwith up to the Clouds
> With him I flew, and underneath beheld
> The Earth outstretcht immense, a prospect wide
> And various: wondring at my flight and change
> To this high exaltation. (5.86–90)

But recall Raphael's counsel to Adam: "Heav'n is for thee too high / To know what passes there; be lowlie wise" (8.172–73). As Raphael had taught earlier, there is so much for Adam and Eve to search and know on Earth that they should be content to keep their knowledge within bounds:

> Commission from above
> I have receav'd, to answer thy desire
> Of knowledge within bounds; beyond abstain
> To ask, nor let thy own inventions hope
> Things not reveal'd, which th' invisible King,
> Onely Omniscient, hath supprest in Night,
> To none communicable in Earth or Heaven:
> Anough is left besides to search and know. (7.118–25)

In an even earlier lesson, Adam understands Raphael's point that only "In contemplation of created things / By steps might we ascend to God" (5.511–12). So, by being "lowlie wise" of the created things in their place, Adam and Eve will gradually gain the knowledge that God will communicate of Heaven:

> till by degrees of merit rais'd
> They open to themselves at length the way
> Up hither, under long obedience tri'd,
> And Earth be chang'd to Heav'n, and Heav'n to Earth. (7.157–60)

Eventually, after "long obedience" to God and study, along with care of their place on earth, *while on the earth,* human beings will find "the way / Up hither" as they legitimately ascend upward toward heaven. This ascent would be a wonderful reward for Adam and Eve, but what is astonishing is the cosmic event it would precipitate: the literal de-struction of what I have been calling the Christian-pagan dyad, not because the boundary between earthly and the spiritual will be penetrable by human beings (Angels have already had free passage between both realms), but because the spiritual-earthly dyadic structure will give way to something more basic, as "Earth be chang'd to Heav'n, and Heav'n to Earth" (7.160). If there had not been a Fall, heaven and earth would have ceased to be the two aspects of a structure in opposition, since heaven and earth would have become *one.*

But there is a problem with the idea that human beings can help work toward earth being "chang'd to Heav'n, and Heav'n to Earth" (7.160):

"earthy heaven" can only come about if human beings stay rooted in the earth, as Raphael expressed it in an earlier lesson:

> So from the root
> Springs lighter the green stalk, from thence the leaves
> More aerie, last the bright consummate floure
> Spirits odorous breathes.   (5.479–82)

Although Creation may flower as spirit, it must be rooted in the earth if it is to live at all. If pulled free of the earth, not only will the root of the plant that grips the earth die; the "aerie" leaves and the "odorous" flowers will die as well. Eve would have done well to remember this, for it is not as Satan suggests, that God intends "to keep ye low and ignorant" (9.704). As with everything else native to the earth, Eve and Adam, as rooted in the earth, should make no attempt at an ascension if this means they must pull free of their place, since a plant pulled from the earth will surely die. To understand this further, we need to consider just what happens when a "bright consummate floure" (5.481) forgets that she too is rooted in the earth, forgets that she is the "fairest *unsupported* Flour" (9.432; italics mine).

Eve is thoroughly *of* the Garden. As the *genius* of the Garden, Eve has (to borrow Spengler's words) "roots in the earth that [s]he tends," an "earthboundness of being," as she grows in "the fruitful earth that grows up along with [wo]man." (*Decline of the West*, 89–90). Eve and Adam would be happiest if they sought "No happier state, and know to know no more" (4.775) than what they know of their place in the Garden. But as Eve did want to know more, her lapse can be seen as an effort to gain a *knowledge* outside of the earthly Garden where she is rooted, not a knowledge of the Garden and Creation itself (which, except for a single tree, she and Adam have the opportunity, and are quickly developing the mental talents, to know quite well). She desired what immediately after her fall she believes is within her grasp: "knowledge, as the Gods who all things know" (9.804)—knowledge reserved for a Creator.

Seen in these terms, the Fall comes about because Eve seeks to pull herself free of Creation (to uproot herself from the Garden) so as to gain a god's eye view of Creation. Eve's fall is the tragic consequence of a failed ascension. Indeed, immediately after the Fall both Eve and Adam mistakenly believe that they have succeeded at pulling free of the earth:

> As with new Wine intoxicated both
> They swim in mirth, and fancie that they feel
> Divinitie within them breeding wings
> Wherewith to scorne the Earth.   (9.1008–11)

Had Adam and Eve only waited, they would have ascended to heaven "by degrees of merit rais'd" (7.157); now, however, they only fancy themselves ascended, though sadly, the earth has truly been "scorned." As Eve's fall results from a move away from the earth, it is the opposite of the humility of one rooted in the earth, as the word "humility" derives from "humus," earth. The momentary lack of humility that rips Eve from the earth is the source of the wound felt by the earth. To illustrate this idea, one might imagine a great tree that had reached too high for its roots in the earth to continue to support it and in consequence falls. Now the crater left by such a *fall,* as with Eve's fall, would truly be a wound that the earth would feel. Because our difficulties resulted from our desire to pull ourselves free of the earth, our greatest postlapsarian hope should be in one motion to heal the wound felt by earth and re-root ourselves in the earth, a desire quite the opposite of what medieval theology aspired to.

Stephen Fallon has astutely noticed that in *Paradise Lost* Milton takes "a poet's revenge" on the dualistic philosophers by "dressing the philosophies of Descartes and Hobbes in diabolic clothing," attributing to the devils the metaphysical views of Milton's age.[26] Milton's startling account of the Fall makes a similar assault on dualistic medieval theologians. To many of these Christian thinkers, giving too much favor to the earth is what happened at the Fall: a privileging of the not-spiritual earthly. Many modern environmentalists take this Christian tradition of privileging the spiritual at the cost of marginalizing the earth to be the source of much of our current woe.[27] But in Milton's reading of the Fall, Eve initiates the Fall as she momentarily pulls *away* from the Earth as would a dualistic theologian. In other words, in *Paradise Lost* medieval theology's attempt to counterbalance Original Sin through a one-sided privileging of the spiritual becomes, with absolutely delicious irony, a likeness of Original Sin! This understanding of the Fall also radically destabilized medieval theology's misogynous suspicion that Eve was a little too earthly. As *Paradise Lost* celebrates Eve's connection to the earth, her downfall only occurs when she is momentarily duped (by a dualistic theologian in devil's clothing) into believing she should turn away from the earth. The "poet's revenge" aside, in *Paradise Lost* we have a reading of the biblical Fall, friendly to both Eve and the earth, that has for three centuries been taken as entirely plausible.

To understand just how human beings and the earth share a single wound, we need to further explore Milton's description of the Fall. The imagery surrounding Eve's and Adam's fall does not merely depict their rootedness in the earth. Milton is not prepared to relegate Mother Earth, as personified, to the status she occupies in works such as *The Faerie Queen.* (As

Walter Kendrick expresses it, Spenser's Mother Earth "is subject to no personification and possesses little of what one could call character."[28]) Mother
Earth is lovingly personified during the fall of Eve, leading one critic, Richard
DuRocher, to ask a long overdue question: "What is the personification of the
Earth doing at this pivotal moment in *Paradise Lost*?" This is an important
question, since as DuRocher notes, "For all its originality and importance,
the significance of this figure has virtually escaped critics' attention."[29] Adam
is not present at Eve's fall, God is nowhere to be seen, even Satan has
slithered away as Eve nears the moment of Original Sin. There is only Eve—
and the Earth:

> Earth felt the Wound, and Nature from her seat
> Sighing through all her Works gave signs of woe,
> That all was lost.   (9.782–84)

And at Adam's fall the Earth is again present:

> Earth trembl'd from her entrails, as again
> In pangs, and Nature gave a second groan,
> Sky lowr'd, and muttering Thunder, some sad drops
> Wept at compleating of the mortal Sin
> Original.   (9.1000–1004)

Now if Nietzsche (or even one of the Church Fathers) had written these
scenes, one might have expected Earth's presence, but she would have likely
felt pleasurable trembling as Eve privileged the flesh, "ingorg'd without restraint" (9.791). But in Milton's account the Earth was wounded. Why? Du-
Rocher's interpretation is provocative: "Seen in the sequence of the Earth's
personifications throughout the poem, this figure makes a turning point in
Milton's argument. Through anthropomorphic imagery of childbirth, Milton
shows that during the Fall the Earth reverses the process of Creation" ("The
Wounded Earth in *Paradise Lost*," 94).

There is certainly much to suggest that there is "anthropomorphic imagery of childbirth" at the Fall. DuRocher argues that there is a parallel between the mining taught by the fallen angel Mammon, as related in Book
One ("Men also, and by his suggestion taught / Ransack'd the Center, and
with impious hands / Rifl'd the bowels of thir mother Earth" [1.678–90]) and
the idea that "Adam and Eve's sin likewise seems to involve a violation of
Mother Earth's creative power" ("The Wounded Earth in *Paradise Lost*,"
101). When personified, DuRocher argues, Mother Earth's "body" may bring
forth naturally in birth (as in "The Earth obey'd, and straight / Op'ning her
fertile Womb teem'd at a Birth / Innumerous living Creatures" [7.453–55])
or may unnaturally have her treasure taken from her (as in Mammon's dese-

cration of Mother Earth). Milton's use of the word "pangs" to describe what the Earth felt is telling, since from the sixteenth century through Milton's time "pangs" was generally limited to either "death pangs" or "pangs of childbirth."[30] For DuRocher, "Eve's Fall is at first unlocalized, but as the depiction of the Earth after Adam's Fall indicates, it is felt in the vital, creative part of Mother Earth, her womb" ("The Wounded Earth in *Paradise Lost*," 114).

DuRocher states that "at the Fall Milton's Earth registers both sympathy with human suffering and sentience of its own injury" but encounters difficulty in arguing that "during the Fall the Earth reverses the process of Creation," because he is at a loss to explain what brought about the wound. He can only conclude that "some kind of external injury . . . actually befell the Earth" ("The Wounded Earth in *Paradise Lost*," 112, 94, 114). On the other hand, if we do not think in terms of a literal childbirth but rather a child's own foolish act that causes a separation from the Mother Earth, then the wound becomes the site (the place of "rootedness") where human beings and the Earth became separated. If a child is tragically taken from its mother through a momentary lapse in obedience by the child, we not only say that the mother feels her own wound at having lost the child; we also rightfully say that the empathetic mother feels the child's wound at having lost the mother. In this sense, the child's and mother's wound are the same, not only because the child's act in pulling them apart created a single wound that they share, but simply because in their profound sorrow, they each share the wound by feeling it for their own sake and the sake of the other. Indeed, as long as they continue to feel the wound, though a great distance may separate them, they will always be together in the sorrow they feel. So we might say, though it sounds contradictory, that whereas the act that brought about the wound separated human beings from the Earth, through the act of feeling the single wound of the Self-Other, they are still, in a certain sense, together. This is a radical de-struction of the idea that spiritual Christians (even after the Fall) must be separated from the Earth.

The full tragedy of Eve's lapse becomes clear to her when she learns that she will be permanently uprooted from her place. Though there is "A voice of weeping heard, and loud lament" (183) when the "parting Genius" of the Nativity ode is forced from his place, we as readers are not privy to the "lament." But in Book Eleven of *Paradise Lost*, when in similar language the parting genius, Eve, reveals herself by "audible lament" (11.266), we hear Eve's speech when Michael informs her that she must leave her place (the Garden). As Death is the punishment for disobedience to God, Eve's lament is all the more astonishing as she now "feels the wound" she shares with the Earth, when she learns of the coming separation:

O unexpected stroke, worst than of Death!
Must I leave thee Paradise? thus leave
Thee Native Soile, these happy Walks and Shades,
Fit haunt of Gods? where I had hope to spend,
Quiet though sad, the respit of that day
That must be mortal to us both. O flours,
That never will in other Climate grow,
My early visitation, and my last
At Eev'n, which I bred up with tender hand
From the first op'ning bud, and gave ye Names,
Who now shall reare ye to the sun, or ranke
Your Tribes, and water from th' ambrosial Fount?
Thee lastly nuptial Bowre, by me adornd
With what to sight or smell was sweet; from thee
How shall I part, and whither wander down
Into a lower World, to this obscure
And wilde, how shall we breath in other Aire
Less pure, accustomed to immortal Fruits?   (11.268–85)

In her penultimate speech in *Paradise Lost,* on coming to understand that
she must leave the Garden, Eve has a moment of painful clarity in which her
existence comes into focus even as it falls away from her with news of the
impending exile. And it is not a life in focus, as existentialists might have it,
because she is faced with the prospect of her own death (she has known that
she has been facing death ever since her fall), but rather because she clearly
understands here that she (along with Adam) has been a "spirit of the place"
called the Garden. It is not her existence per se that Eve laments, but her
existence as a *genius loci,* an existence so interwoven with the Garden that
Eve is in essence asking, What will happen to *us:* Eve, Adam, the flowers, the
bower—to the Garden that roots us all? "How shall we [Adam and Eve]
breath in other Aire / Less pure, accustomed to immortal Fruits?" (11.284–
85). And of the plants: "Who shall now reare ye to the sun?" (11.278). When
Eve learns of the exile from the Garden (as she "feels the wound"), she
realizes both that she is a "spirit of a place without a place" *and* that the
"place" is equally without a spirit, which paralyzes her with fear of the separation of her life from the place of life that both nurtured her and had been
nurtured by her—which will mean death for all.

Geoffrey Hartman wrote of Milton that "His lines in the Nativity ode on
the 'parting Genius' left their imprint on almost every major poet in the
following century," as they diffused into the countryside in search of the
exiled Genius.[31] What they failed to see, however, was that, perhaps with
greater insight, Milton had already caught a glimpse of the Genius, as the
poet himself pined for a more authentic Christian encounter with the Earth.

I referred to Oswald Spengler to suggest that his enterprise (in a limited way) parallels Milton's own in *Paradise Lost,* in that both thinkers proceed from the conviction that human beings were once so thoroughly rooted in the earth that (because of this humble peasant rootedness in the earth) the earth was nothing less than a Paradise. To Spengler this was not a question of biblical interpretation but rather an historical fact. This said, we can view the achievement of *Paradise Lost* as having delivered Christianity to the fold of environmentalists who hold that our foolish acts have brought ecological devastation to the earth. Indeed, Milton goes so far as to suggest that this foolish uprooting of ourselves from the earth was the pivotal act in human history—and the source of all our current sorrow. But this sorrow may offer the greatest hope of renewing our earth-bound peasantry, lost with Paradise. Because feeling the wound may offer the best chance at healing our loss, shared with the earth, *Paradise Lost* may itself be seen as an attempt to have us again confront our Original Sin of believing anything less than that we are all "Adams" (in Hebrew literally "creatures made of Earth") who, faced with our earth-bound nature, may either choose to renew the bond or scorn it along with our future.

Rutgers, Camden

NOTES

Though I am very grateful to Diane McColley, Albert Labriola, and Richard DuRocher for the generous guidance they have provided throughout this project, I owe a special debt to Diane McColley for suggesting what at first seemed outrageous but now seems utterly obvious: that Milton might be read "Greenly."

Epigraph: Martin Heidegger, "The Country Lane," trans. by Michael Heron in *Envoy* 3 (1950): 72.

1. On the matter of Milton's monism, Stephen M. Fallon has persuasively argued that the mature Milton developed a "monistic conception of the relationship between body and soul" that was "an affront to any of the available dualistic conceptions, including the Platonic, the Christianized Aristotelian, and the Cartesian." *Milton among the Philosophers: Poetry and Materialism in Seventeenth-Century England,* (Ithaca, N.Y., 1991), 99. Although Phillip J. Donnelly has recently suggested that Fallon may have erred in "treating 'matter' (*materia*) and 'body' (*corpus*) as synonymous" ("'Matter' versus Body: The Character of Milton's Monism," *Milton Quarterly* 33 [October 1999]: 79.), my present essay, which contends that Milton deconstructed medieval theology's dualistic representations of Christianity, is in many respects built upon Fallon's general arguments regarding the monism (especially Hebraic) at work in *Paradise Lost.*

2. Jacques Derrida, *Of Grammatology,* intro. and trans. Gayatri Spivak (Baltimore, 1974), xlix.

3. Martin Heidegger, *Being and Time,* trans. John Macquarrie and Edward Robinson (New York, 1962), 44.

4. Heidegger, *Being and Time,* 44.

5. See Edward John Van Buren, *The Young Heidegger: Rumor of the Hidden King* (Bloomington, Ind., 1994). Also see John D. Caputo, "Heidegger and Theology," in *The Cambridge Companion to Heidegger,* ed. Charles Guignon (Cambridge, Eng., 1993), for additional research connecting Luther and destruction.

6. Caputo, "Heidegger and Theology," 272–73.

7. Martin Luther, *Luther: Lectures on Romans,* ed. and trans. William Pauk, Library of Christian Classics (Philadelphia, 1959), 214.

8. Van Buren, *The Young Heidegger: Rumor of the Hidden King,* 162, 161.

9. Oswald Spengler, *The Decline of the West: Perspectives of World History,* 2 vols., trans. Charles Francis Atkinson (New York, 1928), vol. 2, 89–90. All references to Spengler are to this edition and are cited parenthetically in the text.

10. Both *pagan* and *peasant* first derive from the Latin *pagus.* In the words of Eric Partridge: *pagus* in all probability derives from *"pangere,* to stick (something) into (esp. the ground), to fix firmly, and therefore akin to *pax." Origins: A Short Etymological Dictionary of Modern English* (London, 1958), 463. Also see notes 12 through 14 below.

11. Generally Theodosius I is credited with attaching our present meaning of *pagan* to *pagus* at around 400 B.C. Certainly by the time of Augustine, *pagus* as meaning "pagan" was widely in use.

12. This interpretation (which is admittedly my own) of *pagan's* origin from *pagus* is certainly debatable. Though it has been suggested from the sixteenth century onward (probably beginning with Denys Godefroy) that *pagans* means *civilians,* since they stand in opposition to Christians, "the *soldiers* of Christ," more recently Pierre Chuvin, while acknowledging that *pagus* suggests "a man whose roots . . . are where he lives," takes this to mean that "pagans are quite simply 'people of the place,' town or country, whereas the *alieni,* the 'people from elsewhere,' were increasingly Christian." *A Chronicle of the Last Pagans,* trans. B. A. Archer (Cambridge, Mass., 1990), 8–9.

13. I am not arguing that Milton, master wordsmith, is forging a new meaning for either *peasant* or *pagan* directly, as each word is used by the writer only once in his poetry. I merely wish to suggest that, in a broader sense, Milton is challenging us reconsider just what we mean by pagan—and Christian.

14. Bruce W. Foltz, *Inhabiting the Earth: Heidegger, Environmental Ethics, and the Metaphysics of Nature* (Atlantic Highlands, N.J., 1995), 164.

15. For a further analysis, see Martin Heidegger, *Nietzsche, Volume 1: The Will to Power as Art,* trans. David Farrell Krell (San Francisco, 1979), 200–10.

16. Lynn White Jr., "The Historical Roots of Our Ecological Crisis," in *The Ecocriticism Reader: Landmarks in Literary Ecology,* ed. Cheryll Glotfelty and Harold Fromm (Athens, Ga., 1996), 10. The immediately following references to White are also to this page.

17. Stella Revard, *Milton and the Tangles of Neaera's Hair: The Making of the 1645 Poems,* (Columbia, Mo., 1997), 74.

18. Cedric Brown, *John Milton's Aristocratic Entertainments* (Cambridge, Eng., 1985), 54.

19. Richard Neuse, "Metamorphosis and Symbolic Action in Comus," *ELH* 34 (1967): 58.

20. For a consideration of Milton's sources for the Sabrina myth, see John D. Cox, "Poetry and History in Milton's Country Masque," *ELH* 44 (1977): 634.

21. Diane Kelsey McColley, *Milton's Eve* (Urbana, Ill., 1983), 126.

22. An explanation of my use of *dominion* is in order here. In "The Historical Roots of Our Ecological Crisis," Lynn White charges that much of the ruthlessness toward nature in the modern West can be attributed to Genesis 1:28, where man is indeed given "dominion" over the earth. For two decades White's view gained influence, but in 1989 Jeremy Cohen published a

book-length treatment on the influence of Genesis 1:28, concluding that, "with regard to Genesis 1:28 itself, the ecologically oriented thesis of Lynn White and others can now be laid to rest. Rarely, if ever, did premodern Jews and Christians construe this verse as a license for the selfish exploitation of the environment." Jeremy Cohen, *Be Fertile and Increase, Fill the Earth and Master It: The Ancient and Medieval Career of a Biblical Text* (Ithaca, 1989), 5.

Building in part on Cohen's work, Jeffrey Theis recently explored, in environmental terms, the influence of Genesis on *Paradise Lost.* Considering not only Genesis 1:28 but Genesis 2:15, where Adam is put "into the garden of Eden to dress it and to keep it," Theis notes that, unlike in the history of the West, there is a "literal interpretation (and thus, a misinterpretation) of [Genesis] 1: 26–28" in *Paradise Lost:* Satan's understanding of dominion and rule. By contrast, Theis argues that in the epic Adam and Eve's perception of their relation to the earth is largely derived from Genesis 2:15 (echoed in *Paradise Lost* in the instruction Adam receives "to Till and keep" Paradise [8.320]), which Adam and Eve choose to interpret "through physical actions that culminate in an environmental practice which fuses work in Eden with worship." As was intimated by McColley, through their gardening practices Adam and Eve reveal their interpretation of "dominion" as to "to Till and keep" the specific place (the Garden) they inhabit. Therefore, "instead of standing outside of nature and subduing it," says Theis, Adam and Eve stand "within it," and their "task of tilling and keeping the land helps complete the natural world." Jeffrey S. Theis, "The Environmental Ethics of *Paradise Lost:* Milton's Exegesis of Genesis I–III," in *Milton Studies* 34, ed. Albert C. Labriola (Pittsburgh, 1996), 74, 71, 64. I believe my argument that Eve is a *genius loci* in *Paradise Lost,* caring for the specific place called the Garden, builds upon Theis's insights.

23. Michael Lieb has noticed that when Adam and Eve "led the Vine / To wed her Elm" (5.215–16), there is also a blending of fertility and fecundity: "the underlying image undeniably relates to the basic sexual metaphor of propagation. Adam and Eve cause a wedding to occur between plant and plant, so that barrenness may be avoided." *The Dialectics of Creation: Patterns of Birth and Regeneration in Paradise Lost* (Amherst, Mass., 1970), 73. Jeffrey Theis builds upon Lieb's insight by suggesting that the "marriage metaphor . . . links the controlling act of gardening with the loving and productive act of marriage. . . . This creates a complex whole within which nature and human beings are (in modern environmental terms) an interrelated ecosystem." Theis, "The Environmental Ethics of *Paradise Lost*," 72.

24. Not only the genius of the northern wood and Adam and Eve rise in their morning to brush off the dew and otherwise tend their respective places; angels also have a similar vocation, as "in Heav'n the Trees / Of life ambrosial frutage bear, and vines / Yield Nectar, though from the boughs each Morn / We brush mellifluous Dewes" (5.426–29). So it seems angels may not be as Lynn White suspected, "mobile as the Saints themselves," but firmly rooted in the heavenly place they tend. White, "The Historical Roots of Our Ecological Crisis," 10.

25. Donald M. Friedman has aptly remarked of these lines: "in response to its nurse the natural world of growing things grows, fulfills its intrinsic nature, becomes more like itself under her tutelage. Milton intensifies the point by his play on 'gladier,' in which the attributed delight of the flowers on encountering Eve is registered as more emphatic and healthier growth. The natural response to the hand of Eve is for vegetation to grow better and happier." "The Lady in the Garden: On the Literary Genetics of Milton's Eve," in *Milton Studies* 35, ed. Albert C. Labriola (Pittsburgh, 1997), 130.

26. Fallon, *Milton among the Philosophers*, 136.

27. I am, of course, speaking in a very general (and admittedly imprecise) way about Christianity—as unfortunately environmentalists often do. Certainly many medieval theologians followed Augustine in holding that "he who extols the nature of the soul as the chief good, and condemns the nature of the flesh as it were evil, assuredly is fleshy both in his love of the soul and

MILTON'S GODS AND
THE MATTER OF CREATION

Juliet Lucy Cummins

<hr>

I

IN *PARADISE LOST* Milton creates two Gods who are also one, plac-
ing a doubleness of identity at the source of being. Scholars have recognized that Milton identifies God with prime matter in the poem, but the
relationship between the omniscient, omnipotent being in heaven and the
inanimate matter of chaos has not yet been adequately explored. In this essay
I argue that the two divine identities are constructed in terms of hierarchical
oppositions that privilege God's heavenly persona over his base material
potency. The divine persona is male, whereas prime matter is female; the
Creator is free, whereas matter is constrained; and God describes his persona
as "self," implying that the matter of chaos is other. The binary structures that
distinguish God's self from prime matter support a masculinist ideology by
ensuring the ascendancy of traditionally masculine terms such as action,
volition, freedom, and spirit. However, Milton's identification of God with
both terms of the binary oppositions projected in the poem partially subverts
these traditional hegemonies by conflating the antitheses on which such
relationships are based.

God's two identities are positioned at either end of a material spectrum,
so that they are united by their common materiality and divided by their
degrees of refinement. God's heavenly persona, I argue, is constituted by the
purest form of physical light. This means that he comprises both the coarsest
and the most refined states of matter. The paradoxical identity and difference
of God's two dimensions in the poem give rise to shifting perspectives on God
and the universe he creates. From a dualistic perspective, God's self is distinct from and superior to prime matter and created things. Yet the poem also
offers the monistic view that the two aspects of God are complementary parts
of a unity and that the universe is an integrated whole composed of inter-
dependent elements.

The play between the monistic and dualistic conceptions of God is at its
most apparent in Milton's depiction of Creation. The God who is distinct
from prime matter instructs the Son to "ride forth" (*PL* 7.166) and effect

81

Creation, while he remains withdrawn from the creative process.[1] And yet
Raphael describes the Son creating the world from the Father's material and
vital identities. Although God is retired in heaven, the Spirit of God infuses
his virtue and warmth throughout the circumscribed matter of Creation.
Whereas scholars have generally seen the "vital vertue . . . and vital warmth"
(7.236) as playing a minimal role in the creative process, I contend that they
convey the divine spirit and vitality to matter. These properties come directly
from God's celestial being without diminishing it, just as the matter from
which the world is formed is a portion of God's infinite material potency. The
created world that results from this fusion of the two dimensions of God combines qualities deriving from each: the passive feminine principle and the
active masculine one. Feminine matter acquires the power of self-generation
from God's masculine virtue and warmth, initiating metamorphic processes
of nature that emulate the original creative act.

As all things originate from a being with a dual identity, the structures in
the created world reflect the divided yet unified nature of the divine being.
The diachronic relationship between Creator and creature is at once dependent and autonomous. Everything in the universe of *Paradise Lost* is "of
God," since everything is composed from God's material and vital identities.
And yet God is also a transcendent being who is unknowable in his entirety,
and his rational creatures are "Authors to themselves in all" (3.122). Similarly,
synchronic relationships between created things are at once hierarchical and
evenly balanced. The relationship between the sexes originates in God's two
dimensions, his feminine material potential and his masculine vital power,
which combine to create the world. Gender thus partakes of the same paradoxical structures that inform the divine being: masculinity is superior to
femininity, yet the two are mutually dependent, complementary properties.
All structures in the universe that Milton creates are subject to this play of
absence and presence, since all derive from the same source.

Milton's paradoxical portrayal of God and his Creation is an important
aspect of his celebration of poetry as a means of revealing truths that transcend logic. In a philosophical climate in which reason was increasingly seen
as a secular faculty equivalent to logic, as "nothing but *Reckoning*," to use
Hobbes's definition,[2] Milton offers a poetic form of "right reason" as the key
to discovering truth. Poetry and theology share a certain superiority to logic
in Milton's works, and in consequence share a relation to each other. In the
Art of Logic Milton criticizes logicians who "irresponsibly confuse physics,
ethics, and theology with logical matters," and in *Of Education* he contrasts
the "contracted palm" of logic with "that sublime art" of poetry, which can
give students "an universall insight into things." In *The Reason of Church-
Government* he identifies the source of poetic insight as the "eternall Spirit

who can enrich with all utterance and knowledge."[3] After seeking illumination from this "Spirit" in *Paradise Lost* (1.17), Milton aims to "assert Eternal Providence" (1.25) and to "see and tell / Of things invisible to mortal sight" (3.54–55). This prophetic conception of poetry forms part of a cultural opposition traditional in the West between poetry and philosophy, or at least between a mystical form of poetry and a rationalist expression of philosophy. As Gerald L. Bruns distinguishes the two enterprises,

The poet's naming is not conceptual determination but a calling of what is singular and ungraspable as such. In the history of the West philosophy originates as that which tries to rationalize this naming, that is, to interpret or make sense of it; but poetry can never be part of this interpretation. Philosophy tries to stabilize the world conceptually by means of the logical determination of what poetry brings into the open, but poetry refuses to be stabilized in this way.[4]

Paradise Lost "refuses to be stabilized" by philosophical reason, instead resisting and subverting what, in the poem's terms, is a simplistic means of understanding the world. Rather, it depicts "what is singular and ungraspable," recounting such "Almightie works" through dramatic narrative, imagery, and rhetoric so that "heart of man" may "comprehend" (7.112–14), at least insofar as human hearts are capable.

II

The critical acceptance of God's materiality in *Paradise Lost* has been a long time coming. Denis Saurat's proposal in the 1920s that John Milton was a materialist and a pantheist met with decades of resistance.[5] In the 1950s, 1960s, and early 1970s, scholars such as William B. Hunter, Michael F. Moloney, Walter Clyde Curry, William Empson, J. H. Adamson, and Leland Ryken all rejected the possibility that Milton's God was material and immanent in nature.[6] More recently, there has been a growing awareness of the importance of Milton's materialism in the epic, and a greater willingness to recognize his heresies.[7] John Rumrich mounted a persuasive case for the materiality of Milton's God in the 1980s and 1990s, showing for the first time how this doctrine assumes poetic form in *Paradise Lost*.[8] Rumrich argues that Milton presents chaos in the poem as "the infinite material dimension of God, which has not yet been ordained for creation," "the part of the deity . . . over which the eternal father does not exercise control." According to Rumrich, chaos in *Paradise Lost* constitutes "the potential for otherness" and so makes possible both freedom of the will and the existence of evil.[9] The majority of scholars are now on Rumrich's side. Dennis Danielson, John Rogers, D. Bentley Hart, and Roy Flannagan have adopted a similar position, and Harinder Singh Marjara and Stephen Fallon agree that Milton's God is "not clearly immaterial."[10] However, Milton's identification of God with the substance of Creation has received little critical attention.

There is ample evidence in *Paradise Lost* that prime matter is an aspect of God, despite the history of critical denial. Raphael offers support for the association between God and prime matter when he describes created things as consisting of "one first matter all" immediately after telling Adam that "All things proceed [from God], and up to him return" (5.472, 470). The construction of a material cycle of being that is centered in God implies that God is the source and end of matter and is material himself. Milton's God refers to his own materiality when he tells the Son that chaos is "boundless,"

> because I am who fill
> Infinitude, nor vacuous the space.
> Though I uncircumscrib'd my self retire.   (7.168–70)

The words "fill" and "nor vacuous" intimate that chaos is material, and the strong biblical "I am" (Exod. 3:14) substantiates the view expressed in *Christian Doctrine* that prime matter is an aspect of God.[11] Yet God's definitive "I am" is followed by an implicit "I am not." God's statement that he "retire[s]" from chaos would appear to support the argument that he is immaterial, were it not for the words that precede it.

Attempts to reconcile this contradiction, that God both fills and is retired from chaos, have been the source of critical creativity. Denis Saurat explained the lines by suggesting that God creates matter and being by retracting his will from certain parts of himself, a theory that is now widely discredited.[12] A. S. P. Woodhouse's argument that "matter in its disordered state is indeed in God's presence, but not in his *active* presence" raises the question of what God's passive presence might constitute.[13] John Rumrich offers the most convincing interpretation of the lines, explaining the contradiction they contain by attributing to God a split identity. He argues that "although God's self— his actualized, volitional persona—is absent from chaos, 'the heterogeneous and substantial virtue' of his material potency remains, filling the infinite."[14] But if prime matter is a "dimension" of God, as Rumrich argues, then as a matter of logic it *is* God and must constitute part of the divine "self." Milton's simultaneous identification of and distinguishing between prime matter and God's self are gestures that challenge the efficacy of logic in the realm of spiritual truths. These lines effectively construct two Gods who are also one: a material logos and a transcendent deity. Milton faces the dilemma of his contemporary Jacob Bauthumley, who asked, "God, . . . what shall I speak of thee, when in speaking of thee, I speak nothing but contradiction?"—and resolves it by refusing to resolve it.[15] The poetic medium provides Milton with a means of celebrating God's immanence and transcendence at the same time and of rhetorically demonstrating the Creator's mysterious nature.

Milton uses the allegorical figure Night to represent God's base, material identity. A. B. Chambers's argument in the early 1960s that Night is identifiable with prime matter has been overlooked, but the evidence in support of this argument is compelling. The epithet "Sable-vested *Night*" (2.962) evokes an association between prime matter and darkness that occurs in classical literature and is employed by contemporaries of Milton such as Robert Fludd.[16] Milton explicitly connects prime matter with darkness in *Paradise Lost* when he refers to the "dark materials" of chaos from which God may "create more Worlds" (2.916). Milton's portrayal of Night as a passive figure is consistent with the Aristotelian, Neoplatonic, and Stoic conceptions of matter as incapable of independent action per se, an idea evident elsewhere in *Paradise Lost.*[17] Many of the words Milton uses to describe Night have associations with prime matter. Satan's description of Night as "unessential" (2.439) is meaningful in the context of the Aristotelian position that matter lacks essence. Similarly, the description of Night as "unoriginal" (10.477) indicates that matter is uncreated (*OED* 1). That Night's nature is "*Eternal*" (3.18) is implied by Milton's view that prime matter is a dimension of God, and its status as the "eldest of things" (2.962) evokes its paradoxical difference from God as a "thing" that precedes all others. Milton's use of the allegorical Night to represent prime matter forms part of a philosophical heritage in which matter is dark, unessential, passive, and feminine.

The representation of prime matter in feminine terms makes sense in terms of the poem's internal structure and the philosophical history with which it engages. Despite some critical support for W. B. C. Watkins's observation that matter is "the feminine aspect of God" in *Paradise Lost,* the view that Milton portrays prime matter as "equivocal[ly] gender[ed]" is also popular.[18] This view is based on the assumption that the Anarch represents the first matter.[19] However, the use of a male figure to represent prime matter would run contrary to a long philosophical tradition associating prime matter with femininity, given expression in Plato's *Timaeus,* where the receptacle from which the world is formed is compared to a mother.[20] Further, as Rumrich himself observes, it would be inconsistent with the Platonic description of matter in *Christian Doctrine* as "the nurse of all generation."[21] Milton's identification of both God and Night with prime matter suggests that Night represents God's alter ego, the shadowy and feminine dimension that complements his masculine "self" (7.170). Milton's God is "Dark with excessive bright" (3.380) and comprises both light and darkness, masculinity and femininity, spirit and matter. The visual oxymoron conveys the contradictory and mysterious nature of the godhead, providing an "inaccessible" (3.377) image of a being who cannot be seen.

Milton's identification of God with prime matter in *Paradise Lost* indicates that prime matter is metaphysically good in the poem, just as it is "good, and it contain[s] the seeds of all subsequent good" in *Christian Doctrine* (YP 6:308). Many scholars have found Milton's theory of matter to be at odds with his presentation of chaos in the epic.[22] Milton's chaos is described in terms emphasizing that it is indeterminate, impersonal and uncontrolled: it is "The dark unbottom'd infinite Abyss" (2.405), "Th' unfounded deep" (2.829), "Outrageous as a Sea, dark, wasteful, wilde" (7.212). It is a region of confusion and conflict represented by an "Anarch" (2.988) who tells Satan that "Havock and spoil and ruin are my gain" (2.1009). Further, Milton's chaos is metaphysically evil in Augustinian terms because it represents an absence of form and therefore of individual being.[23] Belial fears losing "this intellectual being" in chaos by being "swallowd up and lost / In the wide womb of uncreated night" (2.147, 149–50), and Satan claims that chaos "with utter loss of being / Threatens him" (2.440–41). Regina Schwartz suggests that the dramatic presentation of a hostile abyss partly undermines Milton's theodicy, which depends upon a good first matter.[24] Rumrich and other scholars have reconciled Milton's poetry with his theodicy by maintaining that chaos is good or morally neutral in *Paradise Lost*.[25] Rumrich argues that chaos is ontologically deficient but that "for the materialist Milton, deficient ontology does not necessarily imply a loss of being that results from evil."[26] However, this argument is hard to reconcile with Milton's presentation of the falls of the angels and humankind as descents into ontological chaos.[27] Moreover, the view that deficient ontology is evil in *Paradise Lost* explains the warlike state of Milton's chaos and the hostility of its Anarch. And yet the metaphysical evil of chaos is not at odds with Milton's presentation of matter as good.

In *Paradise Lost* Milton draws a distinction between prime matter and chaos, a distinction given allegorical form in the characters of Night and Chaos. Chaos is the "Infinitude" that God "fill[s]" (7.169, 168) and so is not the material dimension of God. It is the limitless space outside the created universe or, in abstract terms, a principle of disorder and indeterminacy. The first matter that fills chaos is good because it possesses a kind of essence that derives from God. In the *Art of Logic* Milton departs from Ramus in making the unusual claim that prime matter is the "common essence" of all things (YP 8:234).[28] This conception is evident in *Paradise Lost* in the depiction of the creation of all things from the "one first matter" (5.472). Milton's representation of the matter of chaos in the epic is indebted to the Aristotelian view that formless matter is good in potential but appears to be base "by virtue of concurrence."[29] The metaphysical evil of chaos makes prime matter "apparently imperfect" (YP 6:308) because matter's passive goodness is powerless in the absence of God's active virtue. The "embryon Atoms" (2.900) of prime matter are blown about randomly by "warring Winds" (2.905) and "must ever fight / Unless th' Almighty Maker them ordain / His dark materials to create more Worlds" (2.914–16). But matter's imperfection is only apparent. The latent goodness of chaotic matter appears when God puts forth his formative virtue at Creation and activates matter's tendency to become "more refin'd, more spiritous, and pure" (5.475).

III

The medium of poetry allows Milton to construct God's masculine persona in terms that evoke both its identity with and its distinction from prime matter. Milton's God describes his "self" as "retire[d]" (7.170) or removed from the matter of chaos which is "disperse[d], propagate[d] and extend[ed]" infinitely (*Christian Doctrine;* YP 6:308). God's celestial self is "invisible / Amidst the glorious brightness where [God] sit'st / Thron'd inaccessible" in heaven (3.375–77). Further, God's persona is not subject to the constraints imposed upon prime matter. The powers of "Necessitie and Chance" (7.172), which control prime matter, are themselves subject to God's will. However, the opposition between God's two identities is not absolute. Both prime matter and the divine self are "uncircumscrib'd" (7.170), the former physically and the latter ontologically. Both are metaphysically good, but where prime matter is passively so, God's volitional goodness is "free / To act or not" (7.171–72). There is thus both continuity and disjunction between the two aspects of the divine being.

The paradox of the identity and difference of God's "self" and prime matter finds substantial expression in Milton's depiction of God's material being. God's two identities are unified by their common materiality and separated by their respective degrees of refinement. Whereas God's feminine aspect is matter in its basest form, his masculine self is the supremely refined condition of matter.[30] Miltonists have generally either assumed that God's masculine persona is immaterial or have not discussed the issue in any detail. However, Milton repeatedly describes God's persona in physical terms. God is positioned in "the pure Empyrean where he sits / High Thron'd above all highth" (3.57–58) and is placed in physical relation to the material angels who surround him in "circuit inexpressible" (5.595). When God speaks, heaven is filled with "ambrosial fragrance" (3.135), a refined physical substance that presumably emanates from the deity. Further, Raphael's account of created things becoming materially more refined "as neerer to him plac't or neerer tending" (5.476) contains the implication that God's masculine self is the pure substance toward which creatures proceed. In a cosmos where rarefied substances "contain / Within them every lower facultie" (5.409–10) and "spirit . . . contains within itself . . . the inferior substance" (body), it follows that God, "the source of all substance," is also the purest substance of all (YP 6:308–9). This kind of logic compelled Milton's fellow materialist and political adversary, Thomas Hobbes, to form the opinion that God was "a most pure, simple, invisible spirit corporeal."[31]

The divine substance is identified in the invocation to light with which Book Three of *Paradise Lost* begins:

> Hail holy Light, ofspring of Heav'n first-born,
> Or of th' Eternal Coeternal beam
> May I express thee unblam'd? since God is light,
> And never but in unapproached light
> Dwelt from Eternitie, dwelt then in thee,
> Bright effluence of bright essence increate.   (3.1–6)

The Johannine phrase "God is light" (John 1:5) acquires an unorthodox meaning in the context of Milton's monist materialism, indicating here that the deity is a supremely refined material being. Many seventeenth-century writers "thought light to consist of material particles" or to be otherwise corporeal,[32] providing a contemporary scientific basis for Milton's depiction of it. Denis Saurat argues that light in this passage is the Son of God as it is the "first-born" of heaven, and he suggests that light was the first divine matter from which all things were created. However, as Maurice Kelley replies, it is not the Son but the Father who is the material cause of the universe.[33] Kelley, Albert R. Cirillo, and Merritt Y. Hughes maintain instead that divine light is metaphorical.[34] Cirillo argues that Milton follows "the Christian-Platonic tradition" in distinguishing between "the immaterial light which is God" and "material light," which is created.[35] But a close examination of the opening lines of the invocation indicates that Milton's language is constantly conflating this distinction.

"Holy Light" is identified in line 1 as the light of Creation ("ofspring of Heav'n first-born"), anticipating Raphael's description of "Light / Ethereal, first of things" (7.243–44) springing from the deep. Then in line 2 it is identified with "th' Eternal Coeternal beam," or the light that is God. The function of the conjunction "Or" that begins line 2 is initially ambiguous. It could be suggesting that the light invoked is *either* physical light *or* the light of God, or it could be asserting that both kinds of light are the same. The declaration in the following line that "God is light" sustains this ambiguity. Milton then clearly identifies the two kinds of light with each other in the next three lines. The reader or listener might assume with Kelley, Cirillo, and

Hughes that the "unapproached light" in which God has "Dwelt from Eter-nitie" is "th' Eternal Coeternal beam." However, the following phrase, "dwelt then in thee," asserts that the "unapproached light" of God is the same as its "effluence," the physical light that is first addressed in the invocation. The light of Milton's Creation is an emanation from God's bright "essence," a word that Milton uses elsewhere in *Paradise Lost* to mean a spiritual entity and a constituent substance.[36] As God's essence is "increate" or uncreated, so too is the effluence from it. Physical light comes directly from God and differs only in its degree of purity from "unapproached light."

Milton's depiction of light and darkness supports his presentation of God as a material being who is at once divided and unified. Many of the epithets Milton uses to describe light and night partially dissolve the opposi-tion between them. Night is the "eldest of things" (2.962), and light is "first of things" (7.244), implying that both originate in time. And yet the adjectives "unoriginal" (10.477) and "increate" (3.6) designate both light and darkness as uncreated. But light and darkness could be always contained within God and only alienated from the divine being at a particular point in time. This explanation of the paradox is consistent with Milton's comment in *Christian Doctrine* that God "disperse[s]" and "propagate[s]" matter rather than shut-ting it up within himself (YP 6:308). It also accords with his description in *Paradise Lost* of visible light as an "effluence" of God who "is light" (3.6, 3). Darkness and light are *"Eternal"* (3.18), "Or of th' Eternal Coeternal beam" (3.2), because they are aspects of God, but they are also born as the separate, physical entities from which the world is created.

Milton's portrayal of God as both transcendent deity and material logos simultaneously supports and subverts the logocentric structures on which the poem relies. The relationship between God's celestial self and his material potency is structured according to a number of dichotomies such as self and other, male and female, transcendence and immanence, active and passive, free and constrained, order and disorder, light and darkness. The construc-tion of these oppositions supports traditional Western hegemonies and is one means by which Milton privileges a masculinist perspective in the poem. However, by identifying God with both terms, Milton also dismantles the binary structure of these oppositions. This strategy resembles deconstructive practices in the twentieth century. Jacques Derrida's critical response to classical metaphysics is partly anticipated by Milton's "reading" of that same tradition in *Paradise Lost:*

an opposition of metaphysical concepts (for example, speech / writing, presence / absence, etc.) is never the face-to-face of two terms, but a hierarchy and an order of subordination. Deconstruction cannot limit itself or proceed immediately to a neutralization: it must, by means of a double gesture, a double science, a double writing, practice an *overturning* of the classical opposition *and* a general *displacement* of the system.[37]

Both Milton and Derrida make "double gestures," but their motives are diametrically opposed. Derrida displaces hierarchical systems in order to undermine them, to show that "there is no metaphysical concept in and of itself."[38] Milton, on the other hand, displaces them to show that there is no concept which is *not* metaphysical in and of itself. Whereas Derrida's strategy challenges the integrity of the logocentric tradition, Milton's celebrates the miraculous nature of God and his Creation. Everything in the Miltonic cosmos is "of God." All the traditional evils—matter, darkness, femininity—are aspects of God and are therefore good. Even evil is not an independent principle for Milton but a mere corruption of goodness, a degradation of material and spiritual purity. Evil is diminishing toward the status of non-being, becoming a metaphysical nonentity.[39] And yet Milton's "double gestures" also allow him to assert that God is a transcendent being, that his creatures are distinct from him and that evil is a moral and spiritual reality. These poetic contradictions are at their most blatant in Raphael's account of Creation, in which Milton paradoxically depicts God as a detached deity and the matter and vitality out of which all things are made.

IV

In rendering Creation poetically, Milton can portray God as present and absent simultaneously. Milton's God both participates in and "retire[s]" (7.170) from the process of Creation. When he sends the Son on a "great Expedition" (7.193) to create the world, the narrative voice records that he also "went / Invisible, yet staid, such priviledge / Hath Omnipresence" (7.588–90). The paradox of God's simultaneous absence and presence from the creative act is partly elucidated by Milton's construction of the Spirit of God as an aspect of God himself. In *Christian Doctrine* Milton argues that the "spirit of God" that moves upon the face of the waters in Genesis 1:2 is not the Holy Spirit but God's power or the Son (YP 6:282, 6:304). In *Paradise Lost* God sends his "overshadowing Spirit and might" (7.165) with the Son to effect Creation, and this Spirit spreads its "brooding wings" over the abyss (7.235). The Spirit of God cannot be the Son, since it accompanies the Son on his creative mission. However, the Spirit is associated with divine power through juxtaposition with the word "might" and again in Raphael's description of the Spirit emanating "vertue" (7.236). The Spirit of God's infusion of virtue or divine power into the circumscribed mass has no scriptural precedent and serves to support Milton's original hypothesis in *Christian Doctrine* that the Spirit brooding over the abyss in Genesis is "God's divine power, not any particular person" (YP 6:304). God is present at Creation through the spirit and power that are part of God's celestial self, but God's infinite being remains undiminished in heaven.

The monistic portrayal of God as encompassing both masculine and feminine material identities allows Milton to represent Creation pantheistically, as a sexual union of the two. God's feminine and masculine dimensions coincide in the parallel images of the Spirit of God making the abyss "pregnant" (1.22) and of the Spirit infusing matter with "vital vertue . . . and vital warmth" (7.236). These images have generally been interpreted as figurative descriptions of Creation that support the binary oppositions of male / female and God / matter. Michael Lieb, for example, observes that "inherent in the description is the sexual metaphor of the male (God) impregnating the female (matter)."[40] However, the identification of God with matter collapses these distinctions and makes Creation a literal form of divine self-impregnation. Something of God's masculine power and virtue coincides with a portion of his feminine, potent goodness, leading to a physical union of the two aspects of the divine being.

Proponents of the view that Milton's God is material have tended to overlook the physical nature of God's masculine self and in consequence have discounted the role played by masculine agents in Milton's Creation. For John Rumrich and John Rogers, the image of the Spirit "brooding" detracts from the masculine nature of its virtue and warmth, which for Rumrich "seem predominately masculine" and for Rogers are "ambisexual."[41] Their opinions that the Spirit's virtue and warmth are not fully masculine support their arguments that Creation in *Paradise Lost* is not a physical union of male and female agents. Rogers claims that the "semimasculine power of the Holy Spirit" is "exclud[ed] from the procreative equation," and Rumrich appears to agree that it has no significant procreative effect. Whereas Rumrich acknowledges "the design of a masculine, artistic, paternal God" in the process of Creation, Rogers describes Creation in *Paradise Lost* as "a self-sufficient feminine process."[42] Both emphasize the unusually prominent feminine imagery in Milton's Creation, and each perceives created things to be detached from the Creator.

It is my contention that Milton portrays the Spirit of God's virtue and warmth as masculine, formative, and vitalizing forces originating in God and operating upon prime matter to cause it to develop into the created world. God's masculine self converges with his feminine material identity at Creation when he literally "put[s] . . . forth [his] goodness" (7.171). Raphael recounts that

on the watrie calme
His brooding wings the Spirit of God outspred,
And vital vertue infus'd, and vital warmth
Throughout the fluid Mass.   (7.234–37)

Milton's portrayal of the Spirit of God as God's power implies that the Spirit is
capable of conveying God's own physical properties to prime matter: his
vitality, active power, and warmth. The two dimensions of God are unified
when the feminine, potential goodness of prime matter interacts with the
masculine, active virtue of God's self. The result is a world that is positioned
between two poles of a material spectrum, which are both divine: the base
prime matter from which things are created and the holy light to which they
proceed.[43]

Milton portrays the Spirit's infusion of virtue and warmth into prime
matter as an impregnation that makes prime matter generative. In the invocation to Book One, the narrator explicitly recalls that "from the first" the
Spirit "Dove-like satst brooding on the vast Abyss, / And mad'st it pregnant"
(1.19, 21–22). The feminine activity of brooding is distinct from the masculine impregnation that follows. In Raphael's parallel account of the Spirit
spreading brooding wings then "infus[ing]" (7.236) the mass with virtue and
warmth, the word *infus'd* carries the sense that the mass has been inseminated (*OED* 5). The representation of the Spirit impregnating matter in
Paradise Lost participates in a contemporary discourse about the Spirit of
God's function in Creation. In the seventeenth century the Spirit's metaphorical impregnation of matter was used to explain matter's original or continuing power of motion by mechanists and vitalists alike.[44] Thomas Hobbes
referred to this tradition to explain the initial communication of virtue to
matter ("Which vertue must consist in Motion"), after which matter operated
mechanically according to a chain of causes.[45] Similarly, the mechanist and
Epicurean atomist Walter Charleton held that *"at their Creation, God invig-
orated or impregnated* [atoms] *with an Internal Energy, or Faculty Motive,"*
and it was from the motion of atoms "that all Concretions derive their *Virtue
Motive."*[46] The idea was particularly prominent in alchemical and vitalist
literature, where it was employed to explain the infusion of material substance with reason and a vital power of self-motion. Thomas Browne equated
"that gentle heat that brooded on the waters" with "the Spirit of God, the fire
and scintillation of that noble and mighty Essence, which is the life and
radical heat of Spirits."[47] Sir Matthew Hale, the prominent judge of the
Commonwealth and Chief Justice under King Charles II, wrote: "this Motion of the Spirit on the face of this Abyss . . . did transfuse into this stupid,
dead, and unactive *Moles* certain activity and vital influence, whereby it did in

general affect that which *Aristotle* calls the common Life of Bodies, namely, Motion; and the several parts thereof were impregnated with several kinds of vital influence, varied and diversified according to their several parts and uses."[48] The context of contemporary philosophy indicates that the "vital vertue" and "vital warmth" that emanate from the Spirit of God in *Paradise Lost* are responsible for the vital and rational characteristics of matter in the created world.

The virtue and warmth matter acquires at Creation are masculine properties that activate its feminine potency. As Harinder Singh Marjara comments, "the action of the male principle on the female" was a common vitalistic way of explaining the "generative processes in inanimate nature."[49] The word *virtue* derives from *vir,* the Latin word for man, and in the early modern period virtue was almost universally considered to be a male power operating upon matter to cause change. When the Spirit of God infuses matter with "vertue" (7.236), the word *vertue* carries its primary meaning of divine power and also acquires a secondary meaning of a "power, efficacy, or good quality inherent in" material things (*OED* 11a and b). "Vital warmth" was regarded as a masculine, generative property by Milton's contemporaries.[50] The association derives from classical biology, notably from Aristotle's view that "vital warmth" was contained in the semen, and that the semen contained the principle of soul.[51] Similarly, the Stoics thought of God as an intelligent creative fire or "seminal reason" that caused natural things to grow. In *Paradise Lost,* God's virtue and warmth endow the female mass with masculine reproductive properties, preparing it for the creation of the world.

Milton depicts the next stages of Creation as a sexual interaction of divine virtue and warmth with prime matter. Once the "fluid Mass" (7.237) contains male properties, it is transformed from its originally "void" (7.233) or "idle" (7.279) state into a "warme" (7.279) "Womb . . . / Of Waters" (7.276–77). The "vital vertue" and "vital warmth" in the waters fertilize the fluid matter that contains them, causing the earth's conception as an "Embryon immature" (7.277). God's virtue activates the passive goodness of matter, giving it form and substantial being. Similarly, God's warmth conveys the life principle to matter, making it capable of producing the vital earth. Milton's depiction of God's warmth as "vital" draws upon an association between heat and vitality that was dominant in diverse strands of early modern philosophy. The Italian Neoplatonist Marsilio Ficino maintained that "Life, just like light, consists of natural heat"; the influential alchemist Paracelsus wrote that fire "hath power and vertue to vivifie whatsoever else lies hidden in other things"; and the physician William Harvey held that "the blood alone is the true innate heat" containing spirit.[52] The origins of life and the soul were generally thought to lie in the combination of "radical heat" and "the first-born" or "primigenial moisture."[53] This notion informs Raphael's description of the earth's conception in the "circumfluous Waters calme" (7.271) that have been penetrated by God's vital warmth. The earth receives spirit and vitality from the warm waters which will ultimately contribute to the creation of living things.

The embryonic earth evolves into a "great Mother" (7.281) through the operation of the same powers. Raphael reports that:

> The earth was form'd, but in the Womb as yet
> Of waters, Embryon immature involv'd,
> Appeer'd not: over all the face of Earth
> Main Ocean flow'd, not idle, but with warme
> Prolific humour soft'ning all her Globe,
> Fermented the great Mother to conceave,
> Satiate with genial moisture   (7.276–82).

Vital virtue and warmth work imperceptibly within the amniotic waters to fertilize the earth while it is still in a foetal state. Milton depicts God's vital warmth or "warme / Prolific humour" as a property of the "Main ocean." The words "Prolific" and "genial" also recall the active, generative powers attributed to male virtue by Milton's contemporaries. Rogers assumes that there is no "higher, preexistent *agent* of parturition" in the "sudden and unexpected transformation of a fetal earth to a pregnant Earth Mother," and Rumrich contends that Milton represents the feminine "Womb . . . / Of Waters" as impregnating the Earth.[54] But the waters do not impregnate the earth; rather they "[Ferment] the great Mother to conceave." The word "Fermented" alludes to a contemporary vitalist explanation of certain forms of autonomous generation as comparable to the fermentation of yeast. As Walter Pagel maintains, sixteenth and seventeenth century writers agreed that the ferment was "a spiritual force joined to a body . . . capable of . . . seminally impregnating any object."[55] A ferment is not expended with the creation of an embryo, as a male seed would be in human reproduction, but continues to be operative. The prominent vitalist Jean-Baptiste van Helmont held that the prime mass was transformed by the ferment, "a Power placed in the Earth" by God, into a pregnant state from which it could self-generate.[56] In *Paradise Lost*, the powers of virtue and warmth "placed in the earth" by the Spirit of God cause the embryonic earth to conceive natural things and then to give birth to them and to herself simultaneously.[57]

The operation of God's masculine power and goodness within the earth stimulates the creation of inanimate and animate things, with God's Word merely precipitating the processes of creation. After the earth has conceived, she becomes "Satiate" or saturated with the "genial moisture" with which she has been conceived and inseminated: that is, moisture that is both generative and conducive to growth. Containing both the male and female principles, the earth becomes generative herself and, at the Word's command, gives birth to vegetable and animal life. The waters "generate / Reptil" (7.387–88), and the earth's "fertil Woomb teem[s] at a Birth / Innumerous living Creatures, perfet formes" (7.454–55). The presence of God's active power within the earth begins an ongoing process of refinement as "further ferment is engendered by the fermented mass ad infinitum."[58] The potent goodness of matter is activated by the ferment—God's virtue and warmth—so that it is "by gradual scale sublim'd" (5.483) toward divine purity.

The interaction of God's masculine qualities with feminine matter initiates the metamorphic processes of nature in the created world of *Paradise Lost*. These processes reproduce the original act of creation on a smaller scale. Within the microcosm of the human body, the heat of the ferment facilitates digestion, enabling human beings to turn "corporeal to incorporeal" (5.413). As William Kerrigan suggests, the "concoctive heate" (5.437) with which Adam and Eve digest food derives from "the 'vital virtue . . . and vital warmth' (7.236) infused into matter by the Spirit of God, the life-heat."[59] God's virtue and warmth also operate in the macrocosm to continue processes of generation and sublimation begun at Creation. After the Son "Transplant[s]" light "from her cloudie Shrine" (7.360) to the sun, the sun assumes the masculine function of the Spirit of God. "[W]ith one vertuous touch / Th' Arch-chimic Sun" (3.608–9) causes the alchemical "ripening" of metals in the earth to a higher physical state, producing "many precious things / Of colour glorious and effect so rare" (3.611–12).[60] The sun's masculine virtue activates the feminine potency of the material earth, producing both inanimate and animate things.[61]

The critical perception that God's virtue and warmth are insignificant in Milton's Creation and that feminine agents predominate in the creative process has led to a distortion of Milton's representation of gender in general. Echoing his contention that Milton assigns active roles to female agents in creation, Rumrich argues that Eve embodies "problematical inconsistencies, and thus [a] challenge to a rational theodicy," "because she is too perfect, though the poem comes down with its highest authorities on the side of male superiority."[62] Whereas Rumrich understands Milton's representation of gender to be confused or inconsistent throughout the poem, Rogers identifies a discrepancy between Milton's Creation and his treatment of gender elsewhere. Maintaining that Milton depicts Creation through images of feminine autonomy, Rogers observes that "Raphael (and no doubt Milton) must respond with 'contracted brow' " to Adam's observation that Eve seems "in herself complete" (7.548). The feminist portrayal of Creation, Rogers continues, is also inconsistent with Milton's prose works, since it "underwrit[es] a politics far more liberatory in scope than the compromised egalitarianism of the most radical of Milton's political pamphlets."[63] These perceived inconsistencies dissolve, however, when it is realized that Milton's Creation is not an exclusively feminine process at all. Milton's "compromised egalitarianism," characteristic of his writing as a whole, is also evident in his representation of the physical processes that constitute Creation in *Paradise Lost.*

Milton portrays the feminine agents in Creation with unusual sympathy, but he nevertheless maintains a masculinist bias. Most classical accounts of Creation, notably Plato's *Timaeus,* depict matter as a lifeless receptacle that is entirely passive in the creative process. This influenced orthodox Christian constructions of Creation such as that of Saint Augustine. Milton's attribution of some kind of essence or being to matter in *The Art of Logic* is a departure from the Neoplatonic view that matter is "the negation of Good, unmingled Lack," "a dead thing decorated."[64] The matter of *Paradise Lost* is substantial rather than "Lack," and it responds spontaneously to God's virtue. In Raphael's account of Creation, material phenomena are assigned active verbs such as "Sprung" (7.245), "Brought forth" (7.315), "flourish't" (7.320), "waterd" (7.334), and "generate" (7.387), creating the impression that natural things willingly participate in their own creation. The relationship between paternal, commanding deity ("Let ther be Light" [7.243]) and matter ("Light / . . . / Sprung" [7.243–45]) is one of interaction and response, with matter assuming the role of a free and volitional, though obedient, subject. The representation of matter as womb, embryo, and mother creates a substantial and positive feminine presence in Creation, whereas the masculine powers of virtue and warmth that work upon this matter are visually obscure. Nevertheless, it is the masculine agents in Milton's Creation that are dominant and formative: matter is given form and vitality by the Son's commands and by the physical operation of God's virtue and warmth. The gender structure in Milton's Creation reflects the relationship between Milton's male deity and his female material potential: they are divided in an antithetical structure of authority and subordination, yet they are also placed in a relationship of reciprocity.

V

The paradox that Milton's God at once is, and is not, the matter of chaos forms the basis of the structures that circumscribe the created world. To the extent that God comprises both spirit and matter, Milton presents the universe monistically, as an integrated whole that derives its unity from its Creator. However, insofar as God is distinct from the material world, the universe is portrayed dualistically and hierarchically, as a structure of difference and authority.[65] The monistic and dualistic perspectives are logically inconsistent but can exist simultaneously in poetic and metaphysical frameworks that establish a "right reason" transcending logic. These perspectives meet in Raphael's image of the "scale of Nature set / From center to circumference" (5.509–10). This ontological "scale" or ladder is a linear representation of the supremacy of God at the center of the cosmos and the graduated inferiority of his creatures as the ladder reaches toward the outskirts.[66] It positions God in superior relation to his creatures, who may approach but can never reach his exalted state of being. However, the words "center" and "circumference" also evoke the concept of a circle or sphere and the corresponding notion of cosmic unity. This image is consistent with Raphael's description of a cycle of being whereby "one Almightie is, from whom / All things proceed, and up to him return, / If not deprav'd from good" (5.469–71). God is both the source and destination of each creature, the "center" and the "circumference" of the sphere of being. He is the base matter from which they are made and the refined matter to which they proceed. Milton's juxtaposition of linear and circular imagery to represent the ontological relation of Creator and creature effectively conveys their simultaneous identity and difference.

The identification of Creator and creature in *Paradise Lost* is achieved through Milton's portrayal of Creation as a union of God's masculine vitality and his feminine potency. Generally, Miltonists have seen the "one first matter" (5.472) of which all things are made as the only factor unifying God with the world. D. Bentley Hart argues that "it is matter that is the ground of all unity" between God and his creatures, and Rumrich holds that "in matter rests the unity of creation, the possibility for apocalyptic communion, the avenue and vehicle for communicable good."[67] However, the unity of Creator and creature is also achieved by the presence of God's vital spirit in created things. As Michael tells Adam, God's

> Omnipresence fills
> Land, Sea, and Aire, and every kinde that lives,
> Fomented by his virtual power and warmd.   (11.336–38)

In Milton's monist cosmos, God's omnipresence is manifested in the "virtual power" and warmth of created things, properties deriving from the Spirit of God's impregnation of prime matter.

Milton's identification of both matter and spirit with God creates a pantheism more absolute than most. Stoicism, a major source of pantheistic philosophy, distinguished between an active principle inherent in matter, associated with the logos, and matter itself, which was distinct from the logos.[68] As Harinder Singh Marjara comments, "even though [the Stoics] considered the universal spirit as material form, [they] believed in some sort of dualism between this spirit and the other, more tangible, forms of matter on which it acted."[69] Milton's association of both active and passive principles with God creates an uncompromising monism, according to which everything originates in and partakes of the Creator. His God is at once the base matter from which creatures proceed and the spiritualized matter to which they return and is logically identifiable with everything in between.

However, within the poetic "right reason," where logic is not always primary, created things can be divine and worldly at the same time. Because God simultaneously is and is not the substance out of which the world is created, he is both identifiable with Creation and separate from it. Created things are physically separate from the deity due to their different "degrees / Of substance" and their "various forms" (5.473–74), which are the source of their individual essences.[70] And rational creatures are ontologically separate from the deity due to their self-authoring souls. Yet created things also participate in the divine nature, "created all / Such to perfection" (5.471–72), and consequently the unfallen are "United as one individual Soule" (5.610). Even fallen creatures retain their divine origins and divinely given nature, however corrupted they might become,[71] and the redeemed have a common identity in Christ, in whom they "live . . . transplanted" (3.293). These paradoxes support the poem's theodicy as they allow Milton to assert contradictory "truths." The portrayal of God's "self" as distinct from prime matter enables him to maintain that God is omniscient and omnipotent, separate from his fallible creatures and therefore not responsible for evil. God's immanence, on the other hand, presupposes the inherent virtue of Creation and God's creative goodness. Milton's poetic portrayal of God allows him to celebrate human virtue and human freedom, attributing the origins of both to God.

The two-part structure of God's being forms the basis of both the binary oppositions and the unities that characterize the world God creates. This is perhaps most evident in Milton's construction of gender. Gender differentiation in the created universe has its source in the opposition between the feminine prime matter and the masculine virtue and warmth that initiate all subsequent acts of metamorphosis. As gender structures stem from the relationships between God's masculine and feminine identities, masculinity and femininity are at once hierarchical terms and different, complementary forms of goodness. The paradoxical relationship between the sexes is amply expressed by Raphael's description of natural processes of generation:

> the Earth
> Though, in comparison of Heav'n, so small,
> Nor glistering, may of solid good containe

> More plenty then the Sun that barren shines,
> Whose vertue on itself workes no effect,
> But in the fruitful Earth; there first receavd
> His beams, unactive else, thir vigour find.   (8.91–97)

The feminine earth and the masculine sun are each dependent upon the other for the generation of life.[72] Female matter is potent or "fruitful," containing "solid good" that is activated by the "vertue" of the sun. The sun's "vertue" is of itself "barren" and "unactive" but capable of giving "vigour" to the earth's potency. The sun is dominant in the generative process, but the earth is equally necessary to the creation of being. Male and female are complementary aspects of a totality, just as both aspects of the divine being together constitute divine unity.

Milton's two Gods, the volitional transcendent deity and the "I am" of prime matter, both "circumscrib[e] [our] being" (5.825). They contribute physically and spiritually to the matter from which each created thing is formed, and they are accordingly the source of the values and relations that condition existence. The tension between the monistic and dualistic conceptions of God is felt in the presentation of gender, physics, ethics, politics, and metaphysics in *Paradise Lost*. Milton's God is superior to prime matter but is also identifiable with it; Eve is created from Adam and is his "other half" (4.488) and "Sole partner" (4.411), even though Adam is also Eve's "Head" (4.443); darkness is the absence of light as well as its opposite; evil is a spiritual reality but, as it is presented as the corruption of good, it is a metaphysical nonentity; Satan is subject to God even though he is "Prince of aire" and free to control his "Realme" (12.454–55)—our world—till the end of time; Creation is a refinement of chaos, not merely its antithesis; and matter and spirit are continuous. Each pair of conceptual terms used to construct the poem's framework is at once a binary opposition and no opposition at all, reflecting the ontological structure of Milton's God. The logocentric hierarchies of *Paradise Lost* and the radical and egalitarian impulse that subverts them find their ultimate expression in a God who is at once a transcendent, authoritative being and the matter and spirit of his Creation.

University of Western Sydney

NOTES

I am indebted to William Christie, Andrew McRae, and Beverley Sherry for their generous comments and support in the writing of this article.

1. All quotations of poetry are from *Paradise Lost* in *The Riverside Milton*, ed. Roy Flan-

nagan (Boston, 1998), unless otherwise indicated, and are cited by book and line number parenthetically in the text.

2. Thomas Hobbes, *Leviathan*, ed. Richard Tuck (Cambridge, 1991), 32.

3. *Complete Prose Works of John Milton*, gen. ed. Don M. Wolfe, 8 vols. (New Haven and London, 1953–82), 8:208, 2:402, 2:404, 2:406, 1:821. References to Milton's prose will hereafter be taken from this edition and cited parenthetically in the text as YP, with volume and page number. Kathleen M. Swaim demonstrates the pervasiveness of Ramistic logic in *Paradise Lost*, including its influence on Milton's poetic. However, Ramism is not hostile to mysticism and, as Swaim notes, "It is true that [Milton's] rendering of Christian paradox and mystery transcends the merely logical and in important ways leaves Ramus behind, but it is also true that the Ramistic foundations and philosophy make such transcendence not only possible but preferred." See Swaim, *Before and After the Fall: Contrasting Modes in Paradise Lost* (Amherst, Mass., 1986), 156.

4. Gerald L. Bruns, *Hermeneutics Ancient and Modern* (New Haven and London, 1992), 233.

5. Denis Saurat, *Milton: Man and Thinker* (New York, 1925), 46.

6. William B. Hunter, "Milton's Power of Matter," *JHI* 13 (1952): 558; Michael F. Moloney, "Plato and Plotinus in Milton's Cosmogony," *Philological Quarterly* 40 (1961): 41; Walter Clyde Curry, *Milton's Ontology, Cosmogony and Physics* (Lexington, Ky., 1957), 34–35; William Empson, *Milton's God* (Cambridge, 1961), 143–44; J. H. Adamson, "Milton and the Creation," *JEGP* 61 (1962): 764; and Leland Ryken, *The Apocalyptic Vision in Paradise Lost* (Ithaca, 1970), 36. Scholars of this period who were convinced of Milton's monism by *Christian Doctrine* offered only brief or qualified defences of this position. Barbara Kiefer Lewalski noted in passing the materiality of Milton's God (*Milton's Brief Epic: The Genre, Meaning, and Art of Paradise Regained* [Providence, R.I., 1966], 140), W. B. C. Watkins maintained that Milton did not commit himself metaphysically to a corporeal God (*An Anatomy of Milton's Verse* [Baton Rouge, La., 1955], 63) and John Reesing concluded that Milton's "doctrine of materiality in God . . . is . . . logically contradictory and philosophically inadequate" ("The Materiality of God in Milton's *De Doctrina Christiana*," *Harvard Theological Review* 50 [1957]: 172).

7. For recent studies of Milton's materialism, see William Kerrigan, *The Sacred Complex: On the Psychogenesis of Paradise Lost* (Cambridge, Mass., 1983), 193–262; Stephen M. Fallon, *Milton among the Philosophers: Poetry and Materialism in Seventeenth-Century England* (Ithaca, 1991); Harinder Singh Marjara, *Contemplation of Created Things: Science in Paradise Lost* (Toronto, 1992), 220–39; John Rogers, *The Matter of Revolution: Science, Poetry, and Politics in the Age of Milton* (Ithaca, 1996), 103–176; and D. Bentley Hart, "Matter, Monism, and Narrative: An Essay on the Metaphysics of *Paradise Lost*," *Milton Quarterly* 30 (1996): 16–27. Milton's heresies are the focus of Stephen B. Dobranski's and John P. Rumrich's collection of essays *Milton and Heresy* (Cambridge, 1998).

8. The title of this article is indebted to John Rumrich's "Milton's God and the Matter of Chaos," *PMLA* 110 (1995): 1035–46. My modifications of his title reflect my argument about the split identity of God in *Paradise Lost* and my focus upon the interaction between God's "self" and prime matter in Creation. For Rumrich's work on the identification of God with prime matter, see "Milton's Concept of Substance," *English Language Notes* 19 (1982): 218–33, *Matter of Glory: A New Preface to Paradise Lost* (Pittsburgh, 1987), 61–63, Rumrich, "Milton's God and the Matter of Chaos," 1043, and *Milton Unbound: Controversy and Reinterpretation* (Cambridge, 1996), 118–146.

9. Rumrich, "Milton's God and the Matter of Chaos," 1043.

10. Dennis Richard Danielson, *Milton's Good God: A Study in Literary Theodicy* (Cambridge, 1982), 43–48; Rogers, *The Matter of Revolution*, 103, 113; Hart, "Matter, Monism, and

Narrative," 19–20; Flannagan, *The Riverside Milton*, 542n; Marjara, *Contemplation of Created Things*, 98–100; Fallon (from whom the citation comes), *Milton among the Philosophers*, 122.

11. In *Christian Doctrine* Milton maintains that the first matter "could only have been derived from the source of all substance," that it "exist[s] in God" and that "God produced all things not out of nothing but out of himself" (YP 6:308–9). The evidence for Milton's authorship of *Christian Doctrine* seems overwhelming, despite the recent challenge to its provenance by William B. Hunter (see, especially, *Visitation Unimplor'd: Milton and the Authorship of De Doctrina Christiana* [Duquesne University Press, 1998]). Supporting Milton's authorship of the treatise are Barbara K. Lewalski, "Forum: Milton's *Christian Doctrine*," *SEL* 32 (1992): 143–54, and "Milton and *De Doctrina Christiana*: Evidences of Authorship," in *Milton Studies* 36, ed. Albert C. Labriola (Pittsburgh, 1998), 203–28; John T. Shawcross, "Forum: Milton's *Christian Doctrine*," *SEL* 32 (1992): 155–62; Maurice Kelley, "The Provenance of John Milton's *Christian Doctrine*," *SEL* 34 (1994): 153–63; Christopher Hill, "Professor William B. Hunter, Bishop Burgess and John Milton," *SEL* 34 (1994): 165–93; Dobranski and Rumrich, *Milton and Heresy*, 6–12; Hart, "Matter, Monism, and Narrative," (25 n.1); and A. D. Nuttall, *The Alternative Trinity: Gnostic Heresy in Marlowe, Milton, and Blake* (Oxford: Clarendon Press, 1998), 71n. A committee of experts who examined the manuscript and undertook computer analyses to form an opinion on the provenance of the work concluded that *De Doctrina Christiana* was "a working manuscript under revision by Milton," probably "an ur-text and a transformation of that text effected by a process of revision which primarily consisted of the accretion of material by Milton" (Gordon Campbell and others, "The Provenance of *De Doctrina Christiana*," *Milton Quarterly* 31 [1997]: 110).

12. Saurat, *Milton: Man and Thinker*, 123–25. For critics of this theory, see Arthur Sewell, *A Study in Milton's Christian Doctrine* (London, 1939), 124–27; A. S. P. Woodhouse, "Notes on Milton's Views on the Creation: The Initial Phases," *Philological Quarterly* 28 (1949): 227; A. B. Chambers, "Chaos in *Paradise Lost*," *JHI* 24 (1963): 70; Maurice Kelley, *This Great Argument: A Study of Milton's De Doctrina Christiana as a Gloss upon Paradise Lost* (Princeton, N.J., 1941), 209–11; Harry F. Robins, *If This Be Heresy: A Study of Milton and Origen* (Urbana, Ill., 1963); 87, C. A. Patrides, *Milton and the Christian Tradition*, (Oxford, 1966), 33; and B. Rajan, *Paradise Lost and the Seventeenth Century Reader* (London, 1947), 23, 139n.

13. Woodhouse, "Notes," 226, original italics.

14. Rumrich, "Milton's God and the Matter of Chaos," 1043, citing YP 6:308.

15. *The Light and Dark Sides of God Or a plain and brief Discourse of the light side {God, Heaven and Earth} the dark side {Devill, Sin and Hell}. As also of the Resurrection and Scripture*, (n.p., 1650), 1.

16. Chambers, "Chaos in *Paradise Lost*," 74–75; and Robert Fludd, *The Origin and Structure of the Cosmos (Utriusque Cosmi Historia)*, 1.5, trans. Patricia Tahil with an introduction by Adam McLean (Edinburgh, 1982), 23ff.

17. Chambers, "Chaos in *Paradise Lost*," 76.

18. Watkins, *An Anatomy*, 63; Rumrich, *Milton Unbound*, 141. Michael Lieb, *The Dialectics of Creation: Patterns of Birth & Regeneration in Paradise Lost* (Amherst, Massachusetts, 1970), 59; Rumrich, "Milton's God and the Matter of Chaos," 1042; and Rogers, *The Matter of Revolution*, 15, have referred approvingly to Watkins's view, and Walter Clyde Curry has noted the connection between Milton's God and the Neoplatonic One to which is ascribed "a dual nature, or male and female together" (*Milton's Ontology*, 57).

19. A. S. P. Woodhouse, "Notes," 229; Curry, *Milton's Ontology*, 70–72; Regina Schwartz, *Remembering and Repeating: Biblical Creation in Paradise Lost* (Cambridge, Eng., 1988), 31–32; Rumrich, *Milton Unbound*, 141–42; and Rogers, *The Matter of Revolution*, 130. John Rumrich has recently contended that prime matter is represented by both Night and Chaos (*Milton*

Unbound, 141) and Catherine Gimelli Martin appears to agree, arguing that Night "is allied with the Anarch as an even darker and more vacuous phase of prematter" ("Fire, Ice, and Epic Entropy: The Physics and Metaphysics of Milton's Reformed Chaos," in *Milton Studies* 35, ed. Albert C. Labriola [Pittsburgh, 1997], 108n).

20. *Timaeus and Other Dialogues,* 50d, ed. Benjamin Jowett (London, 1970), 258. Aristotle is also an important figure in this tradition. In the *Physics,* Aristotle claims that matter is analogous to the female and "yearns as the female for the male and as the base for the beautiful; except that it is neither base nor female, except by virtue of concurrence" (*Aristotle's Physics Books I and II,* 192a, trans. W. Charlton, [Oxford, 1970], 21). The "male" for which matter yearns is form, the active principle which causes matter to change and develop. In *The Genera-tion of Animals,* Aristotle holds more definitively that "the female serves as [the] matter" of generated things (732a, trans. A. L. Peck, [London, 1943], 133).

21. Rumrich, *Milton Unbound,* 141.

22. Schwartz, *Remembering and Repeating,* 31–35; Curry, *Milton's Ontology,* 69; Sewell, *A Study,* 127–30; Woodhouse, "Notes," 229; and Rogers, *The Matter of Revolution,* 130.

23. The Augustinian formula that metaphysical evil is the absence of good and of entity is discussed by Peter F. Fisher, "Milton's Theodicy," *JHI* 17 (1956): 28–53; Peter A. Fiore, *Milton and Augustine: Patterns of Augustinian Thought in Paradise Lost* (London, 1981), 12–22; and Fallon, *Milton among the Philosophers,* 168–71. Milton distinguishes between the "proper essence" given by form and the "common essence" given by matter in *Art of Logic,* YP 8:234.

24. *Remembering and Repeating,* 8, 31–32.

25. Rumrich, "Milton's God and the Matter of Chaos"; Fallon, *Milton among the Philoso-phers,* 190–91; Mary F. Norton, "Chaos Theory and *Paradise Lost,"* in *Milton Studies* 32, ed. Albert C. Labriola (Pittsburgh, 1995), 92; Catherine Gimelli Martin, *The Ruins of Allegory: Paradise Lost and the Metamorphosis of Epic Convention* (Durham, 1998), 198.

26. Rumrich, "Milton's God and the Matter of Chaos," 1041. For Rumrich, Chaos personi-fies the absence of God's creative will and is not a psychological agent capable of expressing evil. Chaos's desire for anarchy and uncreation is a result of this personification and accounts for the "strong narrative evidence of the malignancy of chaos" (ibid.).

27. Stephen Fallon associates "downward ontological movement" with evil (*Milton among the Philosophers,* 209). "[T]hough Spirits of purest light," the falling angels become "gross by sinning grown" (6.660–61). They forfeit the "perfet formes" (7.455) which God gave them and devolve toward the "Matter unform'd and void" (7.233) of chaos. They also experience ontologi-cal chaos. Satan describes himself as "Hell; / And in the lowest deep a lower deep / Still threatning to devour me opens wide" (4.75–77), and the fallen Adam complains that he is "from deep to deeper plung'd" into an "Abyss of fears" (10.844, 842).

28. Cf. Peter Ramus, *The Logicke,* 1574 (Leeds, Eng., 1966), 24–28.

29. *Physics* 192a, 21.

30. I am indebted to Beverley Sherry for her suggestion that God's heavenly persona is material. I have since found that Harry F. Robins is also of this view, noting as a possible source "Origen's opinion that God, though a spirit, is yet in some sense material." See Robins, *If This Be Heresy,* 76.

31. *An Answer to a Book Published by Dr Bramhall, . . . Called the "Catching of the Leviathan," The English Works of Thomas Hobbes,* ed. Sir William Molesworth, 11 vols. (Lon-don, 1839–45), 4:312–13, qtd. Fallon, *Milton among the Philosophers,* 40.

32. Ryken, *The Apocalyptic Vision,* 38.

33. Saurat, *Milton: Man and Thinker,* 303–4; Kelley, *This Great Argument,* 93.

34. Kelley, *This Great Argument,* 92–94; Albert R. Cirillo, "'Hail Holy Light' and Divine

Time in *Paradise Lost,*" *JEGP* 68 (1969): 49; and Merritt Y. Hughes, *Ten Perspectives on Milton* (New Haven, 1965), 98.

35. Cirillo, " 'Hail Holy Light,' " 49.

36. *OED* 2a and 2c cite lines 1.138 and 1.425, respectively.

37. Derrida, "Signature Event Context," in *Margins of Philosophy,* trans. Alan Bass (Sussex, Eng., 1982), 329, emphasis in the original.

38. Derrida, "Signature Event Context," 329.

39. On Milton's Augustinian conception of evil, see note 23 above.

40. Lieb, *The Dialectics of Creation,* 59.

41. Rumrich, *Milton Unbound,* 108; Rogers, *Matter of Revolution,* 116.

42. Rogers, *Matter of Revolution,* 117; Rumrich, *Milton Unbound,* 108; Rogers, *Matter of Revolution,* 116.

43. This evolution is at once spiritual and material, abstract and concrete. Milton's God promises to "soft'n stonie hearts" of fallen humanity so that, "if they will hear, / Light after light well us'd they shall attain, / And to the end persisting, safe arrive," yet if they will not, he declares that "hard be hard'nd, blind be blinded more" (3.189, 195–97, 200). The imagery of progress toward light and regression toward internal darkness represents the physical evolution and devolution of fallen beings.

44. On Renaissance interpretations of Genesis 1:2, see William B. Hunter, "The Seventeenth Century Doctrine of Plastic Nature," *Harvard Theological Review* 43 (1950): 204; Edgar Hill Duncan, "The Natural History of Metals and Minerals in the Universe of Milton's *Paradise Lost,*" *Osiris* 11 (1954): 418; and Marjara, *Contemplation of Created Things,* 213.

45. *Decameron Physiologicum: or, Ten Dialogues of Natural Philosophy,* (London, 1678), 130.

46. *Physiologia Epicuro-Gassendo-Charltoniana: Or a fabrick of science natural upon the hypothesis of atoms* (1654; reprint, with indexes and a new introduction by Robert Hugh Kargon, New York, 1966), 126, 269. See also John Henry, "Occult Qualities and the Experimental Philosophy: Active Principles in Pre-Newtonian Matter Theory," *History of Science* 24 (1986): 340.

47. *Religio Medici* in *The Religio Medici and Other Writings of Sir Thomas Browne* (London, 1906), 36.

48. *The Primitive Origination of Mankind Considered and Examined According to the Light of Nature,* pt. 4, ch. 2 (London, 1677), 293 (emphasis in the original). Hale identified himself as occupying a middle ground between mechanism and vitalism: see Alan Cromartie, *Sir Matthew Hale: 1609–1676* (Cambridge, Eng., 1995), 208. However, as Cromartie writes, "Hale differed from his atomist opponents in insisting on an active principle (apart, that is, from the motion the Almighty originally gave) in a naturally passive material world" (203).

49. Marjara, *Contemplation of Created Things,* 212.

50. Ibid., 168–71.

51. In *The Generation of Animals,* Aristotle wrote that "the semen contains within itself that which causes it to be fertile—what is known as 'hot' substance" (736b, 171), and he also maintained that, because of the male capacity to produce semen, "male animals are hotter than female ones" (765b, 387). For his view that the material of the semen contains the principle of soul, see 737a (173). The second-century physician Galen borrowed the conception of vital heat from Aristotle, making it even more influential in the Renaissance: see Fallon, *Milton among the Philosophers,* 104–5.

52. Marsilio Ficino, *Three Books on Life,* bk. 2, ch. 2, ed. and trans., with intro. and notes, by Carol V. Kaske and John R. Clark (New York, 1989), 169; Paracelsus, *Of the Chymical Trans-*

mutation of Metals and Minerals, trans. R. Turner, (London, 1657), 11; and William Harvey, *Disputations Touching the Generation of Animals,* ed. and trans., with intro., by Gweneth Whitteridge (Oxford, 1981), 374.

53. For a seventeenth-century critique of the scholastic conception of creation from celestial heat and primigenial moisture, see Jean-Baptiste van Helmont, *Works,* trans. by J. C., (London, 1667), 726–30. The view that vital heat is celestial was held by the sixteenth century Italian physician and philosopher, Girolamo Cardano, discussed in *The Cambridge History of Renaissance Philosophy,* ed. Charles B. Schmitt and Quentin Skinner (Cambridge, 1988), 250. For the debate about the origins of vital heat, see William B. Hunter, *The Descent of Urania: Studies in Milton, 1946–1988* (Lewisburg, Pa., 1989), 122–23.

54. Rogers, *The Matter of Revolution,* 116 (emphasis in the original); Rumrich, *Milton Unbound,* 108.

55. *Joan Baptista Van Helmont: Reformer of Science and Medicine* (Cambridge, 1982), 87.

56. *Oriatrike or Physick Refined,* trans. John Chandler (London, 1662), 31.

57. John Rogers claims that the doctrine of the ferment exalted female self-sufficiency as it "swept away the necessity of outside impregnators and created an image of vital matter as self-sufficient, self-moving, impregnable" (*The Matter of Revolution,* 119). In suggesting that fermenting matter generates autonomously, Rogers denies the male gender of the ferment within it.

58. Pagel, *Joan Baptista Van Helmont,* 80.

59. Kerrigan, *The Sacred Complex: On the Psychogenesis of Paradise Lost* (Cambridge, 1983), 220.

60. On the concept of "ripening" metals see Duncan, "Natural History," 393, 412–15; and Lyndy Abrams, "Milton's *Paradise Lost* and 'the sounding alchymie,' " *Renaissance Studies* 12 (1998): 267–68.

61. Stevie Davies argues that "the bisexual poet receiving inspiration from a bisexual deity is, throughout the poem, seen to create a bisexual world." According to Davies, the bisexuality of the world gives rise to "sexual desire" in nature and is the basis of nature's fertility. She sees "the source of the concept of the androgynous creator and androgynous world [as] unmistakably Hermetic." However, Davies does not identify God with the material world, but rather attributes the androgyny of the world to the influence of the bisexual Spirit of God "brooding" on the abyss: see *The Idea of Woman in Renaissance Literature: the Feminine Reclaimed* (Sussex, 1986), 195–96, 197, 198. See also Hermes Trismegistus, *Hermetica,* ed. and trans. Walter Scott, 4 vols., (Oxford, 1924), 1:119, where "the first Mind" who creates "a Maker of things" is described as "bisexual."

62. Rumrich, *Milton Unbound,* 111, 110. Although the portrayal of Eve is beyond the scope of this essay, it will be evident from the following discussion that I do not find support for Eve's perceived inconsistencies in Milton's presentation of creation.

63. Rogers, *The Matter of Revolution,* 117, 122.

64. Plotinus, *The Enneads* (London, 1969), 1.8.4, 2.4.5; 69, 107.

65. Marshall Grossman makes a similar claim in the different context of the relationship between history and eternity in *Paradise Lost.* He argues that "*Paradise Lost* presents two constitutions of man's temporal being. One, prelapsarian and monistic, posits a continual refinement in perception in which knowledge increases faith and faith increases knowledge until man 'improv'd by tract of time' (5.498) ascends to the kingdom. The other, postlapsarian and dualistic, implies a cognitive hierarchy in which the sphere of essence stands above that of protean appearance" (*"Authors to Themselves": Milton and the Revelation of History* [Cambridge, 1987], 195).

66. Flannagan, *Riverside Milton,* 491n.

67. Hart, "Matter, Monism, and Narrative," 22; Rumrich, *Matter of Glory*, 66.

68. According to Diogenes Laertius, the Stoics "hold that there are two principles in the universe, the active principle and the passive. The passive principle, then, is a substance without quality, i.e. matter, whereas the active is the reason inherent in this substance, that is God" (*Lives of Eminent Philosophers* [London, 1925], vol. 2, 239).

69. Marjara, *Contemplation of Created Things*, 221.

70. In the *Art of Logic* Milton holds that it is "only through form" that a thing can be said "to *be that which it is*" and so identifies proper essence with individual being (YP 8:234; emphasis Milton's). Cf. Spenser's description of created things coming into being through their forms in the Garden of Adonis: "All things from [Chaos] doe their first being fetch, / And borrow matter, whereof they are made, / Which when as forme and feature it does ketch, / Becomes a bodie, and doth then inuade / The state of life, out of the griesly shade" (*The Faerie Queene* 3.6.37, ed. Thomas P. Roche [Harmondsworth, Eng., 1978], 471).

71. As Peter A. Fiore argues, "Milton believes that [heavenly] essences are destroyed only insofar as it is possible for them to be destroyed. Their natures, in virtue of the fact that they exist, are entities; and if they are entities, they are good." See *Milton and Augustine: Patterns of Augustinian Thought in Paradise Lost* (London, 1981), 15. See also Fallon, *Milton among the Philosophers*, 169–71.

72. Similarly, Stevie Davies argues that "Male solar light and female lunar light do not polarise experience into units of solitary opposition, but 'communicate' back and forth, desiring return to unity. 'Two great sexes' define Milton's universe as a dynamic duality whose end is not diversity (though diversity is a beautiful and fascinating aspect of its process) but the urge of love into greater nearness" (*The Idea of Woman in Renaissance Literature: the Feminine Reclaimed* [Sussex, 1986], 197).

MILTON'S PASSIONAL POETICS, OR
PARADIGMS LOST AND REGAINED

Michael Fixler

I. The Anti-Cartesian Project

To [logic and rhetoric] Poetry would be subsequent, or indeed rather
precedent, as being lesse suttle and fine, but more simple, sensuous, and
passionate.

Milton, Of Education

By *intuition* I understand, not the fluctuating testimony of the senses,
nor the misleading judgement that proceeds from the blundering constructions of the imagination, but the conception which an unclouded
and attentive mind gives us so readily and distinctly that we are wholly
freed from doubt about that which we understand. . . . [It] springs from
the light of reason alone.

Descartes, Rules for the Direction of the Mind

I BEGIN WITH SOME DEFINITIONS, distinctions, then distinctions begotten of distinctions, and finally some soundings of a larger general hypothesis about culture and consciousness I pursue elsewhere, a matter
sampled here by way of Milton's poetics.[1] Both the project and the scope of
this essay are readily referable to the opposing claims made in the texts
above, that is, that somehow the intuitive power of the mind is defined by its
limitations.

Milton's intuition, enlarged in *Paradise Lost* (5.582–88) by an extension
Raphael calls "angelic," transcends the mind's merely discursive limits. Descartes feels obliged to exclude Milton's kind of imaginative "blundering" in
favor of that intuitive clarity and distinctiveness by which alone the mind can
close in upon rational certainty. The difference comes down to the extremes
of what Western culture has come to expect from aesthetics and science as
ideally the most transcendent aspects of consciousness. The big thing about
Cartesian intuition is that it yields the ore of truth, the ultimately objectively
valid result.

I argue that Milton's aesthetics is focused on his passional poetics, but
not without its insistence that something written is always to be intersubjectively understood. (*A community of readers consisting of just the writer and*

reader is complete!) By definition a passional poetics would be about how the passion or energy of a force, conventionalized (say) as inspiration, presumes to shape, not just a text, but the affinities of virtual readers to its indefinite means. With that in mind I instance for later discussion the controlled release in writing and reading of the axial space/time forces shaping Milton's *At a Solemn Music* (up, down, backward, forward) as the schematic expression of a protean adaptability in rendering formally correspondent the powers of the mind and the holistic significance of its selected contexts.

Nowadays we are more likely to see how problematic the poem's formalizing presumption is, if only because in this kind of writing the form of the experiencing and the observing mind are the same, set by its instruments self-referentially *within* and *outside*, or even *against*, the world as its object. One way the poem seems to resolve the problem of the self-observing observer is by the conventional division of the poem's own substance and effects into the dichotomy of form and content as complementary or marriageable powers, as in the Voice and Verse of *At a Solemn Music*, whose fusion ignite the poem's accomplishment. Here Voice is not only sounded; it takes in the poem's form as the real sounding board of the kind of literary resonance that sustains the possibility of determinate meaning while persistently avoiding meaning's full resolutions, combining the effects of both semiotic openness and closure.

The distinction of formal openness and semantic closure would hold gradationally as well for any prose writing, where the priority of sense over sound may nonetheless be expected to prevail, but where a given work's underlying formalisms mediate the often wholly disparate self-referential resonance of the writer's and reader's separate contexts. Form, or rather *dynamic form*, is then the portmanteau vehicle of how collectively we deal in our communicational codes with transacting differently referenced self-centerings. If direct self-reference and its displacement upon its linguistic instruments and upon the presumably factual nature of their objects are fundamental to the emergence of consciousness, this division of signifying functions can hardly be surprising, and it no doubt can even be traced within the very evolution of writing itself.[2]

Here I skip over the question of how writing progressively transforms the phenomenality of self-reference to focus on its mature effects, except for one prime consideration. For how, within the terms of my argument, might the literary mediation of a phenomenology of self-reference relate biological to cultural evolution? The short answer is encapsulated in this initially foregrounded difference between Milton and Descartes over the question of the nature of the intuitionary transcendence upon which both agree, but not as to its kind. And then the difference is also a matter that has worked its way into a kind of traditional consensus, having been encoded within the canons and developments of a literate culture peculiarly concerned that at their underlying levels these different modes of thought and language should remain in strong cross-communication with one another.

This is really a necessity, since Western culture's powerful insistence on the discursive precedence of logic runs up against the incipient logical binds generated by the terms of our personal self-reference and the limitations upon logical expression they entail, where it seems our tendencies toward irrational entrammelments on that account can only be circumvented by rhetorical and aesthetic means. I would argue that the ability of a more indeterminately conceived poeticized language to play such a corrective part depends in fact on the kind of monistic assumption that, against Cartesian dualism,[3] most of us now share with Milton's monistic sense of the "one first matter all," (PL 5.472), and that as a monism makes all continuities possible. Yet if monistic assumptions tend to generate gradational models of reality, Milton's gradational monism is not like ours, resembling more the monism of a Spinoza who conceived that the imagination is the ultimate resource in a substantial world given to conatus or automatic self-persistence—a concession to Cartesian world mechanics.

But then the extent to which the formal aspect of life, of thought, and even of writing itself may be 'automated' by our nature or by its habits is a question that will here be seen to have also powerfully attracted Derrida's obsessive interests in the formalism of the self-inscribing serial order of numbers to which they seemed to him to be related. I turn to this involvement on Derrida's part with compositional numbers, because, as I have described them in my earlier work, Milton also recognized them. But in the end it is not clear that what for Derrida self-persists automatically through such compositional enumerabilities tells us anything profound about how writing relates to consciousness. Milton is rather more clear about the relation than one might suspect, believing that for a proper poet what self-persists is the mind's unconscious self-identity with its own shaping powers, which in turn hold the purified essence of what it means to be dynamically possessed of a godlike consciousness.

This identity subsists in a well nurtured consciousness because it subsists within the diffusion of one first matter all as everlasting matrix of emergent and happy-tending possibilities. Since this underlying matrix generates as well the ordering powers of the mind, it can only be manifest indirectly, being otherwise diffused throughout all the world orders until it might undergo a kind of millennial recycling. At that point it would effectively return to its original Edenic condition, for which the prototype would have been expressed in Milton's Eden itself by the dance of Pan, the Graces, and the Hours that we look at later. In any case, whatever *rationale* the automatic self-persistence of mental habits entails, is hardly a rational affair in any ordinary sense. As Wittgenstein remarked, language did not begin in ratiocination; nor, I add, did it begin in a poetics that turns the logos or the world's exact or expressible realities into an always indefinitely fictive image, a mythos.

It would begin with an instinct for balance, in every sense. And nowhere is the need for balance more evident than in the paralogistic ways of a holistic thinking that has to subsume the observer within the whole being observed, producing symbolic figures (like Christ in and out of the world) as an index of the mind's need for some formally invariant totalizing device for projecting its shaping power. This is not ordinary logic but the logic of an intuitive holism, one in which mythos as the spirit of story has an advantage over science as logos, the spirit of logic. Yet as the spirit of logic eventually shows us, there is a tough referential problem at the heart of any attempt to grasp the whole of things holistically, a problem usually fudged by some equivocal style of writerly presence (or absence) that ends up confusing the teller with the tale. Descartes starts certain of his self-referential *cogito* but then leaps uncertainly to the certainty that God exists to underwrite the rationality of an essentially aesthetic presumption, the world's perfect design.

In either case, the outright illogic to which any self-centered holism leads constrains us to focus on its backgrounded and foregrounded elements. For self-reference is transactionally variously centered: on the writing self, or among individual readers, or on the cultural commune—or on anyone or anything else for that matter possessed of systematicity. Since systems are cyclic and all cyclicity (for example, the biological or literary feedback loop) is recursively self-referential, sooner or later transactional language's circularizing elements lead to inconsistencies, paralogisms, contradictions, and paradoxes. In poetry these are both enhanced and obscured by poetry's ties to the reigning mythos, and in prose by ties to the dominant logos or its logical paradigm. But suppose we see whether self-referential circularities are only now, or have always been, evident to Western poetic or mythic paradigms and endemic to its logic, as part of that even more primitive or nativist process that tells us a good deal about the constancies underlying certain paradigm shifts.

Thus Patricia Churchland begins her Darwinian *Neurophilosophy* by calling attention to the fact that the mind's central feature is traceable to the elemental feedback loop of the primitive cell's bipolar stimulus and response phases.[4] Over time cultural evolution complicates the loop's adaptive phases into styles of perceptual representations and responsive enactments, which is where we take the big leap from biological to cultural evolution, or, more particularly, to a fascinating equivocity about writing and mental phases right smack within the originating Platonic moment that defines so much of West-ern culture. Interestingly the equivocity is centered on the Greek word *aes-thesis,* wherein a distinction of effects and meaning as both *experiential sensation* and *representational perception* seems to catch Plato's eye (for example, *Theatatus* 163d–166e, 188e–192c), remaining thenceforth the seed for separable intuitions of a representational logic (Cartesian) and an experiential aesthetics (Miltonic), each embedded in the Platonic legacy.

But for Plato himself the experienced knowing of a recognitive intuition could never quite fully realize itself in mere physical representations of its ultimately metaphysical object, where metaphysics stands for a persistence (here of experiences) always short of mortally material completions. Looked at this way, it would seem that Plato saw a representation/enactment problem to be all but explicitly inscribed in Western philosophy by virtue of the fact that as writing reflecting *on* itself *as* writing, *in* writing, and *on* the truth claims *of* writing, the whole compositional art begins to take on the aspect of a circularly self-regarding exercise in consciousness raising. It is as if (1) the history of consciousness were (2) to inscribe itself as consciousness, (3) aware of its own consciousness.

The problem in both writing and consciousness can be described as a matter of exponentiating orders of self-reference and their self-concealing tautologies. For beyond some three or four levels of such metalinguistic circlings, even a good head may begin to spin, with the trick of keeping steady being more rhetorical concealment to spread the effect out. This kind of self-referential entrammelment is already hinted at in the Plato who writes philo-sophically that philosophy cannot be written. Having stumbled upon the inherent problem, it is as if Plato then has to displace it onto his quarrel with the rhetoricians who claimed that wisdom was teachable as/in writing. But that the problem is as innate as anything recoverable by the immortal soul's anamnesis is suggested by how its simplest analogues, in those figure/ground pictures we have all seen, confound us by forcing us to realize we can never simultaneously see figure as ground or ground as figure except as *alternatively* phased aspects of the scene. In effect Plato displaced the illogic of his own procedure onto writing as representational (back)ground, privileging instead as truly philosophic the actional or experiential claims of oral dialectic.

Thus in Letter VII (343a) he treats writing much as a compositional extension of a merely literary formatting procedure *(gegrammene tupois),* setting out a paradigm of a philosophical method which immediately exposes its own limitations in its inability, in writing, to grasp the knowable, when the only knowables worth knowing are transcendental Ideas or Forms, inaccessi-ble except to a type of intuitionary experience that presumably somehow includes what we have called the Cartesian and Miltonic varieties. Say we wanted to know a circle, Plato's method begins. But immediately left unsaid with the choice is that for Plato the circle as pure Idea or Form is *the* generative pattern of all phenomenal circles, as well as a symbol of that perfection in circularity entirely unknowable except by intuitive approximation. The implication is that only in some transcendental unity of being might one *experience* the ultimate perfect circularity (in the *Phaedrus* it is glimpsed as a *representational stage* communicated within a kind of Apollonian rapture), symbolized by the heaven-directed cycling of its justified pattern of aeonically perfected time. Not elsewhere or anyhow.

But such as it is, this fugitive intuitionary experience is only just valid (philosophically) when it is sustained by the *intimate intersubjectivity* of a master and disciple dialectically engaged face to face. Thus for Plato, subjecting the quest for the truth of the circle to the threshold test of intersubjectivity means that both master and disciple continuously engage in a circularizing recursion of discursivity through the four stages of naming, defining, illustrating, and the difficult fourth. Circularity is the key, since at the fourth stage no two may alike and quickly reach to the consummation of actually experiencing the *knowing* of the circle. But since this is the social test of true knowing, the stages are run through over and over again, until some ineffably shared intuitivity intersubjectively supervenes. Weird. But one sees the point.

The procedure's analogue in the *Phaedrus* has as its object knowing Love, where the circularity of essence peculiar to Love (the quintessential intersubjectivity) would seem meant to ground its logic, whether physically or displaced on the idea of an inspirational or infused and transfused reciprocating force animating two people and the individual consciousness and the Idea in the world.

Given the collective flabbiness of all the things vaguely supposed, the circularizing method seems inordinately robust in producing memorable literary results. It is as if it were adapted to an expectation that what the mind knows, and wants to know, is best explored in how we construct such knowing. On that presumption, it does not seem far-fetched to see smuggled into the method of Letter VII both a directed gradient toward metaphysical knowledge of the circle and the radiant *intimations* that the object as circularity builds into a scalar method going nowhere except into *intersubjectively shared* near-mystical intuitions—which is why or how Plato's formatting scale becomes the model for so many later literary accounts of such experiences.

The relevance to Milton appears in how the circularizing of the format symbolically informs the theodicy by which in the *Phaedrus* Plato justifies the significance of the four madnesses or *mania* of which Socrates is mythopoetically possessed. Its climax as a scaled inspirational ascent reaches toward the intuitionary revelation the Good is also Beauty, Justice, and Truth, all convergently unfolding at the highest stage and final end of its drive toward knowing experientially something of the love driving the cosmos (245b–248). At this point the logic of dialectic is left behind, and at the least a circularizing method, clued to the intersubjective involvement of a master and disciple, substitutes for the circle as self-justifying Idea. For Milton, as we will see, the circle as form thematically informs everything about the visionary content of his theodicy, elevating the beauty of recursive circularizing with varying experiential effects over its more passive intellectual representations. Intersubjectivity, the one-on-one of writer and reader, is at the heart of the poetic transaction and its hypothetical breakout from the sometimes subjective solipsism within which poetry might be written. This is written poetry's opening concession to the objectifying constraints of the Western logos.

Note that the *Phaedrus* is the only one of Plato's dialogues with but two persons, its Phaedrus a disciple in the presence of a master who may bring him no further than *communionally* to know how to know love itself. Here also one names, defines, and represents an experience only knowable in some final intuitionary leap never spelled out, which lies just beyond Socrates' extended mythopoetic dithyramb. Yet however powerfully evoked, in the dialogue the experience shifts narrative gears, interrupting the more prosaic dialectic and narrative, so that it became a highly influential model of the poetic "soaring" Milton imagined as a sort of higher level poetic ignition that, as in *At a Vacation Exercise*, uses its booster rocket to take poetic inspiration into a holistic spatial orbit with temporal resonances. Even the embedding of the poem within *Prolusion 6* points back to the way the embedded inspirational ascent in the *Phaedrus*, in embodying the palpable physicality of its soaring context, became a traditional prototype and model of transcendental revelation.

Compare, for example, Augustine's experience with Monica at her deathbed in the *Confessions*, or even Wordsworth's shared epiphany with Dorothy in *Tintern Abbey*, with Paul's passional ascent (in 2 Cor. 12:1–6), where the embodiment is a palpable physicality, evoked as the price of revelation, as in Paul's thorn in the flesh. What we must not lose sight of here is that the real playoff in such visionary processes is between their *intersubjective* authority and the *objectifying* authority of the rational logos, an opposition dramatically juxtaposed within the hierarchy of the four Phaedran raptures by the madness of Dionysus and Apollo. Following Nietzsche's exaltation of the Dionysian over the Apollonian power, Heidegger exalts the incomprehensible intimacies of shared intersubjective or poetistic intuitions, but on terms that barely reveal to us their nativist or biological, as against their cultural origins. Behind his usage, I think, is the fact that Wittgenstein identifies the underlying limitation more objectively as the saying/showing or enactment/representation conditions of the logical positivist language game, ultimately a problem he thought referable not to logic but to biology.

But it is important to the rest of this argument that we focus on the deliberate mystification involved in Heidegger's distortion of the situation. For what he elicits from this language game is the heroic moral imperative given Germany to express itself profoundly through "the variously named conflict of the Dionysian and the Apollonian, of holy passion and sober representation." Yet precisely because he identified the double-mean of the traditional fourfold with Nazi Germany's metaphysical destiny, Heidegger was forced to abandon these terms after the war, converting them instead into his famous but far more enigmatic 'fourings'—the Apollonian aspect of the Being/consciousness duality (as *Sein* and *Dasein*) becoming *Des Gevierts* or *Being* (over-written by its own erasure), an object of Apollonian representation, the other or Dionysian *Das Geviert* becoming the object of the aesthetic experience by which rapturously consciousness *knows* Being.[5]

With this I come to one of the major cruces of my larger argument about the relationship of culture to consciousness in peculiarly Western terms, namely the identity of the saying/showing or enactment/representation opposition with the crashing collapse in the twentieth century of Western logical certainty and of the Cartesian quest for it. As Wittgenstein effectively tells us, the biological root of this collapse inheres in Kurt Gödel's startling logical or mathematical proof of the metacognitive nature of the reality of this limitation. The fact that, as phase dependent alternations of the language game, both saying and showing cannot be given at once, and that this results in a formalizable logical dilemma, tells us that while the logos may be good at representing reality, experience is most at home in fact within the intersubjective terms which always need some mediating mythos. Or, as Wittgenstein said of Gödel's undecidability and incompleteness theorem of 1931, its proof merely translates the dilemma into symbolic logic.[6]

Roughly, the idea is that since propositional logic's *closures* cannot be achieved without courting the unprovability or inconsistency of its axioms, a feint at incompleteness, or a shift into the different systematics of figurative language, can be made to seem as if it were avoiding the trap. The trap was always there, and in ancient Greece it took the intersection of a lively poetics, writing, a newly fledged logic, and an intuitive grasp of a deeply dynamic formalism to help spring it in ways a mind such as Plato's sensed. Perhaps that is part of his attribution to anamnesis or unforgetting the knowledge of numbers and geometry with which we seem to be born. But of course in this context Plato had in mind how peculiarly Pythagorean forms and numbers become generatively intervolved with our sense of emergent meanings, for these, as a good deal of recent and converging cognitive research suggests, derive from some of our deepest nativist or heritable biological limitations.

Apparently the number of things we can organize, explain, and remember are subject to the same limitations governing the optimal units of grammar, the ordering of sequences, or the limiting of the orders we can conceive in metacognition or metalinguistically, as knowing about knowing, or talking or even writing about language about language. And because there is always a kind of surreptitious and spontaneous poetics eking out our logic, it has sometimes seemed as if there is a magical autopoetic power in nature that human poetics grasps as an art, a spontaneous tendency sometimes loosely referred to by cognitive psychologists as "going Pythagorean." Writers possessed of both this power and a sense of archaic tradition (Seamus Heaney is one of them) are not ashamed of taking as inspiration the native tendencies and *habitus* welling up within them as a privileged formal alacrity. Heidegger attributes to the passional animus a force whose spontaneously shaped effects for him, as for Plato, may key structures of transcendence, which pretty much fits the character of how Milton's *At a Solemn Music* would seem to work.

In Heidegger's terms, the animus foregrounds itself out of a background describable as the unconscious coordinations of all the physical, linguistic, and cultural systems intervolved with our conscious interactions in the externalities of Being. But then a permanently backgrounded deposit of typically representational memories and anticipatory reflexes, a *habitus* both natural and acculturated, may extend itself deeply through the penumbra of latencies involving the (emphatically non-Freudian) preconscious and unconscious levels of the mind, an extension taking in progressively everything upon which a mature mind may call—say, in so complex an act as reading a Miltonic theodicy keyed by its four inspirational raptures.

Best of all, as readers we do not even need to think about it, for somewhere at the furthest individual reach the mind seems already to have produced the shape of that mythos/logos homology of which *Paradise Lost* is analogically merely a sophisticated variant. And here in particular both the anti-Cartesian Heidegger and the Derrida of *Dissemination* may relevantly help show us why both seem at time overtaken by the wonderfully capricious poetic or irrationalizing bent native to the logic-blocked mind.

But before developing these connections, I remark upon a convergence of matters here and in essays by Richard Strier and Stella P. Revard that appeared in a previous issue of *Milton Studies* (*The Writer in His Works*).

The convergence bears first on the object of the Miltonic version of these matters and then on the manner of its literary intermediation. Strier is first in making two major points, each susceptible of the enhancement I urge in my own unrelated mapping of Milton's work and outlook upon Heidegger's thought, and Heidegger's upon Milton's. For Heidegger may be said to represent the element in Milton that, as Strier reminds us, has literally bedeviled our sense of Milton ever since Blake argued he was of the devil's party, writing freely of Satan and "in fetters" when he wrote of God.[7]

Strier's second point is that if the durability of the Blakean effect is always present but backgrounded, then notably foregrounded would be Milton's displacement of his "grand argument" onto Eden's powerful beauty. For if the poem justifies God's ways at all (a debatable matter), they are justified in ways allowing us to read Miltonic theodicy as *biophilia,* that is, as analogically a justification of the ways of life to man, where "life" is a totalizing construct homological to the foregrounded aspect of God as All in All. Strier's question then turns on the validity of reconsidering what it is that the poem refers to as the sign of its object. Revard's essay speaks indirectly to the "proemial" relationship, or transactional manner, of poet and reader within the inspirational premise.

Following a complementary interpretation of the classical "proem," I suggest that the question of the poem's subject, or more technically the signified of its sign, is rather seriously compromised by the presence of a legalistic God it ostensibly tries to justify. But he is not the only divine player on the scene. On my reading, then, Milton's differential proemial relationship to both the poem and the reader effectively manages (in the concealed illogicism of its method) to shortcut the problem, a shortcut blessed by Milton's other God, the God of the poem's mythos rather than of its logos. I call the Janus-aspected pair of Miltonic divinities his two Gods. "The hidden wayes of his providence," Milton wrote, "we adore & search not; but the law is his reveled wil." Ernest Sirluck long ago drew attention to this text by taking it as the logical and deliberate, even emphatic, affirmation by Milton of the dominant God of will and law,[8] the God in the conventional view of Miltonic theodicy.

But in context Milton's emphasis on law is specific to his divorce troubles, whereas the God whose unsearched ways are adored, the God of providential contingency and random unfoldings, indeed the God who offers his creatures their freedom, seems far more important to Milton's poetics and poetry, just as this God would belong to Strier's case for Eden being the real center of the theodicy in *Paradise Lost,* or to Revard's case that the poem's four invocational proemia count for a good deal. They count for the doubled pair of the poem's fundamental relational ways of signifying. The first pair consists of the conventional sign/signified relationship over which the writer presides, which however is not precedent but subsequent to the binary self-referentiality of the writer and reader, a relationship again "proemially" initiated by the writer. Thus just as writer and reader are a homologously related set, so too sign and signified are analogously related, with all brought within the interanimations of their own fourfold.

Authorial precedence then is "proemial," we are told—and I have availed myself of the idea—"because it constitutes the necessary precondition for making distinctions and generating form."[9] For example, the four proemia go beyond the conventional mediation of poetic matter through inspirational power, or even as an esemplastic power shaping the whole poem, for gradationally the rapturous stages of such mediation set up poet and poem in a kind of sacramental probing of all degrees of intimational communion peculiar to poetic communication. In Milton's poetics, I suggest, poetry is virtually a transacted *ad extra* grace—but only if both virtual poet and virtual reader (the generic reader in Milton's mind) are providentially and truly brought together in their intersubjectivity. This kind of conditional sacramentality,[10] dependent for its powers on a highly intimational and intuitionary transaction, reconciles his seemingly divergent aims to write poetry doctrinal to a nation yet addressed to the fit few.

But as such it depends upon the presumption in his poetics that recessed with poetic communication is the possibility, not the necessity, of a *communional* relationship, a possibility that does not work by either/or open and shut switches but by way of a poetry technically capable of producing unprecedented degrees of intimational resonance. Or, the poetic transaction is about the psychologistic effects of elective affinities in embodied minds each drawn together from both ends of the continuum of consciousness, from the synapses of the nervous system to our idiolects for delighting in Plato or the swing of the Pleiades.

But it follows that the parity of such attunements must be unimaginably adjustable over time, and Milton might half have expected the consequences. Consider, we are not readers Milton imagined; nor is Milton the virtualities that in reading and discussions we turn him into. Yet for all their variability, the relationships, as with the poem itself, are both shaped by figure and figuratively shaped, with the shape perceived in writing as structures of transcendence and structures of reality.

On these terms the teleology within which Milton wrote *Paradise Lost* and in which traditionally he has been read simply or even easily turns into other things among non-teleologically minded readers—given especially that the invariant which shapes the poem allows remarkable latitude for just such transpositions. In the traditional mode the teleological structures of transcendence seem clear enough and might look most familiar in the three-part structure of Dante's *Divine Comedy* or the four-part invocational structure of *Paradise Lost* (and a good many other such homological literary constructs), all as non-trivially related to the boldly schematic character to which the homologically thematic space/time accountabilities of the mind may be keyed. But the structures shaped toward transcendence, as we have progressively become aware, are peculiarly tricky things. Are they causally produced in nicely systematic schemes? Or do our intuitions of them correspond to something as arbitrary perhaps as the undecidabilities of quantum coherence and decoherence.

In any case, structures of transcendence use immediately formal means to bridge the gaps between causal and seemingly mysteriously caused consequentialities. Here because Heidegger is Milton's fellow-mysterian in some of the ways of the mind, the fact that he finds a doubled but simplified 'fouring' shape in reality to abet his approach to such mysteries serves to highlight for us how and why Milton's comparably monistic way of discerning such structures matter. But then there is Derrida, who gets into Heidegger's fouring act by appropriating the most obscure mess at its fountainhead to his theory of disseminative *différance,* only to further obscure the matter by a denunciation of the role of number-based compositional teleologies in bridging causal gaps, even as he may be said to deploy them for precisely such ends.

This is not surprising, since his opposing of a holistic dynamic formalism by an atomistic and anarchically disseminative one explicitly points toward the self-contradictory tensions within these related approaches, tensions whose outlets characteristically verge toward whatever kind of apocalyptic shapings of historical meaning the age may sanction for a Milton, a Heidegger, or a Derrida.

Gaps in causality *are* mysterious. But mysteriousness may also beautifully resonate semantically. The literary transaction, always full of logical gaps, transacts meaning and resonance. Let us focus on the resonance, which is one of the most pronounced effects of Milton's poetry, coupling it with the indifferent results of Milton's causal logic and the legalistic divinity justifying it. Here resonance is to drink, so to speak, more or less in the spirit of A. E. Housman's memorably exact lines, "malt does more than Milton can, / To justify God's ways to man." Always. For resonance embraces and transcends our own scepticism. Resonance reverberates throughout all the intersubjective transits of a textual code, between every one of its widely disparate authorial and readerly contexts, with these transits between production and reception being about as complex a meeting of minds as may be imaginable.

Which means that, like everything complex, resonantial transits are likely to find and work around the simple attractors that complex dynamics manage to situate at whatever points of coherence may become available. For the more complex the processes, the more likely they are to factor down into a root simplicity, or, in short, the more likely they are to exhibit a regularity running widely across many such reductions. (And what is so exhibited may well be the unconscious target of our intuitionary apprehensions.) Reversibly, the tendency in chaos theory to focus on complexity as primary seems merely the recognition that an underlying simplicity of shaping schema and initial conditions (a nativist, heritable simplicity)[11] may generate vast recomplications.

For we crave simplicity, such as the seeming limiting simplicities of just those three or four things we can ordinarily apperceive or experientially *subitize* at a glance *as a set* (a composite thing that is also the fractal that samples the whole of things), mostly within the right brain, and essentially count out or narrate in the explanatory demands largely handled by left brain. In this sense the simple set is transcendental. For if it is true that human counting (and thence all of mathematics) evolved out of the survival value for us of the primitive ability in many forms of life to recognize patterns constrained to some minimalist but protean *undifferentiation* of immediate space/time conditions, it would not be surprising that language would avail itself of the crucially simplifying constraints upon the ways it can sequence explanatory language.

Consider how much foregrounded information you take in at this very instant, and factor it into the possibility that it is quite possible to seem to go far beyond such minimalist conditions, yet without transcending our inborn and still sovereign limitations. It is possible because these are also the basic generative conditions attached to such formal simplicities and to our survival. Leaping through my theory, I suggest that counting is the rudimentary abstract of all serial or explanatory representation, a proto-narrative fitted to any and every situation.[12] Out of such blandness comes ineffable beauty. But a certain fundamental indeterminacy as to the actual number of a subitized set (say, four items, plus or minus one) seems necessary to creating the differentials that we translate into meaning. Or at least it is an uncertainty in sequencing that becomes fairly consequential in writing.

For example, in the series *1, 2, 3, 4,* the *4* roughly signifies as abstraction what the mathematician Brian Rotman calls "the terminal stasis and imprisoning boundary of binary thinking." By the same token the series *1, 2, 3* . . . is for Rotman the sign of serial counting extended ad infinitum, as the dotted ellipsis after the 3 stands for the space where open-endedness can be co-opted for infinitistic thinking or, I add, as a point of recursion spiraling back to rebeginnings.[13] Note that the relative number values apply to the smallest as well as largest 'systems' discernible as pattern to the mind, as if both the micro- and macro-cosmic aspects of the continuum were subject to the same perspectival preference for types of closure marked by a property indifferently available at every turn, and to be taken at need as an index of open-endedness. I call the enumerable fuzziness a molecular property because primitive phonology, grammar, rhetoric, and narrative all build informational difference into equivocal junctures subject to the structural equivalents of word and phrase structures, nouns, verbs, modifiers, and prepositional markers, the last being possibly a later refinement in proto-grammar, along with tense, plurality, and gender, all resting on simple combinatorial units, generally four plus or minus one.

Narrative syntax has units peculiar to itself, with one of them being the clusters or sets distributed into that degree-zero of invariant sequences,[14] then most effective when by its rule of four, plus or minus one, a set deviates from itself. A fine but common instance are the seasons: "No spring, nor summer hath such grace, / As I have seen in one autumnal face," writes Donne in *The Autumnal,* where held in reserve is the "missing" fourth or wintry element completed in a nearby development. Extremes being excluded from the Eden of *Paradise Lost,* Milton's glancing account of the fruits Eve heaps from "the Trees of God" on the table, welcoming Raphael as visitant, is a complex reductive subtraction: "All *Autumn* pil'd, though *Spring* and *Autumn* here / Danc'd hand in hand" (*PL* 5.394–95). Further, degree-zero sets seem fractal-like nodes of homological recursions scaling up and down throughout the whole conceptual/expressive field, the rhetorical extreme being the synecdoche of the part/whole trope in the microcosmic/macrocosmic correspondence theory central to Renaissance anthropology and seventeenth-century poetics, Milton's theory.

Fractal and synecdoche would seem then to frame that sense of homological consistency and constancy triggered in readers prone to grasp analogical associations or thematic connections instinctively. Note that while analogy specifies resemblance (as when we know the ways in which we think by the ways we observe others thinking), homology presumes a type or generic identity enabling the resemblance to be seen, both specifiable by the most simplified regularities imaginable. That is why the simplifying three/four regularities we find in set/narrative (homology/thematic analogy) interactions as a whole so often seem unconsciously presented or spontaneously configured. Generally I take the unconscious to be backgrounded elements of native and habituated layerings of practice, in styles attractive enough to have been variously explained and obscured by Freud, Jung, and others who tend to load all rifts of the unconscious ore with pronounced Lamarckian-style psychological and ideological programs.

Some such programs may be useful as heuristics, but when their moment is gone they can become stultifying mystifications. Phenomenology and cognitive science largely ignore these ways of accounting for the unconscious as the mind's field of emergent operations, and for the most part so shall I, the exception being Derrida's attack in *Dissemination,* via Heidegger, upon the 'phallogocentric' nature of such simply yet holistically structured or 'formalist' literary writings—of which in principle Milton's *Paradise Lost* would be an egregious example. I note here that my whole precedent account of how the phenomenology of simple numbers enter into the problematic of writing's formalisms had been long grasped by Derrida, as is fairly consistently indicated by his practice in *Dissemination,* yet with a virtuosity confessedly calculated to bewilder the reader looking for expository linearity. It is a virtuosity with a long rhetorically justified tradition in compositional mystification, of the kind practiced by Milton who, in his *Art of Logic,* appeals to it is as an art of *crypsis.*[15]

It is an art that presupposes the unconscious proclivities of readers who are generally blissfully unaware of the constraints and possibilities to which, on dynamically formalist terms, they are responding. Heidegger uses these proclivities to suggest the near mystical affinities between the signifyings of Being (*Sein*) to consciousness (as *Dasein,* the mind's "being there" to Being). For insofar as this consciousness is fused within a glorification of an experiential aesthetics taken as always overriding language's mere representational powers, it resolves itself in the always elusive unity of being, challenging the phase dichotomies of a typical Wittgensteinian saying/showing dilemma. For if Wittgenstein detested the mystifying of such things, Heidegger seems positively to relish it, possibly as a way of cultivating the divination of his murkiness he often seems to expect from his readers.

And nowhere is this divinatory or intuitionary style of reading more called for than in the contexts of those earlier mentioned fouring constructions that, it would seem, belong among the Renaissance "thought-forms" Ernesto Grassi, Heidegger's former pupil and colleague, traced as objects of Heidegger's particular interest.[16] But then to that extent Milton's tendency to reflect the Renaissance past and foreshadow the Romantic future out of which Heidegger comes suggests a deep rather than superficial historical continuity within the ways in which their thought tended to be shaped, a continuity involving automaticities that bring into question the meanings so shaped, or rather what we make of them. Or so Derrida would have us confront such matters.

II. Rapture as Form-Engendering Force

These Numbers enumerate themselves, write themselves, read themselves. By themselves. Hence they get themselves remarked right away, and every new brand [*marque*] of reading has to subscribe to their program.

Derrida, "Dissemination"

Whose mind soever is fully possest with a fervent desire to know good things and with the dearest charity to infuse the knowledge of them into others, when such a man would speak, his words . . . like so many nimble and airy servitors trip about him at command, and in well order'd files, as he would wish, fall aptly into their own places.

Milton, *An Apology*

As I suggested earlier, the Derridean wonderment about these self-enumerating ways of the underlying compositional numbers of a text seems to have been largely inspired by the Heideggerian fouring constructs Derrida himself foregrounded within "Dissemination" proper, and which by way of Heidegger's writings on Nietzsche (from which my section heading on the form-engendering force of rapture comes) seem to have become associated for Derrida with the role in Western intellectual history of a mysteriously self-inscribing programming machine without which its philosophy could never have been written or taken the shape it has.

But most immediately these numbers serve Derrida to betoken an actually automated style of serial compositionality whose provenance, he knows, has also always been subject to the vagaries of mystification and demystification. It starts with this old problem of *conatus,* of self-persistence that is an automaticity, letting the body think for you. Milton surely would have recognized Derrida's sense of something automatic at the heart of one's compositional alacrity. The difference comes when of themselves writing's airy servitors falling nimbly into place are taken infallibly as agents of an actually transfused inspirational power, one metaphysically justified yet still modeled inveterately on a sexuality a good deal more than merely metaphoric.

For Milton in *Animadversions* (YP 1:721), the provenance of this power is clear: the poet is as the minister who "by the faithfull worke of holy doctrine, [is] to *procreate* a number of faithfull men, making a creation like to God's, by infusing his spirit into them, to their salvation, as God did into him"—that is, if the poet has not expended too much of his best or procreative substance in coitus with an unresponsive wife. Derrida focuses on the teleological 'abuse' of these compositional numbers to project a cultural sense of a patriarchal order wherein semen is at the root of dissemination, which in this aspect it was his purpose to deconstruct as object and by example. But then, as Derrida himself realizes, if you want to show that linguistic dissemination is non-teleological you emphatically *should not* replace one ideological teleology with another (Freudian and Marxist), without asking what exactly is it about these numbers that gets to make them seem so sexually potent and teleologically directed.

For his purposes the easiest way to make the point about these beguilingly peccant numbers is to use them compositionally and then to defy the reader who tries to find in them the true order they inscribe. "Dissemination" itself is the first written and published of *Dissemination's* four parts, though in the volume it is the concluding section, and not until the fourth written section (which becomes the first) is there a serious stab at explaining the numerical and non-metaphysical basis of a disseminative linguistics of *différance.* "Two/four, and the 'closure of metaphysics' can no longer take, can indeed never have taken, the form of a circular line enclosing a field, a finite culture of binary oppositions, but takes on the figure of a totally different partition" (*Dissem.*, 25). Yet this totally different figure still bears a metaphysical trace insofar as it comes to the X of erasure over ~~Being~~ or *Des Gevierts,* Heidegger's nihilistic sign for a self-canceling sign-infested ontology.

Its Heideggerian counterpart is *Das Geviert,* or the joyous epistemic fouring fourfold of earth, sky, time-bound mortals, and timeless immortals. Both constructs were Heidegger's post-war replacements for the Phaedran Dionysian/Apollonian double-mean he had borrowed by way of Nietzsche's fashioning of them for his self-delineation in the character of a Dionysian artist/philosopher alienated by an unalloyed Apollonian cultural paradigm for world order. Dionysus presides over Heidegger's elevation of *Das Geviert* into the type of ecstatic enactment in language that takes one so far out of this representational world as to be scarcely communicable, though *Des Gevierts,* as the Apollonian order in its nihilistic and self-erasing ontological identity, is not too hard to understand.

In the latter guise Heidegger's ~~Being~~ is more similar to Milton's legalistic God, who charges the poem with all the meanings still debated in some of our more ratiocinative glossings. Seldom do we admit that as a mass of inconsistencies and internal self-contradictions, its consistency is too much to expect and its logic too devious to understand. But much harder to grasp, though apprehension is easier, is Heidegger's aestheticized Being, who presides over the varieties of its and our becomingness, most in our aesthetic intake (in ways that count), of that play of shadow, trace, or sign, effectively appropriating *our* wit for discerning *its own* covert manifestations. Milton has it the other way around. As a poet *he* appropriates the model of the artist-God listening to the unfolding of his own work-in-progress, appropriating to himself this theomorphic divinity of sensibility to signal to us, through layerings of allusive intimations writ in the book of nature *and* writing, of this presence of which he is the instrument.

But then the *design* of the Miltonic work in progress (for the poem as effect can only be completed by the reader) is truly audible only to the creator whose ear listens delighted. In this conceit the poetic Milton is both inside and outside his own creation, at liberty in the service of the providential God to release into the cosmic/poetic dance the stately legalistic God whose self-justifying ways introduce all the discord of the *concordia discors* the real world can handle, yet in their motions and motions of mind then most regular when most irregular it seems. In part the thematic relationship of Milton's two Gods to Heidegger's two fouring constructs I illustrate by way of translating the 'fouring' in the Heideggerian *Des Gevierts* or ~~Being~~, and *Das Geviert* with Milton's world-bracketing 'quaternion,' the sense of Milton's word relating to Heidegger's opposed fourings as differential values bearing on apprehending 'presence' through the absence and presence of plenary meaning.

But Milton uses the term 'quaternion' with a distinctly 'archeteleological' difference. His Adam and Eve know by inspirational instinct that their "Unmeditated . . . prompt" and eloquent prayer is of an order elemental to Chaos's emergent mediation of primal substance, "the eldest birth / Of Nature's Womb, that in *quaternion run / Perpetual circle, multiform.*" (*PL* 5.160–82; emphasis mine). The same figure in *The Reason of Church-Government* spontaneously occurs to Milton as the rounding-out shape of an ending, but with a difference in the way the determining telos or end will manifest itself in the homeostatic foreverness of an invariable bliss.

Yea, the Angels themselves, in whom no disorder is fear'd, as the Apostle that saw them in his rapture describes, are distinguisht and *quaterniond* into their celestiall Princedomes, and Satrapies . . . through the great provinces of heav'n. The state also of the blessed in Paradise, though never so perfect, is not therefore left without discipline, whose golden survaying reed marks out and measures every quarter and circuit of new Jerusalem. Yet it is not to be conceiv'd that those eternall effluences of sanctity and love in the glorified Saints should by this meanes be confin'd and cloy'd with repetition of that which is prescribe'd, but that our happinesse may orbe it selfe into a thousand vagancies of glory and delight, and with a kind of eccentricall equation be as it were an invariable Planet of joy and felicity. (YP 1.752; emphasis mine)

Note well that if we read *Paradise Lost* as a packet of genres, this quaternion seems in the invariant design of Creation's origins and ends to ground the otherwise *multiform* and mere outwardness of their appearances. But to suppose as much means critically foregrounding the invariant design, and here Derrida effectively challenges our ability to do so, because the design itself he thinks of as hopelessly fraught with the burden of an arch-eteleological shape viciously circular by its very nature. Or is that its phallogo-centric operator really only benumbing our awareness of how these self-same numbers, by their self-inscribing alacrity, insidiously deceive us—or even *conceive* within us purposively on behalf of a dominating patriarchy?

Well, there is a difference between a writing reducible to Derrida's simple counting algorithm and the assurances that the inspired alacrity trace-able to such numbers had for Milton, or even for us. Yet if numbers remain the ghosts within the writing machine, how did they ever get there and who or what do they really serve? If Milton might have supposed that they functioned through all those messenger angels of grace riding connectionist traces, shadows, and signs of presence in the beauty concealing *materia prima,* he would also have had to suppose that as gracious riders they were at the service of all readers somehow morally tuned in to the requisite degree of providential design, in all and in whatever kind of meaningful connections available to them. Is this too much to ask?

Derrida has at least a seemingly plausible answer that takes the line of the Freudian and Maoist logic he professed at the time of *Dissemination,* namely that the automaticity concealed in the age-old patriarchalism of these inscriptive numbers must in the elaborateness of their claims collapse into anarchical incoherence—or ultimately into a type of headless apocalyptic. Still he is obliged to demonstrate that the numbers work, that they guide our compositions and reading, and the procedure he follows in *Dissemina-tion* and *The Truth in Painting* is to extend himself 'proemially' over a self-referential abyss, where he can comment on someone else's calculated four-folding as a way of distancing himself (not too successfully) from the fact that, in exposing these numbers as the cancer of a self-destructive civilization, he is really talking about his own meta-referential urgencies.

Recall that in current parlance the proemial encompassing of a text would relate first to the nominally explicit relationship between the writer and his work, and then to the implicit relationship between the writer and his reader. But the effect of Derrida's proemial invocations of usurping numbers and their effects obscures both sets of relationships. For what is usurped is an order of arrangement that must be driven by some power, and Derrida tacitly admits as much. "Dissemination" proper admits to being a quasi-surrealistic commentary on a thoroughly surrealistic commentary by Philippe Sollers in *Nombres* on compositional numbers, with both Sollers and Derrida tending to treat them as arbitrary counters devoid of the kind of grounding function

they have in scientific meaning. But the subject is writing, not numbers—
except that the numbers keep intruding themselves and dominate as well the
writer's proemial relationship to his reader.

Here the Derridean numbers are grossly exaggerated into a largely
mystifying in-matter, a transactional pass for those who already know the
score, which in fact few outside readers could really be expected to grasp.
Why should we as readers know that the work's seeming beginning (added as
"Hors Livre" but not "hors texte") is really its supernumerary fourth part, a
status rendered ostentatiously uncertain so as to invest the whole book with
an overhanging question it could not occur to us to wonder about: Is this a
book in three or in four parts? And what in the name of relevance might such
a question signify? We are not likely to be tuned in to Brian Rotman's point
that a threeness of sequencing signifies open-endedness and a fourness signifies closure. Or to wondering about how such numbers inscriptively might
index some deep minimalist proclivity in all of us. Indeed I doubt that Derrida himself grasped the depth of the matter he himself roiled so energet-
ically, for what his repeated returns to such questions (and they are many) tell
us is that he was groping after a cognitive phenomenon no ideological answer
might satisfy.

So if "Two/four, and the 'closure of metaphysics'" can no longer be conceived as binding a work to definitive meaning, he has to go on to postu-
late that there is a much larger gap that keeps all meaning open-ended, a
gap marked by the nihilistic X of erasure over *Being*, or as sign (as Nietzsche seems to have remarked) of the decentered spot in the cosmos where
Copernicus has landed us. This then is turned into a categorical *antiformalist*
pronouncement: "The gap between the empty 'form' and the fullness of
'meaning' is structurally irremediable, and any formalism, as well as any
thematicism will be impotent to dominate that structure" (*Dissem.*, 21). But
in fact this impossible gap is in the very act of his book bridged, or trans-
gressed and circumvented by Derrida himself, that is *apophatically* (his word
for doing what you say cannot or is not to be done).

Later in *Dissemination* Derrida invokes Gödel's theorem, which elsewhere he associates with the strange power Plato ascribes to the primordial
cosmogonic fouring of the *khora* in the *Timaeus*. This Greek word is hard to
translate, sometimes signifying the receptacle or generative matrix of cosmogony, which is identified in the dialogue itself as a "she," the "nurse," at
once "virgin" and "mother" of the physical fouring formalism, the paradigm
of fourness as the underlying constituent of the variable arrangements by
which the One becomes the Many of everything in a cosmos that is both
being and becoming. By the same token, the *khora* as the substantial inter-

mediary in the reciprocal transformations of the One into the Many and the Many into the One (Milton's and the Renaissance's Pan in Proteus) elides the logic of separation. Analogously for Derrida, one of the consequences of the Gödelian formalization of a proof that opposites cannot be excluded from a *closed* system is a kind of nullification of the Aristotelian excluded middle, which in turn leads to the supposition of a category of things belonging to neither side of the opposition.

As Derrida observes in *Dissemination*, "An undecidable proposition, as Gödel demonstrated . . . , is a proposition which, given a system of axioms governing multiplicity, is neither an analytical nor deductive consequence of those axioms, nor in contradiction with them, neither true nor false with respect to those axioms. *Tertium datur,* without synthesis" (*Dissem.,* 219). And what counts about such undecidability "is not the lexical richness, the semantic infiniteness of a word or concept, its depth or breadth, the sedimentation that has produced inside it two contradictory layers of signification (continuity and discontinuity, inside and outside, identity and difference, etc.). What counts here is the formal or syntactical *praxis* that composes and decomposes it" (*Dissem.,* 220). What counts is the principled bind by which there is no *logical* bridging of the gap between the irreducible undecidabilities of a "formal . . . praxis," and the fact that the gap is continually bridged, as Gödel himself pointed out, by leaving incomplete or open-ended its "system" of discourse.

Since for Derrida there is no *hors texte* outside the non-closure of writing, he is caught in a bind of his own making. In *Dissemination* the "third" given by excluding the law of the excluded middle is essentially the circularizing teleologies of closed systems inscribing themselves within paralogisms. What his own writing betrays is—as his "two/four" endlessly disseminated sign/signified relationships would suggest—that no writing is altogether enclosed within writing; that when we pretend it is closed, we are really only finding ways of concealing from ourselves and possibly others the fact of its openness; and that with such fourfolds—plus or minus one—we have in fact opened the system up to rational explanation, the system of the Pythagorean tetractys as one of the ways in which the compositional numbers have been traditionally mystified.

Milton's one, little-known compositional use of the Pythagorean tetractys (the correlative of the generative *khora*) may serve here as a useful illustration. It seems that in the underlying ground plan of *Paradise Regained* Milton hid a tetractys *without closure.* That the poem manages to avoid closure is hardly surprising, since all of Milton's major poems end with someone going somewhere else. It is well known that, having finished *Paradise Lost,* Milton was quick to pick up on the suggestion of Thomas Ellwood (the poem's first reader) that it was somehow incomplete. This can be taken in a sense related to but not the same as the obvious one.

I mean that because of the emptying out effect achieved by the fourfold proemial mediation, the reader is arguably held at the bottom of its descent pattern (where the last proemium ends), which induces a palpable need for a symbolic restoration of emergent meaningfulness, something already there when now *we* come to the supplementally ascending poem. For this is what formally *Paradise Regained* delivers in the extraordinary mounting *tetractys,* which according to R. D. Jordan structures its remarkably recessive symbolic progression.[17] Thus counted off with each successive book is a set of temptations ostensibly calibrated by Satan himself, all mounting to a crescendo summing up to the classic Pythagorean sequence, Book One with 1 temptation, Two with 2 temptations, until by the end the notation for the series would be the tetractys, that is $(1 + 2 + 3 + 4) = 10$. What does it do?

Well, as generative form this *non-apparent* tetractys could only serve the author's compositional or ironic design, albeit opaque to the rest of us. Perhaps as implicit symbol for the tropism toward harmony in Creation, the structure might have expressed for Milton a touch of the power by which Jesus recovers, in becoming Christ, an accelerating crescendo of insight, a sort of Platonic anamnesis, a Heideggerian 'unforgetting' of the fact that as the demiurgic Word he existed before the world's creation. Yet given its utter opacity, I doubt Milton had more than a compositional utility in mind, a type of written formatting device of which the reader need know nothing, its part in the coherence of Milton's overall project indirectly transmitted within the combined effect of the two poems, in the manner in which *L'Allegro* and *Il Penseroso* achieve their effects. For what the reader does get is a firmly communicated real-life sense of an elusive but certainly open-ended backgrounded order—just as the world is mostly to us a backgrounded, open-ended, but elusive order.

No one reads by foregrounded counting of this kind, though its automaticities are implicit to the composite actualities in which our embodied minds are immersed. For while we do not count as we read, neither is calculation missing in the composite and dynamic design of the myriads of algorithms insensibly pulsing through the sum total of the somatic and neural substrates of our mind. Being aware here would overwhelm our abilities to be aware, which is why such algorithms seldom surface to either the writer or reader's awareness, except when their vectors cross some threshold from their inherent complexity to the few seeming regularities by which we can deal with them—perhaps as those elementally subitized homological sets we turn into the narratively thematized explanatory orders of our analogizing consciousness.

In "Plato's Pharmacy," the second of *Dissemination's* four parts to be written and published, Derrida tells us that the *Phaedrus* infuses into Western writing an equipotent dose of poison and remedy, indirectly referring these to the phallogocentric operation but not in fact to the open/closed nature intrinsic to the natural number series. Holistic closure seems to him an absurdity, and in the literal "closure" or end lines of "Dissemination" proper (not in fact what appears to be the actual closure of *Dissemination*, 366), he strategically positions the notation $(1 + 2 + 3 + 4)^2$, that is, the Pythagorean tetractys squared. Moreover, this uncertain "closure" comes very soon after Derrida's own figurative ideogram for the phallogocentrism he attributes to the unsquared version of the tetractys as Western writing's underlying formalism, nothing less than the Freudian Oedipus as a stacked fourfold columnar phallus (Oedipus at Colonnus), ejaculating semes in a spectacular display of patriarchal dissemination (*Dissem.*, 364–65).

Perhaps the squaring translates the placement between Oedipus and "closure" of the two unattributed citations of Heidegger's rendering of fouring constructs, *Des Gevierts* and *Das Gevierts.* Yet Derrida also seems well aware that as a practical matter the homological fourfold may have evolved to evade paralogisms. But he is not interested in foregrounding how this rhetorical prophylaxis might work, since the fourfold function has a limited and justifiable teleology of its own, at least within the Lamarckian sense of the evolutionary function earlier touched on: it provides patterns that seem to guide meaning to some end. Derrida knows the construct serves preeminently to avoid inscriptive closure, the systemic closure of an argument fraught with self-referentialities at every level and therefore best left open-ended. But he seems at times more obviously interested in the sexual substrate of the inscriptive paradigm, even if he has to insist on it at Heidegger's expense.

Thus Heidegger is chided without being named, in the so-called add-on beginning of "Hors Texte" (*Dissem.*, 4–5), and part of the parody seems implicitly to delve at the source of the Heideggerian inspirational rapture or *Rausch* (rush) with an origin or cognate development from the Sanskrit *rushys,* or sexual ejaculation or orgasm. It is an ancient tradition, this notion of generative semen as best substance of the humours concocting spirit and mind. And, as is well known, it was central to the Stoic material monism revived in the Renaissance with the allegorization of the occulted *materia prima,* derived from castrated Saturn's genitalia flung through the firmament into the sea as the *logoi spermatikoi* or *rationes seminales,* from whence up foamed Beauty or Venus on the half shell—as conceived by Botticelli, on a suggestion from Ficino.

And without stretching the matter, this would explain Milton's invocation of the Eros/Anteros myth of Plato's *Symposium* (203b–e; YP 2:254–55), part of the second version of the myth of the Charioteer soul in *Phaedrus* (250–251c), where in yielding to the needs of sexual expression, the soul—being relieved and renewed in physical beauty—is enabled to separate its essence from the "accidental" physicality of things, bringing it back to the ideality of its immortal form. The great German classicist, Ulrich von Wilamowitz-Moellendorff, thought the passage the most astounding in Plato, and as I show elsewhere, it occasioned Wallace Stevens's identification of the fourfold in *The Comedian as the Letter C* as uncannily derived from the "mint of dirt / The green and barbarous paradigm."[18]

But the sexuality of form and content in their linguistic dynamics is an old story for Renaissance writers, and it is related to the sexuality of the abstract powers given number properties in apocalyptic writing. In "On a Newly Arisen Apocalyptic Tone," Derrida boldly appropriates to his style of meditation Kant's polemic in "On a Newly Arisen Superior Tone" against the *schwärmerei* or enthusiasm of the Platonizing numerologists who saw in Kant's own general fouring emphases a warrant for reviving its mystique.[19] Displacing one equivocal irrationalism, apocalyptic, onto another, numerology, Derrida goes on to describe this apocalyptic tonality in others, by apophatic technique licensing himself to indulge in some apocalyptic totalizing himself, rising to a particular height with the emotionally charged images of American evil projected by the film *Apocalypse Now!*

The strange modulation in this essay, from Kant's concern with numerological enthusiasts to apocalyptic fantasies, relates, I think, to the recessed connection between Kant's polemic against numerical enthusiasts and apocalyptic's general prepossession with the simplifying numbers of eschatological designs. Deeply ingrained within all apocalyptic is a longing for the simplified order one might presume as underlying the formal order of a textualized history, one for which there is no *hors texte.* There is an analogous apocalyptic tonality to the way the nihilism within one of Heidegger's fouring constructions is redeemed by the life-enhancing plenitude of the other fouring. But in every case the implicit logic in this medley of apocalyptic resonances would seem grounded in the presumption of a monistic continuity between the complexities of the reality perceived and the simplicities to which we would rather subject them.

In the absence of some immediate historical urgency (though they might pop up here and there), the Renaissance approach to the unifying monism indexed by such compositional numbers was more magical than apocalyptic, where magic took as its object of poetic manipulation the occulted connectivities within reality. Here the type was a Prospero poet attuned to the traces of divinity secreted within everything, a single substance freely given to shape whatever order reveals to the *ingegno* or ingenious wit the seeming benevolence, more often than not, of the world's demiurge. In the old style the quintessential Renaissance magus was Pico della Mirandola, for whom the occulted concatenations of the many worlds held together by numbers or their allegorical formulae were legion. "Bound by the chains of concord, all these worlds exchange natures as well as names with mutual liberality. From this principle . . . flows the science of all allegorical interpretation," as well as the power over the levels of worlds or orders available for aesthetic and poetic transformation.

Pico's principle, extended by what he called "the Orphic theology," is in a sense the imaginative energizer of ideas attributable in a larger way to Ficino, whose translations, replete with extensive commentaries—as Michael J. B. Allen pointed out—are the real source of the formal Plato invoked by Renaissance writers whenever they invoke the doctrine of the rapturous frenzies or *furores*,[20] with their conjunctive doctrine of an internality of form in things and the mind. But as in his oration *On the Dignity of Man,* no one in so controlled a "rapture" so fully incorporated into practice the homology and analogy of the Neoplatonic *Phaedrus* as Pico did, exemplifying for those like Milton who knew how to read its presence in the conjunctive doctrine of an internality of form and its energized form of shaping power. We look then next at what the heading below signifies.

III. INTERNAL FORM AND THE MILTONIC ALLEGORY OF INWARDNESS

> call up unbound
> In various shapes old *Proteus* from the Sea,
> Drain'd through a Limbec to his Native form.
> Milton, PL 3.603–4

For though I do not know what else God may have decreed for me, this certainly is true: he has instilled into me, if into anyone, a vehement love of the beautiful. Not so diligently is Ceres, according to the Fables, said to have sought her daughter Proserpina, as I seek for this idea of the beautiful, as if for some glorious image, throughout all the shapes and

forms of things ("for many are the shapes of things divine"); day and
night I search and follow its lead eagerly as if by certain clear traces.

Milton, Letter 8 (the quotation is from Euripides)

As an occulted constant, the invariant generator of a ubiquitous thematics,
the alchemical "Native form" of a conceivable Proteus would depend, as the
charlatan in Ben Jonson's *The Alchemist* knew, on a power of character. For in
the effects of elements and humours well-mixed in the magus there is be-
spoken a homology of internal form without which there can be no control
over their analogically correspondent manifestations. In principle the homological invariance would dominate the thematic variety of manifold types of
expression, which is the ulterior point of the power presumed in the famous
ethos of composition passage of Milton's *An Apology.*

The power Milton describes as having shaped his own moral history is
fully accordant with the powers by which he was graced to discern divine
presence in the beauty of the many traces he transmuted into his verbal art.
When he says that "he who would not be frustrate of his hope to write well . . .
ought himselfe to bee a true Poem, that is a composition, and patterne of the
best and honourablest things" (YP 1:890), the nearly identical "composition"
and "patterne" refer reciprocally, in some kind of oscillational interchange-
ability, to his character and to his ability to write. The idea is not unlike the
one by which Milton in the *Art of Logic* (CM 11:38–39, 42–43, 56–57)
describes internal form as precedent to the merely sufficient causality of
external form in the shaping of discourse toward its perfection. Or in a current reformulation, "the form within the form frames the enclosing form."[21]

In *An Apology* the form governs both a hierarchy of value and Milton's
progressive and (materially) spiritual growth through the externalization of
the shaping power of ideal love. (Compare the internal form of the Good in
Plato's *Republic,* 509b–511e.) The temporal stages of Milton's *paedeia* move
from the particular to the abstractly ideal, from Petrarch and Dante, who
were inspired by an actual Laura and Beatrice, thence to the heroic writings
of Tasso and Spenser, which idealize love at a more abstract but still mundane
level, and further to a third level, at which the Socratic and Platonic philosophy of love endows it with a mystic or allegorical shadow of its supercelestial
reality. Finally, at the fourth level is reached the most "abstracted sublimi-
ties" of visionary or transcendent experience of heavenly love—the model for
which, as noted above, is expressed by Paul, and by Revelation's apotheosis of
the chaste within the love of God to which the internal form aspires, as if
driving toward its own self-unification.

Tweak the focus a bit, and the four stages of the Miltonic mythos resolve into a fairly standard transposition of the scalar counting by which Plato homologically set up the *Symposium* and *Phaedrus,* and even the four stages of philosophical method in Letter VII. By standard I mean compared to the ways in which the same hierarchy shapes a type of textuality that easily accommodates itself to the progressive extension of the Cartesian logos in time. Jacques Hadamard, for example, who studied how the mathematical mind tends to map the course of its most characteristic inventions, draws from its processes the sequence "preparation, incubation, illumination, and verification"—which corresponds closely to the classic mystic version of "awakening, purification, illumination, and unitive vision." Since most Western maps of this order descend from common Platonic, Neoplatonic, Christian, and Scholastic genealogies, corroborating each other from every side, the tradition by which one and the same dynamic form balances mythos and logos may well at times lose itself in metaphysical baffles. It remains strong, however, in such cultural pockets as classically based French education, whether philosophical, scientific, or literary.

Although, as Geza Szamosci points out, Western scientific schemas do not make the top level transcendental, as hierarchical series they remain partitioned along lines that move from pluralities of being and knowing to their respective unities.[22] These series being all homologically related and analogically applied, it would seem to be the reinforcing effect of the two functions we innocently absorb along with its patterning. But not in a Darwinian, rather in a Lamarckian, sense, which allows us to give a purpose to the unfolding design of our lives, especially where it seems the design is implicit as internal form within all the many parallel holisms of mind, their objects, and their differential aspects,

Many years ago Ernst Cassirer, in reviewing Paul Oskar Kristeller's major work on Ficino, remarked upon its failure to mention something as important as Ficino's discussion of the doctrine of "internal form," an idea Cassirer thought vital to the very formation of Western intellectual consciousness.[23] When in the early 1970s I ran into Kristeller at a Renaissance Society conference in Durham, New Hampshire, I asked about Cassirer's remark. Why indeed? Why if the Neoplatonic idea of internal form plays so great a role in Western literary culture, and why if it seems consistently to be identified with the Ficinian interpretation of the Phaedran hierarchy, is so little of its fact and theory ever systematically discussed? Kristeller thought a moment, shrugged, and said that for his part he simply took it for granted. Internal form in all its Platonic manifestations was patently self-evident to any one trained within the Western classical tradition.

One is left wondering. Take the curious Western sense (powerfully expressed within the last three hundred years) that the unfoldings of historical patterns both conform to our sense of emergent actualities, and yet in their "scientificity" obey an implicit sense of historical inevitability most corroborated by the mythic shapings of the past, an idea that comes down to saying we can impose a mythic order upon history, because we actually find its pattern continually re-emerging. This idea was Vico's theory of the fourfold cyclicity of historical development, expounded in his *La scienza nuova,* the source, among many derivatives, of the "Vico-cyclometer" upon which Joyce structured *Finnegans Wake.* Where does this logico-mythic formal sense come from? We know the old, altogether mythic examples. But whence derives the authority we find in Hegel's philosophy of a dialectical science of history that unfolds in a pattern of four stages, the form of which Marx took over, his final phase being the famous withering away of the state? Here, as in the constructions of Freud and Jung, the validity of such constructions as so-called scientific explanations cannot be referred to empirical verification, nor to predictive ideologies, nor to culturally specified ends indelibly writ, Lamarckian style, onto the political or historical unconsciousness of a culture.

Rather, we seem to improvise upon mind-forms whose value-added effects belong to the question of an ethos of writing influenced by the ways in which the configurations we are shaped to configure tend to generate particular thematic orders. Vico boldly called his science "poetic" and made the shrewd point that the mind tends to recognize the cyclical orders (if so they be) that humans have in fact themselves constructed.[24] Elsewhere in the larger project I reconstruct, on phenomenological and historical grounds usefully provided by independent research, the outline of a neuro-linguistic origins for how collective and paradigmatic patterns seem truly to shift in a kind of rhythmic oscillation that could give rise to this underlying sense of a collective regularity in historical progressions. Interestingly, the Western way of handling this sense really derives from the fairly unremarkable rhythmic alternations in our individual thinking, and the ways these, under the right circumstances, like fireflies at night in certain tropical parts, become collectively synchronized.

In sum, we anticipate the patterns that we are more prone to recognize and lock on to, and the anticipations key the resonances we hear in the meaningfulness of their emergent realization, if not their revelation. The resonance phenomenon works, I think, by attractions and attractors analogous to those seemingly quite different ones that work up and down the whole biophysical and cultural scale.[25] But at the level of introspection, attractors may intuitively snap us on to the communicational urging upon us of the design within things. If this be resonance, then we need a discipline to keep our ears vibrating, or perhaps trembling.

Consider, for example, Milton's interpretation of the patterning of events transformed into the saving patterned resonances of his *Samson Agonistes*. The four successive antagonists (Manoa, Dalila, Harapha, and the Messenger of the Philistines) dialectically and progressively clarify Samson's mind to the point where the revelatory epiphany of immanent and imminent divine presence and intervention will occur. That is, they represent Samson's prior history of blunder and mind-blindness. But now his experience is subtly framed and held within a pattern he himself has relationally constructed. In short, to put a beautifully executed play into such violating terms, Milton exploits what today would have to be called a neoformalism of process conditioned by the formal dynamics of how events seem to structure the unfoldings of their larger designs, thwarted though the latter may seem by the randomness that forces choices upon us.

The insight he projects out of his own political and existential dilemmas, and thence onto the patterning of the self-redemption of a helpless Samson in *Samson Agonistes,* falls in a way plangent to intuition on the resonance of its last important phrase, the grinding play of the "uncontrollable intent" in events, with the Chorus here echoing the earlier grinding necessity, but devoid of Samson's passionate revulsion at the earlier grinding. With "all passion spent," the communal catharsis is there, acknowledging Necessity as the God of law realigned at last with the always uncontrollable intent of the emergent God of providential design who underwrites our freedom to choose even blindly, that is, intuitively. It is a poetic insight (not a political one), and it is meant to be ours. There is an unpredictability before the event in all complex systems, the interim being sustained by a patient faith in the human instinct for order. The faith is tantamount to complexity theory's attribution of a subtle patterning force to the attractional power describing or defining the existence of self-organizing systems, qua system.

We accept the challenge as readers and in real life, I submit, because the odds fool us, not because we are assured by some history of outcomes, or because there seems to be a calculus of reducibility so sure across the physical board that it becomes hard to think outside its configurations. We almost expect that when the internality of cultural or even biocultural form is revealed, it will seem formally reducible to the transcendent homologies and proportions we have circularly derived out of our natural gifts and limitations, and have intuitively assented to because such simplicities make our complex lives possible.

If internal form all but visibly governs the outward function of Milton's proemia in *Paradise Lost,* there is a hint of a collateral semiotic function in how the proemia focus the poem's meaning in relation to the reader. To mediate the semiotic play of the overall sign/signified status of their poems as theodicies, and the author/reader relationship in each, Dante and Milton use their elaborately simple formal constructs to allow themselves to step self-referentially into their own production as virtual figures, shaping to a conformable order the design evolving out of the two relational sets. They are outside and inside the worlds they observe, having perfected a knowledge of virtualities we are only beginning technologically to grasp.

Although as poets they are hardly able to predict the values they will transact within the contingent designs completed by contemporary or even later readers, for both of them the excess of some "uncontrollable intent" is referable to the providence that knots the two sets of relationships, the poet and his poem to the poet and reader, across many transverse referents and concerns, diverging from and converging toward the ostensible power of love as metaphysical source of their subject and its poetic manifestation. This is Dante's *forma universal di questo nodo,* to which Beatrice leads him, *alla alta fantasia,* his high-raised fantasy, the crystallizing insight at the end of *The Divine Comedy,* in the last canto of *Paradiso,* the love that moves the sun and stars (91, 142–45). Inscribed within its refulgent circle, love is the horizonal human form, the attractor as peak or high point of the climactic rapture, the bracket closing upon the proemia of Dante's poem, one each invoking the proper muse for the lead into each of its three parts, capped by that fourth vision of love in the last canto of *Paradiso,* the vision recapped as experience in the Miltonic epiphany powering *At a Solemn Music.*

But knotted within the androgynous fusion of sister powers evoked there as Voice and Verse is the trace of Milton's fallen world, from which the enraptured flight takes off and to which it returns, the trajectory subsuming in a simplified gesture the hoped for recovery of the lost Edenic moment expressing, in Strier's interpretation, the theodicy in *Paradise Lost* as the arrested sequence of the real seasons shadowing its dynamic stasis—described with cormorant Satan on a branch overseeing the scene he overshadows without seeing its allegorical depth.

> The Birds thir choir apply; airs, vernal airs,
> Breathing the smell of field and grove, attune
> The trembling leaves, while Universal *Pan*
> Knit with the *Graces* and the *Hours* in dance
> Led on th'Eternal Spring.   (*PL* 4.264–68)

As Heidegger might suggest, the shadow reality of a world capable of falling from meaning invests everything in Eden. A fall from meaning is into meaninglessness. Without the uncanny presence of meaninglessness there is no sense in or of the fullness of meaning in an Edenic theodicy. Conversely, the effect of what seems to me the most poignant of all the immediate effects of the Fall upon nature is Eden decentered, not devoid of all meaning but with a meaninglessness suspended over it, now lost within a sea devoid of human reference, "an island salt and bare / The haunt of orcs and seals and sea mews clang" (*PL* 11.834–35). The absence is more powerful even than the earlier presences of semiotic plenitude within the Botticellian image of Eternal Spring, which is why I find in the music of falling to which God's own ear listens delighted (*PL* 5.616–27) the ground bass of Creation's express *concordia discors*, its almost antinomian patternings of an irreparably flawed reality, a reality that if it is not meaningful risks terrible meaninglessness.

Note that at this level we transcend enactment and representation, since meaningless cannot be represented as such, only derived as experience from what is represented, or from what we so represent to ourselves, as the suicide may do before his suicide.

IV. The Fantastic Intimacies of Universal Form

Blest pair of *Sirens*, pledges of Heav'n's joy,
Sphere-born harmonious Sisters, Voice and Verse,
Wed your divine sounds, and mixt power employ
Dead things with inbreath'd sense able to pierce,
And to our high-rais'd fantasy present
That undisturbed Song of pure concent,
Aye sung before the sapphire-color'd throne
To him that sits thereon,
With Saintly shout and solemn Jubilee,
Where the bright Seraphim in burning row
Their loud uplifted Angel-trumpets blow,
And the Cherubic host in thousand choirs
Touch their immortal Harps of golden wires,
With those just Spirits that wear victorious Palms,
Hymns devout and holy Psalms
Singing everlastingly;
That we on earth with undiscording voice
May rightly answer that melodious noise;
As once we did, till disproportion'd sin
Jarr'd against nature's chime, and with harsh din
Broke the fair music that all creatures made
To their great Lord, whose love their motion sway'd
In perfect Diapason, whilst they stood
In first obedience and their state of good.
O may we soon again renew that Song,
And keep in tune with Heav'n, till God ere long

To his celestial consort us unite,
To live with him, and sing in endless morn of light.
                                    Milton, *At a Solemn Music*

As we see it now foregrounded, the formal execution of Milton's rapture-engendered poem expresses the holistic transparency of its experienced shape as a pleroma of all that is meaningful, soaring up, down, sweeping backward and forward in a curiously familiar and to many an automatic gesture. Yet surely the world as poem must transcend this familiar self-sacralizing signing of the cross, especially if the poet discovers in the enactment of the sign its redemptive rather than any atoning value. So perhaps because the gesture seems, but for Milton cannot be, sacramental in its conventional sense, it might have been inscribed itself as evoking an alternative form of sacramentality, one gauged to the poet's gradient of exquisitely intersubjective intimacy with his readers, even as soaring into the poem's empyrean he falls back into a world-time referred to its *arche* and *telos,* the beginning and circularizing end of its earthly horizon.

This would be consistent with the poem's experiential design, since its representational effect still remains, I think, less powerful than its gestural insistence on the reader's participation in its motions. And insofar as we make the poem ours, we go along with it: Why not, for we do not really want to foreground to full consciousness the merely technical arts involved—like the elision of homology into analogy, and so on. For in any case the homology itself, becoming in our motions the meaning-redeeming space/time coordinates of the world, enforces the final analogy. Yet, thence slipping back into Milton's circle of time, do we at the moment, savoring the fantasies of consummate completion in our work or lives, really come up with the sense of having analogically checked something homological within the experience against the other typical meaningful or meaningless shapes of reality?

The answer depends upon how we take to the verve of Milton's art, or to the manner of his engaging us in the motions of his mind—whether all at once, from his opening words, or not at all. To be sure, we grasp how Milton sets us up. For where, as in *Paradise Lost,* the fit reader is not explicitly acknowledged until he or she has made it to the midpoint (that is, in the Dionysian proemium of the invocation to Urania in Book Seven), in *At a Solemn Music* the proemial Milton absorbs us into a sublime that seems to have left behind its most "egotistical" part. Only *seems* to have left behind, because it is still the poet's theomorphic or godlike horizontal presence that is projected in the emergent shape of the poem itself, which gives the poem its great egotistical or subjectivist surge of meaning. Here Milton's intuitive tact is what I meant earlier by describing it as exquisite. For if, for example, the *I* as a pronoun of subjective presence never appears in the poem, its absence makes way for a liturgical kind of collective intimacy.

And only after the original force of the poem seems to have run its course, well past the downward turn at midpoint, is the self-centering persona there again in that inclusive "we on earth," to whom and for whom the power speaks, giving us a purchase on a mythical probe of salvational space and time. Here the only correlate belonging to us is the extent to which we are already within or outside its gradient of inclusions and exclusion, within the circle of this literary "we" as central subject agency. The gradient also probes the relational pattern enacted, since this "we" is both an intersubjective or doubled first-person "I-Thou" relationship (the archaic "thou" keeps the referent distinct from this nuanced other) and a more impersonalized entity. The latter would seem to be part-way between the solipsistic subjectivity at each end of the transaction; or rather part-way between what may be the situation of the writer at the beginning and that of the reader at the end of the transactional process.

Being part-way also means that within the transactional medium we intervolve with our reading the poem's sliding shifts between private and public codes. If the poet seems to enact himself gesturally within the initial burst of the poem's energy, the effect may really depend upon divesting the gesture, as I think Milton does, of its encrusted ecclesiastical formalism, setting it within its primal human self-reference against our ordinary world horizons.

And there it invites us to share its theomorphic confidence against the more diminishing scale of the world's defining space/time horizon. Again, the sign is refracted through the double-gendered expressive power of the sphere-born Sisters, *their* affects extending to us as virtual members of the same inclusive choir, the "we" who await the completion of this space/time quaternion. The meaningfulness presumably inheres in the expression of the poem's energized rush, and the rush itself is formally transmitted by the symbolic trajectory of a gestural encompassment, the graceful transaction of which is, like grace itself, a *gift*. But with that having been said, and with all that by now has already been said—given then to whom?

The question is not facetious, for either the poet somehow defines us or, absent its particular addressees, his poem ends up in Bartleby's dead letter office. Poetry, Stevens said in his most important critical essay, "The Noble Rider," helps people live their lives. But not all people. Poets, Stevens says in a way that does not endear him to everybody (but which Milton certainly would have understood), write for an elite (CPP, 661). For such poems as *An Ordinary Evening in New Haven* or *Paradise Lost*, there has to be either more or less than that limp entity, the community of readers. There has to be either a great concert of understanding, something like Milton's Invisible Church, or the intimately semi-public communion with one another of the first and second violins in the caressing separateness of one of the movements in Beethoven's last quartet. We read by ourselves these days, not in communities. At best, we share an intimacy of some rarified idiolect, catching nuances as if in the practiced familiarities of kinship or closeness.

Presumably one of the earliest uses for primitive language was to expand the already highly developed abilities to subitize and count, to homologize and thematically analogize in dealing with the increasing complexities of ordinary personal relations. Social intelligence develops out of the immediate circle, where "thee" and "me" is defined by another, a three, or as the four with whom we relate and play off our relations with each other at any given moment. Four is the maximum. Five turns out to be too large for the inner circle.[26] Yet all such intimacies in writing remain largely symbolic, implicitly exploiting the differences by which, as ways of deepening our understanding, we must inevitably read privately what has been placed in the public domain.

Poetry, once more, Stevens said, helps people live their lives. But not all people. "In the generations of thought," Stevens wrote, "man's sons / And heirs are powers of the mind," adding, "How then shall the mind be less than free / Since only to know is to be free" (*The Sail of Ulysses,* CPP, 465). Recall that Milton the poet sees himself as a minister infused by a procreative power he transfuses into others, within the round of the *circuitus spiritualis* transacting the transactional power of occulted substance (for they were one and the same), which presumably turned every act of communicating into a possibly *communional* evocation of a faintly procreative presence. The presence is more literally in a power of attunement as a motional quickening of spirit by the fusion of formal sound and sense than in some symbolic power of atonement in the implicit gestural sign.

Quickening is procreative, a kind of new birth in attentiveness to the presence of power, much as the Attendant Spirit in *Comus* intimates how the power of the Lady's voice is conditional on its reception: "I was all ear, / And took in strains that *might* create a soul / Under the ribs of Death" (561–63; emphasis mine). The antithetical response seems to be that of an equally receptive but purely aesthetically attuned reader or auditor, indeed a Comus who feels within the "rapture" of the song's delivery a presence pleasurably blessed by sensuously narcotic effects. In any case the poem is not for deaf eunuchs. The Attendant Spirit embodies the regenerative response to poetic song, and Comus reflects its purely seductive nature. Implicit in the one is the sexual power of spiritual procreation, and in the other its pleasure in itself, art for art's sake. For Milton, apparently, poetry is, at the level of its material or substantial power, a surrogate form of licit or illicit sexual intimacy. So where does that leave the latter-day reader?

Certainly not in an either/or Cartesian situation. As an old Dutchman I knew once observed, some people are "a little married"—though there might be no point in conceiving the degrees of how little "a little married" may be, when we start thinking of symbolic degrees of linguistic surrogacy in sacramental, biological, and kinship relations.

It is an evident but hardly overworked fact in linguistic theory that a community of language will always extend, emulate, and eventually displace the prior biological claims of the blood community, and perhaps or especially along lines calculable, for example, by Hamilton's Rule for the play of altruism and selfishness according to the degrees of genetic kinship.[27] Children of immigrants can testify how a community of language, including slang or idiolect, often counts more in the fostering of intimacies and social ties than even biological kinship. In the relational terms of the literary transaction, we might say that the elective affinities of the poetic transaction exploit to their advantage the same gradient by which from infancy onwards we learn to gauge the differences between central and salient subjectivity and intimacy and the merely proximate or more distantly discernible relationships on our immediate social horizon.

For how intimate can a community of language be within a transaction typically reduced to the writer and a reader? Especially when they are separated by centuries of homologically different projections of their figures, and no less on the thither side among readers whose minds at the time may be partly or altogether elsewhere than in the embrace of textual intimation. What then becomes of the sacramental conceit presumably underlying the success of the resonantial transaction? Well, it would seem to depend upon cutting some slack in the gradient of relationship. Or to vary the figure, if the fit audience is only few, as Milton expected, there is still, for example, plenty of room left over for a Dryden in the outer court of the gentiles. There Eliot's ideal English classicist has scope to turn *Paradise Lost* into his Cartesian *The State of Innocence,* where every couplet of clear and distinct language is a microcosmic fourfold, its two chiming lines each symmetrically balanced across its predictable caesura. All Sympathy Lost. Fractalized underlying forms do not an identity make. Homologies need commensurable analogizing to restore thematic resonance and meaning to their forms.

What such examples suggest is a problem of absence at the essence of an art that seems to force us to choose between transparent and shadowed effects, as against the degrees of acoustic shadowing at the depth of which there was ostensibly what the ancients called *hyponoia* or deep meaning. In the aesthetics of occulted substance and internal form deep meaning intimated its presence as a certain *je ne sais quoi* of effect and affect, within an admiration of wonder—properties attributable to what Jonathan Culler calls "signs not given to perception," transactional imperceptibles that remain to "tantalize" us while scarcely registering upon us as readers.[28]

Then, as the semiotic air was clearing in the late seventeenth century, Leibniz discovered the problem of logical indiscernibles or imperceptibles, which are or may be, I suggest, the counterpart of those mythopoetic and constructive Miltonic indiscernibles homologically dependent upon the same large internal forms, and which still haunt, still resonate, as the absent analogies we fail to supply the shapes they demand. Here Claes Schaar's study of Milton's recedingly discernible allusive "vertical context systems"[29] is both intriguing and discouraging. It is good, for example, to find the depths of *Paradise Lost*'s resonant allusiveness so well charted, and yet I miss in Schaar the corollary recognition of Milton's well-thought-out poetics to which the poetry is theoretically justified, a poetry of subtle intimations continually probing the possibilities of connectional or intersubjective intimacies.

But who then is this Miltonically targeted "fit reader," who, with only the haziest intuition of how Milton's poetry justifies his poetics, would still not willingly let his work die? Well, he or she is as real as that still cherished chimaera, the equally imaginary common reader, or at least one more common to a community of readers more preferred by itself self-referentially than others. The worst that can be said of such a community of readers may be said by asking, Can we really imagine a community of intersubjective intimacies? Not really, though we can imagine ourselves in a concert hall responding in an intensely personal way to a publicly played piece of music. Except that this is a music that calls upon a dimensionality of unheard sounds, as in the *Ode on a Grecian Urn* Keats echoes Plotinus on the quality of an "unheard" music sweeter than heard, piping "to the spirit ditties of no tone." For the audible music of poetry always tacitly presumes its own gradient tapering off at the inaudible end of which are the many unheard effects heard by different kinds of competent readers.

It is a music that comes of listening to poetic music, as many poets would expect of both their common and uncommon readers. And insofar as listening is not entirely an art that can be taught, it is an art that in some sense has to be disinterested and has to orient itself to whatever there is of the writer's presence. For it is as false a notion that the writer no longer exists, as that we need only consult our communities of partisan interest to see what we can wittily fish out of ourselves. Yeats as arrogantly and with equal justice imagines in his stead a Catullus among the shades scornfully contemplating his academic readers, among whom I include myself. But clearly writer and reader depend on one another, depend, that is, on styles of connection that cannot be specified by ideological or partisan considerations that have nothing to do with aesthetic appeal and affinities. Poetry has its obligations, but in a world where aesthetics subserves the simplest grounds Stevens spelled out, that it help people live their lives, leaving people themselves to sort out how.

In that sense, Milton builds his readerly preferences into the poem, for if he presumed his ethos to inhere in the compositional pattern of his work, he would have presumed as well some analogous connectionist condition touched or signified by the trembling and true ear. Here the poet's technical effects do not displace but have precedence over the ideas they convey, as Macaulay knew in listening for the resonances the poet planned for our ear to resolve, as a musician might, or as Virginia Woolf seems to have been arrested by the layering upon layering of allusiveness in *Paradise Lost.* No wonder that their agreement as to Milton's liberality followed. To that extent Macaulay and Woolf make explicit the point Claes Schaar seems to have been after, that the recovery of deep or allusive meaning in Milton is less about meanings than about effects over which we can't claim rights, or as if they were subject to evidentiary contradiction in a court of law. This hardly privileges a recherché allusiveness, though allusion is the passport to all our separate contexts.

One summary point. Reading pragmatically presumes a communion of minds sustained by formal continuities that at every turn abstract a quite material and dynamic formalism from the living processes of thought and language, not unlike the materiality linking Milton's monism to the formal force poetry shared with sexual potency. He wrote presuming continuities sustained by traces of particular patterns literally consonant with those holistic and totalizing realities he imagined us as sensing and responding to in like terms. If they are part of how a *Paradise Lost* does in fact enlarge our perception of living within an order of elusive presences continuous with the seamlessness of some acute experiencing of the world, we might think its sacramentality as actual and as fugitive a grace as any offered by life itself.

I have been talking about a different approach to reader response theory, seeing that what we have has failed us so miserably in its self-justifying agendas. In evolutionary terms, reading a poem as rich in such presences distantly but still directly follows from the phenomenal refinement of our abilities as hunter-gatherers to follow the spoor of our objectives, the traces and signs lying about in such subtle abundance that only a finely honed intuitive grasp of their patternings could give us this survival advantage: to invent a culture capable of understanding the survival value of a life-enhancing *aesthesis.*

I now come back to biophilia, or what happens if Richard Strier's reading of Milton's existential theodicy is extended to nesting the Miltonic God of law subordinately within the more generous embrace of his God of emergent design. Thereby we may be led more sympathetically toward a comparable moment in the deeply studied biophilia justifying E. O. Wilson's sociobiological project of consilience. Wilson himself is of that fundamentalist background where Milton's biblical frame of reference would be second nature to any literate reader, as indeed of the very shape of that secular veneration of the miraculous accident of life and mind for which he seeks a mythos commensurable to the shape and power of its logos. In a sense Wilson knows it is already there and looks for it in whatever traces elicit its presence. So, in probing for convergences among all the disciplines involved in our collective self-understanding, he starts from the feeling of the passage in Milton's Eden hard by the passage looked at earlier; universal Pan's encompassing of time and space in dance with the Graces and Hours.

It is an interesting choice: a block of dissimilitudes to deepen an excess, that we may hear in the dissonant harmony of its *concordia discors,* the resonances of life approaching what it is to be.

> Not that fair field
> Of Enna, where Proserpin gathering flowers
> Herself a fairer flower, by gloomy Dis
> Was gathered, which cost Ceres all that pain
> To seek her through the world, nor that sweet grove
> Of Daphne, by Orontes and the inspired
> Castalian spring, might with this Paradise
> Of Eden strive.   (PL 4.268–75)

For Wilson the passage bespeaks Milton's love of life, a love modeling our connection with the whole of something—less than *Gaia,* and most immediately extended to the fractured community of understanding, to scholars and scientists who ought to be able to come closer to a pooling of their ways, if we are somehow to get at our interactive involvement in these processes.[30]

Milton's theodicy, then, would not be a discursive theodicy, an argument that in the end must collapse in the logical inconsistencies and internal self-contradictions all theodicies court. Quite simply, it seems to me, it is a theodicy of affect, an evocation of the world in an everlasting human-centered but writing-arrested reality, indeed more like Botticelli's *Primavera,* with its Ficinian view of the eternal dance of Pan, of All, graced with the contingency of the humanly marked seasons and hours, irregularity scaled to a nearly arrhythmic regularity of purposeless design. If we hear that resonance, as one way or another we must, either within or outside the poem, we hear as well in the haunting clang of sea-mews absent all human presence, a celebration of the accident of our being here, even at the cost of having to reflect upon the enigma of purposeless design.

For Shakespeare's Player Queen in *Hamlet's* play within the play seems always to have the last word: "Our thoughts are ours, their ends none of our own" (3.2.232). To presuppose an end is to conceive the design as in some sense already accomplished. Not to presuppose an end allows its evolutionary course to be discovered in the enactment. Darwinism is a view of the biological whole that assumes the self-organization of life to be its own end. But although culture follows from our evolution as a species, as culturally evolved individuals we tend to substitute the Lamarckian ends projected from our daily experiences of causes and their effects. We would rather believe that we have always followed a path than that we have meandered. Because we need to think so.

But when we translate this kind of directionality into the literary terms of a historicized cultural narrative, what surfaces is the extent to which many of us take history and our moment within it on unwitting apocalyptic terms, as Milton and others have sometimes done, as if the past as text were laid down long ago to be read by us always at the present's edge, as if, really, it had been written to make sense of this express moment of our unique existence—the world at last responding to our intersubjective demands upon its seemingly cold objectivity. As with Christianity, or any version of the teleological mythos, our ends, being ours, must explain themselves, according to this perspective, within some purposive frame, setting against the world's being the consideration of how our wills and ends may conform to one another and to the world's. Nietzsche felt this when he proclaimed himself the only god-like mind in a metaphysical void.

But I refer now to some telos, less grand than speculative, the end even of this very project I broach here, and of its bearings on how the purposeless gene, with no end but its self-perpetuation through all species, generates the complex human pursuit of the acculturated mind's irritated pearl of self-immortalization, as if a breed of abstract ideas (no more) were autonomously capable of endless self-perpetuation.

In a way the emergent climax of that form makes immortality the end of all of Milton's major poetry. And it takes us back to where we began, the intuitionary power of the imagination and its role in knowing *how* we know. Here Milton may well be a key to the most intractable problem facing the human mind's contemplation of its own nature. But from there anyone is welcome to start again: perhaps with some such idea as that the "magnanimity" of Milton, and his Adam and Eve, corresponds not so much with heaven but rather with what for us nowadays amounts to the same thing, the circular anthropic principle of current cosmology and its one irreducible self-referential question: How is it that the human mind seems uniquely to exist, as if only to ask of the cosmos from whence it derives exactly this question?

Tufts University, Emeritus

NOTES

Special thanks to Julia Dubnoff for illuminating discussions of Plato's *Phaedrus* and to Steve Bretzius for calling Derrida on numbers to my attention; thanks as well to Margaret Gooch of the Tisch Library at Tufts University and to Tufts University itself for subventions of long standing. Quotations of Milton's prose are, unless otherwise noted, from *The Complete Prose Works of John Milton*, 8 vols., gen. ed. Don Wolfe et al. (New Haven, 1953–82), hereafter cited parenthetically in the text as YP, with volume and page number. All references to Milton's poetry are to *John Milton: Complete Poems and Major Prose*, ed. Merritt Y. Hughes (New York, 1957), hereafter cited parenthetically in the text by work and line number.

1. "Milton's Passional Poetics" pointedly refers to my earlier "Milton's Passionate Epic," in *Milton Studies* 1, ed. James D. Simmonds (Pittsburgh, 1969), 167–91, to, among other reasons, recognize Simmonds as organizer of the tercentenary series with which he conceived founding *Milton Studies*. Other works of mine that led to the larger project, *Proteus Unbound, or An Art That Nature Makes,* and to this particular project, are "The Apocalypse in *Paradise Lost*," in *Gravity and Ease: Essays on Paradise Lost* (Berkeley, 1969); "Plato's Four Furors and the Real Structure of *Paradise Lost*," *PMLA* 92 (October 1977): 952–62; and "Unexpressive Song: Form and Enigma Variations in *Lycidas*, A New Reading," in *Milton Studies* 15, ed. James D. Simmonds (Pittsburgh, 1981). See also "The Orphic Technique of 'L'Allegro' and 'Il Penseroso,'" *English Literary Review* 1 (spring 1971): 165–77; and "Milton's Magnanimous Reader," *Modern Philology* (February 1985): 310–14, which is an article reviewing Dennis R. Danielson's *Milton's Good God: A Study in Literary Theodicy* (New York, 1982), Michael Lieb's *The Poetics of the Holy: A Reading of Paradise Lost* (Chapel Hill, 1981), and John T. Shawcross's *With Mortal Voice: The Creation of Paradise Lost* (Lexington, Ky., 1982). Also relevant is my "All-Interpreting Love: The Name of God in Scripture and *Paradise Lost*," in *Milton and the Scriptural Tradition*, ed. J. Sims and L. Ryken (Columbia, Mo., 1984).

2. See Denise Schmandt-Besserat, *How Writing Came About* (Austin, Texas, 1996).

3. On the rejection of Descartes in current philosophy and particularly in approaches to the nature of the embodied mind, see, among others, George Lakoff and Mark Johnson, *Philosophy in the Flesh: The Embodied Mind and Its Challenge to Western Thought* (New York, 1999); Antonio Damasio's several works on the impossibility of non-emotive or disembodied reason, notably *Descartes' Error: Emotion, Reason, and the Human Brain* (New York, 1994) and *The*

Feeling of What Happens: Body and Emotion in the Making of Consciousness (New York, 1999); and Keith Devlin, *Goodbye Descartes: The End of Logic and the Search for a New Cosmology of the Mind* (New York, 1997).

4. Patricia Churchland, *Neurophilosophy: Toward a Unified Science of the Mind-Brain* (Cambridge, Mass., 1986).

5. Heidegger, *Nietzsche*, vol. 1 of *The Will to Power as Art*, trans. David Krell (New York, 1979), 103–4; Heidegger, *The Question of Being*, trans. W. Kluback and J. B. Wilde (New York, 1958); and Heidegger, *Poetry, Language, Thought*, trans. A. Hofstadter (New York, 1971).

6. For Wittgenstein's remark on "consistency proofs," of which Gödel's is the best known, see *Philosophical Grammar*, ed. R. Rhees, trans. A. Kenny (Berkeley, 1974), 304. "Gödel's proof," said Wittgenstein elsewhere (in *Gödel's Theorem In Focus*, ed. S. G. Shanker [London and New York, 1988], 181), "develops a difficulty which must appear in a much more elementary way. (And herein lies, it appears to me, Gödel's greater service to the philosophy of mathematics, and at the same time why it is not his particular proof which interests us.)" See Karl E. Schorr's "Form in Logic," in *Problems of Form*, ed. Dirk Baecker, trans. M. Irmscher with L. Edwards (Stanford, 1999), 64–77.

7. Richard Strier, "Milton's Fetters, or, Why Eden Is Better than Heaven," in *Milton Studies* 38, ed. Albert C. Labriola and Michael Lieb (Pittsburgh, 2000), 169; and Stella Revard, "Milton and the Progress of the Epic Proemium," ibid., 122–40. See also Kathleen Swaim, "Myself a True Poem: Early Milton and the (Re)Formation of the Subject," ibid., 67, who argues that Milton was involved in a thoroughly pro-Cartesian project. I obviously disagree with Swaim, though I find attractive her suggestion that "the formal order of *Christ's Nativity* follows the model of the rhetorical . . . antimetabole (e.g. 1, 2, 3, 4, 3, 2–1)" (74), a type of chiasm (as I described it in "The Apocalypse in *Paradise Lost*") in which the sequence is a recursive fourfold. Heidegger appears as "Lucifer in the Light of Being," by David E. Cooper, in the *TLS*, August 25, 2000, 12–13, a review of two books on Heidegger that sets out a view of Heidegger not unlike my own. The essence of Milton's monistic ontology far more resembles that expressed in Alfred North Whitehead's process philosophy, though the contrasts Heidegger highlights are more relevant to this argument.

8. Ernest Sirluck, *Paradise Lost: A Deliberate Epic* (Cambridge, 1967); the passage cited is from *The Doctrine and Discipline of Divorce*, YP 2:292.

9. Elena Esposito, "Two-Sided Forms in Language," in Baecker, *Problems of Form*, 83.

10. For contexts relating to the possibilities of a communional resonance in poetry, see Courtland Baker, "Certain Religious Elements in the Doctrine of the Inspired Poet," *English Literary History* 4 (1939): 301–2; and, more particularly, Fixler, "Ecclesiology," in *A Milton Encyclopedia*, 8 vols., ed. William B. Hunter Jr. et al. (London and Toronto, 1978–80), vol. 2, 190–203.

11. As Murray Gell-Mann observes, complexity is measurable by the shortest or simplest sequence to which the totality of that complexity may be reduced; see *The Quark and the Jaguar* (New York, 1994), 34.

12. On the subitizing/counting or narration functions, their localizations, and the developmental and possibly evolutionary roles to which they relate, see first George Lakoff and Rafael Nuñez, *Where Mathematics Comes From: How the Embodied Mind Brings Mathematics into Being* (New York, 2000); then Brian Butterworth, *What Counts: How Every Brain Is Hardwired for Math* (New York, 1999), passim; and, more generally, Stanislas Dehaene, *The Number Sense: How the Mind Creates Mathematics* (Oxford, 1997). Also see, most particularly, Keith Devlin, who in *The Math Gene: How Mathematical Thinking Evolved and Why Numbers Are Like Gossip* (London, 2000), persuasively integrates the enumerability of the number sense with the

proto-language theory of Derek Bickerton's *Language and Species* (Chicago, 1990), something I aim at in my own theory. Here I register my difference with Mark Turner, whose groundbreaking work in cognitive literary studies—*Reading Minds: The Study of English in the Age of Cognitive Science* (Princeton, 1991) and *The Literary Mind: The Origins of Thought and Language* (Princeton, 1996)—is comprehensive and indispensable. My problem is that Turner takes cognition as synonymous with storytelling, an idea best summed up by Daniel C. Dennett's thumbnail characterization, in *Consciousness Explained* (Boston, 1991), of consciousness as a narrative center of gravity—which largely seems to shift consciousness to the left brain. But that could only be half the story, albeit the visible and effectively the most important half. Dennett, for example, also recognizes the prior significance to consciousness of the immensely generative matter of pattern recognition, which I trace to what is divided between two functions: one that grasps or apprehends a set the memory can handle, and of that set generates our sense of its homologies, and another that thematically narrates such sets in analogical form. These two then are among the most primitive of the deeply *asymmetrical*, rather than the obviously *symmetrical*, features of the brain's hemispheric or bipolar nature.

13. Brian Rotman on serial closure, personal communication. The open-endedness is in some sense the subject of his *Ad Infinitum—The Ghost in Turing's Machine: Taking God out of Mathematics and Putting the Body Back In* (Stanford, 1993). The series 1, 2, 3 . . . more readily suggests the most primitive form of closure in the sequence, "one, two, and many." Cf. the often noted number-sense relationship of French *trois* and *tres*. In the more general sense relevant to implicit Gödelian sequences, the difference is expressed by Dirk Baecker in his introduction to *Problems Of Form:* "Mathematics is the model of simultaneous closure and openness," 1.

14. On the degree zero, see the Belgian "Groupe Mu" who, in their *General Rhetoric*, trans. P. B. Burrell and E. Slotkin (Baltimore, 1981), 30–34, 99, 134, foreground such sets. It is extraordinary that basing themselves as they do on Quintillian's *quadripartita ratio,* and faced with normative series of always four items, plus or minus one, they seem too embarrassed to say anything about numerosity or the number sense—as were it a monomaniacal taxonomy. The plus or minus 1 rule is fundamental to all scaling of constancies in our frame of reference.

15. On crypticism and mystification, see Baecker, introduction to *Problems of Form*, 202n. 2, referring to George Spenser-Brown's *Laws of Form* (London, 1967), and on how, when backgrounded, "the knowledge of the 'laws of form' in traditional society is labeled, and thereby handed down, as 'mystical knowledge.'" For Milton on *crypsis*, see *Logic*, in *The Works of John Milton*, 18 vols., ed. F. A. Patterson et al. (New York, 1931–38), vol. 11, 297–99, 471, 483–85. References to this edition will henceforth be parenthetically cited in the text as CM, with volume and page number.

16. Ernesto Grassi, *Heidegger and the Question of Renaissance Humanism: Four Studies,* trans. U. Hemel and J. B. Krois (Binghamton, N.Y., 1983), and Grassi, *Renaissance Humanism: Studies in Philosophy and Poetics,* trans. W. F. Veit (Binghamton, N.Y., 1988).

17. R. D. Jordan, in *"Paradise Regained* and the Second Adam," in *Milton Studies* 9, ed. James D. Simmonds (Pittsburgh, 1976) 261–63, distributes the temptations into the classical sequence of the *tetractys* apparently without being aware of what he has done, seeing no more in the series than a token of the Decalogue. See the discussion of "signs not given to perception" below. The point of Milton's Jesus' progressively "unforgetting" his former identity as demiurge would seem to go back to both a Gnostic and a Unitarian edge implicit, I think, in Paul, 1 Cor. 8:6.

18. Wilamowitz, cited by Josef Pieper, *Enthusiasm and Divine Madness: On the Platonic Dialogue Phaedrus,* trans. Richard and Clara Winston (New York, 1964), 87–88. Wallace Stevens, *Complete Poetry and Prose,* ed. Frank Kermode and Joan Richardson (New York, 1977),

25. References to this edition will henceforth be cited parenthetically in the text as CPP, by page number. See especially the "four daughters" of 35–36 and the significantly different but unpublished draft version of *The Comedian, or From the Journal of Crispin,* CPP, 985–95.

19. N.b. the packaging of Derrida's polemic with Kant's in *Raising the Tone of Philosophy: Late Essays by Immanuel Kant, Transformative Critique by Jacques Derrida,* ed. Peter Fenves (Baltimore, 1993). Relevant here is what Kant saw as the misprision of such things as the fouring layout of his own writings and his attribution of the two basic sets of constructivist fouring categories to the mind's innate tendencies. One set is the representational category of the categories of space, time, number and causality—my own concerns here—and the other the enactional category of quantity, quality, modality, and relationship. Schopenhauer invoked in effect the invariant of these categories when, as did Kant himself, he rightly referred the discovery of the "system" back through Plato and Pythagoras to the Hindus, first by referring his own major work to its foundation in his earlier Kantian *The Fourfold Root of the Principle of Sufficient Reason,* trans. E. F. J. Payne (Peru, Ill., 1974), 1, and then also in the prefatory reference to the fourfolding of *The World as Will and Representation,* 2 vols., trans. E. F. J. Payne (Indian Hills, Col.), vol. 1, 1958, xx–xxiv.

20. Pico della Mirandola, *Heptaplus,* trans. C. P. Glenn Wallis, P. J. W. Miller, and D. Carmichael (Indianapolis, 1965), 78–79. Milton's debt to Pico in the *Areopagitica* has been often remarked. See, for example, Fixler, "The Orphic Technique of 'L'Allegro' and 'Il Penseroso.'" On Ficino's Plato as *the* Plato of the Renaissance, see Allen, *Marsilio Ficino and the Phaedran Charioteer* (Berkeley and Los Angeles, 1981).

21. There are good discussions of Milton's "internal form" in Michael Lieb's *The Dialectics of Creation: Patterns of Birth and Regeneration in Paradise Lost* (Amherst, 1970), and *Achievements of the Left Hand: Essays on the Prose of John Milton,* ed. Lieb and Shawcross (Amherst, 1974). On the underlying form of underlying form, see David Roberts, "Self-Reference in Literature," in Baecker, *Problems of Form,* 43.

22. For a usefully contrastive branching of the Indo-European 'fouring' line of descent in Indian scriptures, see Brian K. Smith, "The Veda and the Authority of Class," in *Authority, Anxiety, and Canon: Essays in Vedic Interpretation,* ed. Laurie L. Patton (Albany, N.Y., 1994), 67–93. On the structure of mathematical thinking, see Hadamard, cited by Dehaene, *The Number Sense,* 172, and Geza Szamosci, *The Twin Dimensions: Inventing Time and Space* (New York, 1986). On the mystical paradigm, see Evelyn Underhill, *Mysticism: A Study in the Nature and Development of Man's Spiritual Consciousness* (New York, 1969), pt. II, ch. 2–5. For how the transformational power was conceived in the Renaissance, see D. P. Walker, *Spiritual and Demonic Magic: From Ficino to Campanella* (London, 1958), 20–24, 119–25, and Gordon O'Brien, *Renaissance Poetics and the Problem of Power* (Chicago, 1956). On how the raptures were specifically tied in with musical theory of the Renaissance as it concerned belief in the energizing and occult effects of the union of music and poetry, see Frances Yates's *French Academies of the Sixteenth Century* (London, 1947), ch. 4.

23. Cassirer, "Ficino's Place in Intellectual History," review of Paul O. Kristeller, *The Philosophy of Marsilio Ficino* (New York, 1943), *Journal of the History of Ideas* 6 (October 1945): 483–501, esp. 498–500, for internal form. Cassirer's point is also intriguing in that it may have come up in the celebrated debate between himself and Heidegger at Davos, where to Heidegger's disgust Cassirer tried to get him to see that he was really some kind of neo-Kantian.

24. *The New Science of Giambattista Vico,* trans. T. G. Bergin and M. H. Fisch (Ithaca, N.Y., 1994), passim.

25. For how quantum coherence and decoherence and the uncertainty principle of their alternations might effect the working of the brain, see Johnjoe McFadden, *Quantum Evolution* (New York, 2001). Uncertainty is always informational uncertainty, on which the resonance

phenomenon subsists. For Milton and the certainty of uncertainty, see the opening pages of Catherine G. Martin's *Milton and the Ruins of Allegory* (Durham, N.C., 1998). To appreciate her point we must realize that, as information theory demonstrates, the greater the degree of controlled or formal linguistic uncertainty in aestheticized language (as against "clear and distinct" language), the greater its semiotic resonance, or the stuff of which the redundancies of emergent meaningfulness come. A suggestive beginning on the matter is made by Wai Chee Dimock, "A Theory of Resonance," *PMLA* (October 1997): 1060–71, especially in her bold invocation of Einstein's fourfold space time model as somehow the unexplained cosmic ground of the literary resonance phenomenon.

26. Robin Dunbar, *Grooming, Gossiping, and the Evolution of Language* (London, 1996), ch. 4.; Geoffrey F. Miller, *The Mating Mind: How Sexual Choice Shaped the Evolution of Human Nature* (New York, 2000), ch. 9; and Devlin, *The Math Gene.*

27. For Hamilton's Rule, see William D. Hamilton, "The Genetical Theory of Social Behaviour," *Journal of Theoretical Biology* 7 (1964): 1–52.

28. Jonathan Culler, "Toward a Linguistics of Writing," in *Framing the Sign* (Norman, Okl., 1988), 223–24, and Culler, *Structuralist Poetics* (London, 1975), 253–54, 257–58. Then there is Milton's older contemporary, Owen Feltham, whose *je ne sais quoi* in "On the Admiration of Wonder" bespeaks the wordlessness of response at fine writing, while in "Of Poets and Poetry," he conceives of the poet who "shall often raise himself a joy in his raptures, which no man can perceive but he." *Resolves* (1628), reprinted in *Seventeenth Century Prose and Poetry,* ed. A. M. Witherspoon and F. J. Warnke (New York, 1963), 311, 320.

29. Claes Schaar, *The Full-Voic'd Quire Below: Vertical Context Systems in Paradise Lost* (Lund, 1973).

30. In *Consilience: The Unity of Knowledge* (New York, 1998), 332, Presumably it is for this context that Wilson lists Barbara Lewalski as consultant, suggesting a practical degree of consilience perhaps more to the point than this present essay.

DALILA'S TOUCH: DISABILITY AND RECOGNITION IN *SAMSON AGONISTES*

Susannah B. Mintz

I

IN HIS MID-1650S sonnet to Cyriack Skinner on the condition of his blindness, Milton makes a now-familiar equation between the loss of his physical sight and both his spiritual enrichment and his political accomplishments. The poem defines the relationship as a matter of "conscience" (10). To have gone blind during the arduous toil of "liberty's defence," the author's "noble task" (11)—and, perhaps most importantly, to have garnered fame for that work—compensates for the mundane disadvantages of sightlessness.[1] "Content though blind" (14), the poet carries on in the satisfaction of a renown that is at once worldly ("all Europe talks from side to side" [12]) and beyond such ephemeral concerns as "the world's vain mask" (13).

Curiously, the sonnet begins by proclaiming the fact of blindness, by dwelling with what sounds like real melancholy over the loss of visual contact with "man or woman" (6) and with the motions of time ("sun or moon or star" [5])—curiously, I would suggest, not because one presumes that Skinner knows full well the state of Milton's vision, but rather because the poem thus foregrounds the very physical condition it would seek to diminish. Yet the avowal of blindness is necessary because the speaker does not "look" blind: his "clear" (1) eyes do not reveal any sign of their impairment.[2] Evidence and interpretation are only indeterminately related, particularly when it comes to the meaning of the body; the visible data (in this case, eyes that are "clear / To outward view" [1–2]) do not carry inevitable, immediately recognizable significance. Such eyes must be scrutinized differently, perhaps more carefully, in order for their sightlessness to be understood.

On the one hand, then, the poem exhibits a need to declare the affliction, to make it "seen" and thus known; on the other hand, it exhibits a desire to rewrite the meaning of that affliction, to retrieve blindness from the negatively moralized connotations of "blemish" and "spot" (2). Both inclinations suggest the important presence of a fantasized audience—other than Milton's amanuensis, for whom recognizable physical symptoms would make blindness more readily detectable—an audience of strangers who, insistently and in a manner now unavailable to the speaker and subject of the poem, *see*. And there is another invisible presence, too—that person, real or imagined, who describes to the speaker the appearance of his eyes, thereby assuring him that they are free of flaw.[3]

But can such an assessment be trusted, either by the speaker or the reader? How can we be sure of what the speaker's eyes look like, and thus know how to understand them? The uncertainty implied by the declaration in the poem's first lines (these eyes are clear although they are really blind)— the fact that the meaning of blindness is open to interpretation but also subject to cultural prejudice—points to the way in which bodies are discursive sites of ideological contest and encoded by societal expectation and myth. The sonnet describes "these eyes" (1) as "Bereft of light" (3), "idle orbs" (4) that have "forgot" their "seeing" (3)—how to do it, that they did it, or even what it felt like to see. Thus blindness is, initially, equated with a morally suspect inactivity (not "seeing" is somehow equivalent to not "doing") and with a kind of mental dulling (to forget is to lack thoughtfulness, to not be an acute or dependable caretaker of one's behavior or duties). Yet the sonnet is also anxious to assure its readers, its addressee, Cyriak Skinner, and its own author alike that blindness does *not* signify all those qualities, that it is *not* what it might seem to be: an indicator of internal as well as physical weakness.

In order to protect its subject from a set of cultural associations that read blindness as a mark of shameful insufficiency, the poem has recourse to the interpretation on the other side of the binary. What allows the speaker to forge on in his disabled state, to continue "Right onward" (9), is conscience. With no guilt to haunt him over not having done something important with his sight (i.e., his life), and with no troubling sense of having gone blind poring over the wrong things, the speaker can reassure himself that his blindness derives from the righteous defense of liberty—a claim that ultimately figures the blind man as one of God's chosen servants. In the act of revising visual impairment, from a condition of loss, idleness, loneliness, or indignity to a sign of spiritual triumph, Milton's poem thus articulates the classic double-sided trope of blindness as both a sign of perceptual or ethical inadequacy and a mystical gift. As is that of Homer and Tiresias, the speaker's blindness is an "ennobling mark,"[4] a sign of prophetic power; but the specter of helplessness or *lack* of discernment simultaneously haunts the poem's confidence. Whether or not Skinner ever queried Milton in the way the poem indicates— "What supports me dost thou ask?" (9)—seems less significant than the question's role in urging the sonnet into being. The implication is that blindness *requires* support, and that the speaker's ability to carry on in the face of such a tragedy also requires explanation. The point is not that loss of sight would not have presented serious difficulties to any seventeenth-century person, especially an avid reader like Milton, but rather that the poem's triumphant analogy of blindness as a mark of special status necessarily invokes, because it also depends upon, an ideology of corporeal normality whereby blindness is encoded as a disability. If one is invited to sympathize with the speaker and to wonder, with Skinner, how such a man could possibly persevere, that sympathy is quickly maneuvered into admiration for the activity that produced the blindness. The impaired physical condition becomes a cause for wonder, a multivalent sign of the writer's dedication to a cause, his prodigious reading, and the privilege of being liberty's spokesman. The blind man, first perceived as an aberration and a monstrous failure, is next a marvel, the prophetic seer.

This dichotomy works to the speaker's advantage, but only because he is able to effect the transformation rhetorically. Blindness is both a loss and a kind of gift, a show of the individual's commitment to a cause but also the converse of that sign, a manifestation of possible inadequacy. The poet's ability—his need—to frame his condition as an ennobling characteristic simultaneously denies and discloses a worry that it might be the opposite, which reveals in turn an inveterate prejudice against corporeal failings. If there is no essential meaning inherent in the body's particularities, then eyes "clear / To outward view" must be accounted for, given discursive meaning, no less than the blindness they paradoxically obscure. Milton's need to confirm the "normal," unblemished appearance of his eyes, as well as the moral probity that their clarity is meant to signify, points to the culturally enforced meaning of the body. It is precisely the disjunction between physical evidence and internal truth initially posited in the poem that makes its final reversal possible. In other words, just as the visible clarity of the eyes belies their blindness, so too might physical blindness conceal a greater truth about one's subjectivity. The overall trajectory of Milton's sonnet seems to follow such an impulse to challenge negative cultural assumptions about the blind person. But in its insistence on being "Content *though* blind" (14; emphasis mine), the poem takes pride in blindness only as a synecdoche, the signifier of a far more profound referent—the ethical integrity proven by the author's larger political and theological activities.[5] Two central questions thus raised by "To Mr Cyriack Skinner Upon His Blindness" are: first, how such a text manages to turn its own construction of physical disablement as a misfortune into the reward of spiritual or mental accomplishment; second, what that slippage means to a study of Milton's use of the body, specifically a disabled body, as a means of examining the cultural mechanism of interpretation—that is, how we understand and make meaning from what we "see."

Blindness does not play a consistent role throughout Milton's work. Such familiar phrases as the outraged "Blind mouths!" (119) of *Lycidas,* or

God's commandment in *Paradise Lost* that "They who neglect and scorn, shall never taste; / But hard be harden'd, blind be blinded more, / That they may stumble on, and deeper fall,"[6] represent a conventional interpretation of the impaired body as a sign of ignorance and depravity. On the other hand, the invocation to Book Three of *Paradise Lost* expresses hope that the loss of sight is a threshold to heightened powers of insight and imagination, aligning the poet with other "prophet[s]": "Blind Thamyris, and blind Maeonides, / And Tiresias and Phineus" (3.35–36). *Samson Agonistes* presents a subtler picture of a "disabled" body, one that complicates the kind of neat dichotomies, evident in these other examples, that underwrite moral and political absolutism. Moreover, exclusive critical focus on blindness as both a literal fact of Samson's imprisonment and a metaphor for moral lapse has distracted us from the drama's pointed use of other senses—particularly hearing and touch—as equally important to the interaction of knowledge, subjectivity, and ideology. Indeed, the poem deploys multiple tropes of embodiment and sensory experience to call attention to the ways in which *all* bodies are conditioned by cultural expectation. Samson and Dalila both, for example, occupy a position of corporeal otherness. If Samson's liminal body complicates the codes that organize and formulate meaning, calling into question the stability of frames of reference, so too does Dalila, as woman and Philistine, question the poem's "normative"—that is, male and Israelite—embodied subject. But whereas Samson clings throughout the poem to the social order that demarcates his identity, Dalila attempts, in a singular dramatic moment, to cross the threshold that separates them and make physical contact across the barrier of difference. In what follows I will argue, focusing on the liminal nature of both "disability" and Dalila's request to "touch" (951), that Milton's late work participates in an overt way in his continued commitment—perhaps a renewed commitment—to the notion of truth as ambiguous and contingent, to a world in which contradictions and multiple interpretations are allowed to proliferate.

As a judge, Samson is neither ordinary mortal nor God (the very fact that he can accuse himself of strutting about like a "petty god" [529] bears witness to this), and as Joseph Wittreich has pointed out, Samson is not a king either. He is a man—but one of superhuman bodily power; but then he is disabled, differently "abnormal": lacking sight, overly attuned to sound, "half-dead" or half alive, enlightened and benighted, *indeterminate* ("Can this be he[?]"— the Chorus cannot immediately determine [124]). Once blind, Samson is neither monster nor marvel, and yet he is both, God's chosen saint and the violent avenger whose every action, every motive, comes under question. In a word, Samson is ambiguous, manifesting the duality of the disabled body and its apparent reporting of God's designs, resisting easy associations of extraordinary embodiedness as either evidence of a divine plan or a sign of punishment. Yet Samson's own use of the word "mean" (207) to complain that his "wisdom" is no better than average, particularly in contrast to his "Immeasurable strength" (206), emphasizes the degree to which his sense of himself is defined by separateness; being "typical" in any way undermines his sense of unique identity. Samson cannot recognize how the very indeterminacy of his own body—the fact that no single or precise meaning can be attached to it—makes him *like* others, how he, too, like Dalila, is bounded by the narratives of ideology. *Samson Agonistes* repeatedly demonstrates the constructedness of difference and suggests that the ability to establish recognition across boundaries—figuratively to receive and accept Dalila's request to touch, rather than rigidly enforcing cultural categories—may be a crucial step toward personal, social, and spiritual renewal. In this way, the poem reconfigures the dynamics of power and discourse that limit its world (as well as Milton's own) to categorical thinking, and it stands as a culmination of Milton's lifelong foray into the intricacies of national, gendered, and religious identity.

II

What might *disability* mean to a late-seventeenth-century English poetic imagination? Just as modern ontological categories of gender and sexuality do not pertain to the early modern experience, in which the categories of "male" and "female," "homosexual" and "heterosexual," exist in a less absolute biological distinction from one another, so too, according to Nicholas Mirzoeff, "the simple binary opposition between the able-bodied and the disabled . . . [does] not exist" in early modern England.[7] Lennard Davis points out that such concepts as "normalcy" and "normative" do not enter the language until the mid nineteenth century; before the notion of a middle-class norm took hold, Western culture perceived of the body in terms of an "ideal" according to which *any* human body, by definition, is imperfect. Yet the Renaissance humoral body—fluid, fungible, unstable—was nonetheless susceptible to frightening impermanence and thus subject to the control of discursive practices aimed at solidifying what the body failed to solidify on its own. And despite a burgeoning scientific discourse that sought to rescue the understanding of corporeal anomalies from the realm of superstition and the supernatural, early modern cultural and literary representations of the body suggest potent fears about "difference."

As with race, class, sexuality, and gender, the category of "disability" serves to create and stabilize the boundaries of a culture's acceptable body.

Far from residing inescapably within the body itself, "disability" is a discursive effect, not an absolute biological entity "but rather a set of social relations,"[8] or, in Peter Stallybrass's words, "a site of conflict."[9] Rosemarie Garland Thomson, one of the pioneering theorists of contemporary disability studies (so-called "freak discourse") writes that disability is "not so much a property of bodies as a product of cultural rules about what bodies should be or do,"[10] a historically specific construction that enables and guarantees "normalcy." The body coded as "abnormal"—at once excessively visible yet ignored at the margins of culture, the subject of intense cultural work and the derided object of scorn or pity—ensures the transparency of the normative body, the only one fully recognizable from within the dominant culture's discourse. "Ableness," no less culturally determined than disablement, masks the fragility of its identity by using the disabled body as its demonized other. So long as there are bodies whose attributes can be denominated as "freakish," "extra-ordinary," or grotesque, Thomson posits, the "privileged, idealized figure" of Western culture is made "symbolically free" from "the vagaries and vulnerabilities of embodiment."[11]

The disabled body is threatening not simply because it exposes the body's capacity for disease and decay. It is also a repository for all that the normative conception of identity must eschew, thus serving an interrelated set of cultural needs: to instantiate deviance and immorality; to visualize personality traits as written on the body or to explain the latter via the former; to segregate groups of people by solidifying difference through prominent bodily features; to metaphorically render psychological or spiritual exceptionality. In her introduction to *Freakery: Cultural Spectacles of the Extraordinary Body*, Thomson writes that the "singular" or "exceptional" body is "never simply itself"; it rather "betokens something else, becomes revelatory, sustains narrative, exists socially in a realm of hyper-representation."[12] Before the eighteenth century, unexpected, unusual embodiment was typically interpreted within a religious context as the manifestation of divine punishment, and the body so encoded could be made to serve a moral, societal function, to literalize a range of sins from gossiping and idleness to adultery and blasphemy. For Western philosophers from Aristotle to Bacon and Montaigne, "the differently formed body is most often evidence of God's design, divine wrath, or nature's abundance, but it is always an interpretive occasion . . . alternatingly coveted, revered, and dreaded."[13] Deformed infants were routinely (and legally) euthanized in ancient Sparta and Athens,[14] and the great philosophers granted their approval: "With regard to the choice between abandoning an infant or rearing it," writes Aristotle in the *Politics*, "let it be lawful that no cripple child be reared."[15] Aristotle considered bodily dysfunction so metaphysically debilitating that the deaf, for instance, were deemed "senseless and incapable of reason," "no better than the animals of the forest."[16] Augustine, too, disparaged the deaf, claiming that "those who are born deaf are incapable of ever exercising the Christian faith."[17]

The ancient belief that "abnormal births were an evil sign"[18] is evidenced by the word "monster," whose various roots, *moneo,* to warn, and *monstro,* to show forth, encapsulate the dual meaning. In the early modern period, monstrosity was an especially overdetermined arena of cultural activity. The exceptional body could be interpreted as a *lusus naturae,* one of nature's jokes or mistakes, its excessiveness (a body with too much or even too little of what is considered "natural") deriving from the *copia* of nature itself. Popular superstition held that unusual births were the product of the interaction between women's mysterious bodies and their unruly imaginations, which could impress upon a developing fetus both the mother's mood and whatever startling scenes she might chance upon. Thus a harelip might be the result of having seen a rabbit during pregnancy, or a winestain birthmark the infant's burden for a mother who witnessed (or participated in) shameful drunkenness.[19] Similarly, deformed infants were often attributed to women's propensity for sinful weakness; a common charge leveled against religious nonconformists was that their blasphemy would issue forth in monstrous births. Fascination and horror for a whole range of physical anomalies—including hermaphrodites, conjoined twins, dwarfs, eunuchs, and multibreasted women; deafness, blindness, missing or extra limbs and digits; epilepsy and mental disorders—derived from widespread cultural anxiety about the tenuous boundaries of normal human embodiment and found ready outlet in the massively popular monster shows and exhibitions like Bartholomew Fair.[20]

Even the increasingly scientific treatment of corporeal "monsters" in the seventeenth century, initiated by Bacon in 1620 and evidenced by the journal of the Royal Society, reflects what Keith Thomas has called early modern "anxiety, latent or explicit, about any form of behaviour which threatened to transgress the fragile boundaries between man and the animal creation,"[21] and such signs of bodily difference as skin color, blindness, deafness, and lameness had cultural and literary currency as proof of moral deficiency. Renaissance monster ballads displayed cleft palates, missing fingers, and other instances of "prodigious" bodies "to instill fear instead of wonder in the hearts of the common people," and broadsides announced monstrous births as both signs of divine anger and "miracles, indications of God's power over nature."[22] Protestant popular literature and sermons alike were particularly vociferous about the causes of corporeal difference. One ballad exhorted "good Christians all" to "Beholde a monster rare, / Whose monstrous shape, no doubt, fortels, / Gods wrath we should beware."[23] The contemporary idea that the freak externalizes fears about the horrors residing at the core of the self was also articulated in the early modern period; the Calvinist Sir John Davies, for instance, author of a verse collection called *Nosce teipsum* (1599), wrote that the soul "retires and sinks for shame and fear" from the "strange chimeras and monsters" she "espies" in her own reflection.[24]

Literary representations of the *terata* (Greek for both "monster" and "marvel") tend to isolate the abnormal trait in order to magnify its symbolic resonance, removing any contextual particulars of individuality. "Because disability is so strongly stigmatized and is countered by so few mitigating narratives," Thomson suggests, "the literary traffic in metaphors often misrepresents or flattens the experience real people have of their own or others' disabilities. . . . The disabled body is almost always a freakish spectacle presented by the mediating narrative voice."[25] Shakespeare's crippled Richard III exemplifies the literary deployment of disability. In *The Body and Physical Difference: Discourses of Disability,* David Mitchell and Sharon Snyder describe the effect of Richard's corporeal impairment with the following list of "attributes." Richard's hunchback is:

a social burden; metaphysical sign of divine disfavor; evidence of the machinations of a divine plan in history; that a disabled child is retribution for parental weakness; that a disabled subject follows a deterministic trajectory in life; he is the bearer of an entrenched identity (pathetic or vengeful); he is the literal embodiment of the evidence of the fall of man; he personifies the fiendish specter of war; he is singular and exceptional rather than common and ordinary; he can be viewed as the most interior to a social order (the most human in suffering) or the most exiled (lacking in natural human affections). . . . Finally, a scapegoat patterning to the play reiterates exile as a culturally sanctioned historical solution to the social disruption that disabled people are perceived to present.[26]

Implicit in this litany is the idea that the grotesque body functions as a receptacle of sorts: just as the uncontainability it seems to make literal troubles the surface of a culture's dominant narrative, so too does it contain through symbolization "all that must be ejected or abjected from self-image to make the bounded, category-obeying self possible,"[27] all that the culture wishes to reject from its center. Shakespeare's portrayal of Richard III as the quintessential figure of disability shows that the disabled body is threatening in its ambiguity, its liminality, its very indeterminacy—he is only half a person, underdeveloped and "unfinished,"[28] proof of all that can go wrong and the wrong that can be done; he must therefore be transformed, discursively, into the embodiment of wrongness, so that the body's frightening capacity for being unfair and out of proportion can be safely confined and discarded through him.

III

The notion that disabledness takes its meaning from culture rather than from nature, that it is discursive rather than essential—and that other forms of identity, in turn, are also culturally produced—is powerfully conveyed in *Samson Agonistes* by Samson's repeated references to a fear of being "stare[d]" at (112) and "exposed / To daily fraud, contempt, abuse and wrong" (75–76). Blindness is a sign of alienation (or "annexation," in David Mitchell's words)[29] from his own Danite tribe as well as his Philistine captors. "Eyeless in Gaza" (41) with "both [his] eyes put out" (33), Samson is "the scorn and gaze" (34) of his enemies, a plight that sounds even more intensely negative than the physical pain of imprisonment or the guilt of having trespassed divine command: being "Blind among enemies," Samson complains, is "worse than chains, / Dungeon, or beggary, or decrepit age!" (68–69). But he is also stared at by his own countrymen (not to mention "viewers" of the drama itself). Both the Chorus and Manoa openly express surprise at the visible change in Samson's appearance. Their reaction is an aspect of their dismay at his captive state and, particularly in Manoa's case, slides into a confusion over Samson's past choices, a confusion that at times hardly sounds distinguishable from bitterness or even resentment. It is being objectified and out of control, a "fool, / In power of others, never in [his] own" (77–78), unable to defend or care for himself, that constitutes Samson's ultimate "insult" (113). This point reiterates the idea that the "meaning" of blindness in *Samson Agonistes* is specifically social, determined by others and in turn "otherizing" the self.

When the characters in the poem try to interpret Samson's loss of sight, they evince the same dichotomy between bane and benefit mapped out by the sonnet to Cyriak Skinner. But blindness eludes the static poles of that opposition and therefore participates in what John Rogers has described as the poem's effort "to destroy the entire principle of arbitrarily determined organization, manifested throughout the bodily, religious, social, and political fabric of experience."[30] Because assessments of Samson's condition attach to events that are themselves inaccessible to stable meanings, loss of sight is no more monologically significant than Samson's dubious marriages, the "intimate impulse" (223) and "rousing motions" (1382) that have provoked so much critical discussion, or the climactic event at the Philistine temple. Samson's bodily peculiarities escape, even as they summon, the kinds of polarities and warning tones common to cultural and literary representations of disability both before and after 1671. References to sight pervade the poem—from Samson's lament for his eyes at the start of the drama to the Chorus's assurance of inward illumination at the end—and the characters re-iterate the blindness binary, linking Samson's loss of sight here to his trouble-making and there to his victory over his pagan enemies. The tragedy seems accordingly to follow the same conceptual shift that organizes the earlier sonnet: physical blindness is first bemoaned and then acclaimed, just as the literal impairment of the eyes is juxtaposed with, and perhaps even allows for, interior enlightenment.

Yet the text consistently upends this sort of linear progress, as well as the simple allegorical key that utilizes blindness in the service of stark op-positions of light and dark, righteousness and sin, regeneration and self-aggrandizement. As is well known to readers of the poem, Milton frustrates easy assessment of Samson's actions or of his afflicted body. Are Samson's decisions justified by God's will or merely self-indulgent? Is his blindness a punishment or a gift, a sign of deviance or grace—or, more disturbingly, neither? George F. Butler argues that "the tragedy is fraught with ambiguity," that "there is no indisputable proof" about the meaning of any of the drama's central events, including Samson's blindness.[31] To the extent that the disabled body becomes the site of tensions about how cultures write on their subjects, Samson's body, itself a blurred either/or, transgresses—and thereby reveals—the discursive boundaries that stabilize and guarantee social identity.

At the start of the poem, both Samson and the Chorus read blindness as a mark of alienation from the "prime decree" (85) of Logos, and thus as a mark of the profundity of his spiritual failure. Samson's first speech agonizes over the loss of "light," "the prime work of God" (70), which "might in part [his] grief have eased" (72). Feeling himself even more "vil[e]" than the lowliest worm that sees (73–75), Samson most urgently bewails his blindness as "chief" (66) among all his present difficulties. "Darkness" symbolizes a whole range of delinquencies, from a lack of self-knowledge to questionable decisionmaking, ethical untrustworthiness, and an over-valuation of "bad women" (211). These failings are emphatically summarized by Samson him-self, when he claims to be "Effeminately vanquished" (562), then follows up with a list of attributes that equate loss of sight with emasculated passivity—"blind, disheartened, shamed, dishonoured, quelled" (563), a "burdenous drone," "a gaze" and a "pitied object" (567–68). This catalogue of epithets collapses the *condition* of blindness into the *events* for which Samson was blinded, so that his physical state becomes inseparable from the religious and social laws according to which that state is interpreted. Blindness thus is given no significance outside of ideology (similarly, the sonnet to Skinner situates blindness within the context of Milton's religious and political identity). As a paradoxically visible encapsulation of all that Samson was foretold to be, his prodigious failure, and the triumph of Dagon over the Israelites' God, loss of sight becomes a corporeal metaphor for what David Mitchell has called the "operations of cultural belief."[32]

Blindness only has meaning, of course, through juxtaposition to sightedness. In order that Samson's loss of physical vision can be interpreted as an increase of wisdom or "insight," the poem sets blindness against the dangers of seeing, invoking what Jeffrey Baker refers to as the "old and pious mythology that the blind are free from the dangers of sight."[33] Physical vision is shown to be dramatically unreliable when the Chorus, upon first witnessing the "change beyond report" in Samson (117), wonders if their "eyes misrepresent?" (124); the possibility of such a mistake suggests that actual sight has little to do with the accuracy of one's knowledge and interpretation. The Chorus takes the figure before it to be Samson, changed nearly beyond recognition. But it quickly doubts its ability to attach proper meaning to information obtained through bodily function—Samson can only be Samson if what he looks like accords with his prior aspect, with the past—with the Chorus's *memory* of what Samson "ought" to look like. Since the figure before it does not, it attributes its "mistake" to its eyes, rather than trying to reconcile what it understands of Samson's selfhood to the data received through vision. Moreover, since sightedness threatens the individual with discomfort—as Dalila will say later, "Eyesight exposes daily men abroad" (919) to "many a care and chance" (918)[34]—blindness transforms from a diminishment and incapacity to a potential form of protection from worldly distractions. No longer burdened with witnessing, or being distracted by, the prosaic sights of everyday existence, the blind Samson turns "inward"—a word used repeatedly by critics to describe him[35]—which seems to make him newly capable of examining his mysterious "motives." Thus the "eyes fast fixed" described by the Messenger (1637) can be interpreted as signs of wisdom, and they seem now to denote prayer or serious, important contemplation rather than the dull stare of a "fool" (77) with an unthinking "servile mind" (412); "blindness internal" (1686) becomes the emblem of "fond," "mortal," "reprobate" men (1682, 1685), no longer Samson's own indignity. When the Chorus enthusiastically fantasizes that Samson's "eyesight" might be "by miracle restored" (1527–28), its focus on physical sight metonymically evokes a hope that Samson has also been spiritually restored, reconciled with God. In a similar way, blind Samson is transformed in the Semichorus's estimation from one who was "Despised and thought extinguished quite" (1688) to a champion of virtue whose "*inward* eyes" are newly "illuminated" (1689; emphasis mine). Samson appears regenerated, and blindness has become the mark of a spiritual triumph made all the more significant by his previous despair and apparent dereliction.

Yet such a schematic is complicated by the inaccessibility of Samson's thinking—we can never be fully sure that he gains greater insight, and at the same time, seeing is really no more misleading than any other form of perception. If Samson's blindness is open to interpretation—if, more importantly, it *must* be interpreted in order for it to accrue meaning at all—and if, subsequently, those meanings shift according to cultural and ideological demands, then the events and people to which his blindness seem ideologically attached also become open to interpretation, and other apparent "truths" can also escape discursive efforts to pin them down.[36] I would argue that the trajectory of *Samson Agonistes* resists a linear progression in which blindness ultimately redefines itself as spiritual regeneration. Rather than moving toward an increasingly knowable, "true" Samson, the poem's juxtaposed scenes of dialogue advance in such a way that Samson comes to appear *less,* rather than more, inward-looking and self-aware. His motives become more and more difficult to ascertain as his encounters with others conduct him toward the enigmatic decision to follow the Officer to the temple. Nor does blindness inarguably grant Samson heightened powers of self-consciousness or understanding. Joseph Wittreich has insisted that the poem "is a radical ambiguation of an already equivocal tale" and Samson "a figure of dubious heroism."[37] And as many critics have pointed out (perhaps most notably Stanley Fish), phrases like "of my own accord" (1643) or the ambiguity of the Messenger's description of Samson "*as* one who prayed, / *Or* some great matter in his mind revolved" (1637–38; emphasis mine) confound both the characters' as well as readers' attempts to ascertain the meaning of the event at the pillars—leaving us not with full certainty that Samson has been inspired but rather with what Fish has called an "interpretive frenzy."[38] George Butler concurs, arguing that Milton's poem "dramatizes the ambivalence and uncertainty of those who must interpret Samson's death," and that "the ambiguity surrounding Samson's suicide is a deliberate exploration of how witnesses respond to events."[39] David Gay has also discussed the interpretive tangles of the text, stating succinctly that "*Samson Agonistes* is largely about the act of interpretation, and the Chorus, with its fixed, provisional interpretations of events, portrays the anxiety for coherence and continuity in its most acute and, in places, fallible form."[40]

If, as Butler's reading suggests, both physical *and* "inward" sight are complicated by the text,[41] then the effect of *Samson Agonistes* may be not so much no meaning as multiple meanings: less a state of impossible emptiness than an insistence on the presence of multiple perspectives and an awareness of the cultural forces that erect the borders-between. David Loewenstein protests against readings such as Fish's: "there is no need to turn *Samson Agonistes* into a drama of indeterminacy where all meanings . . . are simply ambiguous and doubtful."[42] Yet we can acknowledge the accumulation of interpretive possibilities without then concluding that the text resides in meaninglessness. Repeated situating of Samson in the context of such terms as "aloof," "separate," and "unlike" emphasizes his singularity, both as a Nazarite among Philistines and as one "separate to" (31), singled out by, God, an identity that depends upon a steady self-sameness, on being "unlike *all others*" (815; emphasis mine). But with Manoa's oft-quoted assertion in mind, I would suggest that Samson's "disability" makes him both "like" and "unlike" Samson, that his blindness recalls who he is (an Israelite chosen by God to deliver his people) even as it renders him other to himself—a *failed* chosen one, elderly and infantile at once, both Dalila's "child / Helpless" (942–43) and "older than [Manoa's] age" (1489). But at the same time as Samson's blindness displaces him from himself, it also dismantles the boundary that distinguishes him from "all others," undermining Samson's claims to uniqueness. Disability serves as a reminder of particularity and of explanatory frameworks, complicating the universalizing tactics of culture. If *Samson Agonistes* denies the opposition between vision and blindness as well as revealing that binary opposition as an effect of discourse, so too does the poem challenge what Rogers calls "the hierarchical logic of political oppression."[43]

Michael Monbeck writes that "the idea that blind people are helpless has often been equated with the idea that they are fools, that they can easily be tricked, manipulated, or exploited by others in ways usually detrimental to themselves."[44] Richard III's corporeal abnormality is used to exemplify a human tendency toward exploitation and malignancy, for instance, but the blinding of Gloucester serves the opposite need, literalizing fears about being vulnerable, unable to "see through" subterfuge. So when Samson calls "that blindness worse than this" (418), he implies that a cognitive or perceptual inability to detect Dalila's deceit was more egregious than, but was also the root cause for, his current, physical sightlessness. Blindness is thus not only a reminder of the insufficiency of Samson's fortitude in the face of temptation but an indication as well of an inferiority narrated as "essential." Now, without the ability to direct his own gaze, Samson cannot experience himself as a conscious, ethically responsible subject; he feels barely alive, his body an inanimate "sepulchre, a moving grave" (102) that contains "a life half dead, a living death" (100). Lost sight becomes a form of double bondage, linking physical incapacity with deadly psychic torment. Trapped within himself, Samson becomes displaced, dies as Samson. To the degree that lack of visual contact limits interaction—which, in Samson's case, is nearly synonymous with violent overpowerment—a blind Samson cannot be Samson.

But his very affliction, that which renders him other to himself, could also conduct Samson to a different conception of self and to a radically new form of intersubjective contact. It is just this possibility, I think, that Dalila represents in the poem, in part because of the many resemblances between her position and his. As critics have frequently suggested, the parallels between Samson and Dalila extend from their own verbal patterns, and the words and images Milton uses to describe them, to their overdetermined roles as victims, betrayers, and potential champions of their people. Such correspondence works to deepen one's sense of the likeness between the two and establishes a kind of verbal foundation against which the moment of failed touch will take on even greater political and psychological significance. When the Messenger describes Samson's "eyes" as "fast fixed" (1637) in the final scene of the poem, "fixed" may mean (in addition to staring) "repaired," thus indicating that Samson has indeed been granted internalized, prophetic vision, with the "fast" immediacy of divine dispensation. But Samson's eyes may also be "fast fixed" in the sense of immobile or rigid, able to "see" in only one direction, according to one point of view. Though clearly the more subtextual connotation, the possibility that Samson's "vision" remains unchanged works against the traditional contention that he has been regenerated, or that his behavior at the temple is divinely inspired—as Butler contends, all attempts to "assess" the meaning of Samson's look and actions "are only speculation."[45] In the context of interpretive uncertainty, it is significant that the language used to demonstrate Samson's attitude precisely echoes the Chorus's earlier description of Dalila in the first moments of their encounter. In contrast to Samson's supine posture, sprawled "at random, carelessly diffused / With languished head unpropped" (118–19), Dalila's upright stance might seem a dramatic emblem of their spiritual states, staged to display her role in his downfall and to prefigure Samson's progress toward the temple, where his stand-up performance will literally bring down the "house."

Surprisingly, however, just as Samson will then stand "with *head* a while *inclined,* / And *eyes* fast *fixed*" (1636–37), Dalila now "stands and *eyes* [him] *fixed,* / About t' have spoke, but now, with *head declined* / . . . she weeps" (726–28; emphasis mine). To the extent that Samson's climactic action at the temple can be read as the eventual fulfillment of his foretold destiny (what Fish describes as "a single action so dazzling in its clarity and force that the moral structure of the universe comes clearly into view"),[46] what does the linguistic allusion to Dalila's prior posture serve to establish? Is the echo merely ironic, working to subordinate Dalila's specious and ultimately insubstantial "victory" over Samson to the latter's far more cataclysmic and righteous gesture? Or is it also possible that the interplay of language between Samson and Dalila sets up a circuity, rather than a linear causality, and disrupts the kinds of judgments that read their exchange as one step along the path toward redemption, so that all of Dalila's words and gestures must be counted as evidence of her self-interested desire for power?[47] The ambiguous repetition of "eyes . . . fixed" at the end of the play does more than simply invoke the earlier description of Dalila's eyes in order to imply that Samson has successfully discarded all that Dalila represents. Samson's eyes are no more fully "regenerated" in the temple scene than Dalila's eyes had conveyed malicious intent toward Samson in the beginning of their exchange. Rather, I believe, Samson continues to share something with Dalila. In the last moments of the poem, he has not fully defeated or discarded her—or, if he has, it is only because he has missed the opportunity to "see" what followed the moment of her "eyes fast fixed": not destruction, but touch; not separation from, but a desire for interaction with. For Dalila's "fast fixed" eyes lead not to devastating violence but instead to her efforts to communicate with Samson, to touch his hand—a slight gesture, as we will see, of enormous philosophical import.

In the face of Samson's refusal to hear or understand her—"In argument with men a woman ever / Goes by the worse, whatever be her cause" (903–4)—Dalila's perseverance becomes the measure of an ethical purpose unique to her in this text: her desire to *make contact* with Samson and to be recognized. Samson's blindness has already shifted him from the stable subject position of privileged Nazarite, for he is "change[d] beyond report" (117), and Dalila herself is already a transitional figure, a woman straddling lines of national allegiance. Here she asks Samson, given their mutual history, to "see" anew, to reconsider the significance of events and their respective roles and identities within those circumstances. Through Dalila, *Samson Agonistes* suggests that blindness is neither a failure nor a compensation but rather that it has instead the potential to *sensitize* Samson to the complexities of perception, meaning, and identity. In turn, Samson might discover that relief from feeling "deadened" lies not in renewed destruction but rather in thinking beyond the oppositional terms of warfare. Blindness could become a trope for perceiving the world and one's self within it in radically new terms, for a "leveling" tendency directed at the arbitrary establishment of social hierarchies. The poem suggests that only by un-writing the narrative of himself as "able-bodied" can Samson recognize *Dalila's* "separateness" and stop "seeing" her as an appendage either of himself or of an undifferentiated Philistine people. In this way, the temple event could be understood as a radically exaggerated and violent refusal of what Dalila offers Samson: parity, contact, understanding.

IV

The popular belief that deficiency in one sense leads to an amplification of others seems to be medically unproven, but it was nevertheless widely believed throughout seventeenth- and eighteenth-century Europe (and still is believed) that blind people had keener hearing and a heightened sense of touch. In two treatises on the body and soul written in 1644, the English physician Sir Kenelm Digby speculated that sharpening of the remaining senses was a necessary compensation for the "defect" of impairment.[48] A hundred years later, the French artist Sébastien Bourdon, describing Nicolas Poussin's painting *Christ Healing the Blind at Jericho* (1651), wrote that "they who have lost their Sight, have a more acute Hearing, and a more sensible Touch."[49] Both of these latter senses figure prominently in *Samson Agonistes*. Despite the poem's attention to Samson's loss of sight, much of its action hinges on the characters' ability to hear and to feel. Yet whereas Samson's dependence on hearing does seem to have finely attuned that faculty in him, normal hearing is not depicted as entirely beneficial; similarly, Samson experiences tactile sensation largely as a kind of torment. What each of these realms of bodily experience (hearing and touch in addition to vision) renders "readable" are the thresholds of subjectivity, and the way in which the body functions as a field of cultural narratives. Samson and Dalila are both liminal figures in the context of sound—both listen to and produce speech, both undergo the perils of hearing and of not being heard. But again Dalila, who is capable of being silent, emerges as the more mobile character, and again Samson denies the similarity of their experiences in terms of hearing. By foregoing the chance to recognize likeness even in difference, he holds fast to the old hierarchies.

In a study of representations of deafness in sixteenth- and seventeenth-century English writing, Jennifer Nelson and Bradley Berens point out that early modern culture was profoundly aural, with the societal importance of talking and listening evidenced by such diverse common practices as attending four-hour sermons or the public ritual of skimmingtons.[50] The ability to hear was so necessary to being informed about one's world—particularly if one were illiterate—that hearing was effectively constitutive of identity, and loss of hearing, conversely, so deleterious to the establishment of self that deaf people were considered less than human. "It should come as no surprise," write Nelson and Berens, "that in early modern England there are virtually no fully realized representations of deaf people."[51] Yet whereas actually being deaf might have relegated an individual to the margins of the civilized world, a temporary condition of deafness could, paradoxically, be taken on or wished for as a way of escaping the irritation or torment of hearing. According to Nelson and Berens, "there are abundant representations of deaf ears" in early modern literature, including sermons, pamphlets, and royal proclamations. This cultural use of "elective deafness" typically takes two forms, both of which reveal the way in which metaphoric loss of hearing reasserts social rank: someone in power may choose to "deafen" his (or, less often, her) ears against the entreaties of a subordinate, or a powerful figure could wish to flee from the world's noise. In both cases, deafness is willingly appropriated precisely because it is temporary, and the very act of shutting out the voices of others works not to isolate or diminish the deafened character (who would have suffered lesser status in actuality) but to underscore the privilege that allows for the assertion of control in the first place. The trope of deafness is thus not a realistic depiction of the experience of an authentically deaf individual but rather a representation of power, tied to the exercise and display of cultural status.[52]

Both of these forms of appropriating metaphorical deafness as an empowering—because momentary and chosen—condition appear in *Samson Agonistes*. First, Samson complains to the Chorus that despite the "loud" (248) tribute paid him by his own deeds, the Israelite governors "persisted deaf" (249); later, Samson himself is "more deaf" to Dalila's "prayers" than "winds and seas" (960–61), despite her entreaty that he "hear" her (766). In each case, disability is pretended as a way of distancing the self from an other who threatens to disturb social hierarchies by crossing thresholds of power; "playing deaf" becomes a way of insisting on difference and reasserting power dynamics, especially when, as in Samson's conversation with Dalila, the boundary between self and other has already been compromised. At the same time, the word *noise* constitutes something of a leitmotif in the poem. If hearing establishes and sustains "normal" identity even more crucially than sight, then it seems fitting that sound has more presence in *Samson Agonistes* than references to deafness. But whereas sound frequently precedes knowledge, the drama calls attention not to the advantages of hearing but rather to the dangers it so often presages. The Philistines generally, and not simply Dalila, are repeatedly associated with noise; so is Samson, in his act of shameful divulgence. The festival for Dagon grants Samson a reprieve from "popular noise" (16); the disaster at the Philistine temple is preceded by a "noise or shout" (1472); and Manoa and the Chorus nervously attempt, in rapid succession, to figure out the meaning of what they hear: Manoa cries, "O what noise? / . . . what hideous noise was that?" (1508–9), "Of ruin indeed methought I heard the noise" (1515), and the Chorus intones that "Blood, death, and deathful deeds are in that noise" (1513). More than simply an indicator of activity or society, noise seems usually to portend some form of ill in the poem, and the discomfited listeners are unable to close their ears.

Nelson and Berens argue that the silence of deafness is desirable only when it can be taken on and discarded as a function of power. Total silence would otherwise be intolerable, since an inability to hear was considered essentially indistinguishable from an inability to speak, which in turn "went hand-in-hand with an inability to reason, hand-in-hand with stupidity."[53] Yet in Milton's poem instances of unpleasant sound suggest something more complicated about "normal" audition—they suggest that although hearing might be necessary to maintain one's position as a fully legitimized subject within the bounds of the dominant culture, it also involves the individual in, and exposes him or her to, the complexities of interpretation. The difficulty of figuring out "what it *means*," as Fish writes of Samson's bowed head at the temple—and the fact that meaning is always subject to some "signifying construct"[54] that organizes such things as disconnected sounds into coherent narratives—is precisely what the disabled body makes apparent. By suggesting, in effect, that hearing is really *not* a certain method of receiving information, interacting with others, or ascertaining meaning, Milton deepens his poem's radical disruption of hegemonic "truth."

David Gay points out that *Samson Agonistes* "consists of dialogue in which words are the weapons of a spiritual warfare," and he also remarks that "speech is perhaps most intensely experienced in the condition of blindness."[55] Although Samson's blindness may not make him hear any more *accurately* (he "hear[s] the sound of words" but their "sense" is "Dissolve[d] unjointed" by "the air" before it "reach[es his] ear" [176–77]), he is nonetheless more dependent on his ability to hear; thus each interaction with Samson takes place through conversation. On one level, words are soothing—Manoa, for instance, counsels his son to "be calm, / And healing words from these thy friends admit" (604–5). But hearing can be a perilous enterprise, even for the sighted. The most obvious examples of the dangers of hearing are Samson's and Dalila's respective experiences of being beset by the petitions of others. Samson tells the Chorus that Dalila, "mustering all her wiles, / With blandished parleys, feminine assaults, / Tongue-batteries . . . surceased not day nor night" (402–4), that she might extract the secret of his strength. The "seal of silence" (49) under which Samson was to keep his pledge is broken not so much by action on Dalila's part as by the pressure of "importunity and tears" (51); "for a word, a tear" (200), Samson "divulged the secret gift of God / To a deceitful woman" (201–2). "She was not the prime cause," Samson agonizes further on, "but I myself, / Who vanquished with a peal of words (O weakness!) / Gave up my fort of silence to a woman" (234–36). What "silence" means to Samson is both not talking *and* not hearing; in effect, he wishes he could have been deaf, immune to the influence of Dalila's speech, which would in turn have rendered him mute. His own "shameful garrulity" (491), placed in the context of the general "noisiness" of the Philistines, ostracizes him; he merits contempt and deserves to be "avoided as blab" (495).

To be bombarded with unmediated sound, condemned to hear too much—unable to claim the power to turn off someone else's words, unable to ignore or "mishear" others—thus seems to be one of the most egregious signs of Samson's humiliation. Hearing becomes a kind of punishment, continually reminding Samson of his susceptibility to the seductions of sound. Samson's "fort of silence" describes his own silence, his own refusal to speak; yet its significance is bound up with the insinuating speech of others—so that his ability to protect that fort of silence has everything to do, if only implicitly, with how vulnerable he is to the sounds of others talking. If Samson gives in to the speech of others, he risks being "noisy," talking too much in the way that his tempters do. Because he could not deafen his ears, he gave into Dalila's entreaties and gave away his secret. (Indeed, as Irene Samuel once pointed out, Samson is *still* guilty of "shameful garrulity," "outtalking" the Chorus, Manoa, Dalila, and even the "windbag" Harapha.)[56] Hearing normally, then, becomes a kind of liability, a sign of vulnerability—and in a sense Samson's punishment is the continued sound of his own voice ringing in his ears. It is almost as if Samson would wish to be further disabled, or disabled differently—not blind, but deaf.

Dalila, for her part, testifies that her own magistrates and princes "Solicited, commanded, threatened, urged" (852) and "pressed" (854), with the priest "ever at [her] ear" (858). As is Samson, she is both a listener and a talker, but Dalila's experience of language shifts more fully than his: unlike any other character in the poem, Dalila is vulnerable to the sound of others' speech, a perpetrator of similarly seductive "noise," *and* capable of silence. She embodies the contradiction of words as both hurtful and healing, reminding us that no individual ever consistently occupies a position of either power or powerlessness, but characterizations of Dalila's words as "honeyed" (1066), or "cunningly" (819) disguising their aggression by appealing to Samson's loneliness or his continued sexual interest in her, are not neutral; the Chorus and Samson utter their judgments based on their own ideological loyalties. Yet Dalila is also the only figure in the text ever depicted as silent or depicted as choosing not to talk. For example, the words she might have spoken to Samson immediately upon arriving at the place where he sits "seem into tears dissolved" (729). By not speaking, even momentarily, Dalila allows Samson not to hear, in a reversal of their former dynamic that offers him the silence he cannot produce on his own. Later in their dialogue, Dalila tells Samson that she "combated in silence" (864) the panoply of arguments used by the Philistine lords to turn her against her husband. In both of these instances, Dalila's use of silence works in a way nearly opposite to that described by Nelson and Berens in their discussion of deaf ears, because as a Philistine and a woman Dalila is never fully in a position of power, and because her goal in each case is not to resolidify the borders of identity but rather to achieve, however tentatively, some form of connectedness and intimacy *across* boundaries of gender and nationality.

To be sure, there are no literally deaf people in *Samson Agonistes,* and to the degree that deafness is used as a metaphor for complex dynamics of power, Milton does not seem particularly concerned to imagine the real plight of the deaf in seventeenth-century England. At the same time, however, the fact that *hearing* comes to seem tenuous and unreliable, and unable to guarantee selfhood or status, contributes to the poem's larger interrogation of the ways in which cultural categories of being and meaning are deployed in the service of potentially repressive ideals. Through Samson's disabled physical self, which sees too little and hears too much, and through Dalila's body, "disabled" because of its gender as well as her marriage across lines of religion and nation, the text seems to imply that no truth of identity is ever wholly stable. By not recognizing the challenge posed by the fact of multiple perspectives—by refusing, in effect, to recognize his *own* disability—the subject position that Samson represents may never be able to hear; indeed, he will always remain "deaf" to the arguments of "the other side" (768).

V

I have been arguing that bodies coded as "different" serve to make visible the discursive imprints affecting *every* body, and that although Samson fiercely defends his status as "singular" against the risk of similarity to others, Dalila consistently manifests an ability to recognize likeness even across ideological boundaries. The most charged instance of this ability is her request to touch Samson's hand—an attempt to make contact that would again rupture, and in a profoundly intimate way, Samson's separateness. Samson is aroused to expressions of rage and anguish by physical sensation perhaps even more than by sound or the loss of sight,[57] so it makes sense that the threat of Dalila's touch elicits Samson's most violent outburst against her. Nowhere does he express relief, for example, that he can no longer be enticed by her beauty; it is the Chorus, not Samson himself, who claims that "beauty, though injurious, hath strange power" (1003), and when they announce her arrival, Samson reveals fear of her *physical* closeness: "let her not come near me" (725).

There is more at work here than Samson's fear that he will again succumb to a woman's sexual influence. Elizabeth Grosz writes that "the freak is an *ambiguous* being whose existence imperils categories and oppositions dominant in social life."[58] Dalila's desire to touch exemplifies respect for the simultaneity of sameness and difference, a paradox that Samson's disabled body also already literalizes. But by responding to her gesture with a warning that he will effectively "disable" her (to "tear [her] joint from joint" [953]), Samson denies the connection and holds stubbornly to a notion of identity irreconcilable with ambiguity or change.

Samson's first words at the appearance of Dalila imply that the conflicts of their relationship take place in a highly charged physical realm. He responds to the Chorus's introduction of her, "Dalila thy wife," with "My wife, my traitress, let her not come near me" (724–25). The apparent antithesis of "wife" and "traitress"—the one connoting loyalty and mutual affection, the other a betrayal of trust—exposes an ambivalence about Dalila and the extent of her presumed treachery. Samson seems invested in these terms as a single category, taking linguistic possession of them in a single, charged unit: "*My* wife, *my* traitress," bringing into contact with himself the very object he professes to shun. Samson's possessiveness intimates a reluctance to let go of whatever "wife" and "traitress" produce in him—and, by the seeming synonymity of the terms, whatever they have in common. By making Dalila Samson's wife, of course, Milton has raised the stakes of their connection; Dalila makes Samson a traitor to himself not simply because he reveals his secret but also to the extent that the emotional intensity and sexual intimacy of their spousal relationship threaten his "inexorable" and "self-severe" autonomy (827). Samson projects onto "[his] wife, [his] traitress" his anger at himself for what he feels when physically close to her—desire, love, a loss of self-defensiveness—even as his linguistic ownership suggests attachment to those very emotions, a continued desire for the very loss of self-unity implied by "traitress" as well as by "wife." (Note that "let her" immediately follows "traitress": "My wife, my traitress, let her not come near me.")

Dalila's final request of Samson, before her invocation of Deborah and Jael, signals a provocative return to this opening line. Where Samson seems to beg, "My wife, my traitress, let her not come near me," Dalila dismisses all that has passed in this exchange and asks, simply, "Let me approach at least, and touch thy hand" (951). She inverts the syntax of Samson's line, first requesting ("Let me"), then specifying ("touch thy hand"), a structural reversal that conveys the incompatibility of their attitudes. Dalila's desire to touch transforms the possessiveness of Samson's "my wife, my traitress" into the intimate image of hands touching—hinting at the even more reciprocal image of hands being held. Whereas Samson explodes outward, casting the burden of irreconcilable feelings onto Dalila in the form of prohibition ("let *her* not. . ."), Dalila allows desire in herself—a desire unattached in the poem to any ulterior motive—and asks him permission. The simplicity and clarity of the line have the force of truth; far from sounding like a sudden sexual invitation, the language is unadorned, the intonation quiet, what John Ulreich has called a "vulnerable passion."[59] Dalila's word "approach" is gentler, more cautious, than Samson's "come," connoting a sense of process by which the two can draw nearer to each other both physically and emotionally—a process furthered by the sense of circularity in Dalila's translation of the language Samson uses.

It is to the threat of nearness implied by that circularity, and to the genuineness of Dalila's desire to touch, that Samson rebounds with his angriest growl: "Not for thy life, lest fierce remembrance wake / My sudden rage to tear thee joint by joint. / At distance I forgive thee, go with that" (952–54). The enjambment on "wake" allows all the possible memories that Dalila's touch might elicit to pile up in the silence between lines. What does Samson want to ward off? It cannot be simply Dalila's presence, nor even the memory of her "betrayal," which has already been referred to time and again in the poem. What power could the feel of Dalila's hand have to arouse such violent anger? The very fact that Samson warns Dalila of this "remembrance wak[ing]" implies that he is already conscious of the potential impact of her touch—a consequence that is inadmissible to him—perhaps because it entails pleasure, desire, even longing. So intense a need to keep Dalila physically at a distance suggests, in fact, that were she closer to him, he might actually take her back. But there is more at stake here than masculine anxiety about the dissolution of erotic involvement. To allow the touch of Dalila's hand would be to accept the considerable ideological ramifications of renewed contact with a member of the opposing group, to penetrate once again, but now in full view of the instability of culturally narrated subjectivity, the barrier between them.

What makes Dalila's gesture so moving, I think, is that it seems so authentic—an act of genuine desire for contact, motivated by true affection rather than embittered aggressiveness. The resignation of "at least," signaling her awareness that her arguments have failed to appease her husband, and the tenderness of the touch, the symbolic meaning of the hand, suggest something far more emotionally gentle, and philosophically profound, than sexual domination or political treachery. Dalila's motives here seem full of integrity and culminate in a wish to touch his hand, to make contact, to restore something like human connection. Her verbal pleas have failed to move him, but her touch carries more radical potential, suggested by the fact that it is her physical gesture, and not her words, that provokes Samson to the brink of violence. When Samson dismisses her with "At distance I forgive thee, go with that" (954), he suggests that distance—remaining aloof, separate, unlike—is all he knows in terms of his relatedness to others. Dalila's desire to touch, however, seems to articulate a serious need to be "recognized," in the psychological sense, as a person—and not as a metonymy of her tribe, her nation, her "feigned religion" (872)—and a literal willingness to "reach out."

Once again, the combination of Samson's troubled body and the liminality captured by Dalila's touch (which Dalila herself also embodies) destabilizes the allegedly fixed differences between the two of them as signifiers of their cultures. It is not merely that Samson, as a Nazarite, successfully resists the seduction of a "forbidden" liaison, or that his repudiation of Dalila finally "returns" him to himself. Samson's disability brings into view the culturally enforced boundaries that would mark him as unique, but his uncompromising rejection of Dalila simply recapitulates the very hierarchical thinking whose political consequences the poem examines. Dalila brilliantly articulates the importance of her gesture in her own words:

> And love hath oft, well meaning, wrought much woe,
> Yet always pity or pardon hath obtained.
> Be not unlike all others, not austere
> As thou art strong, inflexible as steel.   (813–16)

What she seems to be encouraging Samson to recognize is the price of intolerance—political, religious, patriarchal. His repudiation of her stands, on an important level, as a sign of his inability to be "like," to find similarity in a world of difference. If the scriptural text makes such a polarity necessary, *Samson Agonistes* suggests that in the lived world of late-seventeenth-century England it may no longer be tenable. Dalila invites Samson to accept a form of interconnection that is neither condescending nurture nor an antagonistic contest that solves nothing (and would, indeed, simply perpetuate the cycle of violence and upheaval so baldly dramatized in the Judges story, as well as in England's own recent past). Herself a liminal figure—guilty and innocent, implicated and manipulated—Dalila invites Samson through her touch to acceptance of ambiguity, flexibility, change. The relationship between a female, Philistine Dalila, and a disabled Samson challenges the ontological "otherizing" that cultures perform, and that gendered and disabled bodies make especially visible. Samson explicitly calls Dalila "other" (387) when he distinguishes her from the woman at Timna, but I would suggest that the word carries a more loaded, political charge as well—Dalila *is* "other" from Samson. The radical potential of her desire to touch, I think, is akin to the difference between her word "unlike" and Samson's use of "other":

Dalila attempts to locate similarities in difference, whereas Samson insists only on the difference.

The extent to which Samson really is *"not* unlike all others," especially Dalila, is exemplified by systematic linguistic repetition throughout their conversation. Samson's assertion that he married a Philistine woman "to oppress / Israel's oppressors" (232–33) and "begin Israel's deliverance" (225) applies, by Dalila's nationality and religion, to her entrapment of a "common enemy" (856). Samson calls himself "no private but a person raised . . . To free my country" (1211–13); Dalila was pressured by the "public good" to which "Private respects must yield" (867–68). Samson claims to be moved by "impulse," Dalila says that "grave authority / Took full possession" of her (868–69). To Samson Dalila is an "accomplished snare" (230); she tells him to "Hear what assaults I had, what snares besides" (845). Both Dalila and Samson wish to "expiate," both speak of "pardon." But for Dalila, the double telling of Samson's secret (he to her, she to the Philistines) is an element of the past, an "event" (737) registered into the logbook of history. Her interest now is not to dwell on the painful details of what is, simply, a "fact" (736), or to emphasize dualities of crime and punishment, sin and repentance. Instead, she proceeds to investigate her own motives.[60] Samson's use of "expiate," on the other hand, demonstrates a typical kind of either-or thinking—when he tells Manoa, "let me . . . expiate, if possible, *my crime*" (488–90; emphasis mine), he completes the construction in stark dichotomies stripped of motivating or explanatory context.

Both Samson and Dalila use the term "fool" as they consider their roles in this ideological imbroglio. Samson calls himself "Fool, [to] have divulged the secret gift of God . . . Am I not sung and proverbed for a fool," "The mark of fool set on his front!" (201–3; 496). Later Dalila tells Samson, "I was a fool, too rash, and quite mistaken" (907). But although Samson's use of the word measures a palpable humiliation, an escalating, almost hysterical embarrassment that focuses on public determination of the significance of the event, Dalila's "fool" turns inward, as an index of a self caught between individualized motives and community responsibility. Both, too, appeal to "weakness" as a way of defining the impulses that instigated their behavior and of giving shape to their treatment of each other. But Dalila's alternating repetitions of "weakness" and "strength and safety" testify to her awareness of the complexity of multiple allegiances, showing that she feels vulnerable to Samson even as she hopes to protect him from "perilous enterprises" with her own people (804). Dalila urges Samson to join her in admitting weakness, to acknowledge their shared experience of conflicting desires and even identities: "To what I did thou show'dst me first the way," she tells him (781); "Let weakness then with weakness come to parle" (785). But Samson's response voices, through virulent invective against the enemy, the dualistic way in which he tries to control, and finally to deny, the ambiguity of his situation:

> weakness is thy excuse,
> And I believe it, weakness to resist
> Philistian gold: if weakness may excuse,
> What murderer, what traitor, parricide,
> Incestuous, sacrilegious, but may plead it?
> All wickedness is weakness: that plea therefore
> With God or man will gain thee no remission.
> But love constrained thee; call it furious rage
> To satisfy thy lust: love seeks to have love;
> My love how couldst thou hope, who took'st the way
> To raise in me inexpiable hate,
> Knowing, as needs I must, by thee betrayed?   (829–40)

The refrain of "weakness" pounds in opposition to successive repetitions of "love," as if love poses the greatest threat of contamination to the singularity by which Samson defines himself. In the progression of this passage, "weakness"—the inadmissible opposite of Samson's strength—turns quickly into "love"; love presses in upon his increasingly enraged rejection of Dalila's excuses, so that Samson seems unconsciously to confess the love he had as well as the agonizing loss of rigid self-control that love induced. In this context, Dalila's request to reach for his hand must serve as an unbearable reminder of the fragility of an identity founded on solitude and "unlikeness." That Dalila might actually come forward to touch Samson—that she already *has* touched him—proves the permeability of the barrier between them, a barrier that is both inflected by psychological urgency and invested in political and religious antagonisms.

Critics have argued that the poem gives us every reason to believe Dalila's emotions, her sense of bewilderment as well as the wish to be pardoned by Samson, just as we do not doubt Samson when he says of God, "His pardon I implore" (521).[61] John Steadman's claim that we disbelieve Dalila simply on the grounds that the "betrayer" deserves less "credence" than the "betrayed," a surprising oversimplification of the case, is disproved by what Joseph Wittreich calls the poem's many "countercurrents of female affirmation."[62] What Milton seems concerned to question is the very act of interpretation, the differing processes by which Samson and Dalila locate meaning in past events. In a poem where the most—perhaps only—physical act, Samson's temple feat, is only related by the Messenger, whose information is in part hearsay, the reliability and implications of Samson's and Dalila's memories and the perception of truth are continually interrogated.[63] Perhaps this is why Dalila's presence stands out in such high relief: the movement of her speech seems to rush toward that suddenly and quietly profound instant: "Let me approach at least, and touch thy hand. . . . ." She is in a different kind of motion, too, struggling to understand herself with an emphasis on reinterpretation, a process pointedly juxtaposed to Samson's dichotomized thinking. Steadfast in his position, Samson remains unswayed by Dalila's challenge to his point of view, persistently disagreeing with or contradicting her from within his own stubbornly defended frame of reference. So when he tells Dalila, "thou and I long since are twain" (929), he seems to refer to the ideological abyss between them even while unwittingly affirming that they are paired, two of a kind.

The last words of Dalila's speech have seemed to some readers to confirm her repugnant self-interest: "At this whoever envies or repines, / I leave him to his lot, and like my own" (995–96). Yet by another way of reading, Dalila manages one last reiteration of Samson's connection to her. She may assert, on the one level, that she will "prefer" her circumstances to those of her detractors, but on another level she seems also to suggest that "his" lot (Samson's, implicitly) is "like" hers—similar. The recurrent parallels between Samson and Dalila repeatedly disturb Samson's own efforts to position them as polarized antagonists. But where Samson's disabled body seems to defy explanation, Dalila's wordy self-defense has rendered her almost overly intelligible to critics, as if more than one motivation were proof of insincerity, as if she is merely a chain of signifiers endlessly unraveling. In John Guillory's words, Dalila "possesses no consistent identity but displays a shifting mask, the moral sign of deviousness or concealment."[64] I would disagree that the poem's foregrounding of conflicting perspectives leaves us with the impossibility of stable identity; such a claim would disregard the experience of bodily specificity that both feminist and disability theory have taught us to recall. Nor is Dalila merely a symbol, whether for the heroism of Jael and Deborah or the transgressive uncontainability signalled by women's "fluid" bodies, which Samson is said to mimic or reject in his final act at the temple. I want to go further, to suggest that Dalila is an agent of change within the action of the text itself, a boundary-crossing presence that defies ideological intractability. Even more potently than her words, Dalila's singular request to touch reformulates the kind of dualistic thinking—the "simple absolutes" to which even an ambiguously embodied Samson is repeatedly prone—inherent in acts of cultural violence.[65]

VI

Through his portrayal of a physically "freakish" Samson, Milton imperils categories. Because disability is illegible within cultural codes of corporeal and psychological normality, Samson's disabled body is inconsistently interpreted, offering up a range of meanings to the Chorus, Manoa, Harapha, the gathered crowd of Philistines, and the reader; and even the Messenger cannot accurately describe nor interpret Samson's facial expression at the pillars. In Laura Lunger Knoppers's words, "The signs of the body . . . remain subject to appropriation and contradictory interpretation."[66] Samson's disability is *rhetorically* created, at once a mark of identity and of the loss of identity, the sign of Samson's failure to uphold the pledge that makes him "like" himself, yet also what guarantees him as Samson, precisely because lack of sight reveals the seriousness of that pledge. Thus Samson escapes narrative constructing, even as he can only be perceived through narrative—"sung and proverbed" (203), the stuff of "copious legend, or sweet lyric song" (1737). He and his body are diverse signs.

But disability can also serve to stimulate access to different modes of recognition, and Dalila's request to touch signals the possibility of an alternate response to corporeal difference. Rather than trying to contain Samson's blindness in an explanatory narrative of gift or scourge, Dalila's willingness to touch Samson renders him incredibly *ordinary*—simply a body in need of care, like all bodies, which eventually age, suffer impairment, become dependent. More importantly, it represents an effort toward mutuality, a desire to establish connection even as she recognizes Samson's difference from her. Because the setting of *Samson Agonistes* so clearly echoes the circumstances of radical Protestants in Restoration England, while also evoking personal details of Milton's own life—the political tensions of his first marriage, his revolutionary activities, his blindness, his imprisonment—we are encouraged to read Samson's situation as a representation of persecuted regicides who struggled to hold onto a compromised faith. Rejecting Dalila becomes a sign of triumph over the "blindness" of self-involved temptation and a defiant refusal to succumb to the weight of tyranny and oppression.[67] But it is also possible that the choice Dalila offers Samson is to *accept,* rather than to reject. At the moment of her attempt to touch, the text overlays Samson's liminal body and Dalila's generous intent to complicate just the sort of categorical intransigence at work in Restoration politics. *Samson Agonistes* thus seems to me an expression of neither triumphant saintly aggression nor defeat and resignation. It offers instead an emphatic call for what Milton called "perpetuall progression" (YP 2:543)—the intellectual, spiritual freedom one can achieve by resisting received opinions of "conformity and tradition." Samson's inability to acknowledge his own disability—his contingency, his rootedness within certain ideological formulations—shuts down the possibility of mutual recognition and understanding. The poem is thus also a striking portrayal of a failed attempt to reach across boundaries and make contact with others who represent, on some level, aspects of ourselves.

Irene Samuel once urged readers to "take Samson as protagonist of the tragedy, but not our sole concern, allowing the other agents to matter too, and not only as they provide Samson's occasions."[68] I would argue that Milton urges us to consider Dalila's effort to touch—along with Samson's refusal of that offering—as a powerful symbol of both the hopefulness and the failure of the Commonwealth years, depicting a desire to mitigate rigid oppositions without withdrawing into quietism or exploding in radical vengeance. Corporeal experience in *Samson Agonistes* emphasizes indeterminacy, destabilizes hierarchies of power and configurations of gender, and insists that the toleration of difference is possible—if only one could accept the touch of another's hand. Both Dalila's touch and Samson's disabled body transgress the boundaries that tend to stabilize identity, and in this they share a power to force separate individuals to recognize each other in ways that might escape oppositional narratives. For where does touch take place if not in a liminal space of simultaneous separateness and union? And what is disability if not a rebuke to the smug isolation of society's dominant ideal? To take Dalila's hand would be to contest a fundamental ideology underwriting cultural prejudice, one neatly (and perhaps inadvertently) articulated by the Chorus as "safest he who stood aloof" (135).

St. John's University

NOTES

I am grateful to Albert Labriola for his support of this essay. I owe a special debt to Ashley Cross for her thoughtful questions and comments on an earlier version.

1. "To Mr Cyriak Skinner Upon His Blindness," *John Milton: Complete Shorter Poems*, ed. John Carey (London, 1971). All references to Milton's shorter poetry will be to from this edition and cited parenthetically by line number in the text.

2. See also Milton's self-description in the *Second Defense*, where he writes of his eyes that "so little do they betray any external appearance of injury that they are as unclouded and bright as the eyes of those who most distinctly see." The verb "betray" is, of course, a telling one. *The Second Defense of the People of England*, in *John Milton: Complete Poems and Major Prose*, ed. Merritt Y. Hughes (Indianapolis, 1957), 824. The Yale edition translates the first part of this passage as "And yet they have as much the appearance of being uninjured." Both versions suggest the indeterminacy of bodily markers. *A Second Defense of the English People*, in *Complete Prose Works of John Milton*, 8 vols., ed. Don M. Wolfe et al. (New Haven, 1953–82), vol. 4, part 1, 538–686, 583. Subsequent references to Milton's prose will be to this edition and hereafter cited in the text as YP, followed by volume and page number.

3. See Timothy J. Burbery, "The Representation of Samson's Eyes in *Samson Agonistes*," in *English Language Notes* 35 (December 1997): 27–32.

4. Rosemarie Garland Thomson, *Extraordinary Bodies: Figuring Physical Disability in American Culture and Literature* (New York, 1997), 40.

5. Again, the *Second Defense* makes the same point, that the "misfortune" of blindness can be "endure[d]" not only because it can "befall any mortal" but more specifically as one of the "potent gifts" (or as Hughes translates, "superior endowments" [824]) granted to men like Tiresias, Phineus, and so forth (YP 4:584).

6. *John Milton: Paradise Lost,* ed. Alastair Fowler (London, 1991), 3:199–201.

7. Nicholas Mirzoeff, "Blindness and Art," in *The Disability Studies Reader,* ed. Lennard J. Davis (New York, 1997), 384.

8. Lennard J. Davis, *Enforcing Normalcy: Disability, Deafness, and the Body* (London, 1995), 11.

9. Peter Stallybrass, "Patriarchal Territories: The Body Enclosed," in *Rewriting the Renaissance: The Discourses of Sexual Difference in Early Modern Europe,* ed. Margaret W. Ferguson, Maureen Quilligan, and Nancy J. Vickers (Chicago, 1986), 123–42.

10. Thomson, *Extraordinary Bodies,* 6.

11. Thomson, *Extraordinary Bodies,* 7.

12. Rosemarie Garland Thomson, ed., *Freakery: Cultural Spectacles of the Extraordinary Body* (New York, 1996), 3.

13. Thomson, *Freakery,* 1–2.

14. See Michael E. Monbeck, *The Meaning of Blindness: Attitudes toward Blindness and Blind People* (Bloomington, 1973), 28.

15. Aristotle, *The Politics,* trans. J. A. Sinclair (Baltimore, 1964), 294.

16. Quoted in Margaret A. Winzer, "Disability and Society before the Eighteenth Century," in *The Disability Studies Reader,* 75–109, 87.

17. Winzer, "Disability and Society," 91.

18. Robert Bogdan, *Freak Show: Presenting Human Oddities for Amusement and Profit* (Chicago, 1998), 286n. 9.

19. See Anthony Fletcher, *Gender, Sex, and Subordination in England 1500–1800* (New Haven, 1995), 72.

20. For various accounts of early modern fascination with monstrous bodies, see Regina Schwartz and Valeria Finucci, eds., *Desire in the Renaissance: Psychoanalysis and Literature* (Princeton, 1994), 6; Winzer, "Disability and Society"; Jennifer L. Nelson and Bradley S. Berens, "Spoken Daggers, Deaf Ears, and Silent Mouths: Fantasies of Deafness in Early Modern England," in *The Disability Studies Reader,* 52–74; Thomson, *Freakery;* Mark Breitenberg, *Anxious Masculinity in Early Modern England* (Cambridge, 1996); Thomas Laqueur, *Making Sex: Body and Gender from the Greeks to Freud* (Cambridge, Mass., 1990); and Fletcher, *Gender, Sex, and Subordination in England 1500–1800,* who cites a "fascination with hermaphrodites" (40).

21. Keith Thomas, *Man and the Natural World* (New York, 1983), 38.

22. Paul Semonin, "Monsters in the Marketplace: The Exhibition of Human Oddities in Early Modern England," in *Freakery,* 72–73.

23. Quoted in Semonin, "Monsters in the Marketplace," 72.

24. Sir John Davies, *Nosce Teipsum. This oracle expounded in two elegies. 1. Of humane knowledge. 2. Of the soule of man, and the immortalitie thereof* (London, printed for I. Standish, 1608). Quoted in Frances Barasch, introduction to Thomas Wright's *A History of Caricature and Grotesque in Literature and Art* (New York: Frederick Ungar, 1968; orig. 1865), xxx.

25. Thomson, *Extraordinary Bodies,* 10.

26. David T. Mitchell and Susan L. Snyder, eds., *The Body and Physical Difference: Discourses of Disability* (Ann Arbor, Mich., 1997), 14.

27. Elizabeth Grosz, "Intolerable Ambiguity: Freaks as/at the Limit," in *Freakery,* 65.

28. Richard makes his marginality explicit in his famous speech of self-description, calling himself "rudely stamp'd," "curtail'd of this fair proportion, / Cheated of feature by dissembling nature, / Deform'd, unfinish'd, sent before my time," "scarce half made up," "lamely and unfashionable." Even "dogs bark at me," Richard confesses pathetically, as if that were the most pointed evidence of his liminal, barely human status. See 1.2.14–23.

29. David Mitchell, "Modernist Freaks and Postmodernist Geeks," in *The Disability Studies Reader,* 359.

30. John Rogers, "The Secret of *Samson Agonistes,*" in *Milton Studies* 33, ed. Albert C. Labriola and Michael Lieb (Pittsburgh, 1997), 127.

31. George F. Butler, "Donne's *Biathanatos* and *Samson Agonistes:* Ambivalence and Ambiguity," in *Milton Studies* 34, ed. Albert C. Labriola (Pittsburgh, 1997), 208, 211.

32. Mitchell, "Modernist Freaks and Postmodernist Geeks," 359.

33. Jeffrey Baker, "The Deaf Man and the Blind Man," *Critical Survey* 8 (1996): 265.

34. Oedipus's Chorus concurs: "Dreadful indeed for men to see," they intone, since it exposes men to "sight[s] so full of fear." Sophocles, *Oedipus Rex,* trans. Dudley Fitts and Robert Fitzgerald (New York, 1969), "Éxodus," 68.

35. See, for example, David Loewenstein's "The Revenge of the Saint: Radical Religion and Politics in *Samson Agonistes,*" in *Milton Studies* 33, ed. Albert C. Labriola and Michael Lieb (Pittsburgh, 1996), which uses the word five times in the first three pages. Loewenstein's important discussion of the text's "militant religious radicalism" situates *Samson* within a context of revolutionary Protestant discourse which emphasized an internalized experience of the Spirit.

36. Joseph Wittreich makes substantially the same claim about Samson and Dalila's marriage: "If the propriety of their marriage is questioned, whether it was indeed sanctioned by God, that questioning extends to other episodes, most notably the temple disaster, where divine inspiration had also been claimed for Samson . . . Within the text of *Samson Agonistes,* there seems to be a counterstatement for every statement." *Feminist Milton* (Ithaca, 1987), 134.

37. Joseph Wittreich, *Interpreting Samson Agonistes* (Princeton, 1986), xiii, 327.

38. Stanley Fish, "Spectacle and Evidence in *Samson Agonistes,*" *Critical Inquiry* 15 (spring 1989): 572.

39. Butler, "Donne's *Biathanatos* and *Samson Agonistes,*" 208, 212.

40. David Gay, " 'Honied Words': Wisdom and Recognition in *Samson Agonistes,*" in *Milton Studies* 29, ed. Albert C. Labriola (Pittsburgh, 1993), 53.

41. "Milton carefully questions," Butler continues, "whether every 'rousing motion' felt by Samson is an instance of divine inspiration, and whether true inspiration may be determined" ("Donne's *Biathanatos* and *Samson Agonistes,*" 212).

42. Loewenstein, "The Revenge of the Saint," 162.

43. Rogers, "The Secret of *Samson Agonistes,*" 125.

44. Monbeck, *The Meaning of Blindness,* 35.

45. Butler, "Donne's *Biathanatos* and *Samson Agonistes,*" 212.

46. Fish, "Spectacle and Evidence in *Samson Agonistes,*" 572.

47. See John Guillory, "Dalila's House: *Samson Agonistes* and the Sexual Division of Labor," in *Rewriting the Renaissance,* 106–22.

48. Sir Kenelm Digby, *Two treatises: in the one of which, the nature of bodies; in the other, the nature of mans soule, is looked into: in way of discovery of the immortality of reasonable soules* (London: printed for I. Williams, 1645).

49. Quoted in Mirzoeff, "Blindness and Art," 383.

50. Skimmingtons were public processions, usually accompanied by loud music and the banging of pots and pans, that ridiculed henpecked husbands and shrewish wives.

51. Nelson and Berens, "Spoken Daggers, Deaf Ears, and Silent Mouths," 53.

52. See Winzer, "Disability and Society," esp. 102–4, and Davis, *Enforcing Normalcy,* for thorough discussions of deafness, the Deaf, and seventeenth- and eighteenth-century European advances in the study and education of deaf people.

53. Martha L. Edwards, "Deaf and Dumb in Ancient Greece," in *The Disability Studies Reader,* 35.

54. Fish, "Spectacle and Evidence in *Samson Agonistes,*" 585.

55. Gay, "Wisdom and Recognition in *Samson Agonistes,*" 38–39.

56. Irene Samuel, "*Samson Agonistes* as Tragedy," in *Calm of Mind: Tercentenary Essays on 'Paradise Regained' and 'Samson Agonistes' in Honor of John S. Diekhoff,* ed. Joseph Anthony Wittreich Jr. (Cleveland, 1971), 235–57, 246.

57. That Samson is keenly sensitive to touch and to the feel of things on his skin is made immediately evident in the poem by the "choice of sun or shade" that characterizes the bank toward which he is led. More drastically, he experiences his body as a place of exquisite torment, so that his "griefs . . . pain [him] / As a lingering disease," the body's decay (617–18), and his thoughts, "armed with deadly stings / Mangle [his] apprehensive tenderest parts, / Exasperate, exulcerate, and raise / Dire inflammation" (623–26).

58. Grosz, "Intolerable Ambiguity," 57.

59. John Ulreich Jr., "'Incident to All Our Sex': The Tragedy of Dalila," in *Milton and the Idea of Woman,* ed. Julia M. Walker (Chicago, 1988), 189.

60. Ulreich argues that Dalila calls forth a psychologically compelling, intellectually vigorous range of influences for her actions, that she is able to "articulate her passion constructively," to "shape her feelings" ("The Tragedy of Dalila," 200).

61. See, for example, Ulreich, "The Tragedy of Dalila," 186, and Susanne Woods, "How Free Are Milton's Women?" in *Milton and the Idea of Woman,* 29.

62. John Steadman, "Efficient Causality and Catastrophe in *Samson Agonistes,*" in *Milton Studies* 28, ed. Wendy Furman, Christopher Grose, and William Shullenberger (Pittsburgh, 1992), 212; and Wittreich, *Feminist Milton,* 119.

63. As Wittreich writes in *Interpreting Samson Agonistes,* "there is no presiding narrator" (119) or "totalized narrative" (125), only characters who disguise or disfigure the truth. "[T]he narrative passages in [the poem] are retrospective" (120), imposing meaning after the fact. See 119–35 in particular.

64. Guillory, "Dalila's House," 114.

65. Daniel T. Lochman, "'If there be aught of presage': Milton's Samson as Riddler and Prophet," in *Milton Studies* 22, ed. James D. Simmonds (Pittsburgh, 1987), 195–216, 197.

66. Laura Lunger Knoppers, "'This So Horrid Spectacle': *Samson Agonistes* and the Execution of the Regicides," *ELR* 20 (autumn 1990): 504.

67. Compare Knoppers's idea that it is Samson's *rejection* of Dalila that "revers[es] the action which made him 'Traitor to myself,'" and thus has a "positive effect" that restores him to himself ("*Samson Agonistes* and the Execution of the Regicides," 499).

68. Samuel, "*Samson Agonistes* as Tragedy," 251.

"NOT LESS RENOWN'D THAN JAEL": HEROIC CHASTITY IN *SAMSON AGONISTES*

Paula Loscocco

M UCH OF THE RECENT WORK on John Milton's *Samson Ago-nistes* has focused on the compellingly complex figure of Dalila, and on how Samson's late and often mysterious words and actions make whatever austere sense they do only in light of his bitterly comprehensive divorce from everything Dalila represents.[1] I too understand what I see as Samson's godly regeneration as the fruit of his repudiation of Dalila, but my understanding is tempered by what I see as the transfer of valuable goods that takes place between Dalila and Samson during the marital agon that constitutes their mutual divorcing. Specifically, I think that Dalila, quite despite herself, embodies more spiritual value and so represents more of a godly opportunity (for Samson) than has been granted her, and that while Samson rejects her with stunning violence, he does not reject the one supremely valuable thing that she inadvertently offers. More precisely, he does not reject the one thing that Samson's God (through Milton) allows Samson to take away from his interaction with her, even if true ownership is never granted to Dalila herself. For at the very moment of her defiantly decisive turning away from Samson, the harlot/wife Dalila is the unlikely vehicle through which a potent form of biblical virtue enters the poem—a virtue that first manifests itself as a severe kind of male heroism but that slowly, silently, invisibly metamorphoses into a purifying and uniquely powerful species of female chastity. This virtue persists in *Samson* long after Dalila has gone, and Samson immediately (if imperceptibly) claims it as his own, as legitimately acquired marital property that becomes for him the rediscovered grounds of his final recovery of Nazarite separation to God.

☙

The road to Samson's recovery of what might be called heroic chastity may have begun two decades before the publication of *Samson Agonistes*, with a writer at the farthest reaches of Milton's acquaintance.[2] During what were for him the dark days of the English republic, John Paulet, Marquis of Winchester, translated (among other things) Pierre Le Moyne's 1647 *La Galerie*

des femmes fortes, publishing it in 1652 as *The Gallery of Heroick Women.*
Whether or not Milton was familiar with Winchester's volume—we know
only that he wrote his 1631 *Epitaph on the Marchioness of Winchester* for
Winchester's first wife, Jane Savage—the close parallels between his and
Winchester's readings of biblical passages make the *Gallery* a suggestive analogue for Milton's *Samson.* Given what I will show to be specific textual overlap between these two works, overlap involving contemporary and polemically charged ways of deploying particular figures and stories, we might want
to raise (if not answer) the question of whether Milton knew the *Gallery.*

Renowned by royalist partisans as the "great loyalist" for his service to
Henrietta Maria, his three-year resistance to a parliamentary siege of his
estate, and his fifteen-year imprisonment by the republican government,
Winchester seems to have been ideologically drawn to Le Moyne's *Galerie.*
Le Moyne had written his book as a valedictory tribute to Anne of Austria,
Queen Regent of France during the minority of Louis XIV: after praising her
for having held France together from the death of her husband, Louis XIII,
to the impending Peace of Westphalia, he identifies female governance as a
stop-gap measure that will come to a happy end with the imminent majority
of Anne's sons.[3] The implicit and sexualized parallel between the French
Regency and the English Interregnum—in which royalist men found themselves excluded from power, dependent on women to conduct their legal
and financial affairs, and desperate for a restoration that would convert civil
emasculation into renewed political potency—becomes manifest as Winchester works his way through Le Moyne's book.

In his final chapter on Mary Queen of Scots, for example, Winchester
deploys terms that in 1652 England necessarily invoke the fate of Charles I.
Bitterly lamenting the "Tragical Spectacle" of being forced "to see three
Kingdoms dishonoured upon a Scaffold: [and] To see a Head which hath
born two Crowns, laid under the Ax of an Executioner," he bemoans Mary's
execution as a "Tragedy" that "is not only Inhumane but Monstrous" and
shameful: "*England* applauds this horrid Act, which will be deplored by all
Europe."[4] And in his "Translators Address," Winchester frankly asserts that
though he presently "find[s] no Queen here," he fervently hopes that if the
Gallery's lessons are "well applyed" by the "Ladies of this [English] Nation"—ladies who are both his addressed readers and the effective regents of
their husbands' involuntary minorities—then "Crowns" might one day return
to "this land of trial" (*Gallery,* n.p.). Given the pointedly polemical resonances of the *Gallery* in post-regicidal Britain, I refer in the pages that follow
exclusively to Winchester's 1652 English translation, which closely follows Le
Moyne's 1647 French original.

What makes the *Gallery* particularly suggestive in terms of Milton's *Samson* is how the book's political agenda causes it to disrupt and reconfigure traditional ways of using gender and sexuality to define what it calls "Heroick Vertue" (*Gallery,* 35).[5] This is especially apparent in the book's first few chapters, where biblical heroines are unreservedly praised for using deceitful female wiles to defeat men who are God's and their country's enemies. This may explain Winchester's peculiar absorption with the *Gallery:* a disenfranchised royalist grasping at the best (biblical) straws he can find, he seems to resonate to the descriptions of women like Jael (who in Judges 4 thrusts a tent-stake through the temples of sleeping Sisera to secure an Israelite victory) or Judith (who in the Apocrypha beheads the drunken Canaanite leader, Holofernes, for the same reason). Both heroines rise above the restrictions of their station to take vengeful action against political foes, and they do so righteously and to godly acclaim.

Whatever their (evident) political appeal to Winchester, however, the most remarkable aspect of both stories is their subversion of the traditional antifeminist trope of a seductive woman ensnaring an innocent man. Judith uses all of her formidable "Beauty and Graces" and her "attractives [*sic*] and graceful charms" to trick and murder Holofernes. And Winchester goes out of his way to report that her beauty is "bold and victorious," her graces "magnanimous and conquering," her attractives "violent," and her charms "forcible," adding that "She is equally dangerous and graceful, and wounds even by that which delights: Not onely her eyes are piercing, and the lightning which God hath placed in them doth dazel the sight; but even her very feet contributed to the victory, and the tyes of her Buskins have suprized *Holofernes* by the eye, and enslaved his Soul" (*Gallery,* 30). Nevertheless, Holofernes alone is held responsible for a sexual self-deception that is mercilessly traced to its roots in his own emasculating carnality. "[B]ound up" and "more fastned by the fume of wine and the vapours of sleep, then he would be by six great cords and as many chains," the great (and distinctly Samson-like) captain dreams of a compliantly "mincing" Judith, who is neither more nor less than the projection of his own erotic fantasies: "*Judeth* is there alone what War, Glory, and *Nabuchondonezer* were before. But it is not this [true] *Judeth* whom vertue, zeal, and these Angels have brought: It is a *Judeth,* not unlike a cheating dream, which hath transformed a Heroess into a mincing Dame; and this mincing and imaginary *Judeth* shall be suddenly overthrown by the true and chaste one" (31–32). That Holofernes is undone by his own effeminate carnality, and Judith's devastatingly potent heroism secures an Israelite victory, clarifies the gendering of Winchester's argument here: Judith's example "teacheth men that Heroick Vertue proceeds from the Heart, and not the Sex" (35), and "Women are advertised, that [because] they have Hearts of the same matter, and as well derived as those of Men," they are capable of the same kind of "Heroick Vertue" (37). Carnal self-imprisonment transforms the strongest soldier into an effective woman, and an heroically virtuous woman guards a "Hero's *Soul*" within her "Brest" (21).

Winchester's portrayal of Jael is even more radical in the gendered implications of the heroism it describes, because it figures— and righteously defends—godly and Israelite heroism as a political betrayal that is grounded, even more sharply than with Judith, upon female sexual treachery. Fallen and dying, Sisera looks up to see a Jael whose bloody act "adds new lustre to her eyes, and a second grace to her face":

His eyes, which to him had been ill Advisors and unfaithful guards, and had suffered themselves to be suprised by beauty and sleep, bewail the mortal errour they had committed, and seem willing to cast forth with their blood and tears the pleasing poyson which they had taken in from the looks of *Jahel:* Besides they turn up and down in their last pains, as if they sought her out to reproach her of Infidelity; And the very sight of *Debora* and *Barac* hapning to be present at this Tragick spectacle increases their torment and begets in him a second confusion: The victory of his Enemies proves a torment to him. (*Gallery,* 19–20)

As with Judith, Winchester here defends not "Tragick" Sisera but ostensibly treacherous Jael, first on practical grounds, and then on moral and ultimately religious grounds. Yes, he concedes, women have "some dangerous charities and courtesies whereof we [men] must beware," but this only explains why "sometimes the presence of Women have defeated those who could not be overcome by strategems or armed Legions. . . . This Woman was worth an Armie" (22). And though he grants that her "breach of faith seems in that action very evident; [and] cabinet and chamber-declaimers cannot fail to fill their Common places therewith, and to compose a piece against the infidelity of women," he insists that such hostile responses represent not just an error but an irreligious repudiation of the "holy Ghost himself," who "inspired" Jael "with a prophetick mouth" to heroic action:

There was . . . prudence and conduct, addresse and courage in this action of *Jahel;* and particularly fidelity which is questioned was herein couragious and magnanimous: It was fortified with zeal, and consecrated to Religion. . . . I know very well that she could not engage unto them [Sisera and the Canaanites] a second faith against the first which she owed to God against the Law of her forefathers and to the ruine of that holy nation: A treaty of this nature had been an Apostacie of State and Religion: and she could not have kept her word without the breach of her faith, without betraying her brethren, without sinning against God and *Moses.* (24)

Contrary to expectations and appearances, then, and precisely like Judith, Jael performed an act of political-qua-sexual treachery that Winchester insists is "an Heroick Act of fidelity towards God whom she obeyed" (25).[6]

•?

The parallel between the *Gallery*'s justification of its heroines' murderous breaches of sexual and political faith, and Dalila's defense of what Samson vehemently denounces as "wedlock-treachery endangering life,"[7] is a suggestive one, especially when we consider that no such parallel can be drawn between *Samson* and the scriptural accounts upon which the *Gallery* is based. This is particularly evident in the case of Jael, whom Milton's Dalila forcefully invokes in her final speech. In Judges 4, Jael only offers Sisera refuge, on the basis of the alliance between her husband, Heber the Kenite, and Jabin, the King of Hazor; her breach of faith, consequently, is solely a breach of the laws of hospitality. In the (Genevan) Apocrypha, by contrast, Judith prays to God for "deceit of . . . lippes" (Judith 9:10), she goes to Holofernes dressed literally to kill (10:3–5), Holofernes's heart is predictably "rauished" at the sight of her calculated beauty (12:16), and she later reports triumphantly to the Israelites that her "countenance hathe deceiued him to his destruction" (13:16).[8] If Winchester departs from biblical precedent by transferring the motif of sexual treachery from its source in Judith to the otherwise innocent story of Jael, however, so in his own way does Milton. As I indicate below, Milton embeds Jael within Dalila's spectacular performance of a betrayal whose sexual structure corresponds to that of Judith's, even as the debased moral, political, and religious meaning of Dalila's actions is represented as the spiritual inverse of the exalted value that both the Apocrypha and Winchester attribute to Judith's actions.

As the following discussion suggests, Milton allows Dalila to incorporate Jael (and, less directly, Judith) into her self-defense, in ways that recall the polemically motivated Winchester, for several historically specific reasons. First, doing so allows Milton (through Samson) forcefully to reject the royalist politics that contemporary portrayals of Judith and Jael, including but not limited to Winchester's, so often embodied,[9] a politics that the republican Milton necessarily understands as idolatrous, carnal, and effeminate.[10] Secondly, bringing these biblical heroines into his drama enables him quietly to retain (for Samson) the nevertheless immensely valuable and attractive model of implicitly masculine heroic virtue that underlies such politically abhorrent characterizations. Finally, these heroines free Milton silently to open a door to the very different—and distinctly feminine—virtue of heroic chastity, a chastity that emerges in *Samson* as a supremely potent force, arguably motivating and informing all of Samson's subsequent actions and inactions, speeches and silences.

At the end of her and Samson's marital agon, in what is her final speech in Milton's poem, Dalila meditates upon the relativity of mortal fame, invoking Jael as she does so:

> My name perhaps among the Circumcis'd
> In *Dan*, in *Judah*, and the bordering Tribes,
> To all posterity may stand defam'd,
> With malediction mention'd, and the blot
> Of falsehood most unconjugal traduc't.
> But in my country where I most desire,
> In *Ekron, Gaza, Asdod*, and in *Gath*
> I shall be nam'd among the famousest
> Of Women, sung at solemn festivals,
> Living and dead recorded, who to save
> Her country from a fierce destroyer, chose
> Above the faith of wedlock bands, my tomb
> With odors visited and annual flowers.
> Not less renown'd than in Mount *Ephraim*,
> *Jael*, who with inhospitable guile
> Smote *Sisera* sleeping through the Temples nail'd.   (975–90)

The parallels between Winchester's Jael, closely allied as she is to the apocryphal Judith, and Milton's Dalila, finally identified here with the biblical Jael, are illuminating. Like Winchester's Judith and (especially) Jael, Dalila both raises and dismisses the charge of female sexual deception, acknowledging that her actions will be described by some as "falsehood most unconjugal" and so "defam'd, / With malediction" as a "blot," while simultaneously denying this reading in favor of a more heroic and salvific one. Also like Winchester's Jael, Dalila justifies her heroism by asserting the primacy—"Above the faith of wedlock bands"—of what she had earlier described as "all the bonds of civil Duty / And of Religion" (853–54). Finally and more generally, as a woman whose inner fortitude manifests itself in violently heroic action and whose godly and national motivations render her exempt from sexual or moral accounting, Dalila recalls those royalist heroines whose external femininity figures (male) political disempowerment and whose inner (and male) fortitude reveals their status as tropes, not of women, but rather for men.

To the extent that Dalila in her role as "the famousest / Of Women" embodies the gendered polemics of a royalist volume such as Winchester's, she stands as a charged emblem of a political and religious culture that Milton in the dark days of the Stuart Restoration despised and defied, and so she rightly functions as the detested object of Samson's venom. Samson fiercely rejects Dalila's assertions of supra-marital fidelity by insisting on her conjugal status: "Being once a wife, for me thou wast to leave / Parents and country" (885–86). And his firm refusal to grant her any kind of inner or masculine fortitude commits him to endless charges of specifically female sexual deception: "That specious Monster, my accomplisht snare" (230), "that fallacious Bride, / Unclean, unchaste" (320–21), "a deceitful Concubine" (537), a "Hyaena" with the "wonted arts" of "every woman false like thee" (748–49), "a pois'nous bosom snake" (763), an "Adder" (936). That Samson counters Dalila's claims of biblical heroism with denunciations of her carnal effeminacy recalls Winchester's portrayal of the lust-bound Holofernes. At the very least, this parallel confirms her damning hold on the two great realms that she herself has claimed as her own—the tyrannical realm of "civil Duty" and the idolatrous realm of ecclesiastical "Religion"—and so helps to explain if not excuse the savage ferocity of Samson's repudiation.

If Milton exorcises the carnal effeminacy that he associates with royalist politics, however, loading both into Dalila's all-too-eager arms and sending them with her out of the poem, a literal scapegoat, he still retains the invaluable model of (masculine) heroic virtue that underlies royalist representations of biblical heroines. In other words, Milton fuses royalist politics and carnal effeminacy in such a way that Dalila, in her emergent role as polemical icon, assumes the carnal effeminacy that had been Samson's—as in Winchester it had been Holofernes's[11]—and now is only hers. And it is just this kind of homeopathic takeover, consonant as it is with Milton's head-note on tragedy, that frees Samson once again to the possibility of heroic manhood.[12] Indeed, what Milton salvages for his hero from Dalila's final speech is just this idea of an individual, internal, godly potency, of an "Heroick Vertue" whose separation from carnal effeminacy (of macho Holofernes, of seductive Dalila, of early Samson) genders it quietly but unmistakably masculine. To the degree that Dalila is excised from Samson's life and Milton's poem, that is, the model of biblical heroism that she introduces in her final speech paradoxically persists. Dalila may be gone, but through her going Jael and Judith remain, spectral and (at least partially or temporarily) masculine figures that increasingly haunt and hover over Milton's hero, guiding him back to godly intimacy.

☙

We can discern the persistence, the haunting, the inadvertent transfer of heroic virtue, from Dalila to Samson, as soon as or even before she stops speaking. As has often been noted, the caustic conclusion that immediately follows Dalila's final speech—"She's gone," the Chorus hisses, "a manifest Serpent by her sting / Discover'd in the end" (997–98)—is at some odds with her own remarkably rising final tone, a tone that Janel Mueller's prosodic analysis identifies as "muscular" (70) and that I would describe as "Heroick." Indeed, a distinctly heroic tone enters Milton's poem with Dalila's invocation of Jael, a tone that transfers itself to Samson, as a kind of recovered masculinity, almost as soon as Dalila speaks and leaves.

Dalila's own speech is clear, powerful, and cumulative in its heroic authority. Though she begins conditionally and negatively, with "perhaps . . . defam'd," she swiftly locates herself and her "desire"; she insists on her own agency in enjambed lines that assert her power "to save" and to "cho[o]se"; and she sets herself within an ascending sequence of heroic names, from "*Ekron*" to "Mount *Ephraim*" and from her own "nam'd" self to "*Jael*," a sequence that allows her, like Judith and Jael, to reinscribe murderous crime ("Smote") as salvific heroic action.

When Samson first opens his mouth after Dalila's departure, he speaks, though to very different ends, in the same powerful and rising tone that characterizes Dalila's last words, manifesting in his own voice the persisting presence of Jael. "So let her go, God sent her," he tells the Chorus when she leaves (999), with a serene confidence that stands in marked contrast to his own earlier and simmeringly sarcastic words, just prior to Dalila's final speech, repulsing her touch:

> Not for thy life, lest fierce remembrance wake
> My sudden rage to tear thee joint by joint.
> At distance I forgive thee, go with that;
> Bewail thy falshood, and the pious works
> It hath brought forth to make thee memorable
> Among illustrious women, faithful wives:
> Cherish thy hast'n'd widowhood with the gold
> Of Matrimonial treason: so farewell.   (952–59)

This same quiet confidence marks Samson's dialogue with Harapha after Dalila has gone, with the perhaps gratuitously parodic effect of deflating the strongman's posturings: "The way to know were not to see but taste" (1091), Samson observes cryptically. And when he eventually rises to full speech, he echoes Dalila on Jael with uncanny precision, though as he does so he moves correctively away from her and towards the biblical heroine that he shows her to have mis-invoked. "I know no spells, use no forbidden Arts," he declaims to Harapha;

> My trust is in the living God who gave me
> At my Nativity this strength, diffus'd
> No less through all my sinews, joints and bones,
> Than thine, while I preserv'd these locks unshorn,

The pledge of my unviolated vow.

. . . .

Then thou shalt see, or rather to thy sorrow
Soon feel, whose God is strongest, thine or mine.   (1139–55)

Like Dalila, Samson asserts himself forcefully ("I," "My trust," "me," "my Nativity," "my sinews," "I," "my . . . vow," "mine"), though unlike her he finally asserts not himself but his "God," a difference that sets his final superlative ("strongest") against hers ("famousest"). Like her, he locates himself firmly in time and space, though he again does so "in the living God," as opposed to in an earthly kingdom; like her, too, he asserts a supra-human "vow," though (again) it is to God as opposed to any (carnal) country or religion. Finally, Samson claims an immortality, in the form of his own ever-"living God," that utterly trivializes Dalila's assertions of fame among "Women . . . / Living and dead."

Jael is even more tangibly present when Samson, in his dialogue with Harapha, at long last clarifies what has been a stubborn problem in the poem—namely, Samson's competing loyalties to God, country, and wife. Until Jael enters the poem, which means right up through his agon with Dalila, Samson cannot resolve this problem and so cannot escape the charge of an aggressive sexual double standard when he claims for himself a priority of loyalty to religion and state, a priority that he denies his wife. Once Dalila provides the model of Jael, though, with its clear hierarchy of "piety" (993), "country" (as Dagon's state), and only then "wedlock bands," Samson is suddenly freed to the same heroic logic:

But I a private person, whom my Country
As a league-breaker gave up bound, presum'd
Single Rebellion and did Hostile Acts.
I was no private but a person rais'd
With strength sufficient and command from Heav'n
To free my Country.   (1208–13)

At first, Samson both refutes Harapha's earlier charge of "private" or "Single Rebellion" and, paradoxically, embraces that same charge, asserting his status as a "private person" freed by treachery from political allegiance. But he then refines his point in crucial ways, arguing that he was in fact "no private but a person rais'd / . . . from Heav'n." Not his wife's and not his country's, but then not even his own, in the end he is only God's. Samson's progressive logic here is, luminously, Jael's, though it is not, in any way, Dalila's: sidestepping her damning assertions of self, country, and fame, Samson derives his argument from the biblical heroine she both invokes and spectacularly misapprehends.

Potent though Jael's presence may be here, in the post-Dalila lines of

Samson Agonistes, restoring to Samson the implicitly masculine heroic virtue that he (Holofernes-like) had lost when he unlocked his lips to Dalila, Jael is but half the story here, and she is finally the less important if more visible half. For when Jael enters the poem in Dalila's last speech, Judith enters as well, though she does so silently and invisibly, leaving her traces only later and then only in the form of omissions and ellipses, in what is not said and not done. In so doing, Judith embodies the one essential virtue that Samson had lost and—through Judith, who comes in (like grace, perhaps) on the wings of Jael—now regains: a silence that is the perfect sign of (female) chastity.

☙

Judith comes closest to the surface of Milton's poem in the last fragment cited above, when Samson identifies himself as "no private but a person rais'd / With strength sufficient and command from Heav'n / To free my Country." Samson's claim of human weakness empowered by God to political effect is Judith's as well, and, indeed, Milton's lines on Samson roughly correspond to Winchester's on Judith: God makes "Haughty spirits . . . all discern that Crowns depend on his Favour, and not on the strength of their own Hands" (*Gallery*, 37). The parallel is intensified by the fact that Winchester's lines on Judith (like his later ones on Jael, noted above) reverberate with allusions to the biblical Samson: "This were the way to be truly powerful, to take Towns, and overcome Armies; not with Canons and other Arms, but with broken Pots and the Jaw-bone of an Asse" (*Gallery*, 36–37).

Even more resonantly, Samson's late and Judith-like claim of being "a person rais'd / . . . from Heav'n" is also structurally parallel to his original Nazarite self-representation as "a person separate to God" (31). To hear this parallel is to hear that Samson in his conversation with Harapha knows himself to be what he once was, which is "a person separate to," "no private," only God's own—though the (Judith-like) ascription of all agency to God in the later formulation suggests a return that is also an ascent. And to hear Samson recall his original Nazarite purity is also to remember, yet once more, the sole pledge of that purity, which is *silence:* "Under the Seal of silence" (49), "the secret gift of God" (201), "my fort of silence" (236), "The mystery of God giv'n me under pledge / Of vow" (378–79), "the sacred trust of silence / Deposited within thee; which to have kept / Tacit, was in thy power" (428–30), "God's counsel . . . his holy secret" (497), "my . . . hallow'd pledge" (535).[13] (The list stops when Dalila enters the poem.) "I was his nursling once and choice delight," Samson grieves in a retrospective summation whose every syllable measures incalculable loss: "Under his special eye / Abstemious I grew up and thriv'd amain; / He led me on" (633–38). Samson was once God's infant and His son; he was also God's virgin child, and perhaps intended as His virgin spouse; he was therefore necessarily "Abstemious," turned away from the world, self-restricting, sealed, silent, *chaste*.[14] And in his godly chastity, finally, he was essentially *female,* in the peculiar sense of that word that Juan Louis Vives has in mind when he identifies virginal chastity as the state of being "mother, spouse, and daughter to that god, in whom nothing can be but it be thine."[15]

   To set Vives's 1523 *The Instruction of a Christian Woman* next to Milton's 1671 *Samson Agonistes* is to discover just how precisely Samson's recovery of godly intimacy is figured as a kind of traditional, Christian, female chastity (though that chastity is also gendered male to distinguish it from effeminate carnality). Virginity for Vives involves silence, invisibility, and sealing, but it is all of these separations not for themselves but only for or (in Samson's word) "to" God. "[I]t were better" for a maid "to be at home within and unknown to other folks, and in company to hold her tongue demurely, and let few see her, and none at all hear her" (*Instruction,* 102), Vives writes. It were even better "If thou join a chaste mind unto thy chaste body, if thou shut up both body and mind, and seal them with those seals that none can open but he that hath the key of David, that is thy spouse. . . . [For thou art] married unto him . . . [which] maketh thee like unto the church, . . . the spouse of Christ" (*Instruction,* 104). If a maid has to leave home and "go forth at door," he adds, in a crucial amplification that unambiguously perceives in chastity the possibility and indeed necessity of a specifically female heroism (not unrelated to Winchester's later "Heroick Vertue"), she must

prepare her mind and stomach none otherwise than if she went to fight. Let her remember what she shall hear, what she shall see, and what herself shall say. Let her consider with herself that something shall chance on every side that shall move her chastity and her good mind. Against these darts of the devil flying on every side, let her take the buckler of stomach defended with good examples and precepts, and a firm purpose of chastity, and a mind ever bent towards Christ.   (*Instruction,* 109)

If Vives's image of chaste heroism faintly suggests Samson on his way to Dagon's temple, with his "mind and stomach" prepared, "remember[ing]," "consider[ing]" within, with a defense of "good examples" and "a firm purpose of chastity," it more vividly recalls the Lady in *A Mask Presented at Ludlow Castle,* alone in the woods at night, startled but not astounded, visibly seeing the "unblemish't form of Chastity" (215).[16]

   The memory of *A Mask* is clarifying, however, for Samson is not (in Vives's terms) a virgin, though he is, perhaps, again, chaste; and there is much that this blind man does not see, though he is, perhaps, again, "inward[ly] . . . illuminated" (1689). And at the end of Milton's poem, Samson may be, once again or perhaps fully for the first time, God's chosen spouse, admittedly

guilty of having violated his sacred marital trust:[17] "Thou has broken, thou
false woman, the most holy band of temporal law, that is to say, thy faith and
thy truth. . . . What greater offense can [women] do; or what greater wicked-
ness can they infect themselves withal that destroy their country and perish
all laws and justice?" (*Instruction*, 112–13). But he is now chastened and so
chaste, re-embraced and re-embracing. "And which is best and happiest yet,"
Manoa asserts, blindly hoping, "all this / With God not parted from him, as
was fear'd, / But favoring and assisting to the end" (1718–20). In Vives, there
are but two virtues left a married woman, whose spiritual and emotional
domain is drastically straitened from that of a virgin: "These two virtues that I
mean be chastity and great love toward her husband. The first she must bring
with her forth of her father's house," as Samson, God's nursling, once did,
before he gave it away to Dalila. "The second," he continues, "she must take
after she is once entered in at her husband's door; and both father and
mother, kinfolks, and all her friends left, she shall reckon to find all these in
only her husband. And in both these virtues she shall represent the image of
holy church, which is both most chaste and most faithfully doth keep truth
and promise unto her spouse, Christ" (*Instruction*, 112). Late, in the dark,
stumbling painfully, Samson may have learned to separate from loving father,
from communal chorus, from carnal wife; to close the divide he should never
have allowed to open between his Father's house and his Husband's door;
and to "find all . . . in only [his] husband," who is Christ.[18]

Once we begin to discern Samson in his role as God's recuperated
spouse—a perception that we owe to hearing Judith in Samson's claim of
being "a person rais'd / . . . from Heav'n," and to hearing in this phrase the
structural echo of Samson's original claim of being "a person separate to
God," with all its painful train of chaste silences violated—a number of previously invisible details come (almost) into view. So, too, does Judith, who
emerges as an increasingly powerful figure hovering just out of Samson's and
our vision, an informing presence or, more accurately, a guardian angel of
God, perhaps even God's own guarding spirit.

Judith is never mentioned in *Samson:* she operates under a sign of
(chaste) silence and invisibility which becomes, increasingly, Samson's own
sign in the poem after Dalila leaves. Notoriously, however carefully we trace
the evidence of Samson's recuperation, we are never sure that such recuperation takes place. Samson rarely speaks. When he does, it is often in ways that
are inexplicably different from previous ways he has spoken. And his late
speeches are often ambiguous or (as in Judges) riddling. Apart from a handful
of scattered couplets, Samson responds to Dalila's final speech with silence:
whatever transfer of heroic virtue takes place occurs apart from the poem's
actual language, in the white spaces between the words on the page, though

we sometimes think we see evidence of that transfer having occurred when he does speak. Similarly, in the forty-two lines between his third refusal to accompany the Officer ("I will not come" [1342]) and his decision to go ("I with this Messenger will go along" [1384]), Samson speaks with a radical uncertainty that may suggest an utterly blind faith in God but that also, and perhaps more significantly, tells, reports, communicates little to us (or possibly even to him):

> Yet that he [God] may dispense with me or thee
> Present in Temples at Idolatrous Rites
> For some important cause, thou needst not doubt.
>
> . . . .
>
> Be of good courage, I begin to feel
> Some rousing motions in me which dispose
> To something extraordinary my thoughts. (1377–83)

Samson's assurances of "courage" and of the needlessness of "doubt" are set against his own unknowing ("may," "some," "Some," "something"). And though earlier he had insisted, "my riddling days are past" (1064), by the time he leaves with the Officer, his language has returned to its original (and biblical) riddling state, in which words function as barriers, closed doors, seals set against intruders that can be opened only by the One who has the key. "I am content to go," he tells the Officer: "Masters' commands come with a power resistless / To such as owe them absolute subjection; / And for a life who will not change his purpose?" (1403–6). The Officer may hear: "I obey my civil masters, to save my life." Samson may mean: "I obey God, at the cost of life (or: for eternal life)." We can only conjecture, because Samson himself may not know, and because the poem never provides an answer. "I have learn't / To fence my ear" (936–37), he tells Dalila; after she leaves, he may have learned as well to "fence" his mouth.

Once Dalila has departed, Samson (re-)learns how to use language chastely, silently, directing it inward and upward, shutting up and sealing off meaning from any and all outsiders—Harapha, the Chorus, the Officer, Manoa, the reader. In so doing, he moves ever closer, in his own increasing silence and darkness, to the similarly imperceptible figure of Judith that I have claimed hovers over the poem's end. And it is at this end, at Dagon's temple, when Milton famously departs from Judges in having Samson stand in silence (instead of praying aloud), prior to his final public words and actions, that Samson and Judith seem finally, powerfully, catastrophically to merge.

In the engraving before the *Gallery*'s third chapter, an imposing figure of Judith dominates the folio-sized field, wielding a sword in one hand and Holofernes's head in the other. She dwarfs a much smaller background image in which the same heroine, just prior to action, stands next to Holofernes's bed, surrounded by angels. In his text, Winchester bypasses Judith triumphant and focuses (almost exclusively) on the quieter, less dramatic Judith, a narrative shift that makes her internal preparation for heroic action both the substance and meaning of her story. (This narrative shift loosely parallels Milton's own procedure in *Samson,* especially after Dalila's departure, when the prolonged emphasis on the dark and immobile hours leading up to Samson's final act suggests that the drama that matters here is primarily internal, invisible, inaudible.) Judith appears in the (originally Catholic) engraving accompanied by "the Angel of *Israel,*" who brightens the dark night, but only for Judith, much as the pillar of cloud that guided the Israelites out of Egypt illuminated their way but was dark for their pursuers. "[T]his intelligent night is discreet, like that of *Egypt,*" Winchester writes; "it knows how to distinguish the faithful, and to put a difference of persons. That which is cloudy and dark for others shall be light for us" (*Gallery,* 29–30).

All other aspects of Judith's story are similarly active in their immobility, bright in their darkness, eloquent in their silence, though always and only for an audience of One. Describing Judith's "arms" or weapons, Winchester writes:

These arms, though divinely reinforced and purified with a Heavenly ray, could not have overcome alone. They effected nothing but after prayer, fasting, and tears. And though these [arms] which are spiritual, and of an invisible temper have not wrought upon the sight of *Holofernes,* yet they have done it upon the heart of God, and opened a passage whereby Safety came upon his people, and Death upon his enemies. *Judeth* is ready to give a beginning to both. (30–31)

As Winchester's reference to "prayer, fasting, and tears" suggests, Judith's final power lies in her chaste management of her own widowhood, in a Vives-like sealing off from engagement with the world that produces the state of immobile silence required for divine inspiration and subsequent heroic action. It is, intriguingly, a self-sealing that resembles nothing so much as the parallel sealing of Samson in Milton's poem. "She not being able to renounce her Youth," Winchester writes,

nor to be rid of her Beauty, which were to her like suspected Domesticks, and hard to be preserved: she kept them continually shut up; and likewise fearing lest they should make an escape, she weakned them by Prayer, Labor, Fasting, and Hair-cloth. She grew warlike by these Domestick and Private Combats, and prepared herself all alone, and in one single night for this famous Field, in which the Fortune of the Assyrians was ruined by the Blow received from the hand of a victorious Woman, and the Head of a vanquished Man. (34)

I have suggested that Judith enters *Samson* through Dalila's invocation of Jael, and that she at least partly structures the silences and sealings that increasingly close Samson off from external view and understanding. I would add now that to set Winchester's text next to Milton's is to illumine and open, at least as a possibility, at least partially, what is so powerfully dark and closed about Samson's final words and actions: "[He] grew warlike by these Domestick and Private Combats, and prepared [him]self all alone, and in a single night for this famous Field." That this (perhaps illusory) illumination is withheld from us, in the end, may be its final significance, since it compels us to reproduce Samson's own trustful gropings in the dark, and we do.

In the endlessly prolonged moment before she slays Holofernes, Judith is shown by Winchester to be possessed of a holy "confidence" and "boldnesse," which are paradoxically modest, submissive, faithful, and zealous, and which serve to "enlighten her face":

her eyes are lifted up toward Heaven, as if they did shew the way to the prayers she sends thither in silence. . . . There is nothing which so pure a soul, and so holy tears may not obtain; and the voice of this silence is too powerful and pressing not to be heard. But though it were strong enough to penetrate Heaven, and to make itself to be heard of God, yet it reacheth not the ear of *Holofernes*. (*Gallery,* 31)

Milton writes, of a parallel moment:

> which when *Samson*
> Felt in his arms, with head a while inclin'd,
> And eyes fast fixt he stood, as one who pray'd,
> Or some great matter in his mind revolv'd.
> At last with head erect thus cried aloud.
> . . . .
> This utter'd, straining all his nerves he bow'd;
> As with the force of winds and waters pent,
> When Mountains tremble, those two massy Pillars
> With horrible convulsion to and fro
> He tugg'd, he shook, till down they came, and drew
> The whole roof after them with burst of thunder
> Upon the heads of all who sat beneath,
> Lords, Ladies, Captains, Counsellors, or Priests,
> Thir choice nobility and flower, not only
> Of this but each *Philistian* City round
> Met from all parts to solemnize this Feast.
> *Samson* with these inmixt, inevitably
> Pull'd down the same destruction on himself. (1635–58)

Prior to action, Judith and Samson stand ready and "armed," heads upright or inclined, eyes turned inward or upward, praying or (with the final unknowability of Milton's chaste text) "as" if praying ("or" not), perfect riddles to "*Philistian*" listeners who have neither the eyes to see nor the ears to hear the impending and entirely ironic fulfillment of Dalila's parting fantasy of "solemn festivals" honoring a "tomb" begirt with "flowers." And, in the end, both these inspired figures turn the "pent" or inward power of heroic chastity outward, to devastating, visible, aural effect. This is, we might recall, precisely the catastrophic power that *A Mask*'s Lady so feared to unleash. Though she unlocks her lips to guard her chaste intactness, in the end she refrains, protecting Comus from an heroic and sacred "arm" that she, a lone virgin facing a single threat, may not be ready or yet truly need to use:[19]

> Thou hast nor Ear nor Soul to apprehend
> The sublime notion and high mystery
> That must be utter'd to unfold the sage
> And serious doctrine of Virginity.
>   . . . .
> Yet should I try, the uncontrolled worth
> Of this pure cause would kindle my rapt spirits
> To such a flame of sacred vehemence,
> That dumb things would be mov'd to sympathize,
> And the brute Earth would lend her nerves, and shake,
> Till all thy magic structures rear'd so high,
> Were shatter'd into heaps o'er thy false head.   (784–99)[20]

Older, chastened, chastely espoused, Judith and Samson do "utter" the "high mystery . . . of Virginity," and the effect is both like and unlike what the young and virginal Lady imagines—brilliant, shattering, and powerfully transformative, yes,[21] but also mercilessly "dumb," dark, "brute," and deadly. "*Samson* with these inmixt," the Messenger reports, "inevitably / Pull'd down the same destruction on himself."[22]

☙

In his 1642 *An Apology against a Pamphlet,* Milton locates traditional female chastity in all its various literary and poetic forms, and then he separates it out, recuperating it as a distinctively "male" virtue on the basis of Revelation: "Nor did I slumber over that place expressing such high rewards of ever accompanying the Lambe with those celestiall songs to others inapprehensible, but not to those who were not defil'd with women, which doubtlesse meanes fornication: For mariage must not be call'd a defilement."[23] All elements of the chaste Samson story are here. There is an heroic virtue that is given to "men," in the particular sense of those actual men and women who have avoided the "fornication[s]" of effeminate carnality. There are "celes-tiall songs" that are "inapprehensible" to all but the heavenly saints, making chastity an elusive and riddling (if ultimately powerful) source of a lifetime poetics. And there is an "accompanying" of the "Lambe," whose meaning first emerges in Revelation 14:2–4 but comes into full clarity only in Revela-tion 19:7–8, where, just after the cataclysmic annihilation of the great whore that is the city of Babylon, to ashes and darkness and utter silence, the "male" virgins are made ready, arrayed in fine linen, clean and white, and given to the Lamb as his spouse, his bride, his chaste beloved. Samson's chastity is, in its end, a bride's virtue that is first rendered male to purify its heroism from effeminate carnality but is then set in female spousal relation to the hus-bandly Lamb—perhaps the same Lamb identified in *A Mask* as "Heav'n itself" that "if Virtue feeble were," in all spousal tenderness "would stoop to her" (1022–23). And the sound of that union is what Milton in *Lycidas* identifies as "unexpressive nuptial Song" (176), the voice of a great multi-tude, the voice of many waters, the voice of mighty thunderings, singing as it were a new, potent, apocalyptic song, a song that is, to all but the hundred and forty and four thousand who are redeemed from the earth, perfectly "inapprehensible."

Barnard College

NOTES

1. See Achsah Guibbory, "*Paradise Regained* and *Samson Agonistes:* The Solitary Individ-ual, Divorce, and the Rejection of Community," in *Ceremony and Community from Herbert to Milton: Literature, Religion, and Cultural Conflict in Seventeenth-Century England* (New York, 1998), 219–27; Janel Mueller, "Just Measures? Versification in *Samson Agonistes*," in *Milton Studies* 33, ed. Albert C. Labriola and Michael Lieb (Pittsburgh, 1996), 47–82; Laura Lunger Knoppers, "'Sung and Proverb'd For a Fool': *Samson Agonistes* and Solomon's Harlot," in *Milton Studies* 26, ed. James D. Simmonds (Pittsburgh, 1990), 239–51; Jackie DiSalvo, "Intes-tine Thorn: Samson's Struggle with the Woman Within," in *Milton and the Idea of Woman*, ed. Julia M. Walker (Urbana and Chicago, 1988), 211–29; and Stella P. Revard, "Dalila as Euripi-dean Heroine," *Papers on Language and Literature* 23 (1987): 291–302.

2. In making this claim, I position myself with critics who argue that Milton worked on *Samson* in substantial ways during the 1650s and 1660s. For a brief summary of the dating debate, see *The Riverside Milton*, ed. Roy Flannagan (Boston and New York, 1998), 792.

3. In fact, Mazarin, Anne's suspected husband, ran France during the Regency, as Le Moyne reminds Anne obliquely at the end of his prefatory address to her; he continued to do so until his death in 1661, long after the majority of Louis XIII.

4. Winchester, *The Gallery of Heroick Women. Written in French by Peter Le Moyne, of the Society of Jesus. Translated into English by the Marquesse of Winchester.* (London, 1652), 159. Further quotations from this volume are cited parenthetically in the text.

5. Though Winchester and Milton operate within the coordinates of what Mary Beth Rose identifies as "the phallic heroics of action" and the ideally feminine "heroics of endurance" (84), the following discussion shows that both authors reconfigure this binary distinction in radical and complex ways: " 'Vigorous Most / When Most Unactive Deem'd': Gender and the Heroics of Endurance in Milton's *Samson Agonistes,* Aphra Behn's *Oroonoko,* and Mary Astell's *Some Reflections Upon Marriage,*" in *Milton Studies* 33, ed. Albert C. Labriola and Michael Lieb (Pittsburgh, 1996), 83–109.

6. In a story that describes political treachery in sexual terms, Jael's "fidelity" to God is identified with her chastity, though Winchester does not explicitly develop the idea of (female) chastity to God until his chapter on Judith. Sexual fidelity emerges in the Jael chapter in relation only to her husband, Heber, whose treaty with the Canaanites is described as a frontier experi- ence that neither infringes upon his core Israelite allegiance nor (consequently) puts his wife at odds with his politics: "The Treatie of *Hebar* with the *Canaanites* . . . was not a surrender of his right, nor a dispensation of his duty; It was an innocent Charm against fire and sword, against Tyrants and oppressors; And the war undertaken against them [the Canaanites] proceeding from the will of God, signified by expresse revelation, and declared by the Regent Prophetess [Deborah], [was such] as he might lift himself without any Treachery amongst the [Canaanite] Troops, and joyn his Arms with the common [Israelite] Arms for the liberty of the people; so *Jahel* with a good Conscience and merit might set her hand to the same work" (*Gallery,* 25).

The rationalizing tone of Winchester's argument here may explain why the Jael chapter ends as it does, with the cautionary story of Joan of Beaufort, Queen of Scotland and wife of James I. Joan proves her perfect marital fidelity by interposing herself between her husband and his murderers, forcing them to kill him through her body in an act that is figured as both a murder and a rape (26–27).

7. *Samson Agonistes* 1009. All references to Milton's poems are from *John Milton: Complete Poems and Major Prose,* ed. Merritt Y. Hughes (New York, 1985; Indianapolis, 1957) and are hereafter cited parenthetically by line number in the text.

8. "[The Book of] IVDETH," *The Geneva Bible: A Facsimile of the 1560 Edition,* intro. Lloyd E. Berry (Madison, 1969), 409–15.

9. For a succinct discussion of mid-seventeenth-century portrayals of heroic women, par- ticularly by royalist writers, see Carol Barash, *English Women's Poetry, 1649–1714: Politics, Community, and Linguistic Authority* (New York, 1996). In the sub-chapter "The Heroic Woman" (32–40), Barash argues that Madeleine de Scudery's *Femmes illustrees* (1642), Le Moyne's *Galerie,* and Winchester's *Gallery* all represent Judith, Jael, and Joan of Arc as "morally powerful and physically attractive" women (37). In "Royalism and the Heroic Woman" (56–62), she explores Katherine Philips's debt to what she describes as a royalist tradition of heroic women. Barash cites the relevant studies (32–33): Erica Veevers, *Images of Love and Religion: Queen Henrietta Maria and Court Entertainments* (New York, 1989); Joan DeJean, *Tender Geographies: Women and the Origins of the Novel in France* (New York, 1991); Carolyn Lougee, *Le Paradis des femmes: Women, Salons, and Social Stratification in Seventeenth-Century France* (Princeton, 1976); and Ian Maclean, *Woman Triumphant: Feminism in French Literature, 1610–1652* (New York, 1977). Sophie Tomlinson explores the relationships between Caroline representations of heroines and the behavior of royalist women during the wartime 1640s and republican 1650s in "She That Plays the King: Henrietta Maria and the Threat of the Actress in Caroline Culture," in *The Politics of Tragicomedy: Shakespeare and After,* ed. Gordon McMullan and Jonathan Hope (New York, 1992), 189–207.

10. Guibbory argues that Milton presents Dalila "as a dangerous figure for idolatry": "In Milton's transformation, the biblical character infamous for her treachery becomes identified with the idolatry of a heathen ceremonial worship that posed an ongoing, seductive threat to

Samson and the Israelites—and to the English" (*"Paradise Regained* and *Samson Agonistes,"* 220). The Chorus's first description of Dalila "evokes the conventional association of idolatry with seduction," she adds, and her "attractiveness is at once powerfully sexual and religiously charged, . . . as Dalila becomes identified with the seductive, idolatrous ceremonies of the Laudian church, newly restored in Restoration England" (220–21).

11. His own "foul effeminacy held [him] yok't" (410), Samson admits, so that, precisely like Holofernes, "into the snare I fell / Of fair fallacious looks, venereal trains, / Soft'n'd with pleasure and voluptuous life" (532–34), "Effeminately vanquish't" by both external and internal women (562).

12. "Tragedy . . . be of power by raising pity and fear, or terror, to purge the mind of those and such like passions, that is to temper and reduce them to just measure. . . . [F]or so in Physic things of melancholic hue and quality are us'd against melancholy, sour against sour, salt to remove salt humors" (*John Milton: Complete Poems,* 549).

13. See Marcia Landy, "Language and the Seal of Silence in *Samson Agonistes,"* in *Milton Studies* 2, ed. James D. Simmonds (Pittsburgh, 1970), 175–94.

14. Samson's quiet punning in these lines may point to the mysterious mutuality or even limited identity of an absolute chastity maintained between a divine "eye / Abstemious" and an "Abstemious I." If so, it is punning that may open in Samson's grief a still lower deep, since each separate bond listed here as lost represents a point of infinite superiority to the parallel bond first posited (and punned) at the start of Milton's own career in *Sonnet 7:* "All is, if I have grace to use it so, / As ever in my great task-Master's eye" (13–14).

15. Juan Luis Vives, "Selections from *The Instruction of a Christian Woman,"* in *Daughters, Wives, and Widows: Writings by Men about Women and Marriage in England, 1500–1640,* ed. Joan Larsen Klein (Urbana and Chicago, 1992), 97–122; 104. All references to Vives's *Instruction* are hereafter cited parenthetically in the text.

16. For a brief discussion of some relevant parallels between Samson and the Lady of *A Mask,* see John P. Rumrich, *Milton Unbound: Controversy and Reinterpretation* (New York, 1996), 90–93.

17. In his conversation with Manoa, Samson admits the consequences that his breach of silence will have for his religion and country: "I this honour, I this pomp have brought / To *Dagon,* and advanc'd his praises high / Among the Heathen round, to God have brought / Dishonor, obloquy, and op't the mouths / Of Idolists, and Atheists; have brought scandal / To *Israel,* diffidence of God, and doubt / In feeble hearts, propense enough before / To waver, or fall off and joyn with Idols: / Which is my chief affliction, shame and sorrow, / The anguish of my Soul" (449–58).

18. We might consider Manoa's plans for Samson's burial in this context. Manoa believes his plans to be simple and concrete, but we, still hearing riddles, understand both as a gesture recognizing Samson's chastely sealed reunion with God and as a purifying reclamation of Dalila's original and tainted invocation of the biblical Jael (at 980–90): "I with what speed the while / . . . / Will send for all my kindred, all my friends / To fetch him hence and solemnly attend / With silent obsequy and funeral train / Home to his Father's house" (1728–33).

19. See Jean E. Graham's "Virgin Ears: Silence, Deafness, and Chastity in Milton's *Maske,"* in *Milton Studies* 36, ed. Albert C. Labriola (Pittsburgh, 1998), 1–17.

20. For a nuanced discussion of *Samson* as an aural recalling of Milton's own poetical career, see Ann Baynes Coiro, "Fable and Old Song: *Samson Agonistes* and the Idea of a Poetic Career," in *Milton Studies* 36, ed. Albert C. Labriola (Pittsburgh, 1998), 123–52.

A speculation on a perhaps separate topic: in the second edition of his 1660 *The Readie and Easie Way to Establish a Free Commonwealth,* in a gesture hauntingly like the Lady's here, Milton "unlocks his lips" for one last prose time before finally stopping himself: "I have no more to say at present" (*Complete Prose Works of John Milton*, 8 vols., ed. Donald M. Wolfe et al. (New Haven, 1953–82), vol. 7, 461. When he does speak again, in *Paradise Lost*, in *Paradise Regained*, in *Samson Agonistes*, he does so, like Samson, in more riddling and elliptical (because poetic) ways, a kind of sealing that is highly expressive and that may also be meant to direct God's vengeful power against his enemies. Did he imagine this, or hope for it, of his last epics?

21. "Victory is not little in the heart of the Conqueresse," Winchester writes of Judith after Holofernes's death: "It is there so great as it is dilated on her face, and her eyes have received thereby a second fire with a new and accessory light. It will suddenly appear far greater in *Bethulia* where the generous Widow is impatiently expected: and to which place she is going to carry, with the Head and Death of the Publick Enemy, the life and freedom of all the people" (*Gallery*, 33).

22. For discussion of the apocalyptic power of chastity in Puritan texts by mid-seventeenth-century English writers, see John Rogers, "The Enclosure of Virginity: The Poetics of Sexual Abstinence in the English Revolution," in *Enclosure Acts: Sexuality, Property, and Culture in Early Modern England*, ed. Richard Burt and John Michael Archer (Ithaca, 1994), 229–50. See Guibbory, *Ceremony and Community from Herbert to Milton*, and Veevers, *Images of Love and Religion* for analysis of the correspondences and differences between Puritan and "ceremonial" representations of chastity during this same period.

23. *Complete Prose Works of John Milton*, ed. Wolfe, vol. 1, 892–93.

"TRUE LIBERTY":
ISOCRATES AND MILTON'S *AREOPAGITICA*

Eric Nelson

I

MILTON ADDRESSED THE TENTH SONNET in the 1645 *Poems* to Lady Margaret Ley, the daughter of James Ley, earl of Marlborough. The elder Ley had served as lord high treasurer and lord president of the council before dying of grief only four days after the forcible dissolution of Parliament on March 10, 1629. In his encomium to this fallen official, Milton observes that Ley's career of public service lasted

> Till the sad breaking of that Parliament
> Broke him, as that dishonest victory
> At *Chaeronéa,* fatal to liberty
> Kil'd with report that Old man eloquent.[1]

The "Old man eloquent" in this passage is the Greek orator Isocrates, and the sonnet refers to the tradition that the aged Isocrates starved himself to death after hearing that Philip of Macedon had defeated the coalition of Athens and Thebes at the battle of Chaeronea (338 B.C.), ending forever the freedom of the Greek city-states.[2] In this context, Milton styles Isocrates as a defender of liberty whose love of freedom was so powerful that he refused to continue living in its absence.

Despite its apparent straightforwardness, this allusion has sparked a lively and revealing scholarly discussion. Annabel Patterson has suggested that Milton's nod to the Greek orator should be read ironically. Isocrates, she argues, was an enemy of "Athenian liberty" who composed the celebrated *Philippus* as part of a "campaign to have Philip assume rule over a united Greece."[3] Accordingly, Milton must have known that he was manipulating the Isocratean biography by casting the orator as a martyr to freedom, and he must have had some polemical reason for doing so. In its particulars, this argument encounters several difficulties. The *Philippus,* for one thing, does not endorse a universal monarchy for Greece but rather exhorts Philip to renounce coercion and to unite the free Greek cities in a joint campaign against the "barbarians" in Asia.[4] Moreover, far from being an enemy of liberty, Isocrates undeniably cherished the Greek ideals of freedom and self-rule and differed from his contemporaries only in praying that all of Greece would one day achieve them.[5] Nonetheless, Patterson is correct that we have good reason to doubt the historicity of Isocrates' suicide as represented in Milton's sonnet. First and foremost, if Isocrates' *Third Letter* is authentic, it was written to Philip some weeks *after* the Battle of Chaeronea had taken place.[6]

In a recent response to Patterson, John Leonard has questioned the relevance of such historical information to the task of interpreting Milton's allusion. He points out that, irrespective of its accuracy, Milton's characterization of Isocrates' death is unsurprising in its context: it accords with the accounts provided by Dionysius of Halicarnassus, pseudo-Plutarch, Lucian, and others, who enjoyed wide repute in the seventeenth century.[7] Dionysius, for example, reports that Isocrates died "a few days after the battle of Chaeronea, at the age of ninety-eight, having decided to end his life with his city's heroes [τοῖς ἀγαθοῖς τῆς πόλεως], when it was still uncertain how Philip would use his good fortune now that he had succeeded to the leadership of Greece [παραλαβὼν τὴν ἀρχὴν τῶν Ἑλλήνων]."[8] By turning to Milton's sources, Leonard underscores the essential point that the Isocrates of the seventeenth century is not the Isocrates of today. In interpreting an early modern allusion to "that Old man eloquent," therefore, we must be careful to reconstruct, not who he was, but how he was perceived during the early modern period.

The debate over the reference to Isocrates in *Sonnet 10* illustrates on a small scale what is at issue in the confusion surrounding Milton's more famous allusion to the Greek orator. That second allusion appears in the title of Milton's best known prose work, *Areopagitica,* and has occasioned a prodigious amount of scholarly discussion. Milton's chosen title for his 1644 attack on parliamentary licensing refers to an oration of the same name by Isocrates, written in 355 B.C.[9] In that speech, Isocrates urges the Athenian assembly to restore the ancestral democracy instituted by Solon and Cleisthenes, a regime in which great powers of moral oversight had been entrusted to the Areopagus (the highest Athenian court). The superficial similarity between the two works has been almost universally acknowledged: both Isocrates and Milton wrote their essays in the style of a formal, classical oration, even though neither work was intended for public delivery.[10] Indeed, early in *Areopagitica* Milton makes the allusion explicit, comparing himself to "him who from his private house wrote that discourse to the Parlament of Athens, that perswades them to change the forme of *Democraty* which was then established."[11]

That, however, is where the consensus ends. In a series of important articles on *Areopagitica,* several Miltonists have advanced the claim that the stated goals of Milton's oration are radically incompatible with those of Isocrates'. According to this view, Milton's essay is an attack on censorship, whereas Isocrates' "urges imposing restraints rather than relaxing them, and the vote of the Athenian assembly against his proposal was a vote for liberty, a vote against censorship."[12] In order to account for this perceived discrepancy in aims, scholars have taken several approaches. Joseph Wittreich has argued that the allusion is ironic: Milton ("essentially a liberal")[13] refers to Isocrates ("essentially an authoritarian") so that he can perform a series of imaginative subversions in which the original Isocratean intent is turned on its head.[14] Paul Dowling, on the other hand, has sought to demonstrate that Isocrates' message in *Areopagiticus* was disingenuous, and, thus, that Milton's allusion was meant to signal the disingenuousness of his own stance toward Parliament.[15] Lastly, several scholars (Stephen Burt is a recent example) have argued that the allusion is not to Isocrates at all but rather to Paul's speech on the Areopagus, as recorded in the book of Acts.[16]

These questions surrounding the Isocratean allusion in *Areopagitica* are, thus, substantially more than matters of obscure, antiquarian interest; they cut to the heart of what is still read as an essentially libertarian document. The scholarly practice of labelling the allusion as misplaced or ironic depends on doubtful readings of both the Miltonic and Isocratean texts. When it comes to Milton's essay, the libertarian reading can be corrected partly through careful examination of the text itself, and, indeed, several scholars have begun the process of demonstrating that Milton's tract is emphatically not "anti-censorship."[17] But the Isocratean side of the question is less straightforward. As we saw in the case of *Sonnet 10*, no matter how thoroughly we read Isocrates, we shall not ascertain the content of Milton's allusion unless we discover how Isocrates was read in the Renaissance and early modern period. In short, we have to understand what it meant to allude to Isocrates' *Areopagiticus* in 1644. Such an understanding leads to a substantially different reading of Milton's essay. It suggests that *Areopagitica* should be regarded, not as a narrow attack on censorship, but as a broader account of true liberty and the best form of republican government—an account that draws strength from the seventeenth-century reading of Isocrates' great oration. Indeed, the Isocrates of *Areopagitica* is no less a champion of liberty than the Isocrates of Milton's tenth sonnet.

II

Those who translated or edited Isocrates during the Renaissance and early modern period took very seriously Cicero's characterization of him as a "magnus orator et perfectus magister."[18] That is, they saw him not only as an "Old man eloquent" but also as a revered teacher of moral and political philosophy. During the period in question, by far the most prevalent form of didactic literature (and of political philosophy in general) was the so-called *speculum principis* (mirror for princes), and, accordingly, the early reception of Isocrates was characterized by a series of attempts to assimilate his works to that mode of writing.[19] The most cooperative Isocratean texts from this point of view were his three "hortatory" orations, *To Demonicus, To Nicocles,* and *Nicocles.*[20] Whereas *To Demonicus* is simply a moral exhortation to a young man, the other two works are more overtly political: *To Nicocles* represents Isocrates' account of the kingly virtues and is addressed to the King of Cyprus (whose father, Evagoras, Isocrates immortalized in a famous encomium), and *Nicocles* discusses the duties of subjects and the merits of monarchy. These three orations were the first printed Isocratean texts and by far the most frequently printed: they appear in literally dozens of editions throughout the sixteenth and seventeenth centuries.[21]

Of the three, *To Nicocles* most resembled a standard *speculum,* and, as a result, it received the preponderance of humanist attention.[22] To take only two examples, Erasmus appended a Latin translation of it to his *Institutio principis christiani* (1516), and Sir Thomas Elyot rendered the text into English in his *The Doctrinal of Princes* (1533). In the preface to his translation, Elyot extols "this litle booke (which in mine opinion) is to be compared in counsaile and sentence with any booke, holy Scripture excepted,"[23] and he refers to it frequently throughout his own contribution to *speculum principis* literature, *The Boke named the Governour.* In Book One of that work, Elyot turns to consider "What order shulde be in lernynge, and whiche autours shulde be fyrste redde," and has this to say about Isocrates:

Isocrates concerning the lesson of oratours, is every where wonderfull profitable, hauynge almost as many wyse sentences as he hath wordes: and with that is so swete and delectable to rede, that after him almost all other seme unsauery and tedious: and in persuadynge, as well a prince, as a private persone, to vertue, the two very litle and compendious warkes, whereof he made one to kynge Nicocles, the other to his frende Demonicus, wolde be perfectly kanned, and had in continual memorie.[24]

In the *Governour,* Elyot is concerned with the proper education of a prince or royal administrator, so it is, predictably enough, *To Nicocles* that receives the bulk of his attention. For example, while discussing the importance of historical study, Elyot notes that "the swete Isocrates exhorteth kynge Nicocles, whom he instructeth, to leaue behynde him statues and images, that shall represent rather the figure and similitude of his mynde, than the features of his body."[25] Elyot's Isocrates was the Isocrates of the *specula*—a *perfectus magister* who left to posterity his inspired view of ideal princely government.

It is against this backdrop that the emergence of Isocrates' *Areopagiti-*

cus has to be viewed. In 1526, Juan Luis Vives, the Spanish humanist who settled in England as tutor to the Princess Mary, released a Latin translation of two of Isocrates' orations: *Nicocles* and *Areopagiticus*.[26] The pairing was far from arbitrary. As Vives indicates explicitly in his preface, he views *Areopagiticus* as the republican counterpart to Isocrates' more popular treatise, "Nicocles de monarchia"[27]:

> It is an old question, which both exercised the intellects of many men, and changed the states and regimes of commonwealths: whether it is more excellent and more advisable for the people to be the judge and lord of its own affairs, or for the regime of the state to be controlled by the care and providence of one man? Many things are said ingeniously and truly on each side [*in utranque partem*] by other men and truly also by the Athenian Isocrates in two orations, of which one concerns popular power [*de populari potestate*], and the other concerns monarchy [*de monarchia*].[28]

Vives's choice of words is significant here: Isocrates, he argues, like other writers of antiquity, had written insightful comments on political life *in utramque partem*—arguing both sides of the question, like any good *rhetor.* Vives draws no conclusion as to which form of government Isocrates preferred. So far as he is concerned, the *perfectus magister* had simply left behind him two guidebooks for human government: one designed for monarchies, in which the *regimen civitatis* is held by a single man, and one for republics, in which the *populus* is judge and master over its own affairs. *Areopagiticus* was the latter.[29]

As to the content of this republican oration, Vives's exclusive interest is in the remarkable moral virtue and wisdom of the Areopagite judges themselves. He describes with great admiration that *perpetuus Senatus* (the Areopagus) and its members: "What sort of manners were found in the Areopagite judges, Isocrates expounds in this oration, and these ancient utterances declare them: 'more holy than an Areopagite, 'more venerable than an Areopagite,' 'more upright than an Areopagite.' . . . For no one was admitted to that council whose mores were not extremely excellent, and who had not given many proofs of his own probity."[30] Isocrates' oration on *popularis potestas* places authority in the hands of the most virtuous, wise, serious, saintly men in the commonwealth. Indeed, Vives takes this characterization of the Areopagite judges so seriously that he ends his epistle dedicatory to Cardinal Wolsey by referring to him as an "Areopagite."

Yet, whereas reverence for the Areopagite judges themselves remained a prominent feature of all early modern editions, future editors expanded considerably on Vives's analysis. In particular, they attempted to cast Isocrates' oration as an account of the ideal form of republican government. This is certainly the approach taken by Hieronymus Wolf of Augsburg, a former pupil of Philip Melanchthon and Isocrates' most important editor of the period.[31] In dedicating his edition to the governors of Nuremberg, Wolf attributes the greatness of their republic, not to the material grandeur and prosperity of the city, but rather to the exemplary form of government they had enjoyed for so long: "For all philosophers approved this condition of states [status civitatum] above all, in which the best and most prudent men thus rule over the citizens, like parents over their children: and the rest of the multitude is ruled by controlling them with the fairest possible laws and with sound teaching. Good men not only live in peace without injury, but are even honored: the impudence of the mischievous men . . . is held in check by appropriate punishments."[32] Thus, Wolf describes an ideal status civitatum as presided over by wise and virtuous men and maintained by fair laws and good discipline.

But it soon becomes evident that Wolf derives this model from someone far more specific than "all philosophers"; the passage is simply a paraphrase of the view he ascribes to Isocrates in his own argumentum for Areopagiticus. That essay begins as follows:

There are principally two plagues for republics: Tyranny, whenever magistrates, prey upon the weak with impunity, and refer their every action to their own lust, avarice and ambition; and Anarchy, when the people, holding the authority of both laws and magistrates in contempt, arrogates to itself complete license of speaking and acting. However neither disorder can be of long duration, but continually one overturns the other, like as those earth-born brothers [the warriors sown by Cadmus, Met. 3].[33]

Wolf sets out two poles for republican governments to avoid: tyranny of the magistrates and popular anarchy. He proceeds to point out that neither of these can maintain itself in the long run, and that one will always yield place to the other. But Isocrates, a "vir aetate gravis, spectataeque virtutis & sapientiae," provides an alternative: "The state between these is the best, and constitutes true liberty [vera libertas], when good laws are held to be sacrosanct both by the magistrates and by the citizens, and the best and most excellent men rule, the rest submit modestly, and the highest regard is paid to the discipline of the young."[34] In this account, Isocrates had identified an ideal status for commonwealths and a recipe for vera libertas: the ideal republic is presided over by the best and wisest men and maintains an equitable balance between magistrates and citizens. It is, in fact, a perfect midpoint between the tyranny of magistrates and popular anarchy. Of equal importance, the ideal republic pays careful attention to the education and discipline of the young, fully aware that a civitas libera requires virtuous citizens in order to survive and flourish.[35]

In support of his reading, Wolf includes a Latin translation of the section of Dionysius of Halicarnassus' *Isocrates* that considers *Areopagiticus*. Much of Dionysius' essay (which was also reprinted in the important edition of Henri II Estienne) pursues the same theme as Wolf's, albeit with a more marked emphasis on the ancient Areopagus' rejection of anarchy:

Truly Isocrates saw that for this reason it [the commonwealth] was in ruins and disorder, namely that now private citizens could not be coerced by the magistrates, but anyone was able, not only to say, but also to do anything they wanted: and all men accounted unsuitable confidence to be popular liberty. Therefore he urges that the republic instituted by Solon and Cleisthenes be restored anew. Reviewing the nature and institutions of which, he said that . . . they judged democratic government to consist not in impudence and boldness, but in moderation and temperance; and liberty not to be established in contempt of magistrates, but with orders being carried out.[36]

The language here sounds very Thucydidean, but Dionysius is more likely recalling a passage from *Areopagiticus* itself. In section 20, Isocrates insists that the ancient democracy did not breed citizens "in such fashion that they looked upon insolence as democracy, lawlessness as liberty, impudence of speech as equality, and license to do what they pleased as happiness."[37] Dionysius also stresses the familiar theme of Areopagite wisdom and virtue. In this ideal republic, he argues, the citizens "did not permit power to someone unscrupulous, but appointed magistrates from among the most excellent men, because they believed that the rest of the citizens will only be as good as their governors."[38]

But the printing of Dionysius' *argumentum* added a new element to the discussion—one that would prove extremely significant. Although Wolf's reading of Isocrates had stressed the importance of good discipline for the young, Dionysius goes considerably farther down this path. Although never questioning the need for good laws (the *bonae leges* of Wolf's essay), his Isocrates favors the benign moral oversight of the Areopagus in lieu of legal constraints. Dionysius highlights the priority of *mores* over legal structures, claiming that, in Isocrates' ideal republic, "it was thought to be more grave to resist those who were more advanced in age by speaking, than to desert ranks [in battle]"[39] and adds that the Areopagus paid careful attention to the education of young men (even when they had passed boyhood) because they believed that "correct studies [*recta studia*] were even more important than a carefully wrought code of laws."[40] The Areopagite judges did not aim to "coerce delinquents with punishments" but rather to educate their citizens in such a manner as to eliminate the need for punishments. The role assigned to the Areopagus in this context is, indeed, much more educative than legally punitive.

We find very much the same reading of the oration in Jan Meurs's

Areopagus, sive de senatu Areopagitico (1624).[41] Meurs argues for the superiority of government by a senate such as the Areopagus, and he draws heavily on Isocrates' oration (which Wolf had earlier dubbed the *Oratio Senatoria*)[42] in order to make his case. He dedicates his work to the Doge and Senate of Venice, beginning his epistle dedicatory with a familiar kind of flattery. He writes of the Areopagus that "if someone compared it with that august senate of yours, he would not go astray entirely"[43] and later adds that the Areopagus was "preeminent over all the councils of Greece,"[44] characterized as it was by *dignitas, auctoritas,* and *virtus.*[45] He then presents himself as one who is "studious of common liberty" (*studiosus communis libertatis*) and submits his work to Venice in payment of a debt owed by all freedom-loving people to the *Respublica serenissima.* At this point Meurs turns to the place of education in the republic. Venice, he argues, had an important insight: "you understood that the great part of public happiness consists in intellectual cultivation. . . . For the human mind, imbued correctly with studies, brings forth wisdom as well as prudence; by both of which it makes itself the master of Fortune, and holds her in its power."[46] Meurs draws on the ancient and Renaissance image of *virtus* subduing *Fortuna* in order to underscore the necessity of a well-educated citizenry for the survival of the polity. He then praises Venice for understanding this imperative: "You, I say, understood this best; and indeed, so that the minds of your youth were first instructed for entering political life in the Republic, you built schools . . . for you clearly believed that no greater benefit, ornament, and bulwark of the Republic could be given by you."[47] It is because the Areopagus shared this conviction (i.e., that the virtuous upbringing of the young constitutes the bedrock of republics) that Meurs praises it. Indeed, later in the work, when he cites *Areopagiticus* explicitly in order to argue that the Areopagite judges "also had the care of morals [*morum cura*], and castigated those living dishonorably,"[48] he means to highlight their preoccupation with a benign, non-legalistic moral education.

This is precisely the thought that we find later in James Harrington's *The Commonwealth of Oceana* (1656). Harrington insists that "the laws of a government, how wholesome so ever in themselves, being such as if men by a congruity in their education be not brought up to find a relish in them, they will be spit at,"[49] and cites Isocrates to make his point:

Now the health of a government and the education of the youth being of the same pulse, no wonder if it have been the constant practice of well ordered commonwealths to commit the care and feeling [*sic*] of it unto public magistrates; a duty that was performed in such manner by the Areopagites as is elegantly praised by Isocrates. The Athenians, saith he, write not their laws upon dead walls, nor content themselves with having ordained punishments for crimes, but provide in such manner by the education of their youth that there be no crimes for punishment; he speaks of those laws which regarded manners, not of those orders which concerned the administration of the commonwealth, lest you should think he contradicts Xenophon and Polybius.[50]

Harrington takes this indictment of restrictive laws "which regarded manners" so seriously that he feels obligated to reassure his reader that the laws in question (i.e., those laws that are trumped by studies) are not the *bonae leges* we encountered in Wolf's *argumentum:* they are not the fundamental laws of the republic. Although he retains the notion that the state should be an "empire of laws,"[51] Harrington wholeheartedly embraces the interpretation of Isocrates' oration we have been excavating. It is of more than passing interest that this is *the* reference to Isocrates in Harrington's defence of republicanism (written twelve years after Milton's essay).[52]

We are left, then, with a fairly clear picture of the way *Areopagiticus* was read in the Renaissance and early modern period: it was cast as Isocrates' "republican" oration (as opposed to the monarchist *To Nicocles* and *Nicocles*), and it was thought to present an ideal form of republican government (one situated perfectly between tyranny of the magistrates and popular anarchy) in which the best and wisest men ruled, and in which the rulers benignly oversaw the moral education of the citizens. There is, however, one final development in the reception of this text to which we must turn before we can complete our picture. Recall that Vives had accepted that Isocrates argued about government *in utramque partem* (i.e., rhetorically, without taking sides absolutely). By the end of the sixteenth century, this lukewarm assessment came under fire. Already in Wolf we find hints of an attempt to recruit Isocrates as a committed republican: in his second preface, for example, Wolf ascribes to Isocrates a deep *amor patriae,* indicating an attachment to the polity of his city. Henri II Estienne (Stephanus), perhaps the greatest classicist of the late sixteenth century, would later make the point explicitly.

Estienne's edition (first printed in 1593) contains Wolf's Latin translation and many of the same *argumenta* for the various orations (both *argumenta* for *Areopagiticus* are the same). He also includes a series of seven *diatribae* (learned discussions) concerned with various issues arising out of the text. One of these is titled *Politica quaedam Isocratis* and contains a reading of the orator's political philosophy. Estienne's opinion is extremely significant and bears quoting at length:

Now, just as Aristotle established honor as the end of political life, in the oration *Areopagiticus* of the writer under discussion we read, concerning men who had administered the commonwealth, that they used to receive praise, and were content with this honor if they had proven themselves just men while in office. But since

Isocrates lived in a democracy, and preferred this regime to any other, it is no wonder that he related his political science or political philosophy (as it had come to be called shortly before this time) to it in particular. And there were certainly a great many other men who likewise greatly preferred democracy to oligarchy and aristocracy (unless perhaps one should rather say that they like it alone), as we gather from the fact that the early orators spoke of democracy as the constitution "par excellence," and Isocrates himself belongs to the number of those who use the word in this way. . . . Isocrates thus shows himself a "political man" in what he says about the best form of democracy everywhere in these orations of his, so much so that one may scarcely find a better master than him. When I say, "politicus," I mean "someone knowledgeable about political science or philosophy." Thus in several places he learnedly discusses what true democracy is (as in *Panathenaicus*), [and] what is the fairest and most stable of all (as in *Areopagiticus*).[53]

Estienne's Isocrates is a republican political scientist, and *Areopagiticus* contains his account of the *aequissima & firmissima* republican government.

Estienne's convictions on the subject produce surprising results in his second *diatriba*. Here, he entertains doubts as to whether *To Nicocles* and *Nicocles* were written by Isocrates at all.[54] He lists several possible reasons for suspecting fraud, including the presumption that Isocrates was better situated to set down precepts "de optimo statu reipublicae" than "de regno optime administrando."[55] But ultimately Estienne's sympathy lies with the following objection: "for a man both born in a democracy, and accustomed to praising democracy extraordinarily, it is not only indecent but even unholy to extol monarchy so highly, and to preserve its memory in literature."[56] Estienne's Isocrates could not argue *in utramque partem*. Indeed, the centerpiece of Estienne's argument is an inconsistency between *Nicocles* and *Areopagiticus:*

Certain things it [*Nicocles*] says contradict those which are read in *Areopagitica*: for there he writes "that the Lacedaemonians are the best governed of peoples [κάλλιστα πολιτευομένους], because they are the most democratic [μάλιστα δημοκρατούμενοι]"; but we read these *Nicocles* as follows, "and again we know that while the Carthaginians and the Lacedaemonians, who are the best governed peoples of the world [τοὺς ἄριστα τῶν ἄλλων πολιτευομένους], are ruled by oligarchies at home, yet, when they take the field, they are ruled by kings." If both passages proceed from the same pen, this writer is surely one of the most self-contradictory who ever wrote.[57]

In order to assert Isocrates' republican pedigree, Estienne went so far as to question the authenticity of his two "monarchical" orations. Estienne's *Areopagiticus* is above all an account of ideal republican government written by a committed champion of republicanism and liberty. This is the *Areopagiticus* Milton had in mind when he sat down to compose his attack on a licensing order in 1644.[58]

III

Having shown that Isocrates' speech was not read as a case for censorship in the Renaissance and early modern period, we will now argue that Milton's *Areopagitica* is not itself an argument against "censorship." The essay constituted a response to a particular statute enacted by the Long Parliament mandating that no books or pamphlets could be printed "unlesse the same be first approved of and licensed" by parliamentary appointees.[59] Milton's opposition to this order derived from his characteristically neo-Roman understanding of the nature of liberty.[60] According to this view, liberty is a status of non-domination to be contrasted with slavery; it is not simply the absence of coercion. If a man lives under the arbitrary power of another man (or group of men), he is a slave and thus unfree, irrespective of whether that power is ever used. The central sources for this view are the *Codex* of Justinian and the writings of Sallust, Livy, and Tacitus, all of which make their presence felt in Milton's tract. In particular, Milton was taken with the argument (expounded clearly at the start of Tacitus' *Historiae)*[61] that learning and virtue cannot flourish in a state of dependence. At the end of his treatise, he considers the cause of England's intellectual dynamism and contemplates how it might come crashing down:

If it be desir'd to know the immediat cause of all this free writing and free speaking, there cannot be assign'd a truer then your own mild, and free, and human government; it is the liberty, Lords and Commons, which your own valorous and happy counsels have purchast us, liberty which is the nurse of all great wits; this is that which hath rarify'd and enlighten'd our spirits like the influence of heav'n. . . . Ye cannot make us now lesse capable, lesse knowing, lesse eagerly pursuing of the truth, unlesse ye first make your selves, that made us so, lesse the lovers, lesse the founders of our true liberty. We can grow ignorant again, brutish, formall, and slavish, as ye found us; but you then must first become that which ye cannot be, oppresive, arbitrary, and tyrannous, as they were from whom ye have free'd us.[62]

For Milton, the parliamentary statute was an enslaving document worthy only of the royal government Parliament had just toppled.

But Milton's argument applies only to this specific statute; he has no quarrel with censorship per se. He states quite openly that "it is of greatest concernment in the Church and Commonwealth, to have a vigilant eye how Bookes demeane themselves as well as men; and thereafter to confine, imprison, and do sharpest justice on them as malefactors."[63] He also writes that, after publication, "if it [a book] prov'd a Monster, who denies, but that it was justly burnt, or sunk into the Sea."[64] The censorship practices of the Christian Roman emperors, for example, meet with his unqualified approval: "The Books of those whom they took to be grand Hereticks were examin'd, re-

futed, and condemn'd in the generall Councels; and not till then were prohibited, or burnt."[65] Milton simply opposes what we might call "censorship
before the fact," or the practice of requiring that books be scrutinized by the
state even before they have made any mischief. He insists that "so far to
distrust the judgement & the honesty of one who hath but a common repute
in learning, and never yet offended, as not to count him fit to print his mind
without a tutor and examiner . . . is the greatest displeasure and indignity of a
free and knowing spirit that can be put upon him."[66] He also observes that the
process of licensing destroys the integrity of an intellectual product: "I hate a
pupil teacher, I endure not an instructor that comes to me under the ward-
ship of an overseeing fist." Ultimately, Milton laments the "disparagement"
brought about "when as dettors and delinquents may walk abroad without a
keeper, but unoffensive books must not stirre forth without a visible jaylor in
thir title."[67]

Milton could, of course, have extended his argument by observing that
all censorship has this enslaving effect—but he emphatically refuses to do
so.[68] Although he seeks "due process" for books, and expresses confidence
that, after careful scrutiny, relatively few books will be found to have harmed
society, Milton never denies the responsibility of the state to "do sharpest
justice" on genuinely harmful books (for example, non-Protestant books).[69]
His complaint is with the pre-censorship of "unoffensive" books, and this
makes it impossible to interpret his allusion as an ironic subversion of the
view on censorship he attributed to Isocrates. For Milton insists that this
particular species of censorship—the only one to which he objects—was first
conceived by the Inquisition: "We have it not [i.e., licensing], that can be
heard of, from any ancient State, or politie, or Church, nor by any Statute left
us by our Ancestors elder or later; nor from the moderne custom of any
reformed Citty, or Church abroad; but from the most Antichristian Councel,
and the most tyrannous Inquisition that ever inquir'd. Till then Books were
ever as freely admitted into the World as any other birth."[70] Indeed, Milton
notes approvingly that "in *Athens* where Books and Wits were ever busier
then in any other part of *Greece*" the "Judges of the *Areopagus*" only censored *(after the fact)* books "either blasphemous and Atheisticall, or Libellous"[71]—three sorts of books Milton explicitly favors censoring (although he
defines these categories much more narrowly than do most of his contemporaries).[72] Because he is quite clear that no preexisting regime (least of all the
Athenian) ever practiced "licensing," he could not be casting the "ancestral
constitution" defended by Isocrates as a licensing regime. Thus, the "ironic"
reading of the allusion falls apart.

Instead, Milton's Isocratic allusion should be taken at face value. By invoking Isocrates' oration, Milton exhorts the Long Parliament to emulate the

ancient Areopagus and to bring ideal republican government to England. As
with Solon and Cleisthenes, who Isocrates tells us "drove out the tyrants and
brought the people back into power,"[73] Parliament, having revolted against a
tyrannical king, must institute enlightened government and preserve the
vera libertas of its citizens. What is Milton's recipe for this felicitous result? Precisely the recipe Isocrates' Renaissance and early modern readers
drew out of *Areopagiticus.* First, Milton emphatically defends the rule of the
wisest and most virtuous men.[74] Indeed, as Sharon Achinstein has observed,
his implicit comparison of Parliament to the Areopagus is both exhortation
and flattery; he treats the licensing order as an aberration in what has otherwise been a very "Areopagitical" administration—that is, one characterized
by the benign rule of the best citizens.[75] Milton begins his tract by attributing
England's liberty to "your faithfull guidance and undaunted Wisdome, Lords
and Commons of *England*" and to "your indefatigable vertues."[76] He also
praises their "civill and gentle greatnesse" and their "prudent spirit,"[77] and,
in the peroration, once again credits their "prudent foresight, and safe government."[78] As we saw earlier, he attributes the intellectual dynamism of his
country to their "mild, free, and human government" and hails them as the
"founders of our true liberty." The very final passage of the treatise makes the
point most clearly: "This I know, that errors in a good government and in a
bad are equally almost incident; for what Magistrate may not be misinform'd,
and much the sooner, if liberty of Printing be reduc't into the power of a few;
but to redresse willingly and speedily what hath bin err'd . . . is a vertue
(honour'd Lords and Commons) answerable to Your highest actions, and
whereof none can participat but the greatest and wisest men."[79] This is
indeed a devious passage, but the message is clear: if Parliament lives up to its
potential, it will give England the best republican government—one by "the
greatest and wisest men."

Milton also wholeheartedly endorses the convictions about moral oversight we excavated from the Isocratean tradition. He repeatedly exhorts these
"greatest and wisest men" to reject legislative enforcement of public morality,
and to opt instead for benign moral education.[80] He insists that "God uses
not to captivat under a perpetuall childhood of prescription" (children, like
slaves, are not *sui iuris*), and he adds that "there were but little work left for
preaching, if law and compulsion should grow so fast upon those things which
heretofore were govern'd only by exhortation."[81] Perhaps his most revealing
comment is that "truth and understanding are not such wares as to be monop-
oliz'd and traded in by tickets and statutes, and standards. We must not think
to make a staple commodity of all the knowledge in the Land, to mark and
licence it like our broad cloth, and our wooll packs."[82] In the context of his
critique of Plato's authoritarianism, Milton proposes a familiar alternative:

[B]ut those unwritt'n, or at least unconstraining laws of vertuous education, religious and civill nurture, which *Plato* there mentions [in *Laws* I], as the bonds and ligaments of the Commonwealth, the pillars and the sustainers of every writt'n Statute; these they be which will bear chief sway in such matters as these, when all licensing will be easily eluded. Impunity and remissenes, for certain are the bane of a Commonwealth, but here the great art lyes to discern in what the law is to bid restraint and punishment, and in what things perswasion only is to work. If every action which is good, or evill in man at ripe years, were to be under pittance, and prescription, and compulsion, what were vertue but a name.[83]

Drawing on the Isocratean tradition, Milton argues that "vertuous education" and "religious and civill nurture" form the bulwark of the commonwealth, and that a true Areopagus secures public morality by participating in those processes. If the government resorts instead to ineffective laws (such as licensing orders), it becomes tyrannical, thus upsetting the precious balance between magistrates and citizens that constitutes the ideal Isocratean republic—that is, the balance of *vera libertas.*

IV

To say that Milton sincerely takes Isocrates as his authority and model in *Areopagitica* is not by any means to cast Milton's great essay as a mere exercise in ventriloquism. Milton's approach to his classical antecedent is, as always, a subtle blend of emulation and correction. In *Paradise Regain'd,* written nearly thirty years after *Areopagitica,* the Son dismisses the illuminati of ancient Greece and Rome as

> Ignorant of themselves, of God much more,
> And how the world began, and how man fell
> Degraded by himself, on grace depending. $(310–313)^{84}$

Milton's "improvement" on Isocrates in his attack on parliamentary licensing addresses this very same perceived deficiency in the classical worldview. Milton leaves his Isocratean model behind to insist that it is the *clash* of ideas that leads men to virtue and spiritual awakening. Isocrates was deprived of this insight by what he did not know, namely that "It was from out the rinde of one apple tasted, that the knowledge of good and evill as two twins cleaving together leapt forth into the World. And perhaps this is that doom which *Adam* fell into of knowing good and evill, that is to say of knowing good by evill. . . . Assuredly we bring not innocence into the world, we bring impurity much rather: that which purifies us is triall, and triall is by what is contrary."[85] For Milton, the fallen condition of man revealed by the Christian gospel renders the "knowledge and survay of vice" necessary for the "constituting of human vertue"—which makes licensing all the more pernicious to the moral development of citizens. The pagan Isocrates simply could not have known how right he was.

But Milton never underestimated what Isocrates *did* know. On the contrary, Milton saw himself as the proud inheritor of a tradition that celebrated the Greek orator as an expert on the value and practice of human liberty. We have seen that *Areopagiticus* was read as an account of the *optimus status reipublicae* written by a committed republican, and that the force of that reading would have been carried by any allusion to the oration in the seventeenth century. This calls into question the familiar claim that Milton did not become a republican until well after the regicide, and that he never drew on classical models to defend republicanism.[86] Indeed, if Isocrates' *Areopagiticus* was read as a classical model for ideal republican government during the Renaissance and early modern period, then Milton's allusion places him in a particular political tradition. His "Old man eloquent" was a champion of true liberty, not unlike himself.

Trinity College, Cambridge

NOTES

I would like to take this opportunity to offer my deepest thanks to Professors Quentin Skinner and Barbara Lewalski for their support and guidance, and for offering indispensable advice on earlier drafts of this essay. I also record a debt of gratitude to Professor James Hawkins and Dr. Simon Goldhill for patiently reviewing my Latin translations, and to Shirley Sarna and Anisha Dasgupta for their careful proofreading.

1. *The Riverside Milton*, ed. Roy Flannagan (New York, 1998), 88.

2. See *Isocrates*, ed. and trans. George Norlin, Loeb Classical Library (Cambridge, Mass., 1928), vol. 1, xi, xliii.

3. Annabel Patterson, "That Old Man Eloquent" in *Literary Milton: Text, Pretext, Context,* ed. Diana Treviño Benet and Michael Lieb (Pittsburgh, 1994), 22–44.

4. See, for example, *Isocrates*, vol. 1, 287, 311. John Leonard makes this point in "'Thus they relate, erring': Milton's Inaccurate Allusions" in *Milton Studies* 38 (2000), 106–7. See also S. Perlman, "Isocrates' 'Philippus'—a Reinterpretation" in *Philip and Athens*, ed. S. Perlman (New York, 1973), 306–17.

5. *Isocrates*, vol. 1, xxxii.

6. See *Isocrates*, vol. 3, 401. The Battle of Chaeronea took place in August of 338 B.C., and Isocrates' letter (if genuine) was written in the autumn of that year. See N. G. L. Hammond, *A History of Greece to 322 B.C.* (Oxford, 1959), 571, and Simon Hornblower, *The Greek World 479–323 B.C.* (London, 1983), 258.

7. Leonard, "Milton's Inaccurate Allusions," 96–121. See also John Milton, *The Complete Poems*, ed. John Leonard (London, 1998), 647.

8. See *Isocrates* 1 in Dionysius of Halicarnassus, *The Critical Essays*, ed. and trans. Stephen Usher, Loeb Classical Library (Cambridge, Mass., 1974), 107.

9. Isocrates' oration was known in Latin either as "Areopagiticus" or as "Oratio Areopagitica." Milton's title derives from the latter. For clarity's sake, in this essay Isocrates' speech will always be referred to as "Areopagiticus," to distinguish it from Milton's.

10. Isocrates claimed that he avoided public speaking because he considered himself a poor orator.

11. *The Riverside Milton*, 998.

12. Joseph Anthony Wittreich, "Milton's *Areopagitica:* Its Isocratic and Ironic Contexts" in *Milton Studies* 4, ed. James D. Simmonds (Pittsburgh, 1972), 103. Hiroko Tsuji goes even further, arguing that "while Milton argues to abolish the Licensing Orders which had the aim of controlling publications, Isocrates argues to restore the authority of the government to control publications." This view is especially implausible, since Isocrates never mentions publications. See Hiroko Tsuji, *Rhetoric and Truth in Milton: A Conflict between Classical Rhetoric and Biblical Eloquence* (Tokyo, 1991), 72.

13. Wittreich, "Milton's *Areopagitica*," 108.

14. Ibid., 102.

15. Paul M. Dowling, "*Areopagitica* and *Areopagiticus:* The Significance of the Isocratic Precedent" in *Milton Studies* 21, ed. James D. Simmonds (Pittsburgh, 1986), 49–69.

16. Stephen Burt, "'To the Unknown God': St. Paul and Athens in Milton's *Areopagitica*," *Milton Quarterly* 32 (1998): 23–30. The clear reference (quoted above) not only to Isocrates in general but to *Areopagiticus* in particular seems to argue against this view (especially since there is no similarly conclusive reference to Paul's speech from Acts 17:16)—as will the case I am about to lay out. Wittreich argues more moderately that Milton may have intended his readers to play both references off against each other ("Milton's *Areopagitica*," 102). If there is any reference to Paul's speech, however, it is surely not to its alleged "toleration" (Tsuji effectively disposes of this argument [*Rhetoric and Truth in Milton*, 74]) but rather to the fact that the Athenians refer to Paul as "a setter forth of strange gods." Milton's argument in *Areopagitica* rests substantially on the fallibility of human judgment; what the Athenians found "strange" (and, perhaps, would have censored) was the gospel itself.

17. See, for example, Stanley Fish, "Driving from the Letter: Truth and Indeterminacy in Milton's *Areopagitica*," in *Re-membering Milton: Essays on the Texts and Traditions*, ed. Mary Nyquist and Margaret W. Ferguson (New York, 1988), 234–54; John Illo, "The Misreading of Milton," in *Radical Perspectives in the Arts*, ed. Lee Baxandall (Harmondsworth, Eng., 1972), 178–92; Mary Ann McGrail, "Bookburning: Milton's *Areopagitica*," *Agenda* 30 (1992): 50–63; and Roy Flannagan, *The Riverside Milton*, 987–94.

18. See Cicero, *Brutus*, ed. and trans. G. C. Hendrickson, Loeb Classical Library (Cambridge, Mass., 1962), 41.

19. For an account of this phenomenon, see Lucia Gualdo Rosa, *La fede nella 'paideia': Aspetti della fortuna europea di Isocrate nei secoli XV e XVI* (Rome, 1984), esp. 5, 25–28. Gualdo Rosa writes: "Quello che Guarino e gli altri umanisti dopo di lui cercavano, nelle prime tre orazioni isocratee [i.e. the three 'hortatory' orations] e nell'*Evagoras*, è piuttosto un codice di comportamento, un 'galateo', destinato da una parte ai principi (A [sic] Nicoclem, Evagoras), dall'altra (Nicocles, Ad Demonicum) ai sudditi, e piu' precisamente a quegli uomini che ai principi si dovevano appoggiare per la loro ascesa sociale" (25).

20. However, *To Demonicus* is now thought to be spurious. See Albin Lesky, *A History of Greek Literature* (London, 1966), 587–88.

21. Gualdo Rosa, *La fede nella 'paideia*,' 41, 113–19. Isocrates' *Evagoras* was also compatible with *speculum principis* literature but was less frequently printed.

22. *Nicocles* (which purports to be the king's own speech, rather than an exhortation to him), although ideologically similar to its companion piece, proved less generically apt.

23. Sir Thomas Elyot, *The Doctrinal of Princes made by the noble oratour Isocrates,* in *Four Political Treatises,* ed. Lillian Gottesman (Gainsville, Fla, 1967).

24. Sir Thomas Elyot, *The Boke named the Gouernour,* ed. H. H. S. Croft, 2 vols. (London, 1880), 74. This passage appears in 1.11, titled "The most commodious and necessary studies succedyng ordinatly the lesson of poetes."

25. Ibid., 82. The reference is to *To Nicocles* 36 (*Isocrates,* vol. 1, 61).

26. John Edwin Sandys, *A History of Classical Scholarship,* vol. 2 (Cambridge, Eng., 1908), 214.

27. Vives clearly believed that *To Nicocles* did not require his attention as a translator: when he compiled his *Satellitium* for the Princess Mary, he included the Latin translation of *To Nicocles* by Ottmar Nachtigall (1515) rather than one of his own making (Gualdo Rosa, *La fede nella 'paideia,'* 134).

28. All translations from Latin are my own; translations of Isocrates' Greek have been taken from Norlin's standard edition. Juan Luis Vives, *Isocratis Atheniensis Areopagitica oratio de republica Atheniensi, Eiusdem Isoctatis [sic] Adiutoria oratio sive Nicocles de monarchia* (Bruges, 1526). "Vetus quaestio est, quae varie tum multorum ingenia exercuit, tum rerum publicarum status mutavit atque administrationes: utrum praestet, consultiusque sit, populum suarum rerum esse arbitrum ac dominum, an unius cura & providentia teneri regimen civitatis? Multa in utranque partem dicuntur & ingeniose & vere, quum ab aliis, tum vero ab Isocrate Atheniens duabus orationibus: quarum una est de populari potestate, altera est de monarchia." This also seems to be the view taken by Christopher Hegendorf, whose edition of *Areopagiticus* was published in Krakow in 1534: he titled the work *Areopagiticus et clarissimi et eloquentissimi Oratoris Isocratis, quo tum recte, tum salubriter respublicas tam instituendi quam gubernandi ratio praescribitur* (Gualdo Rosa, *La fede nella 'paideia,'* 102).

29. Vives uncritically repeats the account of Isocrates' death that inspired Milton's tenth sonnet: "Tantus patriae amator, ut fractis a Philippo Rege Atheniensium rebus ad Chaeroneam, ut primum ea de re nuncius est Athenas perlatus, moerore expiraverit, grandis admodum natu." Leonard remarks on Vives's comments in "Milton's Inaccurate Allusions," 104.

30. Vives. "Areopagitarum mores quales fuerint, exponit oratione hac Isocrates, & declarant prisca illa verba: Sanctior Areopagita, Gravior Areopagita, Integrior Areopagita . . . Nemo enim in consilium illud cooptatus est, cuius mores spectatissimi non fuerint, & qui non probitatis suae multa ediderit documenta."

31. Sandys, *A History of Classical Scholarship,* 268. Wolf's edition was reprinted more than a dozen times throughout the sixteenth and seventeenth centuries.

32. Wolf's "Praefatio Secunda" is reproduced in full in Henri II Estienne [Henricus Stephanus], *Isocratis orationes et epistolae* (Geneva, 1593). "Hunc enim statum civitatum philosophi omnes in primis probant, in quo viri prudentissimi & optimi ita praesunt civibus, ut parentes liberis: & reliqua multitudo aequissimarum legum moderatione honestaque disciplina regitur. boni viri non modo sine iniuria in pace vivunt, sed etiam honorantur: improborum petulantia . . . legitimis supliciis coercetur."

33. See *Isocratis scripta, Quae quidem nunc extant, Graecolatina* (Basel, 1570), 205. "Rerum publicarum pestes duae praecipue sunt: Tyrannis, quando magistratus impune in imbecilliores grassantur, atque ad suam libidinem, avaritiam & ambitionem omnia referunt; & Anarchia, quum populus contempta legum & magistratuum auctoritate, omnem & loquendi & faciendi licentiam sibi sumit. Neutra autem perturbatio diuturna esse potest, sed subinde altera alteram, velut terrigenae illi fratres, evertit."

34. Ibid. "Status inter has optimus est, & vera libertas, quum bonae leges & a magistratibus & a civibus sacrosanctae habentur, & optimi ac sapientissimi imperant, reliqui modeste parent, ac iuventutis disciplinae summa ratio habetur."

35. The converse of this argument (namely, that a free state is required in order to cultivate virtue) will become important later. See Quentin Skinner, *Liberty Before Liberalism* (Cambrdige, Eng., 1998), 36–57.

36. Reproduced in Wolf, *Isocratis scripta,* 203. "Videbat enim Isocrates, eam ita esse prolapsam & perturbatam, ut iam nec a magistratibus privati coerceri possent, sed unusquisque cum diceret tum faceret quicquid collibitum esset: ac omnes importunam confidentiam, libertatem popularem esse ducerent. Suadet igitur ut a Solone & Clisthene constituta respublica veluti postliminio revocetur. Cuius naturam & instituta recensens, ait. . . . Democratiam, eos iudicasse, non in petulantia & protervitate, sed in moderatione & temperantia consistere: libertatem posuisse non in contemptu magistratuum, sed imperatis faciendis."

37. *Isocrates,* vol. 2, 115. ". . . ὥσθ' ἡγεῖσθαι τὴν μὲν ἀκολασίαν δημοκρατιαν. τὴν δὲ παρρησίαν ἰσονομίαν. ἐλευθερίαν. τὴν δὲ παρρησίαν ἰσονομίαν. τὴν δ' ἐξουσίαν τοῦ πάντα ποιεῖν εὐδαιμονίαμ . . ."

38. Wolf, *Isocratis scripta,* 203. "Potestatem improbo nemini permississe, sed spectatissimis viris mandasse magistratus: quod existimarent, tales fore caeteros cives, quales essent gubernatores civitatis."

39. Ibid. "Gravius existimatum esse, dicendo adversari natu maioribus, quam ordines deserere." This Latin translates a corrupt passage in Dionysius' Greek. Usher completes the period using the corresponding passage from Isocrates' oration, which contains a somewhat different thought: "To contradict one's elders or to be impudent to them was then considered more reprehensible *than it is nowadays to sin against one's parents* [ἢ νῦν περὶ τοὺς γονέας ἐξαμαρτεῖν]." For the purposes of this essay, however, Dionysius's text is only relevant as it was known in the seventeenth century. See Dionysius, *Isocrates,* 123.

40. Wolf, *Isocratis scripta,* 203. "Recta studia praestare legum accuratae constitutioni."

41. Merritt Hughes cites Meurs's tract as a roughly contemporary instance of an author praising the "superhuman probity and prestige" of the Areopagus. See John Milton, *Complete Poems and Major Prose,* ed. Merritt Y. Hughes (New York, 1957), 716.

42. Wolf, *Isocratis scripta,* 206.

43. Jan Meurs, *Areopagus, sive de senatu Areopagitico, liber singularis* (Leiden, 1624), 3. "Si aliquis comparaverit cum senatu isto vestro Augustissimo, non omnino aberraverit."

44. Ibid., 20. "Isocrates, in Areopagitica, ait, omnibus Graeciae conciliis praestitisse."

45. Ibid., 17.

46. Ibid., 5. "intelligeretis, publicae felicitatis magnam partem in ingeniorum cultu sitam esse. . . . Animus enim humanus, recte studiis imbutus, ut prudentiam, ita quoque sapientiam sibi parat; qua utraque dominum se Fortunae facit, & in potestate eam sua tenet. Quae res quantum ad Rempublicam bene administrandam valeat."

47. Ibid. "Vos hoc, inquam, optime intellexistis; ideoque, ut instruerentur prius ad Rempublicam capessendam iuventutis vestrae animi, Academias erexistis . . . ita plane existimantes, nullum maius beneficium, ornamentum, munimentum, Reipublicae dari a vobis potuisse."

48. Ibid., 69. "Habebant quoque morum curam; & inhoneste viventes, castigabant."

49. James Harrington, *The Commonwealth of Oceana and A System of Politics,* ed. J. G. A. Pocock (Cambridge, Eng., 1992), 189.

50. Ibid., 190.

51. Ibid., 8.

52. All five Isocratean references in the Harringtonian corpus are references to *Areopagiticus.* Harrington was particularly taken with Isocrates's comment in *Areopagiticus* 61 that (in Harrington's own translation) "I know the main reason why the Lacedaemonians flourish to be that their commonwealth is popular." He reproduces this passage once in *The Prerogative of Popular Government* and a second time in *The Stumbling-Block of Disobedience and Rebellion.*

As we shall see, this passage was also of deep significance for Henri II Estienne, who noted that it directly contradicts a passage in *Nicocles*. See James Harrington, *The Political Works of James Harrington*, ed. J. G. A. Pocock (Cambridge, Eng., 1977), 299, 455, 479, 570, 831.

53. Estienne, *Isocratis orationes*, 16. "Quemadmodum autem Aristoteles politicae vitae finem statuit honorem, sic apud hunc nostrum scriptorem legimus in oratione Areopagitica, de iis qui reipublicae curam gessissent . . . si se in eo munere iustos praebuissent, laudari solitos, eosque hoc fuisse honore contentos. Caeterum quum in democratia viveret Isocrates, & haec politeia illi prae quavis alia placeret, non mirum si suam politicam scientiam sive politicam philosophiam (ut etiam nominari dictum paulo ante fuit) ad eam potissimum contulerit. Atque aliis certe quamplurimis itidem placuisse mirum in modum democratiam prae oligarchia & aristocratia, (nisi forte dicendum potius est eam solam placuisse) ut hinc colligimus quod prisci oratores politeiam de democratia, tamquam κατ᾽ ἐξοχήν, dixerint: & ipse Isocrates eorum sit e numero qui vocabulo illo ita uti sunt. . . . Politicum igitur ita se ostendit noster Isocrates in iis quae de optima democratia passim his in orationibus disseruit, ut vix meliorem quis eo magistrum nancisci possit. Politicum autem quum dico, politicae scientiae seu philosophiae . . . peritum intelligo. Ideoque aliqot in locis quae sit vera democratia (ut in Panath . . .) quae sit omnium aequissima & firmissima (ut in Areop . . .) doctissime disserit."

54. Estienne also acknowledges that, if these two orations are inauthentic, so too is the encomium to Evagoras.

55. Ibid., 7.

56. Ibid. "Homini & in democratiam nato, & democratiam mirifice laudare solito, non solum indecens sed vix etiam fas esse tantis monarchiam laudibus extollere, easque literarum monumentis mandare." Isocrates himself seems to address precisely this concern in the *Antidosis:* "for you will see that I have expressed myself to Nicocles as a free man and an Athenian should, not paying court to his wealth nor to his power, but pleading the cause of his subjects, and striving with all my powers to secure for them the mildest government possible" (*Isocrates*, vol. 2, 225). "φανήσομαι γὰρ πρὸς αὐτὸν ἐλευθέρως καὶ τῆς πόλεως ἀξίως διειλεγμένος. καὶ οὐ τὸν ἐκείνου πλοῦτον οὐδὲ τὴν δύναμιν θεραπεύων ἀλλὰ τοῖς ἀρχομένοις ἐπαμύνων. καὶ παρασκευάζων καθ᾽ ὅσον ἠδυνάμην τὴν πολιτείαν αὐτοῖς ὡς οἷόντε πραοτάτην." Here, Isocrates actually continues by quoting a substantial passage of *To Nicocles*. However, the *Antidosis* only survived in fragments until A. Mystoxides discovered the substantial middle section (73–309) in 1812. See Lesky, *A History of Greek Literature*, 585.

57. I have taken the Greek translations here from Norlin, vol. 1, 91, and vol. 2, 143. "Repugnantia quaedam loquatur iis quae in Areopagitica leguntur. nam ibi scribit καὶ Λακεδαιμονίους διά τοῦτο κάλλιστα πολιτευομένους. ὅτι μάλιστα δημοκρατούμενοι τυγχάνουσιν: at vero in Nicocle haec legimus ἔτι δὲ Καρχηδονίους καὶ Λακεδαιμονίους. τοὺς ἄριστα τῶν ἄλλων πολιτευομένους. οἴκοι μὲν ὀλιγαρχουμένους. παρὰ δὲ τὸν πόλεμον βασιλευομένους. Quis unquam magis sibi repugnantia scripsisse dici potest, si ab unius eiusdemque calamo profectus est uterque locus?"

58. We cannot know which particular editions of Isocrates Milton had access to (unfortunately, no editions survive in the Christ's College Library from the time Milton was a Cambridge undergraduate). But Milton was deeply familiar with Isocrates (he makes the orator part of his curriculum in *Of Education*), and the editions surveyed in this essay were the most significant of the period. Given the content of Milton's *Areopagitica*, it seems clear that the story we have just told was very much the story Milton had in mind in 1644.

59. Reproduced in *The Riverside Milton*, 988.

60. For analysis of the neo-Roman tradition, see Quentin Skinner, *The Foundations of Modern Political Thought*, (Cambridge, End., 1978), vol. 1 (The Renaissance); Skinner, "Machiavelli's *Discorsi* and the Pre-Humanist Origins of Republican Ideas," in *Machiavelli and*

Republicanism, ed. Gisela Bock, Quentin Skinner, Maurizio Viroli (Cambridge, Eng., 1990), 121–41; Skinner, "Political Philosophy," in *The Cambridge History of Renaissance Philosophy*, ed. Charles B. Schmitt, Quentin Skinner, Eckhard Kessler, Jill Kraye (New York, 1988), 389–452; Skinner, *Liberty before Liberalism*.

61. See Tacitus, *Historiae*, trans. and ed. Clifford Moore, Loeb Classical Library (Cambridge, Mass., 1996), vol. 2, 3.

62. *The Riverside Milton*, 1020. The phrase "true liberty" also appears in the epigraph to *Areopagitica*, adapted from Euripides's *Suppliants* (lines 438–41): "This is true liberty, when free-born men,/ Having to advise the public, may speak free." See *John Milton*, ed. Stephen Orgel and Jonathan Goldberg, Oxford Authors (Oxford, 1991), 237. The actual text here is "τοὐλεύθερον δ᾽ ἐκεῖνο. Τίς θέλει πόλει/ χρηστόν τι βούλευμ᾽ εἰς μέσον φέρειν ἔχων:/ καὶ ταῦθ᾽ ὁ χρῄζων λαμπρός ἐαθ . . ." Way translates, "Thus Freedom speaks:—'What man desires to bring / Good counsel for his country to the people?' / Who chooseth this, is famous [lit. "brilliant" or "illustrious"]." See Euripides, *Works*, ed. and trans. Arthur S. Way, Loeb Classical Library (Cambridge, Mass., 1912), vol. 3, 535.

63. Ibid., 999.

64. Ibid., 1003.

65. Ibid., 1001.

66. Ibid., 1012.

67. Ibid., 1013.

68. It is certainly true that Milton's prose in *Areopagitica* often seems ready to burst through the relatively narrow confines of his argument, but it is significant that the argument remains intact.

69. Milton makes clear that he does not mean to tolerate "Popery" or "open superstition" but rather only "those neighboring differences, or rather indifferences . . . whether in some point of [Protestant] doctrine or of discipline, which though they may be many, yet need not interrupt *the unity of Spirit*, if we could but find among us *the bond of peace*" (*The Riverside Milton*, 1022).

70. Ibid., 1003.

71. Ibid., 999.

72. See *The Riverside Milton*, 1022. In *Of True Religion*, Milton claims that "of all known Sects or pretended Religions at this day in Christendom, Popery is the only or the greatest Heresie; and he who is so forward to brand all others for Hereticks, the obstinate Papist, the only Heretick" (1151). Likewise, in *De Doctrina Christiana* (the authorship of which continues to be disputed, however) Milton attacks those "irrational bigots who, by a perversion of justice, condemn anything they consider inconsistent with conventional beliefs and give it an invidious title—'heretic' or 'heresy' " (1159).

73. *Isocrates*, vol. 2, 113.

74. Milton maintains this view throughout his career, even in *The Readie and Easie Way* (1660). In that tract, he endorses a "free Commonwealth; wherin they who are greatest, are perpetual servants and drudges to the public" (*The Riverside Milton*, 1139). He later advocates a "perpetual Senat" (recall Vives's *perpetuus Senatus*) made up of the "ablest men," not unlike "that of the *Areopagus*" (1141–42).

75. See Sharon Achinstein, *Milton and the Revolutionary Reader* (Princeton, N.J., 1994), 59.

76. *The Riverside Milton*, 997.

77. Ibid., 998.

78. Ibid., 1020.

79. Ibid., 1024.

80. Wittreich comes close to making this point in Milton's *Areopagitica*, 106. He notices an affinity with Isocrates' comments on legislation but locates it in Milton's idea that "real and substantial liberty . . . is rather to be sought from within than from without." The affinity, rather, is in the conviction that government should indeed oversee morals, but through education rather than legislation. Isocrates, after all, was committed principally to "paideia," and that is the tradition we have been following.

81. *The Riverside Milton,* 1006.

82. Ibid., 1013.

83. Ibid., 1010.

84. Ibid., 773.

85. Ibid., 1006.

86. Thomas N. Corns, "Milton and the Characteristics of a Free Commonwealth," in *Milton and Republicanism,* ed. David Armitage, Armand Himy, Quentin Skinner (Cambridge, Eng., 1995), 26. For a critique of Corns's view, see Nigel Smith, "*Areopagitica:* Voicing Contexts, 1643–45," in *Politics, Poetics, and Hermeneutics in Milton's Prose,* ed. David Loewenstein and James Grantham Turner (Cambridge, Eng., 1990), 103–22.

MILTON AMONG THE RELIGIOUS RADICALS AND SECTS: POLEMICAL ENGAGEMENTS AND SILENCES

David Loewenstein

IN THE REASON OF CHURCH-GOVERNMENT (probably published in early 1642) Milton vigorously defends the sects against the prelates in terms that would likely have startled his Presbyterian allies: "If we go downe, say you, as if *Adrians* wall were broke, a flood of sects will rush in. What sects? What are their opinions? give us the Inventory."[1] The dramatic outburst of sectarian activity in 1641 and the growing fragmentation of the zealous Protestant tradition were arousing increasing fears that "a rabble of Sects [would] come in"; yet Milton no less provocatively goes on to condemn the pejorative misnaming of sectarians, especially "knowing that the Primitive Christians in their times were accounted such as are now call'd Familists and Adamites, or worse." Notable here is the independence of Milton's polemical voice: well before publishing his scandalous divorce tracts and suffering himself the "aspersion of a disgracefull name" because of them (YP 1:788), Milton cannot be aligned in all respects with the Presbyterians or the mainstream godly who were zealously attacking the Laudian church and promoting a reformed but compulsory national church purged of ceremonial innovations. For *The Reason of Church-Government* says little about a visible church and its government, and Milton's vision of discipline made inward is not confined to any particular church. Furthermore, the tract includes highly provocative statements about the sects, anticipating his vigorous, more general defense of them over two years later in *Areopagitica,* where he dismisses the "fantastic terrors of sect and schism" (YP 2:554) and affirms the combative energy generated by the new sectarianism.[2] Yet in subsequent moments of political and religious crisis, Milton would not always defend or invoke sectarians by name; and if he defended them, he would usually do so in general terms without addressing specific radical religious groups and their leaders or citing them as authorities on controversial political and religious issues. There are no direct references in his revolutionary polemical writings to the Levellers, Ranters, Quakers, Seekers, or other sects—only one specific reference, as we shall see later, to the Fifth Monarchists.

At crucial moments in his polemical career—notably at moments of significant political tension—Milton remains aloof from specific radical sectarian groups or writers, including leading radical agitators with sectarian connections such as the Leveller leader John Lilburne. The issue of Milton's aloofness, it seems to me, has not been adequately explored. Moreover, it complicates Christopher Hill's view of Milton as a radical Protestant heretic and champion of fearless discussion engaged in an ongoing dialogue with fringe groups during the English Revolution.[3] Hill himself has rightly challenged the stereotypical image of the Puritan Milton "as an aloof, austere intellectual."[4] Yet maintaining a certain aloofness with regard to contemporary radical groups and writers—and refusing to profess allegiance to any one group in his controversial writings—could have been an intentional tactic that served Milton's polemical purposes, especially during periods of acute political and religious uncertainty. Compared with Milton's supposed silence about Cromwell after the *Defensio Secunda,* which Blair Worden has claimed "is loud,"[5] Milton's silence about specific radical groups and sects and their leaders is arguably more notable. We need to be more alert to the implications of that silence.

Milton does not always engage in direct dialogue with those to the left of him or with those whose political and religious views are similar to his. He never specifically mentions the Levellers, whose contentious writings demanded toleration for Puritan sects, the abolition of tithes, the reform of "gibrish Lawes," an open popular press, and the principle of popular sovereignty; the Levellers insisted, as did Milton, that "the power of Kings and Magistrates is nothing else, but what is only . . . committed to them in trust from the People . . . in whom the power yet remains fundamentally" (*The Tenure of Kings and Magistrates;* YP 3:193, 202).[6] Their books, radical politics, and leaders had come under vicious assault by "shallow" Thomas Edwards at the end of 1646: Milton uses the contemptuous epithet to dismiss the frenetic Presbyterian author of the massive heresiography *Gangreana,* which presents Lilburne as "the great darling of the Sectaries, highly extolled and magnified by them in many Pamphlets."[7] Yet Milton, who had become part of the political establishment in 1649, could remain aloof from or even silent about troublesome radical groups and their leaders—there was no place for Levellers in the new Republic, nor for fiery Quakers and Fifth Monarchists in the Protectorate regimes. But even before he joined the political establishment, Milton had demonstrated polemical shrewdness in *The Tenure* by refusing to invoke Leveller or sectarian authorities to bolster his arguments against equivocal Presbyterians and in favor of regicide: "This I shall doe by autorities and reasons, not learnt in corners among Scisms and Heresies, as our doubling Divines are ready to calumniat, but fetch't out of the midst of choicest and most authentic learning, and no prohibited Authors" (YP 3:198).

During and after the revolutionary decades, Milton challenged orthodox Puritan fears of sectarianism, deploring, whether by the orthodox godly or other mainstream authorities, the defaming of unorthodox groups "spit at with all the odious names of Schism and Sectarism" (YP 3:348). Yet he would maintain his own polemical authority and independence by defending the sects at some times and at others remaining detached. He never directly invokes the authority and writings of contemporary radical religious groups, nor, most significantly, does he allow such groups or their leaders to speak for him, however closely their political or religious views and language may resemble his. Hill has argued that Milton remained "in permanent dialogue with the plebeian radical thinkers of the English Revolution";[8] yet Milton often maintains a firm independence from particular authors of radical political and religious views, as he self-consciously creates his own polemical voice. The sectarian writers he did develop close connections with—for example, the Quakers Thomas Ellwood and Isaac Penington the younger—were by no means plebeian but instead well-educated, cultured gentlemen. As Milton forged his polemical stance toward sectarians and radical groups during the revolutionary decades, he maintained both distance and sympathetic engagement—and sometimes silence.

MILTON AND THE LEVELLER CHALLENGE OF 1649

First I want to consider Milton's silence with regard to the Levellers during the crises of 1649. This was a climactic year of revolutionary upheaval that saw the regicide, the abolition of kingship and the House of Lords, and the establishment of the Republic—events forced through by the army, supported by many religious radicals, and vigorously justified in Milton's polemics. The year was also a year in which the limits of the English Revolution were being tested. There occurred a series of significant, interconnected disturbances that Milton the controversialist never mentions: the arrest and imprisonment of the four Leveller leaders (Lilburne, Richard Overton, Thomas Prince, and William Walwyn) at the end of March after renewed Leveller agitation against the government and army leaders, the outburst of popular anger at their imprisonment and vigorous petitioning on their behalf in April (including bold petitions to the Commons by women), and the execution of the Leveller agitator and soldier Robert Lockyer for mutiny at the end of that month. Lockyer's heroic behavior at his execution inspired the massive pro-Leveller demonstration at his funeral—this martyred popular hero was, in Lilburne's words, "much bewailed and lamented at London," as about four thousand soldiers, citizens, and women accompanied his coffin wearing the Leveller color of sea green.[9]

Moreover, Milton never mentions Cromwell's crushing of the Leveller mutiny at Burford in May 1649, a crucial defeat for the Leveller movement; nor does Milton mention Lilburne's dramatic trial for high treason in October of that year. Milton also never mentions the remarkable political activities and visionary writings of the agrarian radicals, or "True Levellers," led by Gerrard Winstanley in Surrey: their agitation, protesting a socioeconomic system based on "the cheating Art of buying and selling,"[10] took place concurrently with Leveller-related revolts in the army and engaged Lord General Fairfax on several occasions; indeed, one meeting with the Diggers occurred (on 26 May) as Fairfax returned from crushing the Leveller-inspired mutiny at Burford. These silences in the Miltonic political oeuvre might not warrant our attention except for one significant fact: Milton's first polemical assignment under the Republic was not to break the royal image (as he would soon do in *Eikonoklastes*) but to help break in pieces the Levellers, particularly Lilburne's notorious writings assaulting the new regime. Milton was asked by the Council of State (on 26 March) to refute the first and second parts of Lilburne's *Englands New Chains Discovered*, scathing attacks on Cromwell and the army leadership for betraying the revolution and the Leveller's *Agreement of the People*.[11] But Milton did not do so: he remained silent rather than use his pen against the Levellers.

When Milton took up his official government position in March 1649 it was a time of sharply mounting tensions. Radical and conservative forces in the revolution were clashing as "the Division betweene the Levellers and Crumwellists" was increasing.[12] Disappointed that the Levellers' version of the *Agreement of the People* was failing to be implemented by Parliament, Lilburne had resumed vigorous polemical activity, producing *Englands New Chains Discovered* (with several colleagues) and presenting it to the Commons on 26 February. This powerful indictment of the new regime, where "liberty [is] so much pretended, so deerly purchased," highlighted the disjunction between a vision of revolutionary freedom achieved with great difficulty by the people ("flattered," Lilburne caustically observes, "with notions of being the Original of all just power") and the reality of a new age of centralized, military power cunningly masked by the public discourse of liberty.[13] In the first half of March the Levellers revived their organization and actively campaigned for a new petition to Parliament;[14] they also sought support from sectarian congregations, including Baptist ones. They then published two scathing manifestoes—*The Hunting of the Foxes* (on 21 March) and *The Second Part of Englands New-Chaines Discovered* (on 24 March). In the first text they used the language of theatrical illusion to call attention to the treacherous practices of the army officers "now a moulding . . . a *New Regality*," as the Levellers invoked the grim specter of Charles I and other English monarchs and their prerogative institutions: "we shall shew you how the Court of the High Commission, the Star chamber, the House of Lords, the King and his Privy Councel are all alive in that Court, called the General Councel of the Army." The portrait of Cromwell, whose smooth godly behavior, they alleged, cloaked brutal ambition, highlighted the equivocal politics of "saintly show" that conceals "Deep malice" (*PL* 4.122–23) now operating in England's new Commonwealth: "did ever men pretend an higher degree of Holinesse, Religion, and Zeal to God and their Country than these? . . . You shall scarce speak to *Crumwell* about any thing, but he will lay his hand on his breast, elevate his eyes, and call God to record, he will weep, howl and repent, even while he doth smite you under the first rib."[15]

A few days later Lilburne's hard-hitting *Second Part of Englands New-Chaines* appeared, further reinterpreting the recent events of the revolution from a Leveller perspective underscoring patterns of treachery, betrayal, and "vile Apostacy" that had brought the Commonwealth to its "uncertain and dangerous condition." The events of 1648–1649 had become the occasion for a few, new political masters, including the leaders of the army, to assume their position of power and, in Lilburne's grim account, to practice "a new way of breaking the spirits of the English, which Strafford and Canterbury never dreampt of." Lilburne, who, as did Milton, despised "the odious names" used to brand sectarianism, complained of radical petitioners now "spit at" (in the Leveller's words) "with the names of Atheists, Hereticks, and seditious Sectaries."[16]

Cromwell was now more determined than ever "to break [the Levellers] in pieces"—"if you do not breake them they will break you," he reportedly shouted in the Council of State[17]—and on 27 March, the day after Milton was ordered to refute Lilburne, Parliament issued its own severe condemnation, voting that *The Second Part of Englands New-Chaines* "is highly seditious, and destructive to the present Government," tending to "Division and Mutiny in the Army, and the Raising of a new War in the Commonwealth"; the authors of the tract were "guilty of High-Treason" and, moreover, "all Persons whosoever that shall . . . aid or assist the Authors, Framers, and Contrivers of the aforesaid Paper" would be considered "Traitors to the Commonwealth."[18] At this moment of acute tension, Baptist leaders—"fearing if [they] should be silent"—spoke out, publicly repudiating Lilburne's manifesto ("we neither had nor have heart nor hand in the framing, contriving, abetting or promoting of the said Paper") and appealing to the imprisoned Levellers to abandon their fierce opposition to the regime now endangered by enemies within and without.[19] But from Milton there was no response.

Here was a moment of political crisis when Milton was certainly not "talking to his [most radical] contemporaries," as Hill would put it, but keeping his distance and, crucially, maintaining his silence.[20]

What, in the end, did Milton think about Cromwell's crushing of the Levellers? Did it reveal to him the limits of the revolution of 1648–1649? Did he regard the Leveller writings attacking the infant Republic as an example of what he called in *Areopagitica* those "scandalous, seditious, and libellous Books, which were mainly intended to be supprest" (YP 2:491)? We cannot know for sure. Yet his silence in the spring of 1649 suggests a writer who remained conflicted: Milton was a vocal defender of the army and the new, still unsettled regime; nevertheless, he was unwilling to back in public polemic the hard line Cromwell and the army leaders took against Lilburne and the Levellers and thus to counter the most serious radical threat facing the regime. The crushing of the Leveller insurrection, after all, signified the triumph of military force over the revolution's more radical and populist dimensions—the Leveller challenge having highlighted unresolved conflicts over how much power to invest in the people.[21] The revolutionary political changes of 1648–1649 were forced through by the army, and they did not lead to the more or less democratic transformation for which the Levellers had struggled—the implementation of the *Agreement of the People,* the elimination of tithes, the reform of the legal system, the decentralization of power, the dissolution of the present Parliament and the election of a new one. Curbing radical dissent and agitation, the army had determined how far the revolution would go.[22] It was now, moreover, safer to express antagonism toward radicals. Thus it would be easier to crack down on the extreme antinomian Ranters, as the regime began to do in early 1650; indeed, the Ranters' notorious prophet Abiezer Coppe (whose apocalyptic vision of social levelling was more radical than that of the Levellers) himself soon warned the army leaders that the blood of the Burford martyrs would bring the vengeance of the Lord: "Ye have killed the just—Ye have killed, ye have killed, ye have killed the just," the Ranter proclaimed in *A Fiery Flying Roll,* echoing the words of doom that the epistle of James directs at the rich and powerful (James 5:6).[23] But Milton, who often dared to "utter odious Truth[s]" (*PL* 11.704) in his age, withheld his prophetic voice during this period of internal crisis, thereby maintaining his voice as the Commonwealth's polemicist. He chose to say nothing against the martyred Levellers and nothing in their favor during and after their suppression.

Milton may well have sensed that he could achieve wider influence by, at critical moments, being careful to not engage with specific radical groups and their leaders. Milton's withholding his response to Lilburne reminds us that such polemical silences can themselves be significant, with open-ended and ambiguous consequences. For when he was eventually banished from the Republic, Lilburne published *As You Were* (1652), a tract in which he attempted to display for Cromwell and the army Grandees "the *faces of their Soules*, spotted with *Apostacy*" and "*Ambitious breach of promise*, and hocus-pocus-*juggleing* . . . [a] deformed and *fearfull visage*";[24] and there he enlisted for his cause the Commonwealth's "valiant and learned Champion Mr. MIL-TON," now depicted as his polemical and literary ally. Lilburne in effect transformed Milton's republican *Defense of the English People* into a text that could be used to buttress Leveller ideology and attack the English regime. Presenting himself "as a man that intirely loves [his] native Countrey," Lilburne quoted at length—and in English—from the conclusion of Milton's Latin polemic a passage in which, as the Leveller rightly notes, Milton warns his countrymen and the Rump Parliament to remain vigilant against self-seeking forces that could undermine the achievements of the revolution.[25] In the Leveller's text, the republican Milton becomes a Lilburne-style hero and writer: bold and assertive toward both his enemies and leading countrymen and also patriotic and chivalric.[26] Lilburne admires the eloquent way that the "valiant and learned Champion" routed "the forces of SALMASIUS," and then he notes how Milton advised his own Commonwealth masters "with much *faithfullnes* and Freedome" to conquer ambition and avarice lest in time of peace they "prove base and unworthy" and bring God's wrath upon themselves—a divine hatred greater than the wrath manifested against their royalist enemies. Milton's "excellent and faithfull advice" to his countrymen has thus become a means of supporting and authorizing Lilburne's own polemical authority as a contentious, undaunted writer in exile continuing to challenge the legitimacy of the English Republic.[27] And so by maintaining his silence during the internal crises of 1649 Milton had subsequently—and simultaneously—enabled himself to speak on behalf of the new Republic *and* to win over one of its most vocal and popular radical enemies.[28]

SECTARIAN DISCORD DURING THE PROTECTORATE

At the end of December 1653, for the first time since the defeat of the Levellers, radical agitation against Cromwell exploded again. Alarming sectarian unrest was countered by leading apologists for Cromwell's new Protectorate, including Marvell in *The First Anniversary of the Government*. Maintaining a certain distance from radical agitators, Milton, in the *Defensio Secunda* (May 1654), was more restrained and less direct in his criticism, and at the end of this section I will contrast these two major texts from the Protectorate as responses to renewed fears of sectarianism. Published during a period of vocal sectarian assaults on Cromwell's regime, Milton's work of revolutionary mythmaking represents to a European audience the protector as a godly liberator. Milton similarly presents himself as a bold, heroic defender of the godly Protestant cause, even when in Rome, center of idolatry and superstition, where (during his Italian tour of 1638–39) he had been "unwilling to be circumspect in regard to religion" (YP 4:618).[29] Yet when the *Second Defense* appeared, Protestant unity in Cromwell's England was imperiled by heightened sectarian factionalism; England, the protector would lament, was full of "carnal divisions and contentions amongst Christians" and a "nation rent and torn in spirit and principle from one end to another."[30] Tensions between political conservatism and religious radicalism, ambivalent trends embodied in Cromwell himself,[31] were aggravated by the ambiguous character of the quasi-regal Protectorate and by strident sectarianism. The *Second Defense* presents a vision of Milton and Cromwell the liberator arduously advancing the godly cause during times of war and peace, yet it barely registers the sharp escalation of radical discontent: the saints, who had once hailed Cromwell as a second Moses or Gideon, were now bitterly disaffected with the backsliding protector, demanding "No king but Jesus."

Immediately after Cromwell had been installed as protector in December 1653, fiery millenarian Fifth Monarchists, including Christopher Feake and John Simpson (singled out for satirical treatment in Marvell's *First Anniversary*),[32] began spewing venomous rhetoric and waging a vigorous, well-orchestrated campaign against the new, anti-Christian regime for betraying the revolution. Once hailed as a new Moses leading the saints from the Rump Parliament's bondage, Cromwell was now called "the man of sin, the old dragon, and many other scripture ill names," and identified, as Charles I had been, with the little horn making war against the saints (Dan. 7:8, 21).[33] Cromwell's single-person regime was represented as a more menacing anti-Christian power than the "apostate" Rump, whose dissolution these radical saints considered a crucial step toward the inauguration of the kingdom of Christ.[34] Cromwell's supreme power was as popish as the former king's: "This popery and the old monarchie are one and the same," preached the vehement Feake, aiming to stir up deep-seated popular fears of new popery.[35] On 19 December 1653 one of Milton's "particular Friends," Marchamont Nedham, attended a Fifth Monarchist meeting in which Vavasor Powell, provocatively interpreting Daniel 11:21, suggested that "a vile person" would "obtain the kingdom by flatteries."[36] Nedham would also soon report to the protector on the "mischief" of Anna Trapnel, the flamboyant Fifth Monarchist prophetess who, in a twelve-day trance at Whitehall during January 1654, issued fiery millenarian prophecies in prose and verse assaulting the new Protectorate, including the protector's "great pomp and revenue," and questioning his role as England's new Gideon.[37] Illuminated by the light within, the Quakers too became increasingly pugnacious in their apocalyptic exhortations and confrontational writings, which rejected social hierarchies, denounced temporal authorities, attacked a settled ministry, and alarmed the orthodox godly who complained to the protector and Parliament.[38] Jesus Christ had raised up "his Army . . . in the North of *England*," one Quaker prophet announced, "and is marching towards the South in mighty Power to cut down . . . all the Powers of the Land."[39] In April 1654 George Fox and Edward Burrough issued apocalyptic tracts warning that the dreadful day of the Lord was swiftly approaching, as did John Audland and James Nayler the following month; in October Fox was proclaiming that "The Lord Protector of Heaven and Earth is above all Highnesses."[40] A public scourge of godly ministers and magistrates, the Quakers' "frantique Army" (*First Anniversary*, 299) was aggressively on the move as their bellicose prophets threatened clerical and political authorities with the Lord's language from Ezekiel: "I will overturn, overturn, overturn" (21:27).[41]

Despite such fiery assaults on Cromwell's regime by religious radicals, Milton's *Second Defense* does little to answer them directly, though the religious and political tensions aggravated by strident sectarian rhetoric would soon provoke the protector's angry responses in Parliament. Milton's claim that "in unison we acknowledge [Cromwell's] unexcelled virtue" (YP 4:671) is belied by his brief comments on internal factions, when he observes how "men who are unworthy of liberty most often prove ungrateful to their very liberators" and "like wild horses fretting at the bit [*velut ferocientes equi fraenum indignantes*] try to shake off the yoke, driven not by the love of true liberty . . . but by pride and base desires" (YP 4:683). Yet even here he never specifically singles out "the hot men at *Black Fryers*"—as Nedham dubbed the Fifth Monarchists furiously assailing the Protectorate—though Milton's general formulation likely includes such restless firebrands, along with other rebels against Cromwell and his single-person government.[42] At the same time, Milton's favorable characterization of the New Model Army as sober, godly, and well-disciplined—its soldiers engaged "in careful reading of sacred Scripture" (YP 4:648)—dissociates it from sectarian radicalism and heresies; in fact, its godly soldiers had been inspired by the spiritual egalitarianism of its leading radical chaplains William Dell, William Erbery, John Saltmarsh, and Hugh Peters, and numerous Quakers had served among its ranks.[43] The accusation that it had become a dangerous "Lernaean swamp of all heresies" was made not only by the author of *Regii Sanguinis Clamor ad Coelum* (YP 4:648), Peter Du Moulin, but also by Thomas Edwards, whose *Gangraena* fiercely criticized the many sectaries who had infested the army and radicalized it, with the consequence that sectarian soldiers had usurped pulpits and preached against infant baptism, against tithes, and for universal grace and liberty of conscience.[44] Moreover, Milton highlights the New Model Army's famous sobriety and godliness in a year when Fifth Monarchists were now aiming their fiery invectives at the army, accusing it, in Feake's words, of having "set up old Monarchy in a new disguise" and, in the words of another leading saint, of having "declared themselves *Rebels,* and *Traytors* to Jesus Christ" for supporting Cromwell's Protectorate.[45] Milton's polemical defense of the army as godly thus responds to both its conservative and radical critics, though without engaging directly with the latter. Milton keeps his distance from radical groups, quickly deflecting attempts by the author of the *Clamor* to malign him by linking him with Anabaptist ideas (see YP 4:632–33, 643–44).

Nevertheless, when Milton expresses apprehensions about the new regime and its precarious authority, his concerns do resemble those of discontented sectarians and radical groups, though as a polemicist he is too independent-minded to invoke their allegiance. He perceives the danger of godly power taking on regal forms and vices and expresses acute concerns lest his countrymen and the Protectorate sink "into royalist excess and folly [*in regium luxum atque socordiam prolapsos*]," its architects and representatives pursuing "the same vanities" and thus becoming royalists themselves. Moreover, in a nation so debased, Milton observes, wide suffrage itself would easily become corrupted, with faction resulting in the election of unworthy legislators (YP 4:681–82). (Here Milton refers, though rather skeptically and for the only time in his prose, to a key Leveller issue: that of a wider franchise.) When Milton expresses his fears, using the language of simulation, that "the achievements of genuine virtue and piety" could therefore become in the Protectorate "the mere counterfeit and shadow of these qualities—cleverly feigned, no more [*duntaxat belle simulando*]" (4:682), he recalls Leveller accusations that the counterfeit godliness of Cromwell and his Grandees supported by a Parliament that was a "*mock-Power,* or *shadow,* or *shell* of *Power*" had created "a *New Regality*" in the Republic.[46] At the same time, Milton vigorously attacks Presbyterians over the abuses of the tithe system (4:640, 650–51), still not abolished by Cromwell, that had been repudiated, along with the national church served by a professional ministry, by Fifth Monarchists, Quakers, and many Baptists. Similarities between Milton's concerns and those of radical religious groups may explain why he only briefly criticizes their unbridled attacks on Cromwell without mounting, as Marvell would, a direct assault on dangerous swarms of sectarians. When seen in the context of the regime's other major vindications and Cromwell's political speeches, which soon bitterly condemned sectarian discord, Milton's apology is notable for its unwillingness to make vocal sectarian opposition a major justification for renewed vigilance in the Protectorate.

The outburst of strident religious radicalism had renewed Cromwell's urgent wish to reunite the fragmented godly: lamenting "the nation rent and torn in spirit and principle" when he addressed the Protectorate Parliament in September 1654, Cromwell had called for a period of "healing and settling." The experiment in radical godly rule under the Barebone's assembly, which was dissolved in December 1653, had brought little political and religious stability: only millenarian saints lamented its fall, and Milton himself had little good to say about it in the *Second Defense* (YP 4:671). Asserting his conservative principles, Cromwell denounced Levellers, Ranters, Fifth Monarchists, and sectaries who aimed to abolish the established ministry; he deplored "men of Levelling principles" who "tend to the reducing all to an equality," as well as this age of "prodigious blasphemies; contempt of God and Christ, denying of him, contempt of him and his ordinances and of the Scriptures." He likewise expressed alarm at the apocalyptic rhetoric of "overturning" and "the mistaken notion of the Fifth Monarchy," which fueled "men of discontented spirits" to promote "divisions and distractions."[47] Though the Instrument of Government (December 1653) included a provision expressing tolerance toward those "differing in judgment from the doctrine, worship or discipline publicly held forth," the new constitution also expressed concern about radical sectaries who abuse religious "liberty . . . to the actual disturbance of the public peace."[48] In late 1653 and throughout 1654 such disturbances—as the Protectorate was being attacked in press and pulpit—were preventing that "healing and settling" to which Marvell would allude at the end of his *First Anniversary,* where he depicts the godly protector as "the *Angel* of our Commonweal" who, after the troubling of the waters, "yearly mak'st them Heal" (401–2; echoing John 5:4).

The fiery preaching and rantings against Cromwell by militant saints were provoking sharp critical reactions from both fellow-enthusiasts (who spoke their language) and from the Protectorate's official apologists. John Goodwin, the radical Independent whose revolutionary writing drew upon Milton's *Tenure* and who would differ with the Protectorate, raised probing questions about clamorous Fifth Monarchist prophecies; at the end of 1653 and then a month before the *Second Defense* appeared, he directly challenged bitter visionaries "who publiquely undertake or pretend to know, and predict unto the people, how long the present Government shall stand, and . . . [when] it shall . . . fall" so as to raise "Tumults and Insurrections in the Land."[49] The radical preacher and Seeker William Erbery likewise published a series of provocative queries rebuking the outraged millenarian saints for meddling in state affairs and construing the scriptural prophecies of the kingdom of Christ—*"the thousand years"*—"so carnally, when . . . all the Revelation . . . is a mystery, or spiritual secret."[50] Meanwhile, major vindications of the Protectorate by John Hall and Marchamont Nedham warned of the consequences of sectarian bitterness; thus Hall, who had been employed with Milton by the Republic's Council of State and whose writings drew upon *Areopagitica* and *Of Education,* warned of the instability created by the "pulling down of *Antichrist, Forms, Orders, Ordinances* of *Man,*" and "the plucking up of all *Ecclesiastical* and *Civil* policy" by extreme millenarians proclaiming that all earthly powers should be broken in pieces.[51]

Marvell would respond skillfully to this heady apocalyptic discourse of "pulling down" earthly powers by envisioning a Cromwell who both pulls down and erects "a firm State" anew and whose "sober Spirit" counters the raging spirit of the "frantique Army" of radical saints (*First Anniversary,* 247–48, 230, 299). His *First Anniversary* is a sophisticated work of polemical propaganda; published anonymously as a quarto pamphlet in January 1655, it was printed by the government printer, Thomas Newcomb, who had published Milton's *Second Defense* and advertised in the government-controlled newsbook, *Mercurius Politicus.*[52] Milton's *Second Defense* and Marvell's poem have been closely—and understandably—linked by recent scholars responding to the latter poet's admiration for the dazzling rhetorical qualities of Milton's work.[53] Nevertheless, these two major works of the Protectorate differ in terms of the degree and vigor with which they confront sectarian aggression.

"Despite and contempt by men of Levelling principles" deeply troubled Cromwell, and Marvell acknowledged the need to address recalcitrant radicals who would have "quickly Levell'd every Cedar's top" (*First Anniversary,* 262) in a political poem attempting to sustain the vision of a new regime that hoped to create an ordered, godly nation in the face of sharp contentions.[54] Cromwell's patience toward radical saints who strayed had been sorely tried, though he persisted in strenuous dialogues with sectarian firebrands, including Feake and Simpson.[55] "*The unity of Spirit*" that, ten years earlier, Milton's *Areopagitica* had envisioned as including many schisms and sects in a nation of prophets now seemed a shattered ideal (YP 2:565). Indeed, contrary to Marvell's vision, the "crossest Spirits," it seemed, "whose Nature leads them to divide," had become too recalcitrant to "take their part" in building the godly Commonwealth under the protector (*First Anniversary,* 89, 91).

Yet Marvell's own political proclivities remain complex and ambivalent, combining and negotiating tendencies from both the conservative and radical trends of the English Revolution. As with Milton, he did not simply serve as an apologist for the Protectorate but instead skillfully attempted to bridge key tensions in the period. Thus, in line with the antimonarchical fervor of apocalyptic revolutionaries (including Milton) who envision shaking the monarchies of the earth, he repeatedly diminishes the achievements of "heavy Monarchs": "Unhappy Princes, ignorantly bred, / By Malice some, by Errour more misled" as they "adore" the Great Whore of Babylon; and he promises "with graver Accents [to] shake" their "Regal sloth" (*First Anniversary,* 15, 117–18, 113–14, 121–22). Marvell, however, is also acutely sensitive to Cromwell's wish, especially at this moment of religious and political instability, to avoid unbounded rule, including the saints' strident claim to rule as a result of a direct call from Christ: Cromwell observed the need "to avoid the extremes of monarchy on the one hand, and democracy on the other, and yet not to found *dominium in gratia*" (i.e., a Fifth Monarchist regime in which an elected few ruled until the return of Jesus).[56] So Marvell's Cromwell is truly an artful steersman who saves the ship of state and its "Giddy" passengers from "threat'ning Rocks" (265–78) and avoids steering the Commonwealth into radical seas.

At the same time, Marvell's depiction of radical groups as a "frantique Army" stimulates his satirical imagination and can be associated with the more conservative tone of the Protectorate and its apologists (including newsbooks) combatting challenges from "factious firebrands"; as one apologist observed, "Government can never be safe and settled which is infested with seditious Sectaries."[57] Marvell's satirical catalogue of swarming sectarians evokes, in a highly compressed fashion, a wide range of popular fears and exaggerated representations, the kinds of fears and stereotypes Milton himself sought to combat in his controversial writings:

> Accursed Locusts, whom your King does spit
> Out of the Center of th'unbottom'd Pit;
> Wand'rers, Adult'rers, Lyers, *Munser's* rest,
> Sorcerers, Atheists, Jesuites, Possest.   (311–14)

Antisectarians equated the multiplying sects with the terrifying locusts emerging from the bottomless pit in Revelation 9, a new onslaught of the forces of destruction spreading over the nation.[58] Moreover, they sometimes depicted Quakers as Jesuits in disguise and associated them with sorcery— their extravagant tremblings and shakings seemed testimony of demonic possession.[59] Indeed, Jesuits "Possest" were themselves included in accounts of devilish sectarians endangering the state: Cromwell lamented that "the emissaries of the Jesuits never came in these swarms, as they have done since [these distractions] were set on foot."[60] Furthermore, the "frantick Zeale" of radical millenarians, especially the Fifth Monarchists, linked them with the original Munster Anabaptists, since the saints seemed to breathe "nothing but fire and sword" as they looked "upon their country-men with such an eye as the *Anabaptists* cast upon *Munster.*"[61] Marvell's satirical catalogue therefore reminds us that the protector valued unity among the godly more than religious diversity: Cromwell remained largely unsympathetic to Quakers, Ranters, Fifth Monarchists, and Socinians, as well as to Roman Catholics and Anglicans.[62]

Marvell, in comparison to the cruder antisectarians of the 1650s, is more skillful in his polemical assaults, maintains more control over his sarcastic tone and he is infinitely more capable of urbane compressed expression. His political position is also more complex and less consistently conservative than theirs, as he negotiates the tension between political conservatism and religious radicalism during the Protectorate. His mockery deflates the religious radicals who "deface" the Scriptures and the laws "With the same liberty as Points and Lace" and serves as a rhetorical means of diminishing their threat; yet his sharpness breaks through as he considers their godlier-than-thou zeal ("Oh Race most hypocritically strict!" [*First Anniversary,* 315–17]), reminding us of the powerful anxieties which the "frantique Army" of sectaries and saints could arouse as they contested Cromwell's vision of the godly nation. Furthermore, Marvell's polemical response to sectarian unrest (as I have argued elsewhere) operates at a complex level as he skillfully transmutes the explosive language of extreme millenarian enthusiasm (which Cromwell, in his more exuberant moments, shared with the militant saints) into a means of legitimizing the new regime's power and Cromwell's apocalyptic role.[63] Thus Marvell envisions in Cromwell "a Captain" who alone might "raise / The great Designes kept for the latter Dayes" (109–10)—the Fifth Monarchy and the reigning of the saints prophesied by Daniel (7:18, 27 and 10:14)—in an age full of "thankless Men" (217) who have dangerously misrepresented Cromwell as the agent of Antichrist.

Milton himself, however, never engaged in such a pointed, polemical way with the troublesome sectarian threat during the Interregnum; he maintained sympathy for the sects but continued, in his controversial writings, to keep his distance from specific radical religious groups and their leaders. At times, this is a polemical tactic. But it is also more than that. His aloofness or silence, as we shall see, can be increasingly attributed to his sense that one strenuously works out one's personal religious beliefs, however unorthodox, only for oneself.

MILTON AND SECTARIANS IN THE LATE INTERREGNUM AND AFTER

During the late Interregnum, the spiritually radical Milton refused to depend upon any human authority when it came to matters of inward religion. His radical religious countrymen were themselves not infallible: "Sects may be in a true Church as well as in a false, when men follow the Doctrin too much for the Teachers sake, whom they think almost infallible," Milton observed in 1673 (YP 8:422), recalling *A Treatise of Civil Power* (Feb. 1659), in which, scornful of being "servile in religion towards men," he had stressed that *"no man or body of men* in these times can be the infallible judges or determiners in matters of religion to any other mens consciences but thir own" (YP 7:265, 242–43; emphasis mine). Indeed, the late Milton increasingly committed himself to his own tireless solitary exertions: as his deeply personal epistle to *De Doctrina Christiana* suggests, he sought to work through difficult theological issues by means of his own strenuous exertions, never sparing himself in any way. Milton eschews human authorities and would follow "no other heresy or sect" (YP 6:123)—only Scripture (which he will interpret for himself) and the guidance of the Spirit.

Milton is thus scornful of those who believe "only as the church" or as the state believes (YP 7:242–3, 249, 252). Instead, each believer should labor constantly in spiritual matters—searching, trying, examining them for him or herself. Milton advocates following *one's own conscience* and the guidance of the Holy Spirit within rather than any law of man (YP 7:242), a theme that would find its most dramatic and daring Miltonic expression in the deeply religious, antinomian "rousing motions" of *Samson Agonistes,* when a fiercely defiant, solitary Samson spurns "those who have [him] in thir civil power" (1382, 1367) and follows the impromptu guidance of the Spirit, not the prescription of the law.[64] Indeed, even the apostles, Milton notes in an age when Quakers regularly invoked them as models, "had no dominion or constraining power over faith or conscience" (YP 7:245). And so Milton, for whom human traditions or counsels, or the canons of any church, were fallible, would not invoke the authority of other religious radicals as supreme interpreters of Scripture or matters of religion. *Civil Power* and *The Likeliest Means to Remove Hirelings* neglect the role of the church and organized religion in Protestant experience, and there is no evidence that Milton himself ever joined a gathered church or a separate congregation: he was closely associated with the Quakers in the 1660s but, unlike Lilburne and Winstanley, he did not become one at the end of his life.[65]

The radical spiritual polemicist kept aloof from sectarians (at least in his writings), although, as they did, he sought to be guided by the inward persuasive motions of the Spirit. Consequently, he rejected tithes to support a parochial clergy, demanded the separation of church and state, and denied civil magistrates any authority in matters of religion. His twinned texts, *Civil Power* and *Hirelings,* were both published in 1659, a year of political upheaval and widespread fears about the revival of radical sectarianism; republican and sectarian agitation would bring down Richard Cromwell's regime in April. Radical pamphleteers, including sectarians, would soon again be pressuring the Rump Parliament, restored in May, to sweep away the clerical establishment.[66] During the summer the troublesome Quakers (whose numbers had swelled to several tens of thousands by the end of the decade) were raising the specter of social and religious revolution, thus fuelling fears of radical sectarianism. To the mainstream godly, "the fantastic terrors of sect and schism" seemed more frightening than ever.

In the middle of *Civil Power* Milton, rather surprisingly, refers in favorable terms to one of the Interregnum's principal pieces of antisectarian legislation: "that prudent and well deliberated" Blasphemy Act of August 1650, which the purged Parliament had passed in an attempt to promote moral reform, conciliate moderate Presbyterians, and repress the Ranters and their flamboyant reaction against the restraints and guilt-consciousness of orthodox Puritanism (YP 7:246).[67] Milton sends conflicting signals here: his repudiation of civil power in spiritual matters would hardly please a religiously conservative regime such as Richard Cromwell's; his citation of a strict act against blasphemy, "Execrable Opinions," and "wicked and abominable Practices," however, would. For this was no forgotten piece of legislation; it served throughout the Commonwealth and Protectorate as the only statutory statement of unlawful religious beliefs. It had been cited in Oliver Cromwell's ordinance (August 1654) for ejecting scandalous ministers during the Protectorate—an ordinance intended to help reform the ministry, to approve new public preachers, and to control radical preaching.[68] That loose form of state control had only further inflamed the "frantique Army" of Fifth Monarchists. More recently, the act had been invoked in the 1657 constitution of the Protectorate—The Humble Petition and Advice—to exclude from Parliament persons deemed to profess "atheistical, blasphemous, and execrable opinions derogatory to the honour of God and destructive to humane society."[69] Milton's citation thus enables him to voice radical spiritual convictions while putting distance between himself and radical religious groups.

Milton calls the act "prudent and well deliberated," but *Civil Power* itself was certainly no "prudent" text: it was addressed to a Parliament hoping to draw the bounds of the established church tighter.[70] Its members would call for a day of fasting and public humiliation on account of "many Blasphemies, and damnable Heresies" that had encouraged "the most horrible Contempt of the Ordinances and Institutions of *Jesus Christ*" and of godly ministers.[71] But as Milton retrospectively praises the Blasphemy Act, he introduces a revealing qualification: "although in all likelihood," he adds, "they whose whole studie and profession these things are should be most intelligent and authentic therin, as they are for the most part, *yet neither they nor these unnerring always or infallible*" (YP 7:246–47; emphasis mine). And because parliaments are not infallible, Milton challenges the Parliament to rethink the meaning of blasphemy so as to defuse an inflammatory term used by the orthodox godly to condemn radical sectaries. Most members had been outraged in 1656 by James Nayler's riding into Bristol on a mule—perceived as a horrid, blasphemous impersonation of Christ's entry into Jerusalem—and they savagely punished the charismatic Quaker leader.[72] By invoking the Blasphemy Act in this rather ambiguous way, Milton could maintain his polemical independence from troublesome sectaries. Yet without allowing himself to be identified with any one radical sectarian group, he remains fiercely opposed to *any form* of institutionalized religion.

Addressed to the restored Rump, Milton's *Hirelings* appeared in August 1659—the same month as the pro-Royalist Presbyterian uprising of Sir George Booth.[73] Quaker writings and militant activities, which increased alarm and arousing hostility toward sectaries, helped to provoke Booth's rising in Cheshire and growing sentiment for the return of the monarchy. In a published letter, Booth expressed his fear that religion was threatened "by subjecting us under the meanest and fanatick spirits of the Nation," including "this fanatick Quakeisme."[74] Milton would refer to the Booth revolt—"those Cheshire Rebells"—as he lamented the backsliding nation later in October (*A Letter to a Friend;* YP 7:325), but in *Hirelings* he does not allow himself to be identified with those "meanest and fanatick spirits" who had fuelled the Royalist-Presbyterian insurrection.[75] Despite his own religious radicalism, Milton remains aloof from radical sectarians in a tract offering a sustained, historically based assault on tithing—a key Quaker issue during the Interregnum, including in 1659, when the Quakers' opposition to tithes contributed to the perception that they were dangerous social radicals.[76] Indeed, tithing had remained one of the most contentious religious issues of the English Revolution; religious radicals, including Milton (YP 7:281–90), argued that tithes had lost their divine sanction when the ceremonial law was superseded by the gospel and the Levitical priesthood by an apostolic ministry. Yet while attacking in 1659 a hireling clergy and their "seeming piety" (7:280), Milton never specifically invokes the example and writings of the Quakers (whose millenarian tracts castigated hireling priests) or other contemporary sectarians; rather than allow any sectarian group to speak for him, he continues to assert his own polemical independence and authority.

Nevertheless, as did the Quakers, he deflates the university curriculum used to train the educated, orthodox ministry—"all those piles of sermons, notes, and comments on all parts of the bible, bodies and marrows of divinitie" (YP 7:316). When Milton writes that the pretenses of hirelings are "colour'd over most commonly with the cause of learning and universities," he recalls radical sectaries suspicious of a well-educated, well-paid ministry for dressing up the Word of God with learned scriptural glosses and making a "cloak of carnal interest" (YP 7:317, 313). And when he castigates hirelings as *"greedy dogs,"* borrowing from Isaiah 56 a metaphor for Israel's rapacious religious leaders (YP 7:296), he employs the kind of reviling scriptural language that Richard Baxter complained the Quakers were using to excoriate orthodox ministers.[77] Milton's radical religious convictions are likewise notable as he characterizes the kind of apostolic ministry he admires, one that seems remarkably close to early Quakerism: he observes that "they who after [Christ] first taught [the gospel], were otherwise unlearned men" and had "the spirit to guide them in all truth" (YP 7:302). Most provocatively, he commends itinerant, inspired preachers who preach in informal settings ("we may be well assur'd that he who disdaind not to be laid in a manger, disdains not to be preachd in a barn . . . such meetings as these, being, indeed, most apostolical and primitive") and who model themselves after the apostles (as early Quaker preachers regularly did), for they, though few in number, "preachd to the poore as well as to the rich, looking for no recompense but in heaven" (see YP 7:303–5). Yet when Milton considers the difficulty of removing hirelings and finding ministers "contented to teach *gratis*" (as Paul did), he pauses and tersely remarks: "but few such are to be found" (YP 7:280). Just who those few inwardly inspired ones might be, and where they might be found during this tense Interregnum year of sectarian unrest, Milton never explicitly tells his reader, just as he never cites as allies other religious radicals who vigorously rejected a worldly ministry. In an age of "carnal power," when "grievous Wolves" succeed for teachers and make the gospel a cloak of carnal interest, as *Paradise Lost* grimly envisions, "works of faith / Rarely be found" (12.507–37).

The radical religious Milton of the late Interregnum, then, can be polemically provocative while keeping aloof from specific radical groups (even when his language and views resemble theirs) and never authorizing them to speak for him. Among the late pre-Restoration tracts, Milton mentions only the Fifth Monarchists, in a passing reference in the first edition of *The Readie and Easie Way* (February 1660), where he observes, in a paragraph dismissing states meddling in ecclesiastical matters, that "ther would be . . . no more pretending to a fifth monarchie of the saints" (YP 7:380). Milton's brief criticism, deleted from the second edition, again attests to his independent-minded desire to distance himself from specific religious radical groups, as he makes his own radical arguments and publishes them later in the same month as General George Monck, an enemy to Quakerism who had purged his army of sectaries, had entered London as a savior of religion.[78] One hostile contemporary commentator on *The Readie and Easie Way* (whose attack on Milton included a lengthy peroration addressed to Monck) observed that Milton was happy with "a *Parliament* that would allow *Anabaptisme, Rant-*

ing, Quaking, Seeking, and what not."[79] Yet, as we have seen, the late pre-Restoration tracts do not, except for the first edition of *The Readie and Easie Way,* mention by name any such radical sectarians or kinds of behavior. Rather, Milton maintains a distance as he advances his own radical attacks on the state church and established religion, and, we might add, as he defends the Good Old Cause by reminding his countrymen of the divine light that had illuminated a revolutionary generation of the godly who had sought to act according to it: "after all this light among us," he asks, how could they now allow themselves "to returne back to *Egypt*" (YP 7:462)?

In his last polemical prose work, *Of True Religion, Heresy, Schism, Toleration, and What Best Means May be Used against the Growth of Popery* (1673), Milton chose to speak more directly about specific radical spiritual groups—from Anabaptists to Arminians—and accusations that had been made against them (YP 8:424–26). He registers his sympathy in language that has a personal charge to it: "It cannot be deny'd that the Authors or late Revivers of all these Sects or Opinions, were learned, Worthy, Zealous, and Religious Men . . . perfect and powerful in the Scriptures, holy and unblameable in their lives: and it cannot be imagin'd that God would desert such painful and zealous labourers in his Church . . . who had so often implor'd the assistance of his Spirit." The visionary poet and zealous controversialist, after all, himself yearned to be unblameable and upright in his own life, even if he feared that he might incur blame when his writing expressed controversial and difficult theological notions ("May I express thee unblam'd?" he asks as he invokes "holy Light" in *Paradise Lost* and calls it "Coeternal" with God). But Milton does not appeal to the authority of authors or revivers of sects, "oftimes great sufferers for their Conscience," in order to sustain his own theological positions. He respects diverse radical Protestant groups yet maintains independence from them—preferring his own strenuous exertions in scriptural hermeneutics and "constant reading" (YP 8:435) as the means of discovering and grappling with spiritual truths. He provocatively encourages the selling and reading of books by "Anabaptists, Arians, Arminians, & Socinians" (YP 8:437), and, indeed, he vigorously defends each of these heretical groups and their beliefs, including the rejection of Trinitarian orthodoxy (see 8:424–25)—but not because Milton or readers of these books might become unquestioning followers of any of their beliefs.[80]

From *Areopagitica* to *Civil Power* and *Of True Religion* Milton spurned the credulous following of all human authorities: synods, one's pastor, the Westminster Assembly, even leaders of sects.[81] After all, one might still be a "Sectary" in Miltonic terms if one blindly follows any doctrine "too much for the Teachers sake, whom [one thinks] almost infallible" (YP 8:422); such passive, unquestioning acceptance of a spiritual truth, though the "belief be true," made the truth a heresy, so Milton himself was not about to "post off to another" radical religious leader or group "the charge and care of [his own] Religion" (*Areopagitica; YP* 2:543). Nevertheless, Milton observes, "no Learned man but will confess he hath much profited by reading [sectarian] Controversies, his Senses awakt, his Judgement sharpn'd, and the truth which he holds more firmly establish't" (YP 8:437–38). The same observation could be made about the challenging experience of encountering the controversial theological doctrines at the heart of *Paradise Lost:* for its fit, alert readers, their senses are awakened, their judgments sharpened, and the truth they hold more firmly established through their strenuous engagement with Milton's demanding theology.

In his later writings, then, Milton exhibited sympathy toward radical sectarians and their controversies, but he also maintained his independence and, at tense political moments, silence. This complex stance enabled Milton to negotiate political and religious crises during the Interregnum as he forged his distinctive polemical voice and radical religious convictions. When at the end of *Paradise Lost* he turned to the subject of postlapsarian human history—"to sing the victorious agonies of Martyrs and Saints" and "deplore the general relapses of Kingdoms and States from . . . Gods true worship" (YP 1:817)—he chose not to single out any radical religious contemporaries among his just men who utter odious truths "in a World perverse" (11.701). His closest sectarian connections during the Restoration were with Quakers— his friends Thomas Ellwood and Isaac Penington,[82] the latter the most prominent Quaker in Buckinghamshire (where Milton lived in 1665) and a radical religious figure who suffered "heavy persecution" (12.531), including imprisonment no fewer than six times between 1661 and 1671. Although some of these imprisonments were "long" and hard, Ellwood reports, this dissenter—a kind of Miltonic "just man" unshaken in his radical spiritual convictions—underwent them "with great constancy and quietness of mind" and "kept the faith."[83] Yet in the stark account of secular power and persecution at the end of *Paradise Lost,* Milton presents no Quakers or Baptists or other radical separatists as sons of light in a dark age—those "who in the worship persevere / Of Spirit and Truth" as the "rest, far greater part / Will deem in outward Rites and specious forms / Religion satisfi'd" (12.532–35). The language of radical spiritualism is poignant and unmistakable in the poet's dark depiction of post-apostolic history; his polemical, radical religious voice indeed remains "unchang'd / To hoarse or mute" (7.24–25) as the haunting narrative of spiritual decline evokes the embattled religious world of Restoration England, where dissenters were under a state of siege and militant Anglicanism clashed with the religion of the Spirit. Nevertheless, we find no reforming individuals memorialized here, no radical sectaries, no contemporary martyrs bearing witness to the truth. Lamenting an age when "works of Faith" shall "Rarely be found" (12.536–37), the tragic voice of this radical Protestant poet is embittered, vulnerable, polemical—and tenaciously independent.

University of Wisconsin, Madison

NOTES

An earlier version of this essay (addressing Marvell at greater length) was delivered as a plenary lecture at the Sixth International Milton Symposium in York, England, in July 1999; I am grateful to the participants for their comments and suggestions. I also thank Norman Burns, Thomas Corns, Heather Dubrow, and Michael Lieb for discussing particular points and commenting on an earlier draft.

1. *Complete Prose Works of John Milton,* gen. ed. Don M. Wolfe et al., 8 vols. (New Haven, 1953–82), 1:786–87. Subsequent quotations from Milton's prose are from this edition and cited parenthetically in the text by volume and page number as YP.

2. See Michael Wilding's perceptive account in "Milton's *Areopagitica:* Liberty for the Sects," *Prose Studies* 9 (1986): 7–38. In 1643–1644 Milton also registered his sympathy for "that sort of men who follow *Anabaptism, Famelism, Antinomianism,* and other *fanatick* dreams, (if we understand them not amisse)" (*Doctrine and Discipline of Divorce;* YP 2:278). But he also noted, registering some desire to distance himself from the sects, that by relaxing the divorce law "many they shall reclaime from obscure and giddy sects" (2:355).

3. See Christopher Hill, *Milton and the English Revolution* (London, 1977). Whereas I argue that we need to qualify Hill's argument, I nevertheless consider his book one of the major studies of Milton's ideas in their contemporary context. See also Wilding, who observes that Milton's relation to the sects "remains a matter for further exploration and argument" ("Liberty for the Sects," 22).

4. Hill, *Milton and the English Revolution,* 9.

5. Blair Worden, "John Milton and Oliver Cromwell," in *Soldiers, Writers and Statesmen of the English Revolution,* ed. Ian Gentles, John Morrill, and Blair Worden (Cambridge, Eng., 1998), 243. In fact, Milton is not altogether silent about Cromwell after the *Second Defense:* see also *Pro Se Defensio;* YP 4:703, 720.

6. A number of parallels between Milton and the Levellers have been highlighted by Ernest Sirluck in YP 2:84, 86–87, 89–92, 490n. 15, 542n. 192, 543n. 197, 551n. 228, 556n. 247, 563n. 277, 566–67n. 294, and by French Fogle (discussing the *Digression* to the *History of Britain*) in YP 5:421–22, 454n. 17. See also Hill, *Milton and the English Revolution,* 101–2.

7. "On the New Forcers of Conscience under the Long Parliament," line 12. Quotations from Milton's poetry are taken from *John Milton: Complete Poems and Major Prose,* ed. Merritt Y. Hughes (New York, 1957). For Edwards on Lilburne and sectarianism, see *Gangraena* (London, [Dec.] 1646), pt. III, 153–61 (the quotation is from 153). On the Levellers' relation to sectarianism and radical religion, see Murray Tolmie, *The Triumph of the Saints: The Separate Churches of London* (Cambridge, Eng., 1977), ch. 7; Brian Manning, "The Levellers and Religion," in *Radical Religion in the English Revolution,* ed. J. F. McGregor and B. Reay (Oxford, 1984), 65–90.

8. Hill, *Milton and the English Revolution,* 5.

9. For Lilburne's response, see *The Young Men's and the Apprentices' Outcry* (Aug. 1649), in *The English Levellers*, ed. Andrew Sharpe (Cambridge, Eng., 1998), 181; on Lockyer's execution, see Ian Gentles, *The New Model Army in England, Ireland, and Scotland, 1645–1653* (Oxford, 1992), 326–29.

10. *The Works of Gerrard Winstanley*, ed. George H. Sabine (Ithaca, 1941), 490.

11. *The Life Records of John Milton*, ed. J. Milton French, 5 vols. (New Brunswick, 1949–58), 2:239–40: "That M^r. Milton be appointed to make some observations upon a paper lately printed called old & new Chaines." The *Agreement* was the Levellers' constitutional program, a new social contract based on inalienable natural rights that was first published in November 1647; the third and final version of the manifesto was issued by the Leveller leaders from the Tower of London on 1 May 1649. See *The Levellers and the English Revolution*, ed. G. E. Aylmer (Ithaca, 1975), 88–96, 159–68.

12. Bodleian Library (Oxford), MS Clarendon 37, fol. 32 (letter of 2 March); the letter refers specifically to Lilburne's activities. See also the narrative of political events during early 1649 in Brian Manning, *1649: The Crisis of the English Revolution* (London, 1992), ch. 5.

13. Lilburne et al., *Englands New Chains Discovered*, in *The Leveller Tracts, 1647–1653*, ed. William Haller and Godfrey Davies (New York, 1944), 161–62.

14. On Leveller agitation during this period, see Gentles, *The New Model Army*, 316–25.

15. *The Hunting of the Foxes from New-Market and Triploe-Heaths to Whitehall . . . or the Grandie-Deceivers Unmasked* (London, 1649), 9, 14, 12.

16. Lilburne, with Richard Overton and Thomas Prince, *The Second Part of Englands New-Chaines*, in *The Leveller Tracts*, 184, 172 (title page), 185, 173.

17. See Lilburne, Thomas Prince, and Richard Overton, *The Picture of the Council of State* (1649), in *The Leveller Tracts*, 204; *The Writings and Speeches of Oliver Cromwell*, ed. W. C. Abbott, 4 vols. (Cambridge, Mass., 1937–47), 2:41–42.

18. *Journals of the House of Commons*, 6:174. See also the newsbook *Perfect Occurrences*, no. 117, 23–30 March 1649, on "many exceeding dangerous passages" in Lilburne's "scandalous book" (934); and *A Declaration of the Parliament of England, in Vindication of their Proceedings* (London, 1649), 25. This official defense of the regime against Leveller criticisms was published in late September.

19. Lilburne, *The Humble Petition and Representation of Several Churches of God in London* (London, 1649), 4. This text was published in April; Lilburne's *Second Part of Englands New-Chaines* had been brought to Baptist congregations and "read in several of [their] publike meetings . . . without [their] consent or approbation" (4–5).

20. Hill, *Milton and the English Revolution*, 5.

21. Gentles, *The New Model Army*, 348; *A Paper called the Agreement of the People taken into Consideration* (London, 1649), dated 26 March.

22. Manning, *1649: The Crisis of the English Revolution*, 214.

23. *A Collection of Ranter Writings from the 17th Century*, ed. Nigel Smith (London, 1983), 94.

24. Lilburne, *As You Were* ([Amsterdam?], 1652), title page.

25. Lilburne, *As You Were*, 15–16. For the passage from *A Defense*, see YP 4:535–36. Lilburne's citation of Milton's text was first noted by Don M. Wolfe, "Lilburne's Note on Milton," *Modern Language Notes* 56 (1941): 360–62.

26. Lilburne could have found visual evidence for Milton's chivalric self-presentation in relation to the Commonwealth in the frontispiece to the *A Defense*, which displays not only a harp but a shield with a cross (see YP 4:298).

27. Lilburne, *As You Were*, 16.

28. Christopher Hill notes that the Levellers "continued to speak sympathetically of Milton

as late as 1657." See "Milton and Marvell," in *Approaches to Marvell: The York Tercentenary Lectures*, ed. C. A. Patrides (London, 1978), 17. Hill does not cite specific authors and texts, but he presumably has in mind Edward Sexby's favorable reference to Milton in *Killing Noe Murder* (n.p., 1657), 11.

29. On Milton's self-presentation in the *Second Defense*, see Diana Treviño Benet, "The Escape from Rome: Milton's *Second Defense* and a Renaissance Genre," in *Milton in Italy: Contexts, Images, Contradictions*, ed. Mario Di Cesare (Binghamton, 1991), 29–49; and David Loewenstein, "Milton and the Poetics of Defense," in *Politics, Poetics, and Hermeneutics in Milton's Prose*, ed. Loewenstein and James Grantham Turner (Cambridge, Eng., 1990), 171–92.

30. *Writings and Speeches of Oliver Cromwell*, 3: 437, 438.

31. I refer to a Cromwell who had no wish to undermine "the ranks and orders of men" (*Writings and Speeches of Oliver Cromwell*, 3:435), yet who could speak with millenarian fervor that aroused the radical saints in his famous address to the Barebone's Parliament (4 July 1653): 3:52–66.

32. Marvell links their wild, distracted prophecies with an epileptic Muhammad and his revelations (lines 303–6). Subsequent quotations of Marvell are from *The Poems and Letters of Andrew Marvell*, ed. H. M. Margoliouth, 3d ed., rev. Pierre Legious with E. E. Duncan-Jones (Oxford, 1971), hereafter cited parenthetically in the text, with line numbers.

33. *A Collection of State Papers of John Thurloe*, ed. Thomas Birch, 7 vols. (London, 1742), 1:621; see also 1:641.

34. See John Rogers, *To His Highnesse Lord General Cromwel, Lord Protector, &c.* (21 Dec. 1653): "Antichrist works (now) more in a mystery of Iniquity then ever."

35. A sermon preached on 5 January 1656/57: *State Papers of John Thurloe*, 5:756. See also ibid., 2:128; Christopher Feake, *The Oppressed Close Prisoner in Windsor-Castle, His Defiance to the Father of Lyes* (London, 1654), 105; B. S. Capp, *The Fifth Monarchy Men* (London, 1972), 184.

36. *Calendar of State Papers, Domestic Series, 1653–1654*, 305 (20 Dec. 1653). On Milton's friendship with Nedham, see *The Early Lives of Milton*, ed. Helen Darbishire (London, 1932), 74; see also 44, 45, and Blair Worden, "Milton and Marchamont Nedham," in *Milton and Republicanism*, ed. David Armitage, Armand Himy, and Quentin Skinner (Cambridge, Eng., 1995), 156–80. Nedham himself had earlier voiced his criticisms of the Levellers and Diggers for challenging the new Commonwealth: see *The Case of the Commonwealth of England, Stated*, ed. Philip A. Knachel (Charlottesville, 1969), 96–110.

37. See *Calendar of State Papers, Domestic Series, 1653–1654*, 393 (7 Feb. 1653/54); Anna Trapnel, *The Cry of a Stone* (London, 1654), 50 and passim. For discussion of Trapnel and the Protectorate, see Loewenstein, *Representing Revolution in Milton and His Contemporaries: Religion, Politics, and Polemics in Radical Puritanism* (Cambridge, Eng., 2001), 116–24.

38. *A Second Beacon Fired. Humbly Presented to the Lord Protector and the Parliament* (London, 1654), 10; *Mercurius Politicus*, no. 227, 12–19 Oct. 1654, 3846; Barry Reay, *Quakers and the English Revolution* (London, 1985), 10; Ann Hughes, "The Frustrations of the Godly," in *Revolution and Restoration: England in the 1650s*, ed. John Morrill (London, 1992), ch. 4.

39. William Dewsbury, *A True Prophecy of the Mighty Day of the Lord* (London, 1654), title page.

40. George Fox, *The Trumpet of the Lord Sounded* (London, [April] 1654); Edward Burrough, *A Warning from the Lord to the Inhabitants of Underbarrow* (London, [April] 1654); John Audland and James Nayler, *An Answer to the Booke called The perfect Pharisee under Monkish Holinesse* (London, [May] 1654), esp. 33; Fox, *A Warning from the Lord* (London, [Oct.] 1654), 1.

41. Dewsbury, *A True Prophecy*, 6. See also James Nayler, *A Few Words occasioned by a*

paper lately Printed, Stiled, A Discourse concerning the Quakers ([London?], 1654), 21; Burrough, *A Warning,* 26; George Fox, *To all that would know the Way to the Kingdom* (London, 1654), 5.

42. [Marchamont Nedham,] *A True State of the Case of the Commonwealth* (London, 1654), 14. Milton's Latin here (and subsequently) is cited from *The Works of John Milton,* ed. Frank A. Patterson et al., 18 vols. (New York, 1931–38), vol. 8.

43. Gentles, *The New Model Army,* 94–95, 103, 104–5, 113–14; Reay, *Quakers and the English Revolution,* 18.

44. *Gangraena,* pt. III, preface, and 63. See also Richard Baxter, *Reliquiae Baxterianae,* ed. Matthew Sylvester (London, 1696), pt. I, 50–51, 53–54, 56–57, 61; Austin Woolrych, *Soldiers and Statesmen: The General Council of the Army and its Debates, 1647–1648* (Oxford, 1987), 20–21; Gentles, *The New Model Army,* 101–2.

45. *The Oppressed Close Prisoner in Windsor-Castle, His Defiance to the Father of Lyes* (London, 1654), 39; John Spittlehouse, *Certaine Queries Propounded* (London, 1654), 8. See also [Nedham,] *A True State,* 20; cf. *State Papers of John Thurloe,* 5:756.

46. John Lilburne, *Strength out of Weaknesse* (London, 1649), 4; *The Hunting of the Foxes,* 9. Indeed, Milton's judgment on the failure of the Rump under whose governance the people "had been deluded of their hopes and circumvented by the power of the few" (YP 4:671) resembles earlier Leveller criticisms.

47. *Writings and Speeches of Oliver Cromwell,* 3:435–38; Austin Woolrych, *Commonwealth to Protectorate* (Oxford, 1982), 395.

48. *The Constitutional Documents of the Puritan Revolution, 1625–1660,* ed. S. R. Gardiner, 3d ed. (Oxford, 1906), 416; cf. *Writings and Speeches of Oliver Cromwell,* 3:227–28, 459 (on liberty of conscience). On the extent of Cromwell's "toleration" in the 1650s, see Blair Worden, "Toleration and the Cromwellian Protectorate," in *Persecution and Toleration: Studies in Church History* 21, ed. W. J. Sheils (Oxford, 1984), 199–233.

49. See συγκρετισμόσ. *Or Dis-satisfaction Satisfied* (London, [22 Dec.] 1653), 16–17, and *Peace Protected, and Discontent Dis-Armed* (London, 1654), 63; the latter text was published in April and, moreover, expresses Goodwin's admiration for Nedham's official apology (75–76).

50. *An Olive-leaf: or, Some Peaceable Considerations* (London, 1654), 8; see also 2–4. This text first appeared in January 1654. For Baptist texts castigating subversive Fifth Monarchist language, see Samuel Richardson, *An Apology for the Present Government, and Governour* (London, 1654), 5–6; and Woolrych, *Commonwealth to Protectorate,* 349–51.

51. [John Hall], *Confusion Confounded* (London, 1654), 7; [Nedham,] *A True State,* 14–19, 25–27, 43. For Hall and Milton, see Gordon Campbell, *A Milton Chronology* (London, 1997), 100; David Norbrook, *Writing the English Republic: Poetry, Rhetoric and Politics, 1627–1660* (Cambridge, Eng., 1999), 169.

52. My discussion of Marvell in the following paragraphs is necessarily selective and brief; for a fuller treatment of his poem in terms of the tensions fuelled by religious radicalism, see Loewenstein, *Representing Revolution in Milton and His Contemporaries,* ch. 5.

53. Annabel Patterson, "Literature and Politics in Marvell's Cromwell Poems," *ELR* 5 (1975): 266; Patterson, *Marvell and the Civic Crown* (Princeton, 1978), 71–72; Christopher Hill, "Milton and Marvell," 21–22; Warren Chernaik, *The Poet's Time: Politics and Religion in the Work of Andrew Marvell* (Cambridge, Eng., 1983), 46, 51, 52. For Marvell's response to Milton's *Defensio Secunda,* see YP 4:864.

54. *Writings and Speeches of Oliver Cromwell,* 3:435. Quaker prophets had recently warned the protector that "the mighty day of the Lord . . . is coming, wherein . . . all the tall Cedars shall bow": *This was the word of the Lord which John Camm, and Francis Howgil was moved to declare and write to Oliver Cromwell* (London, 1654), sig. A2r–v.

55. *Writings and Speeches of Oliver Cromwell*, 3:372–73, 504, 546–47, 607–16, 619, 639; 4:309, 440, 867–68; *The Journal of George Fox*, ed. John L. Nickalls (1952; rpt. London, 1975), 274, 289, 350; Austin Woolrych, "The Cromwellian Protectorate: A Military Dictatorship?" *History* 75 (1990): 212.

56. *Writings and Speeches of Oliver Cromwell*, 3:587 (speech of 22 Jan. 1654/55); Woolrych, *Commonwealth to Protectorate*, 366n.40, notes that "democracy" probably refers to the unbounded rule of the Rump, though it may "conceivably refer to the Levellers."

57. E. M., *Protection Perswading Subjection* (London, 1654), 27, 26. See also *The Observator, with A Summary of Intelligence*, no. 1, 24–31 Oct. 1654, 4, 7, 9–10; *The Observator*, no. 2, 31 Oct.–7 Nov. 1654, 27, 30.

58. Ephraim Pagitt, *Heresiography, Or Description of the Heretickes and Sectaries Sprang up in these latter times*, 5th ed. (London, 1654), "The Epistle Dedicatory." Cf. William Prynne, *The Quakers Unmasked* (London, 1655), 1, 3; [Alexander Griffith], *Strena Vavasoriensis* (London, 1654), 25.

59. Prynne, *The Quakers Unmasked*, 5, 6, 7; [Donald Lupton], *The Quacking Mountebanck or The Jesuite turn'd Quaker* (London, 1655); Richard Baxter, *One Sheet against the Quakers* (London, 1657), 8; *The Journal of George Fox*, 142.

60. Pagitt, *Heresiography*, 121–25; *Speeches and Writings Oliver Cromwell*, 3:438.

61. Pagitt, *Heresiography*, 117; William Aspinwall, *The Legislative Power in Christ's Peculiar Prerogative* (London, 1656), 37.

62. Worden, "Toleration and Cromwellian Protectorate," 210–12.

63. See Loewenstein, *Representing Revolution in Milton and His Contemporaries*, 158–62.

64. On the radical religious themes of Milton's drama, see Norman T. Burns, "'Then Stood up Phinehas': Milton's Antinomianism, and Samson's," in *Milton Studies* 33 (1996), 27–46; Loewenstein, *Representing Revolution in Milton and His Contemporaries*, ch. 9.

65. See John Toland's observation in this regard: "he was not a profest Member of any particular Sect among Christians, he frequented none of their Assemblies," *Early Lives of Milton*, 195. See also Jonathan Richardson's life: 237.

66. Among many tracts, see, e.g., Isaac Penington the younger, *To the Parliament, the Army, and all the Wel-affected in the Nation* (London, 1659); Edward Burrough, *To the Parliament of the Commonwealth of England* (London, 1659); Ambrose Rigge, *To all the Hireling Priests in England* (London, 1659). See also Barry Reay, "The Quakers, 1659, and the Restoration of the Monarchy," *History* 63 (1978), 194.

67. *Acts and Ordinances of the Interregnum, 1642–1660*, ed. C. H. Firth and R. S. Rait, 2 vols. (London, 1911), 2:409–12; Christopher Durston, "Puritan Rule and the Failure of Cultural Revolution, 1645–1660," in *The Culture of English Puritanism, 1560–1700*, ed. Durston and Jacqueline Eales (Basingstoke and London, 1996), 217–18.

68. *The Stuart Constitution: Documents and Commentary*, ed. J. P. Kenyon, 2d ed. (Cambridge, Eng., 1986), 315. Its commissioners included reconciled Presbyterians, some respectable Baptists, and some Independents.

69. *Constitutional Documents*, 450–51, 454–55. On the orthodox godly fears of blasphemy and its implications for *Paradise Lost*, see Loewenstein, "Treason against God and State: Blasphemy in Milton's Culture and *Paradise Lost*," in *Milton and Heresy*, ed. Stephen Dobranski and John Rumrich (Cambridge, Eng., 1998), 176–98.

70. Austin Woolrych, "Last Quests for a Settlement, 1657–1660," in *The Interregnum: The Quest for Settlement, 1646–1660*, ed. G. E. Aylmer (London and Basingstoke, 1972), 191.

71. *Journals of the House of Commons*, 7:623–24 (2 April 1659).

72. See Leo Damrosch, *The Sorrows of the Quaker Jesus: James Nayler and the Puritan*

Crackdown on the Free Spirit (Cambridge, Mass., 1996), and Loewenstein, "Blasphemy in Milton's Culture and *Paradise Lost*," 176–81, 185, 187–89, 191–92.

73. See *Journals of the House of Commons,* 7:753–54.

74. *Sir George Booth's Letter of the 2d of August, 1659* (London, 1659), 5–6. See also Barry Reay, "The Quakers, 1659, and the Restoration of the Monarchy," 206–7; Ronald Hutton, *The Restoration: A Political and Religious History of England and Wales, 1658–1667* (Oxford, 1985), 57–59.

75. James Harrington's *Aphorisms Political* (London, 1659), published in late August, is illuminating in this context. It refers to Booth's rising and defeat (7) and is partly a response to Milton's *Hirelings* at a moment of concern about aggressive sectarian activity; Harrington stresses the need for "a National Religion" and an "endowed Clergie" (aphorisms 21–38). This reminds us that *Hirelings* should be considered in this context of radical religious activity that stimulated hostility to sectarianism. Harrington sees Milton's text in the context of the sectarian unrest of 1659 and the pro-Royalist response to that threat.

76. Barry Reay, "Quaker Opposition to Tithes, 1652–1660," *Past & Present* 86 (1980): 98–120; Hutton, *The Restoration,* 47.

77. Baxter, *One Sheet against the Quakers,* 4–5 ("Even dogs, wolves, greedy dogs and hirelings" are among their "railing accusations and reviling words").

78. Monck defended a presbyterian national Church; on his strong antisectarianism, see Reay, "The Quakers, 1659, and the Restoration," 210. On Milton's distance from the Fifth Monarchists in his *Readie and Easie Way,* see also Barbara K. Lewalski, "Milton: Political Beliefs and Polemical Methods, 1659–60," *PMLA* 74 (1959): 200–201.

79. G. S., *The Dignity of Kingship Asserted* (London, 1660), 135; for the peroration, see 179–218.

80. Indeed, Milton, who believes strongly in interpreting Scripture for oneself, clearly distinguishes himself from the Socinians in *De Doctrina,* where he (a believer in Christ's twofold nature) diverges from "those who argue that Christ was a mere man" (YP 6:419); see also Maurice Kelley's note to this passage (n.18).

81. Jonathan Richardson's story about Milton's servant who was "a Zealous and Constant Follower" of "Pretended Divines" conveys something of Milton's disdainful view: "when he came from the Meeting, his Master would frequently Ask him What he had heard, and Divert Himself with Ridiculing Their Fooleries, or (it may be) the Poor Fellow's Understanding; both One and t'other Probably" (*Early Lives of Milton,* 238).

82. Ellwood observes that Milton "bore a good respect" to Penington: *The History of the Life of Thomas Ellwood* (London, 1900), 89. Penington was instrumental in arranging Ellwood's employment as reader to Milton.

83. See Ellwood's testimony concerning Penington, in *The Works of the Long-Mournful and Sorely-Distressed Isaac Penington* (London, 1681), sig. c4r–v.